Ethnography in Unstable Places

Ethnography in Unstable Places

Everyday Lives in Contexts of Dramatic Political Change

Edited by Carol J. Greenhouse, Elizabeth Mertz, and Kay B. Warren

DUKE UNIVERSITY PRESS   DURHAM & LONDON 2002

© 2002 Duke University Press   All rights reserved
Printed in the United States of America on acid-free paper ∞
Designed by Rebecca M. Giménez   Typeset in Quadraat
with Officina Serif display by Keystone Typesetting, Inc.
Library of Congress Cataloging-in-Publication Data
appear on the last printed page of this book.

Contents

Part Three. Resistance and Remembrance

Part Four. Conclusion

Carol J. Greenhouse

Introduction: Altered States, Altered Lives

The essays in this volume explore experiential connections between political instability and social life. The contributors consider situations in which established social routines—including taken-for-granted understandings of society itself—have been altered by transformations of state power. In the absence of routines, other social connections and registers proliferate, some more productively than others. The authors' explorations of the agencies, interests, desires, and identities further lead them to reassess the nature of state power under more normal circumstances; their reassessments extend to some of anthropology's classic representations of the state, politics, and social organization—and ethnography itself. Indeed, the book is as much about ethnography as it is about political transformation; the book's main claim is that these are necessarily connected issues.

Today, the question of how people manage their lives in the midst of dramatic political change engages many scholars in the human sciences, including a widening circle of anthropologists and others for whom ethnography is a primary mode of inquiry. In this exciting new literature, this volume is distinctive in theorizing reflexive ethnography in relation to the junctures of states and subjectivities. Specifically, by eschewing the assumption that states are organizational forms, the authors demystify the conventions of scale that ordinarily would obscure such junctures. They resist the anthropological convention that places states and society at some remove from personal life, as if they were merely neutral or natural settings for action. In the following chapters, such reified notions of "state" and "society" become ethnographic objects in themselves as authors follow the careers of these ideas in contexts of crisis and change. Crisis does not necessarily extinguish the efficacy of taken-for-granted notions of politics or social life as platforms for action or as discrete objects of rational planning. As the authors show, however, maintaining the illusion of states' concreteness calls for new kinds of creative energy on the part of the people who inhabit these states. This is as true for individuals, who act in official capacities as it is for people who do not. In the following essays, such creativity takes many forms. In some cases, it entails survival and renewal as well as new ethical challenges, political forms, and forms of governmentality. In other cases, a failure to survive does not negate the vitality of personal and collective efforts but instead reminds us of the potential force of events. Overall, the essays show that under circumstances of extreme instability and doubt, society itself can become a genre of performance, narrative, remembrance, critique, and hope—even as it loses any stable referent to empirical conditions, places, persons, or predictable propriety (compare Desjarlais and Kleinman 1994).

These essays may be read as outtakes of late-twentieth-century state nationalisms and capitalism rendered ambiguous by decolonization, globalization, and the end of the cold war (the horizons of change closest to this volume's case studies). Most of the essays are set in the 1990s in contexts transformed by state responses to transnationalism and the globalization of capital. (The exceptions address Germany's wartime occupation of Poland and colonial administration in what is now Namibia.) The geographical locations and the specific aims and perspectives of each author differ, but there is a strong overarching theme. Our collective concern here is to expand the limits of ethnography by demonstrating that the connections between the political restructuring of states and personal and collective subjectivity and agency are accessible to ethnographic methods. In each chapter, the contributors reflect on these connections by articulating their own responses as ethnographers to the challenges of dramatic change for contemporary ethnography.

In most of the chapters of this book, the specific context in which states are unmade or remade is one in which the structural tensions between the globalization of capital and the rights of citizens expose critical gaps in states' administrative fabric. Specifically, the absence of effective mediating institutions or established routines (even within state agencies) is marked by highly improvisational maneuvers on the part of state actors as well as among those whose situations put them at the margins (often quite central margins) between public and private sectors. The focus then is not on bureaucratic structures as these "structures" do not, in fact, exist experientially, but rather on the people whose lives—on the job or elsewhere—pressure them to maintain the existence of a social order that their everyday experience does not in fact confirm. Accordingly, the essays focus on the imaginative and performative work that states' spatialized claims to legitimacy and authority charter, as well as on the ways such claims sometimes elide and sometimes enable a host of other, often uncoordinated purposes. The contexts for the studies reported here include colonial, postcolonial, nationalist, postnationalist, and postcommunist societies—precisely at the junctures where one or another element of the taken-for-granted association between state sovereignty, the circulation of capital, and the expectation of some "return" (in the form of rights or livelihood or both) falls away. The chapters point to the practical necessity of reworking conventional representations of agency in such contexts as well as in their embedded forms in classic sociological notions of labor, markets, value, and purpose.[1]

Importantly in this regard, the people featured in the following chapters occupy a variety of status positions, all of them ambiguous in the long run. Some are oppressors, some are oppressed, some are neither or both. In some chapters, the focus is on elites in the employ of the state (German judges, German colonial administrators, European scientists) and personal or collective struggles at or past the margins of the state (orphaned refugee children in Vietnam, Filipino urban squatters, Palestinian feminist activists in Israel). In most chapters, the focus is on ordinary people—neither activists nor elites—who (like those others) recognize their own situations as signs of the times (new middle classes in post-Soviet Russia, Togolese Ewe villagers, urban Polish Jews, English "county folk"). We witness all of them in the midst of their efforts to manage their everyday lives against the palpable transformation of the world they thought they knew but now feel pressed to reassess through the lens of their everyday circumstances.

Another distinctive feature of the authors' approach is their focus on the arenas and media (discursive, technological, institutional, and so forth) through which people assert their ideas of social form. These entail symbolic, discursive, and ritual displacements of the familiar. They also involve literal displacements of people's actual lives (in ghettos, squatter settlements, refugee camps, and work-related relocations, among others) and also, less tangibly, of time (for example, as nostalgia for the past or hopes for the future) and self-identification (for example, as the perception of a break between internal and external worlds, between "them" and "us"). But these ethnographic essays are not (or not just) about finding some foothold of emotional comfort in the middle of turmoil. They are also about the ways the determined momentum of improvisation even in previously unimaginable circumstances makes meaning itself a mode of social action and not merely a reaction. Ritual, commemoration, narrative, law, fetishes, and enactments of various kinds are vital as interpretations of circumstances precisely because they are in themselves confirmations of vitality to the people who are their agents. The chapters detail the specifics of such expressive renewals; some are liberating, others are not. In some contexts, such expressions are the makings of new forms of political action that ultimately challenge conventional notions of where politics is to be found and what it is. The authors make clear that this challenge is as relevant to anthropology as it is to the people among whom anthropologists work.

All in all, the simultaneous reordering of nations, families, people, the skies above them, the ground under their feet, their purses, their ghosts—and the nature of their work (including ethnographic work) are in view here. In these contexts and others, ethnography emerges as a methodology for exploring the zones (literally and figuratively) where people are entangled, abandoned, engaged, and altered by the reconfiguration of states. In the following chapters, contributors take as their field sites those locations where state institutions are drawn simultaneously outward and inward and are made vulnerable by those contradictions (see Gupta and Ferguson 1997).[2] The contributors to this volume treat such structural transformations as problems of consciousness and social action. It is worth remembering that important theorizations of consciousness—those of Marx, Freud, Lukács, Du Bois, and their heirs in contemporary feminism and cultural theory—emerge from fields of struggle for justice and reform not unlike those explored here. Consciousness is the agentive dimension of dialectic—and therefore (like dialectic) necessarily left theoretically open to a wide horizon of objects and outcomes (Comaroff and Comaroff 1991:19–27, 1997:28–29). The contributors examine imperialism, globalization, and the fragmentation of states (concentrating some powers, dispersing others), recognizing that these have pressed state and society into new forms, and, accordingly, have pushed ethnography into new domains. Ethnographic methodology was classically formed in some of the very contexts whose unraveling we witness in these chapters. Under such circumstances both present and past, reflexive ethnography has inescapably legal and political referents and bears an implicitly ethical charge.

The political instabilities in question in this volume are quintessentially modern, involving crosscurrents and confrontations associated with colonialism, economic globalization, the end of the cold war, postcolonial ethnonationalisms and democracy movements, and the bureaucratization of violence, as well as other local and translocal social movements and retrenchments. The pressures against the classical formulation of the nation-state in these cases come from a variety of sources, some internal to the research settings, some external to them: the essays offer fragments of larger stories involving the reconfiguration of states in circumstances of war, political upheaval, colonialism, formation of the European Union, and other transnational activities and arrangements. These altered states reverberate in people's everyday lives, where the fluctuations of state power materialize as the presence and absence of people and resources. Thus, while conventional approaches to social organization make the state an organizational "level" that is removed from everyday life or neutral to it, here the authors interrogate state power at close range in social encounters involving its agents, effects, and imperatives in a variety of forms.

In some of the essays, the experience of learning to function effectively while familiar hegemonic relations are suspended, visibly deconstructed, and recirculated as parts, is explicitly related by the ethnographers' interlocutors as a form of revelation (compare Comaroff and Comaroff 1991, 1997), as if the original and true nature of the "system" has now been revealed. This sense of the present as having opened up to something past or underlying—as if revealing an ontology, which may or may not be the case—is another form of displacement relevant to the volume's theme. The term "displacement" in this context is Spivak's, and she suggests that it reveals what she calls the "phantasmic nature of . . . hegemonic nationalism" (1993:79).[3] The contributors' interlocutors make plain their own preoccupations in this regard, and they are not always with events as such but with reroutings and reformulations of agency—voiced as contemplations of their altered social lives. The experiences that yield such discussions often involve confrontation with revealed agency. To put this more concretely: as states deform, people can see (from the street, as it were) who is doing the state's work.

Writing as an ethnographer, it is difficult to resist the temptation to see ontology in such narratives of unmasking as these chapters present, but to do so is to fall prey to the nation-state's classic myths of self-legitimation—as reflecting the will of the people on their homeland, in its capacity as the sole legitimate agent of their force, and as the template of order. In practice, such displacements as people relate in these pages dissolve any possibility of distinguishing between past, present, and future except in mythical terms (see Greenhouse 1996: part 2). And, turning to the spatial aspect of the metaphor, such displacements do not imply some hierarchy of power's palaces or tenants, as if each were dominant in their season. Rather, they prompt us to question the sense in which conventional discourses of state power—which elide agency and territory in an idiom of bureaucratic organization and jurisdiction—conceal the varieties and contingencies of agency. Webb Keane discusses this in anticipation of a more general ethnographic project beyond his study of ritual, exchange, and power in Indonesia: "The representation of power at once reflects and displaces the hazards to which agency is prone. The hazards of representation, in turn, must be in question wherever we think we have found power on, and in, display" (1997:28–29).

In the break-up of states or in people's spheres of activity beyond state bounds, aspects of the state-controlled hegemonies disaggregate, and their components are taken up by other hands. Even in the extreme circumstances of state collapse (as we shall see, especially in the essays on the former Soviet Union and East Germany), the loss of the old regime does not demolish the question of its power but translates it into questions of its many forms, their dispersal and recommoditization, their idioms and dynamics in the inevitably unsteady nexus of hegemonies that make the state, or take its place, depending on the circumstances. In several essays, the hyperagency of the state is taken up by many hands simultaneously, sometimes expanding it (as in the regimes of terror in colonial Namibia, wartime Poland, and Togo, and sometimes dividing it (as in the Russian mafia and Manila land syndicates). The very possibility of such arithmetic suggests that state power—even under so-called normal conditions—can involve a concatenation of essentially rogue powers (emphatically plural, sometimes legitimated). Indeed, taken together, the essays imply that the state is not the endpoint of some evolution of political forms but only one modality of concentrating and representing human agency that always entails alternative, even rival, forms (see Greenhouse 1996). Writing about states that are in the process of deforming or breaking (and thereby belying officializations of the notion of "process" itself), the contributors show something of the strange array of credits and debits that make state power "real" in the Lacanian sense—beyond representation.[4]

The ethnographies focus on the everyday realities (including crucial

6 Carol J. Greenhouse

everyday ambiguities) of people's lives. There, the dimensions of what are generally theorized as larger structures and processes are gauged from within ethnographic frames. This is unusual, not only in ethnography, but also in political theory.[5] Indeed, the interpretive and reflexive ethnographic approach that—in different ways for different authors—imbues these studies overturns conventions of agency, organization, and place. Like other anthropologists who look at state power from the sites where it is practiced, we have found that this shift in perspective yields more than just another point of view.[6] At a minimum, the perspectives in these essays put the state on the same footing as the people who inhabit it by treating it only and wholly in relation to its social reality—or irreality—"on the ground."[7]

In this sense, political transformations provide more than the context for the ethnographic studies in this volume. They also provide the contents as the upheavals of change reveal that large-scale, so-called structures include the everyday lives of ordinary people—not merely the arenas in which their lives unfold. In standard ethnographic practice (varied though it is), conventions of scale are wedded to those of legal jurisdictions (and sometimes markets); the conventions of temporality are fused to the official renderings of national histories; the conventions of agency are keyed to the canons of biographical narrative (if not police profiles).[8] In contrast, some of the actualities discussed in the following chapters are surprising, but there are also some surprising absences. Be that as it may, readers can expect to find altered states (in the structural sense) and altered lives (in the subjective sense) entwined in practice and in theory.

In this volume, the authors' ethnographic attention to social processes in the course of political reordering yields reflexive insights with respect to ethnography's usual terms for understanding states as formal social organizations. This is a point I wish to emphasize since "reflexive anthropology" generally has a somewhat broader (or looser) meaning. As presented in this volume, the possibility of reflexive anthropology rests on both the long-standing (and always problematic) exchange of knowledge between states and social science and on the authors' consequent sense of implication in the situations about which they write. As former state structures break down in response to crisis or as they are drawn into new transnational partnerships, their horizons of doubt and change encompass the ethnographers along with the people among whom they work. Local people, too, are absorbed in the question of how to understand their own times and take the measure of their potential gains and vulnerabilities. As we shall see, they also find the ordinary discourses of social description inadequate to the demands of everyday life. They have difficulty maintaining their footing along the shifting terrains of large and small scale, inside and outside, then and now. And they sometimes make mistakes. If ethnography is "an assertion of power [and] a claim to 'authority'" (Fox 1991:6), those claims are not the ethnographer's alone; they presuppose a system of institutionalized exchanges of knowledge between the state and social science that political change, by definition, destabilizes.

The volume brings together work by anthropologists whose ethnographic research in contexts of political crisis required them to reassess and expand the conventional limits of ethnographic practice in significant ways. The authors tell their own stories about ethnographic projects involving different scales, locales, historical periods, institutions, instabilities, methodologies, and quandaries, and they also tell us how key parameters of anthropological method, theory, and, in some contexts, ethics came into question in the course of their projects. To put it another way, people's altered lives challenge them—and with them, ethnographers—to redefine order and disorder, losing and winning, cooperation and resistance, oppression and solidarity, mobilization and denial, violence and humane affirmation, structure and agency, hegemony and resistance. Sometimes individuals do this alone. Sometimes they do it in the real or imagined company of others. In these cases, their company included an ethnographer.

For the most part, the people whose situations are the subject of this volume were not active participants in the events that altered the state around them, if action is to be measured by partisan mobilization or collective action. However, neither were they mere witnesses, beneficiaries, or victims. The distinction between acting-on and acted-upon, or between a structural "inside" and "outside," dissolves along with the metaphorical spatialization of the state that puts it above, or apart from, daily life. The state is deeply relevant to people's lives, but not because it acts on them from above or from the outside. Similarly, people may not necessarily act deliberately against the state, yet their acts nonetheless transgress the self-representations of state agencies. Consciousness is by definition "anti-structural," to borrow Victor Turner's phrase from another context (1969). In this collection, then, the ethnographic focus is on people's efforts to position themselves in highly unpredictable social circumstances, and it is those situations that give the book its themes of agency, improvisation, and performance.

Modern Uncertainties

Jürgen Habermas opens *Legitimation Crisis* with the observation that the term "crisis" refers to turning points, that is, to conditions that make outcomes unpredictable; he also notes the origins of this usage in the field of medicine (1976:1). In this volume, crises, by definition, involve conditions in which people (including the state's agents) must improvise with the elements of their social and political technologies and cope with a variety of unexpected disruptions and opportunities. Some of these crises alter the very conditions central to the constitution of social identities—the contingencies bound up in the way people know themselves and others as members of communities, groups, families, or even as individual women, men, and selves.[9] Ethnography in circumstances of political instability is both inviting and difficult, then, in that its ground is inevitably beset with unpredictabilities and dissemblings, however normalized or credulous these might respectively be. Such difficulties are not absent from more stable situations, but, for better or for worse, they are more easily masked. Sometimes unsettled circumstances are liberating; sometimes they expose people to fatal risks. Accordingly, some of these chapters have happy endings while others do not.

Looking into states of crisis as ethnographizable states of affairs, the contributors reflect on what constructions of "normal times" conceal. These are, after all, stories of people coping with extremities of change on home ground for the most part, often among fellow citizens with whom they share ways of life, social logics, at least one language, and, in many cases, the fruits of material and social success. A generation ago, perhaps two, anthropologists were taught to expect that dramatic social transformations lay beyond the ethnographer's grasp (see Malkki 1997). Without ignoring the specificities of the situations in these chapters, we might also ask: What does crisis teach us that we must not unlearn in more ordinary times? The answer implied by this volume is "very little," since there is so much in the current dynamics of change that makes returning to business as usual feel like pretending not to know.[10]

It is in this sense that these stories of political and social instability intersect most fundamentally with ethnographic dilemmas of ethics and understanding: in some cases, their analytical vocabularies are essentially the same (see Mertz in this volume). "Culture," for example, is the hallmark of the human sciences. The term implies some transcendent possibility of solidarity in shared repertoires of meaning, yet in one of the more harrowing contradictions of modern life, and as recent events around the world amply demonstrate, "culture" also serves as a key term of ethnic cleansing and genocide. Thus, if the contributors to this volume draw connections between the sometimes desperate situations they encountered in the field and ethnography itself, this neither trivializes human crisis as if it were merely an academic quandary nor aggrandizes anthropology's self-doubts as if they were the making of world events. In the situations they describe, the authors focus on situations in which people cope with uncertainty by reaching out for some sort of theory of social order or process and then attempting to live that theory. In turn, the authors consider how we might continue to do ethnography now that we know how our terms of art—such as "culture," "ethnicity," and "society"—double, in other circumstances, as the lexicon of fatal triage.[11]

Specifically, our effort here is to raise questions about the discipline's conceptual indebtedness to a particular formulation of the state and its legitimacy and functions now that the formulation has been so palpably altered in theory and practice during the course of the late twentieth century. Especially in this regard, our focus is on the assumption that identity and social contiguity coincide—a key assumption of both representative democracy in any of its communitarian expressions and classic ethnography.[12] Arjun Appadurai refers to this shared nexus of assumption and its contemporary fragility—noting the disjunction between "locality" ("a structure of feeling") and neighborhoods ("as coherent social formations")—as the hallmark of contemporary "postnational formations":[13]

> This disjuncture between neighborhoods as social formations and locality as a property of social life is not without historical precedent, given that long-distance trade, forced migrations, and political exits are very widespread in the historical record. What is new is the disjuncture between these processes and the mass-mediated discourses and practices (including those of economic liberalization, multiculturalism, human rights, and refugee claims) that now surround the nation state. (1996:199)

The potential scope of ethnography is widened by conceptually shifting from structures and social fields to "political locations" (Gupta and Ferguson 1997:38–39) as well as to the modes of agency and performance by which they are made and sustained. Dramatic political change means not only that former institutional structures and social forms are unsettled, but also that multiple structures and regimes function simultaneously and in varying states of incompleteness (see Appadurai 1996: ch. 9). In this regard, some of this volume's authors examine how ✗ people perform their own ideas of society under circumstances of political transformation using the language of community, commerce, culture, and law (Darian-Smith, De Nike, Faier, Lewin, Ries, Rosenthal); others examine states' self-legitimations in these and related media (Freeman and Nguyen, Gordon, Parnell, Zabusky). In all the essays, the state is not an agent in its own right performing this or that function. Rather, the ethnographic focus is on people who claim to act in the name of the state, drawing their salaries and wages from the public payroll, dressing for work—perhaps in uniform, perhaps not—and setting off for their offices or outposts. And where the subject is coercion and resistance, there, too, the authors explore the literal and figurative spaces and media that people design as means for confronting each other.

The essays derive from their authors' ongoing research projects around the world—in Europe, Russia, Africa, the Middle East, and Southeast Asia. The chapters (and the locales themselves) are crossed by colonialism, war, and their aftermath in new national and transnational arrangements (for example, Germans in Poland and Southwest Africa; French in Togo and Vietnam; Americans in Vietnam and the Philippines; the "New Europe"; Palestinian feminists in Israel; the end of the cold war in the former Soviet Union and the former East Germany). In each case, the research was jostled or overtaken by events, and the authors tell stories of discovery in the course of the evolution of their research. In different ways, the contributors convey their sense of surprise—highly constructive surprise—in their encounters with the immediate face of large-scale drama. The essays vary in how much explicit attention the authors give to the reflexive issues in their work. In general, though, and in a variety of ways—some circumstantial, some aspirational—the essays are indicative of the capacity of ethnography to outgrow its conventional limits for the sake of remaining engaged as a human and humane discipline. The authors draw on ethnography itself for their terms of analysis and critique. Overall, we hope the collection will be read as an ethnographic exploration of modern circumstances of political change—as well as an exploration of the ways those circumstances occasion positive ethnographic challenges. We also hope to convey a sense of opportunity in addressing some of the implicit challenges to ethnography, particularly in the domains of politics and law.

Cross-cultural Readings of the Political

This discussion brings us to the chapters themselves. The book is organized in three parts. Here, I introduce each section and conclude with a brief elaboration of the issues that link them. Further discussion of the book's overarching themes and implications can be found in the concluding epilogues by Elizabeth Mertz and Kay Warren.

In the first part, "Law against Culture," the classic theoretical fusion of place, state, and society is taken up as an ethnographic object. The authors consider contexts in which the actors' taken-for-granted notions about how social fields work become important factors in their loss of control over their own circumstances. Carroll Lewin's examination of the Jewish ghettos of Poland in the years of Nazi occupation shows how Jewish leaders consistently overestimated their constituents' value to the Nazis as workers and, in effect, misidentified their oppression as that of a laboring class. The ghetto councils functioned as if they were agents of communities; however, as Lewin shows, there were no terms of struggle that would succeed against total power.

Robert Gordon examines the other side of the extension of law into daily life as he studies vagrancy law in South West Africa after Germany ceded the country (now Namibia) to South Africa. Gordon shows how vagrancy law, which authorized police to arrest natives who were not working, was integral to the social map of the settler society. Importantly, for our purposes, the laws in effect were a substitute for real knowledge of the "natives" inasmuch as the very applicability of the law both presupposed and reproduced the "native" and the "settler state" as identifiable and mutually exclusive entities. Indeed, the act became a surrogate for its own effectiveness, as lawmaking became an end in itself, a ritual performance of colonial control.

Howard De Nike's ethnographic field is the former East German legal profession in the period following reunification (and extending into the present). Many members of the former East German bench and bar were immediately disbarred, and De Nike pursues a double question: first, why and how the public focused on lawyers as the lightning rod for closure on the communist period, and, second, why and how the disbarred lawyers conceptualize and address their own situations in legal terms. In De Nike's essay, law emerges not only as a regulatory regime but also as a discourse of autobiography and generation that links personal and state histories.

The major theme in this section of the book is the local identification and negotiation of the distinction between the interiority and exteriority of legal fields in relation to struggles that for some are for survival and for others are considerably more benign. In each of these chapters, law is associated by the actors themselves with an explicit notion of social field, but in a way that essentially defeats them the ghetto councils invoke a rational legal order, the colonists fetishize the law, and the former lawyers paradoxically attach to the saving power of a liberal rule of law.

In the second section, "Ethnographies of Agency in the Fissures of the State," the theme accordingly turns to contexts in which local constructions of the nation-state are explicitly at issue. These chapters build upon the previous section's sense of problem in the actors' consciousness of law as a dimension of their broader social understanding at specific moments of crisis. And so, these chapters probe actors' understandings of states as fragmentary and open to reworking for particular purposes. These essays are also the most explicit in their reflections on the process of ethnographic fieldwork. This is not a coincidence; rather, the section suggests the extent to which ethnographic categories of agency and social action rely on implicit notions of the reality and stability of states.

Stacia Zabusky makes this reliance clear in her study of transnational scientific cooperation. For the teams of space scientists whom she studied, the "New Europe" is a context in which individuals improvise self-identifications as individuals with "nationality" and, at the same time, as "transnational" researchers within the research institute. In their lives "outside," the institute and science itself have only a virtual reality that is both exciting and disturbing to the people Zabusky knew. Within the institute, the virtuality of national identity is intrinsic to their notion of transnational scientific cooperation; the constant disappearance of the nation is also important to the way the institute actually works as a transnational (non)space. As Zabusky emphasizes in her chapter, this break, or vanishing point, in a sense cancels space in favor of time; the "organization" as such is not a community of working partners with a place of its own but rather is a set of protocols of bureaucratic communication. The distinctions between the personal, the national and the transnational, and the virtual take shape over lunch, at meetings, and in the extracurricular social lives of scientists—and also suffuse the meaning of science itself. As Zabusky shows in her earlier work, the researchers distinguish between "science" and "technology" in terms that they make parallel to the more personal sense of their lives as "excitement" (as individuals) and "science" (as discovery) (Zabusky 1995).

Phil Parnell's ethnographic work is in Manila, the Philippines, among women activists in a large squatter settlement. As squatters, activists occupy both a physical location in the city and a strategic political position in relation to the state. One parcel at a time, they manage to secure title to land through a series of negotiated and legal maneuvers within the arenas they can find (or make) available. Their strategies are effective because they understand the state as a highly fragmented and incomplete composite of agencies; the times, places, and officials to whom they address their demands are not fully coordinated with each other—thus, contradictions can be made to disappear, and seeming impossibilities give way. Parnell recounts his own expectations and surprises as the women he knew worked the internal fissures of the state. They effectively claim for themselves the break between time (the operations of state power) and space (the land to which they seek title), and Parnell considers the implications of their activism for the ethnography of states.

Elizabeth Faier's essay is about feminist Palestinian activists in Israel. Insisting that the space of their activism is outside the state, the Palestinian women she knew were volunteers in self-help organizations for other women, especially in urban Haifa. Their situation is keenly double-edged: as Palestinians they see themselves as marginal in Israel, and as women they see themselves as marginal in the very traditions they defend. They respond to this double bind by specifically and self-consciously reworking the traditionalist notions of honor and sexuality in their own feminist terms. Their activism literally and figuratively engenders their subjectivity, and their self-identity as Palestinians is inseparable from their self-identity as women. As in the other essays in this section, Faier recounts the story of her own fieldwork as integral to the ethnography itself.

In the refugee camps of Southeast Asia, James Freeman and Nguyen Dinh Huu examine the situation of unaccompanied Vietnamese children who were forcibly returned to Vietnam from refugee camps in Southeast Asia. Freeman and Nguyen explore the context of the camps as sites where western social-science terminology—"culture" and "family" in particular—define punishing stakes for Vietnamese children, and where none of the legalities accord children any agency in deciding their own futures. The authors recount the outlines of their ethnographic work, which developed into an ongoing project in Vietnam, a community-based center for training children and young adults the skills that will enable them to earn a livelihood and live on their own.

The third section, "Resistance and Remembrance" extends these issues by examining directly specific modes and sites of engagement with transformed states. In this section, as in the others, people undertake to reconfigure their immediate worlds in relation to—against—critical ambiguities in their cherished notions of social membership. Their efforts often take the form of public or private rituals; accordingly, this section has the most explicit focus on performance.

Eve Darian-Smith, whose ethnographic fieldwork was on the Channel Tunnel, takes us to Kent, England. Faced with the daily confirmation of the proximity of "the New Europe," some people in Kent have revived a traditional rite of territorial boundary marking. In this case, though, the "local" boundary marked is the intangible one between Britain and Europe. This boundary is retraced as people resist thinking of themselves as citizens of the double state of Britain and Europe, with its multiple legal and political centers.

Nancy Ries, writing about social life in Moscow, explores the ways that profoundly altered social systems and practices are made coherent, familiar, and "natural" through everyday narratives. The narrative refrains are laments of difficulty and loss. Ries focuses on their central theme—the flow of money and its seemingly unlimited "power to corrupt." The collapse of the Soviet state has brought about enormous upheaval of what these Muscovites previously imagined as stable social fields and routines. Ries examines people's discursive strategies for locating their own economic and moral positions amid this flux. This means attending ethnographically to people's active husbandry of the symbolic resources with which they might claim a space for their self-identities within the chaos of moral, social, and economic contradictions.

Judy Rosenthal's essay is also about the power of speech. Indeed, her exegesis of Togolese Ewe Gorovodu as political discourse reminds us that the powers of speech go beyond the polarity of the literal and figurative. Vodu possession signals the exchange of bodies (female for male, gods for humans, slaves for masters, northerners for southerners, the ancestors for the living) in a complex, temporary reorganization of agency. Rosenthal evokes local exegetical traditions to argue that trance is a medium of justice. Ewe villages regard possession as the acknowledgment and temporary reversal of specific relationships of oppression and abusive hierarchy. Rosenthal reads Ewe Gorovodu in relation to the current crisis in Togo and as integral to the work of Ewe activists in the thwarted democratization movement.

To summarize, the three sections are in dialogue along the lines of several themes already discussed earlier in this introduction. One major set of themes bridging the essays is their focus on the public negotiation of political fields. All of the essays evoke discourses and devices for improvising, articulating, ritualizing, and insisting on or contesting a break between interior and exterior domains that comprise their own immediate spheres of action.[14] Sometimes these assertions generate new forums for participation (literal political spaces) or allow for new forms of participation in more settled forums. On the other hand, people sometimes make mistakes, or fail for other reasons, with the result that important horizons of difference are swallowed up by the elision of opposed forces.

A second theme is inherent in the authors' attention to the nature of social boundaries, as these are actively constructed and placed in the course of public discussion and debate. As already noted, classic social science treats boundaries as analytically neutral, and the essays refute this in various ways. The construction of boundaries is interesting in itself, and it is especially engaging to consider what they are made of: in these essays, they are made of specific, explicit multiplications and reworkings of history, the future, hierarchy, and other theories of social value, as well as reconfigurations of the social circuitries of agency and power. A related issue follows from this, in that the boundaries in question are also comparative schema involving the construction or refusal of equivalences—for example, the ghetto leader imagining the ghetto as having labor value; the refugee workers who can imagine the Vietnamese children only in relation to their families in Vietnam, the Togolese Ewe practicing trance as a means of acknowledging debts to slaves (Rosenthal 1998). While the situations are obviously different, they reconfigure—or attempt to reconfigure—the contemporary histories of states.

A third set of themes linking the essays focuses on the relationship ⟨ between political crisis, narrative, and agency. Several essays explore occasions in which people claim their agency by means of a narrative performance, in Richard Bauman's (1992:41) sense of the term: "an aesthetically marked and heightened mode of communication, framed in a special way and put on display for an audience." The performances are highly varied, sometimes improvised by individuals and sometimes enacted in more established and collective modes. Sometimes, it seems, the audience is limited to the conversational partnership of the moment (for example, the ethnographer and his or her interlocutor) or even to the speaker herself (and only coincidentally others). The framings are also highly varied, ranging from evocations of other genres (stories, prayers, dreams, dance) to performative commands (legal orders) and coercion (violence). Here, such narrative performances concentrate at the junctures where fields of power refract and fragment. The ethnographer can relate the hermeneutics of narrative performance to the flux of events because that relationship is already explicit: it frames and/or provides the substance of the performance itself. Although the ethnographic exegesis is not collaborative in all cases, in each of this volume's essays, the authors' interpretive analyses do emerge ethnographically.

This aspect of the volume is pertinent to the ongoing critical debate in the discipline about the nature and limits of narrative, text, and representation, including the extent to which narrative might be said to constitute events. The essays point to numerous ways in which the representational and interpretive dimensions of narrative (including ethnographic narrative) are different. To limit discussion of ethnography to its representational aspects is to restrict ethnography to the symbolic dimensions of experience; this limitation is disrupted in fundamental ways by the conditions that make up the contexts of these essays. The interpretive aspect of ethnography engages a hermeneutic dimension of experience, that is, the circumstances in which people struggle to recognize and identify the signs of their own crisis. A dilemma for them, and for their interlocutors (including, sometimes, ethnographers), is to weave these circumstances somehow into an ongoing narrative without depleting the signs of their communicative power. In this sense, the "crisis of representation" (Marcus and Fischer

1986) in anthropology would seem to be less that of ethnographic authority than the pervasive ambiguity or instability of a horizon between the hermeneutic and symbolic dimensions of narrative at any particular moment. Experience simultaneously defies and relies on language. Accordingly, the limits of language and the elusiveness of representation are not problems for ethnographers alone, but rather problems they share with the people whose lives they attempt to convey to readers.[15]

The more interesting critiques of interpretivism focus on the extent to which text fails to cover the surface of social life, that is, the ways in which interpretivists might be predisposed to assume that accessible articulatory practices in the public sphere comprise the full range of articulatory *needs*. This concern has led to interesting ethnographic reflections on language silence, and, as in other humanistic disciplines (where related questions have yet a different genealogy), to broader discussions of the limits of interpretation and representation (see Mertz 1992). These questions are also pressing in this collection, and readers can expect to find multiple confirmations of people's abilities—if not to put their situations into words, then to bring words to their situations. In particular, they show the centrality of narrative to individuals' and groups' articulations of their lives as integral to the society around them. The essays by De Nike, Faier, Ries, Rosenthal, and Zabusky especially address the relevance of narrative beyond its character as a descriptive or symbolic system and probe the limits of language as an issue with implications for ethnography.

The semiotic and hermeneutic aspects of narrative are inseparable from their realization as performances (Bauman 1986). As performers—in their parlors, in trance, or in their offices—the individuals whose speech we hear in this book comment on the past, but their performances neither describe past events nor (except in Darian-Smith's essay) do they claim to be reproducing the past. Rather, in invoking the past, the speakers, dancers, and bureaucrats reconfigure the *present* as meaningful "vis-à-vis"[16]—as temporary, reciprocal, an undoing of past forms, and so forth. Moreover, in treating particular materialities (people, things, forms of access) as signs of the present, the performances also offer a logic of these signs. Invoking the past thus marks the present as temporal, thereby allowing speakers and their audiences to claim a discursive space for themselves in the history of events, although this means something different in each case.

The assertion of temporality in this context should be understood as a political performance in the broadest sense. The performance constructs the present as confirming a particular relationship to the past, ¥ even when that relationship is construed as one of antithesis. Speakers do this consciously, with the expressions of relish or ennui that also mark the occasion as a performance and infuse it with personal style and desires. Further, the acknowledgment of the performance as a performance by the participants themselves allows the ethnographers—along with them—to question the times. They do so by calling the performed rendering of time into question and appreciating the ironies the participants themselves bring to the occasions when the past is drawn close through reminiscence, trance, or preoccupation.[17] Performance produces more than a story; the words and acts that mark performance as performance in effect announce it as a break—a space—for commentary and selective, or partial, contradiction (Hammoudi 1993:vii). Just beyond the essays, one can imagine this space as a new political ground.

Agency, Scale, and Social Fields

The contributors originally prepared their essays for a session at the annual meeting of the American Anthropological Association in Atlanta, Georgia, in November 1994 (with the exception of Elizabeth Faier, who was conducting fieldwork and contributed her essay later). Prompted by the developments sketched out in the preceding section, our common point of departure was the question of how individual ethnographers had experienced the impact of dramatic political change on their own fieldwork and as an interpretive problem. The call for papers posed its invitation simply in terms of the timeliness of some collegial conversations about personal solutions to the methodological and interpretive problems that arise when the "social field" does not exist as a unit of analysis because it no longer exists with any reliability for local people or ethnographers in the domains conventionally associated with politics and law.

We borrowed our definition and usage of "social fields" from Sally Falk Moore (1973), treating them as "normative communities," that is, groups capable of generating and enforcing their own norms, in semi-autonomous relation to other social fields. Given the pervasiveness of political change, including changes in state-local relationships, and currently high rates of world migration (including massive migrations of refugees) it seemed to us that while the idea of the social field was by no means outmoded, world circumstances had unsettled some of its methodological guarantees. In most of the essays, the very idea of a functional social field is something people might wish for, but it is otherwise a wishful construction of people's circumstances—at least insofar as social fields can be aggregated in a way that corresponds to state structures or a social organization that can provide for people's well-being and personal security.

Moore's concept of social fields and her application of it to the study of multicultural and other complex social environments has influenced much modern theorizing about pluralism, especially legal pluralism, in anthropology and law.[18] To the extent that understanding social fields provides both the means and ends of an anthropology of complex societies, the social field concept mediates between formalist and substantivist approaches to law and politics by illuminating the political and social processes intrinsic to any aspect of law's social reality (as norms, rules, judgments, institutions, and so on). The "social field" also defines a scope for ethnographic inquiry, at least to the extent that its emphasis on normative communities suggests a practical link between the feasibility of ethnography and functional social systems. As the chapters indicate, this link is sometimes a limiting condition; we focus on the ways recent world events render the notion of social fields problematic. Still, this does not diminish the fact that attention to the generative intersections of social fields has yielded a generation of important ethnography in the areas of politics and law.

But, in light of twentieth-century transformations of state forms, we ask: Can we understand legalities and politics as normative flows where social fields are in disarray (as in Ries's essay on post-Soviet Russia), or where their coherence is primarily a matter of memory (as in Freeman and Nguyen's essay on refugee children) or hope (Faier's essay on Palestinian activism)? Is the semiautonomous social field an appropriate unit of analysis when there are no mediating institutions between individuals and agents of the state's power (as in Gordon's essay on colonial South West Africa), or where there are suddenly new ones (as in De Nike's essay on reunified Germany)? Can we account for the ways that the idea of a social field operates in the field itself (as in Lewin's essay on the Jewish resistance to the Nazis in the Polish ghettos), sometimes misleading people into overestimating the rationality of their situation or featuring an effective and canny activism (as in Parnell's essay on self-help in Manila)? Can we understand situations where people analyze their social arrangements as involving multiple, simultaneous fields in a constant state of tension? Some of these situations are intrinsic to transnationalism as a personal experience (as in Darian-Smith's essay on the "New Europe" and the ritual reconsolidation of "place" in Kent, and Zabusky's essay on scientists' play with the antimonies of vocation and "big science" in an international research laboratory). Emphasis on social fields as the unit of study tends to direct ethnography toward times and places other than those immediately caught in the extremities of dislocation—for good or for ill (as in Freeman and Nguyen's essay on Vietnamese orphans in refugee camps in Southeast Asia, and Rosenthal's essay on Vodun in Togo). These situations, too, are part and parcel of the current world scene. To anticipate what follows in the essays themselves, social fields operate more obviously in stable organizations than unstable ones, among subgroups more than subaltern groups, as an aspect of hegemony in its settled forms more than in the unrehearsed improvisations of daily life, where the suddenness and unexpectedness of people's encounters with others' designs for them may make resistance inescapably late (as Lewin's essay shows with keen vividness).

Social fields, then, provide a strand of reflexive critique in the fabric of the volume overall. Another strand derives from the ways altered states and altered lives challenge social anthropology's classic premise as to the corollary nature of structure and agency. In the following chapters, structure is agency, but the reverse does not hold. Classically, social anthropology—indeed, modern social science in general—makes "social structure" the template for questions of agency. Social structure itself tends to be viewed in non-agentive terms, as the archive for the intended and unintended effects of individual action. Readers who are familiar with anthropology's ethnographic traditions will readily recognize the ways the twinned notions of structure and agency provide a paradigm for the classic treatment of norms, rules, ritual, and custom in relation to individual action, tactics, interests, and disputes. In general, the volume can be read as an argument for uncoupling this pair of concepts in light of the ways political crises reveal important incommensurabilities, subversions, and alternative discourses that are ordinarily submerged within these terms and their standard usages.[19]

More general readers will have encountered these ideas through the influential formulations of Anthony Giddens.[20] For Giddens agency emerges as a form of inscription, an " 'intervention' in a potentially malleable object-world" (1979:56). "Agency" tends to pertain to individual efforts, and "structure" pertains to the cumulative consequences of those efforts. Rules and norms account concretely for the recursive aspect of social structure, that is, the feedback between the structure and the individual through social systems. The concept of social fields is directly relevant in this context. With the notion of interdependent normative communities, for example, Giddens visualizes a mutually constitutive relationship between individual agents and the social structure and an active dialectic between rules and practices (83). In this way, individual agency is absorbed into and fixed in social structure as more or less a function of time.

The appeal of these formulations is their intrinsic rationale for conceptualizing society, culture, and history as the cumulative work of individuals—the quintessential rationale for a practice-centered ethnography. There are also some difficulties, though, particularly with respect to a definition of agency in relation to an ontology of social effects; this is too restrictive a definition, particularly in contexts of dramatic change. Limited to its impact on structure in this way, agency would seem to be less constitutive of structure than retrospectively derivative of it.

For this reason, such a schema is entirely inadequate to the sorts of crises that some of this volume's essays involve. In their scenarios, the so-called structure is by no means a given; in many cases, it has collapsed, is ambiguous, or is a matter of fundamental contest. In the most extreme cases, the question is not how a "society" registers individuals' ideas and deeds, but, more fundamentally, whether individuals and the cultural groups with whom they identify are even recognized as human beings—human beings worthy of life—by their own compatriots.[21] Circumstances are not always extreme in this way, to be sure, but nonetheless pose urgent questions of recognition; such questions are always relevant, if not mutual. Indeed, in the following chapters, critical aspects of personal self-identity and subjectivity are reworked in the very same contexts of critical risk. For this reason, "race," "nationality," "class," "gender," and others among modern social science's conventional rubrics of identity have no a priori or independent status in these essays; they surface as subject positions but never permanently or completely—and never alone.

In broader terms, the project of reassessment in this volume implies the value of re-examining the ways in which states misrecognize and conceal formulations of agency that they cannot accommodate. I refer to plural formulations of agency to help readers anticipate the highly varied forms and expressions of agency that are central to the cultural accounts that follow. Certainly, in its conventional social science renderings (as above), agency is synonymous with the acts of individuals and their social effects. However, this association of agency with individuality will not be adequate for a reading of this volume, since several essays tell of people whose concepts of agency involve neither individuals' intentions nor their actions—indeed, they might preclude these. The forms and expressions of agency are not determined by individuals on their own, if they are "determined" at all, but rather by the perceived demands of the communicative orders in which they navigate—however fragmentary these orders might be under some circumstances. Agency cannot be considered an analytically neutral term except to the extent that it serves as a reference to the entire problem of how people conceptualize, articulate, and enact their own ideas of relevance in relation to others.

The problematics of agency as just outlined might have particular relevance for ethnographers, given the interpretive challenges of cross-cultural research; however, the issue has emerged along a broad horizon of social science and humanities disciplines in recent years as feminists and other social theorists "rethink the subject" (Faubion 1995; see also Grosz 1994; Weston 1998). Judith Butler captures the sense of that inquiry and what is at stake in it when she writes that "agency is always and only a political prerogative" in that the "subject is never fully constituted, but is subjected and produced time and again" (1993:13). I take Butler to mean that questions of agency are inevitably political in nature whether or not agency is recognized at the level of a political institution's formal practices. It is optimistic, perhaps, to think that the constitution of the subject has an inevitably regenerative quality— sometimes it is reconstituted only to be annihilated. Still, Butler conveys the sort of openness and stakes that readers can anticipate in the following essays.

Discourse, the Social and the Political

One harvest of scholars' recent efforts to acknowledge more fully the ways people experience the world is a growing ethnographic literature at the narrow border between the everyday and the unthinkable.[22] As state-sponsored terror, ethnic cleansings, and war move through households across sites formerly associated with anthropology's classic "village tradition"—in Africa, Bosnia, Central America, Ireland, Oceania, and elsewhere—anthropology itself has changed. And as the collapse or transformation of states exposes their social machinery (or lack of it), classic anthropological questions find their way into unconventional sites—large-scale "systems" are suddenly revealed to be fragile amalgams of improvisatory arenas (Herzfeld 1992; Moore 1993).

The press of world change has registered in anthropological theory, notably in recent writing on translocal and global cultural flows, cultural production, agency, and resistance in our own times and in the past.[23] Some of the conceptual tools in these new exchanges are themselves responses to the dynamics of world change. For scholars in the human sciences, the events that by the mid-1980s tolled the "crisis of socialism" left a legacy of theoretical debate about hegemony, resistance, discourse, and power (Laclau and Mouffe 1985:2).[24] Those debates came to the ground in contexts that had meanwhile been reshaped by new diasporas, social movements, world markets, communicative technologies, and forms of work, among other developments. These changes challenged scholars to rethink and reframe their paradigms of analysis as well as certain of their key terms.[25] The range of reference in these reframings is very wide, bringing into dialogue (and changing the dialogue) among social scientists, philosophers, feminists, historians, psychoanalysts, and literary critics, among others.[26]

Contemporary ethnography has been influenced and to some extent reshaped (particularly at its borders with other disciplines) by these theoretical reassessments. In the mid-1980s, ethnographers were already in a general state of self-reflection about the core tenets of their craft. This self-reflection was related to the same pressures for recognition from social movements and political struggles that concerned theorists of the Left: both were concerned with the self-evident diversity of people's demands for justice and self-representation, and both faced the inadequacies of theory and method that this range of contest made plain. For a variety of reasons, then, both direct and indirect, the project of rethinking socialism—that is, rethinking interests, agency, and hegemony—in a postindustrial, postcolonial world has had a significant impact on the ways in which ethnographers (including contributors to this volume) conceptualize relationships between "the political" and individual experience in the past and present. Given this recent history, as noted at the outset, it should not be surprising that an attempt to engage ethnography in the contemporary settings where life, law, and politics are vividly transformative should yield a reflexive analysis of ethnography itself. The events themselves and ethnography's conceptual terms are already mutually implicated as both histories and practices.

These veins of critique yield numerous lines of ongoing critical debate in anthropology and adjacent (inter)disciplines. Four areas of debate are particularly important for understanding the way this volume's themes and discussions unfold. These are at the horizons where interests yield issues of *agency*; structure yields *discourse*; social fields open to *performance*; and hegemony is revealed as *plural*. Along each dimension (and they are conceptually interrelated), critical discussion has yielded a shift of emphasis as the classic metaphors of social action come under scrutiny from the vantage point of their tendency to overstate the clarity and determinacy of causes and effects. I expand briefly on each of these veins of discussion below.

Socialism's theoretical crisis as influentially formulated by Ernesto Laclau and Chantal Mouffe in *Hegemony and Socialist Strategy* (1985) focused on a critical reassessment of classical Marxist notions of politics as "superstructure" and agency as "interests" (20). The classic notions of politics and agency, they argue, cannot account for the pragmatic specifics of actual political struggles. Actual events unfold around contingencies and instabilities of agency, identity, and society, and any neat distinction between mental and material realities founders on these ambiguities and indeterminacies. Indeed, "causes" always might have entailed other consequences, and social categories are always blurred in practice. Such indeterminacy precludes "the social field from being mapped out in a clear and distinct way" (Guattari 1995:43), specifically in the sense of identifying social groups with characteristic interests or positions in political contest.

It is not only indeterminacy that precludes a bright distinction between material and mental worlds. The concept of discourse, comprising both language and the materializations of speech in social effects and stakes, rests on a critique of the very notion of power as a form of materiality that is presocial or prepolitical (that is, apart from knowledge and experience). Michel Foucault's (1975) idea of discourse and Pierre Bourdieu's (1977:159–71) ideas of "doxa" and "habitus," which together focused on the selective alignments of language and institutional practice as the essence of hegemony, have been influential among ethnographers whose interpretive concerns had already led them to search for ways of acknowledging the contingencies of meaning and the realities of power (see Comaroff and Comaroff 1991:19–27).[27] For ethnographers, the concept of discourse is not limited to dominant institutions' semantic charters; it also refers to the critical visions and alternative charters. This makes "discourse" a useful conceptual tool since it allows one to ask questions about power and meaning without limiting such questions to stable social milieus.

Discourse was integral to the project of reworking the concepts of hegemony, interests, and structure to make them more open to varieties of experience of the contemporary liberation movements. For Laclau and Mouffe, the material and "syntactic" connections between discourse and hegemony are central to their critical aim of making "contemporary social struggles . . . thinkable in their specificity" (1985:134, 3). This requires a more flexible notion of agency than Marx provides, and Laclau and Mouffe approach this task by emphasizing agency over identity, thereby releasing identity from its classical Marxist position interior to fixed class structures and political superstructures. In place of a priori fixed structural "interiorities" and "exteriorities," they develop the notion of "the social" as a "topography" of contingent relations of "antagonism," that is, conflicts over interests that resist "closure" (139, 22). Discourse, in their view, grounds interests and politics firmly within social processes (as subject positions and hegemony). Discourse accordingly makes identity, difference, and "the social" contingent on agency and relations of antagonism in time.

Importantly, the connection between hegemony and communication ("articulatory practices"; 105, 134) on the one hand, and the uncloseable series of relations of antagonism on the other, place the concept of "the social" in real time (in contrast to classic social-science spatializations of "society" as noted above). Laclau and Mouffe refer metaphorically to "political space," but their notion of politics is temporal (for example, in their reference to "differential positions" as "moments"; 105; compare Giddens 1979:63–64). This shift from space to time is significant since, in time, the officialized totalities of the state's self-legitimating claims (and their counterparts in "society") can be unfrozen (Laclau and Mouffe 1985:111; compare Abu-Lughod 1991; Bourdieu 1990:98–111). In the following chapters, the reflexive critique turns on a rereading of place and space, with the result that agency emerges *as time itself*, rather than action *in time*. In general, opening up the spatialized claims of reality of states and societies to expose their circuitries of agency, hegemony, social change, communication, difference, identity, language, and expressivity is one way that an ethnography of crisis provides ground for rethinking the terms of normal conditions as well. The difference between these "states" is not just the efficacy of their institutional structures but also the efficacy of knowledge (from knowledge of solutions to everyday problems to expert knowledge of particular systems). This, too, is an important line of investigation in the following chapters.

Under normal circumstances, the timeless order of society is no less an object of myth than in times of crisis, but in normal times its challengers can be more easily denied. Such denials may also take the form of myth. The mythic dimensions of political self-legitimation make crisis—whether novelty or menace—not altogether beyond anticipation or imagination in the sense that any society's myths by definition encompass the conditions of its own undoing or remaking. Some of the essays—particularly those by Lewin, Ries, Rosenthal, and De Nike—document the efforts of people to apply their mythic and semiotic repertoires to the task of strategizing resistance and survival. In others, notably those by Darian-Smith, Faier, Parnell, and Zabusky, it is the contrast between the state's mythic claims and the multiplication of actual legalities and sites of power that are in view. In Freeman and Nguyen's essay, idealized American models of "family" are to some extent at issue, as these are misapplied to Vietnamese orphans—with serious consequences.

In a variety of ways, then, the authors take up their ethnographic positions at the edges of the state's mythic self-legitimation.[28] From those vantage points, as already noted, "the state" and social fields in crisis dissolve into a composite of agents with unpredictable powers. In no case does the dramatic change in state structure or social functioning eliminate the question of hegemony; rather, it compounds it, as the multiplication of systems of control (however fragmentary) yields hegemonies—plural—and competing logics of patronage, survival, and success. The intersections and gaps between hegemonies emerge as ethnographic issues in all of the essays, and these become occasions for narrative, performance, ritual, legal action, resistance, and lament—among other things. Most importantly for our purposes, these occasions are dimensions of the expressive lives of the people we encounter here, moments that the people themselves mark in a variety of ways. As a result, hegemonies, expressivity, and agency are inseparable in these chapters.

Ethics and Epistemologies

Since the 1980s, anthropologists have grown accustomed to hearing their discipline described as fragmented. Some of these fault lines are made by controversy, and others are produced by neglect—professional or cultural habits of partial recognition or misrecognition. With luck, individual anthropologists find nourishment and inspiration in the proliferating solidarities and intellectual innovation that are supposed by some to be signs of anthropology's disarray. Indeed, one implication of the previous discussion linking hegemony, expression, and agency is that the proliferation of anthropologies (plural) is a healthy sign and necessary step in the development of discipline and the democratization of our profession. Still, there is no denying that "fragments" can have edges sharp enough to graft vulnerability to originality, especially for junior scholars, and that anyone searching for a unified epistemology for anthropology is likely to be frustrated.

The field looks different, though, if one is looking for a terrain of ethical debate. At least from the perspective of what ethnography has to offer against oppression, including the oppression of misunderstanding, the fragmentation of anthropology looks less like disorientation and more like its opposite: engagement with the world as it is. Fragmentation in the discipline, in other words, seems an entirely reasonable and even necessary response to fragmentation in the world. In the contemporary world, where "culture" can mean both life-affirming creativity and the mark of death, we need hardly be surprised—or dismayed—if anthropologists go about their work with different risks and goals in mind. Indeed, we should be dismayed if this were not the case, since it would probably mean that the discipline was so removed from the lived-in world that even a maelstrom could not disturb the surface of our daily professional activity.

The contributors to this volume respond in quite different ways to the situation in the discipline and in the world. These differences involve a variety of questions, focal lengths, frames of reference, and methodologies. Ultimately, however, the authors have in common the ethnographic grounding under each of their various interpretive and reflexive projects. Specifically, they resist the paradigms of culture, agency, time, and space that are central to the cultural self-legitimations of the state and other powerful institutions that operate in the settings X where they worked. Instead, their descriptions of people's lives—ethnography's oldest tool—animate the core of their aggregate response to the problematics of ethnography in circumstances of dramatic change. They are not content to leave "the state" or "power," or, indeed, any aspect of social organization as merely metaphorical totalities—since it is precisely these metaphors that are belied by events. Instead, they look to people's ways of recognizing and acknowledging particular aspects of their own lives' (and others' around them) as social, political, or legal.

Another element in common—and this, too, pertains to recent debates in anthropology and the ethnographic social sciences generally—is a regard for language that begins in the implicit acknowledgment that narrative is both a part of and apart from the experiences one might wish to make known. Moreover, unlike some who worry that an outsider's pen can never get it right, they implicitly acknowledge that whatever the deficits of language might be, they are not the anthropologists' alone. In these essays, we see numerous examples of people's efforts to marshal words for their situations, and to celebrate those unique efforts as signs of their own humanity, no matter how cruel, arrogant, mystified, poignant, or heroic their assertions might seem to distant readers.

In any conventional sense, the ethnographic accounts of these altered states and altered lives "add up" only most doubtfully: indeed, this X is an important concluding point (see also Daniel 1996: esp. ch. 7). One should not expect to reconstruct a unified social or political "field" or "system" from the ethnographic ground reported here. Rather, the ethnographic fragments—and the spaces between them—show where the past has gone, and from where the future will come. The discrepancies between the mythic totalities that have been central to the self-legitimations of the modern nation-state and these ethnographic fragments are, in fact, what allow us to measure the stakes in an ethnographic inquiry of how life, law, and politics proceed. Only a language that stood outside of time and a social universe that could be wholly controlled, could yield the totalities that remain central myths in our own times. To put this another way, the inability to confirm those totalizing claims from ethnographic ground should not disqualify the method. To the contrary, its access to such discrepancies points to a useful future for ethnography and, particularly, the ethnography of law and politics.

Notes

I am grateful to the contributors both for their faithful collaboration on these essays and for their participation in the American Anthropological Association session that was their original context. Beth Mertz and Kay Warren were the discussants for the session, and my thinking toward this introduction was positively influenced by their arguments and examples on that occasion (though I take responsibility for any errors in this essay). It was a series of conversations with Beth Mertz that led to the original idea for the session. I owe a debt of thanks to Richard Bauman, Eve Darian-Smith, James Freeman, Stephanie Kane, Beth Mertz, Phil Parnell, Nancy Ries, Judy Rosenthal, Kay Warren, and Stacia Zabusky, as well as to anonymous readers, for their comments on earlier drafts of this introduction. Kay Warren's extensive comments on the other essays in this volume also raised issues that helped sharpen my thinking. I gratefully acknowledge the hospitality of the President and Fellows of Wolfson College, Cambridge, during the summer of 1995 when I was preparing the first draft of this introduction as a visiting scholar, and also the sabbatical support from Indiana University in 1997 when the essay took something more like its present form. Valerie Millholland's stewardship at Duke University Press has been a tremendous boon. My thanks to Katie Demaree, who prepared the final version of the manuscript, and Joe Becker, for copyediting. Kay Warren and Beth Mertz have been energetic and creative coeditors, and it is a pleasure to acknowledge their very collegial partnership in this project.

1. Anticipating the essays: The wartime ghettos of Poland become forced labor pools. The anti-vagrancy legislation in colonial Namibia becomes a fetish of legal control over "native" labor. The moral geography of Togolese Ewe Vodu deliberately inverts capitalism's routines of redemption (in the double sense of that term). The campaigns of squatters to secure title to property in the Philippines take place in the fissures of the state's administration of title. The organizational basis of feminist Palestinian activism is urban volunteer work, through which women claim a space for themselves that belongs neither to their village families nor to the state of Israel. Russians discursively construct the moral economy of the new Russian underworld as capitalism's mirror. The New Europe is the context for bold reconfigurations of space—literally, via the Channel Tunnel, and figuratively, through international space research. Meanwhile, the reunification of Germany is officially constructed as the end of an illegitimate legal order, such that many members of the former East German bench and bar can no longer earn a living in their professions. Vietnamese refugee children cannot for the most part effectively resist repatriation and assignment to the care of relatives after the war, but some are able to escape the consequences of the flawed assumptions of western nongovernmental organizations (NGOs) as to the will and ability of these families to care for them.

2. Gupta and Ferguson (1997) analyze the spatial dimensions of such projects—spatialities that are central to the legitimation of both states and classic ethnography. Arguing against the flat map of bounded "cultures," where one is always either "at home" or "in the field," they propose that ethnography potentially offers the means of conceptually suspending and reanalyzing just such categories and mappings, and that doing so is necessary for the sake of understanding the webs of commitments and vulnerabilities that make identity both urgent and possible to explore.

3. In her discussion of what she terms the "inscription of displaced space," Spivak asks (Western) readers to suspend their assumptions of congruence between the multiculturality of metropolitan centers and the heterogeneity of decolonized states. In Spivak's view, these involve different forms of subalterity and political address.

4. See Rosenthal's essay in this volume and also Bourdieu 1990; Herzfeld 1987, 1977; Latour 1993; and Strathern 1988.

5. On ethnography, see Daniel 1996; Trouillot 1991: esp. 36; Vincent 1991; and Appadurai 1991. On political theory, see Skočpol 1985 and Warren 1993a: esp. 9–10.

6. See especially Coronil 1997; Ferguson 1994; Gupta 1995, 1998; Gupta and Ferguson 1997; Heyman 1999; Nagengast 1991; and Verdery 1996.

7. See Comaroff and Comaroff 1991, 1992; Daniel 1996; Lazarus-Black and Hirsch 1994; Moore 1993; and Starr and Collier 1989.

8. On scale, see Strathern 1995b; on ethnography as alternative history, see Comaroff and Comaroff 1992; on states' appropriations of history, see Alonso 1994; Bhabha 1994:139–70; Chatterjee 1993; Duara 1995; Herzfeld 1990; and Mertz 1988. On autobiography, see especially Henderson 1989 and Lionnet 1989. On the reflexive implications of law's discursive dominance over issues of temporality in ethnographic practice more generally, see Greenhouse 1996; on the experiential dimensions of legal jurisdictions and their implications for ethnography, see Barnes 1997; Gooding 1997a; and Wagoner 1997.

9. See Anderson 1991; Battaglia 1995; Baumann 1996; Bornemann 1992; Brenneis 1990; Coutin 1997; Espeland 1994; Gooding 1994, 1997b; Green 1997; Kleinman 1986; Strathern 1995c; and Thébaud 1994.

10. To some extent, the call for reassessment is paradigmatically made in response to the Holocaust; Zygmunt Bauman (1989), and, earlier, Hannah Arendt (1967) challenged intellectuals and, in Bauman's case, social scientists specifically, to acknowledge—at the level of social theory—the state's capacity to terrorize and kill its citizens. More broadly, recent assessments of ethnography's epistemological conventions stress the centrality of critical engagement as integral to reformulating the methodological and ethical value of fieldwork for contemporary world conditions (Gupta and Ferguson 1997; Olwig and Hastrup 1997).

11. On this and related points we join a widening circle of conversation among anthropologists and others. In addition to works cited in the text, see Aretxaga 1997 on gender and political subjectivity in Northern Ireland; Comaroff and Comaroff 1991, 1992, and 1997 on colonialism, ethnogenesis, and black consciousness in South Africa; Comaroff and Comaroff 1993 on indigenous African reworkings of capitalism and modernity; Feldman 1991 on political prisoners in Belfast; Freeman 1989 on Vietnamese recollections of war and relocation to the United States; Gordon 1992 on ethnogenesis and genocide against the "Bushmen" of Namibia; Kane 1994 on discourses of development among the Emberá of Panama; Lavie 1990 on Bedouins under military occupation; Malkki 1995 on genocide in Burundi; Marcus 1993 on the negotiation of state power through cultural media; Nagengast 1991 on the collapse of socialism in Poland; Poyer 1993 on the Ngatik massacre (Micronesia); Ries 1997 on post-perestroika Moscow; Rosenthal 1998 on Togolese Ewe Vodu; Steedly 1993 on poetics and political economy in rural Indonesia; Stoll 1993 on Ixil Maya captured in the Guatemalan war; Tambiah 1986 on ethnic fratricide in Sri Lanka; Tsing 1993 on the poetics of marginality in Kalimantan; Warren 1998 on indigenous democracy movements in Guatemala; Welaratna 1993 on Cambodian recollections of war and U.S. resettlement; Zabusky 1995 on international scientific cooperation in Europe; Zonabend 1993 on life in the shadow of a French nuclear power plant.

Ethnography is a flourishing genre, and this is by no measure a comprehensive list; however, these are among the works that have directly influenced the evolution of this project.

12. For important critical discussions of ethnography's "localizing" traditions, see Fardon 1985; Gupta and Ferguson 1997; and Olwig and Hastrup 1997.

13. The phrase "postnational formation" is also Appadurai's (1996:164). His reference is to the recent emergence of important ethnonationalist challenges to the nation-state, which "remind [us] that the nation-state is by no means the only game in town as far as translocal loyalties are concerned" (165).

14. I borrow the imagery of interiority and exteriority from Bahloul 1992.

15. On language as "outside," and the efficacy of signs, see Deleuze 1993. When the local situation is marked by chaos, danger, or violence, the reader's safe distance compounds the problems of ethnographic narrative as a marked and unbridgeable absence; this, too, affects the tone and substance of ethnographic address in some of the essays, especially those by Lewin, Freeman and Nguyen, and Rosenthal.

16. I borrow the phrase in this context from James Boon.

17. See Deleuze 1993:75–80 on Whitman's concept of writing fragments.

18. On legal pluralism's conceptual underpinnings, especially with respect to Moore's essay, see Griffiths 1986 and Merry 1988.

19. The discussion of structure and agency is drawn from a more expanded version in Greenhouse 1996: esp. ch. 3.

20. Giddens 1979: esp. 49–95. Agency emerged as an anthropological issue in the mid-1980s from several sources in ethnography, feminist theory, and sociology. In addition to Giddens, see Ortner 1984: esp. 159. For extensions and critiques, see

Comaroff 1985; Fardon 1985; Strathern 1985, 1987a: esp. 21–31, and 1988, esp. 272–73; for a re-theorization of agency in relation to enactments of authority, see Keane 1997.

21. When state institutions are in crisis, their very vulnerability exposes the ways that they routinely fail to monopolize the effects of agency, revealing alternative and rival formulations of agency beyond those accorded recognition in official practice. Indeed, the questions are still there, even when states do manage to maintain the illusion of their own permanence. Crisis conditions highlight the ways links between structure and agency can fail under any circumstances.

22. I borrow "the unthinkable" in this context—as well as the view of "the unthinkable" as a discursive practice—from Bourdieu's discussion of doxa (Bourdieu 1977:159–71, esp. 170). For recent ethnography in the aftermath of war, see Lan 1985; Malkki 1995; Nordstrom and Martin 1992; Poyer 1993; Stoll 1993; Warren 1993b; and Werbner 1991, in addition to works cited in the text.

23. This is not the place to attempt a synopsis of anthropological theory in the 1990s, but any such effort with respect to the United States would necessarily trace new connections between anthropology and other disciplines. Some of those disciplines are themselves relatively new, emergent in response to developments within the United States and elsewhere—for example, black studies, cultural studies, and women's studies, among others along these and other horizons (see, for example, Baker 1993; Chandler 1996; and Weston 1998). These exchanges of knowledge with other disciplines are also integral to ethnographers' attempts to reconcile their sense of ethical accountability with accountabilities to their discipline and departments. One way of reading the recent methodological and epistemological debates in anthropology and related disciplines is to regard them in relation to a widespread enthusiasm for experimentation in the human sciences, experimentation that is itself integral to an effort to come to grips with the ethical challenges of doing social science.

24. For Laclau and Mouffe the crisis of socialism is a response to a "whole conception of socialism which rests upon the ontological centrality of the working class, upon the role of Revolution . . . as the founding moment in the transition from one type of society to another, and upon the illusory prospect of a perfectly unitary and homogeneous collective will that will render pointless the moment of politics" (1985:2).

25. For reassessments of the working class in relation to a concept of privileged agency of struggle, see Gorz 1982; Laclau 1990; and Laclau and Mouffe 1985. For more general discussion of debates within Marxism—or among Marxisms—see Barrow 1994. For examples of the impact of such debates on social science and humanities disciplines, see collections edited by Dimock and Gilmore 1994 (literature); Elam and Wiegman 1995 (feminism); Hann 1993 (anthropology); and Osborne 1991 (political theory); these collections specifically assess the implications of the crisis of socialism for their own disciplines. For an evocation of the times and their impact on social theory in more general terms, see Moi (1986:9).

26. This discussion, focusing on developments that periodize contemporary anthropology *as* contemporary, is not meant to imply that anthropology's responsiveness to world events is itself new. On the contrary, anthropology has always been shaped by its explicit and implicit dialogues with other public discourses of culturality and multiculturality. While professional anthropologists may be particularly aware of new interdisciplinary conversations around their subject today, anthropology's interdisciplinarity itself is not new. As in the past, contemporary anthropology's interdisciplinary fusions take some of their intellectual shape from contestations in the public sphere over the significance of difference. For general discussion and additional bibliography on these contemporary resonances, see Appadurai 1996; Dirks, Eley, and Ortner 1994; During 1993; and Fox 1991.

27. In anthropology since the 1970s, debates between "materialists" and "interpretivists" have been contentious and sometimes acrimonious, particularly when materialists insist that the interpretivists' refusal to separate the material and the symbolic is tantamount to their failure to distinguish the materiality of power in social life. For materialists, discourse is in effect "just words"; for interpretivists, discourse refers to the relevance of words in the world. For reviews and critical debates, see Moore 1986: esp. 320–29; Strathern 1987b (and replies); and Sangren 1988 (and replies).

The issue of material versus symbolic approaches to power also surfaces in other fields; see Sarat and Kearns 1993 for a sense of at least some strands of this argument in sociolegal studies. For a reflection on related debates in feminism, specifically in relation to Foucault, see Butler 1993. Laclau and Mouffe (1990) also offer their own response to critics.

In anthropology, the debate has brought to the fore issues of agency, formulated as comparative and historical questions. Comaroff 1985; Munn 1986; and Strathern 1988 directly address the reflexive, interpretive, and comparative problems of taking culture and power seriously in their respective reformulations of the concept of agency.

28. This is not a coincidence since classic social theory shares the terminology of Western myths of the nation-state. See especially essays by Parnell and Zabusky (this volume) for their accounts of their conceptual starting points.

Part One

Law against Culture

Carroll McC. Lewin

Ghettos in the Holocaust: The Improvisation
of Social Order in a Culture of Terror

In February 1941, near Warsaw, in the Otwock ghetto that was created by the Nazis two months earlier, twenty-five-year-old Calel Perechodnik, a secular Jew and self-proclaimed Polish patriot, volunteers as a ghetto policeman in order to avoid labor conscription. By the summer of 1942, relocations of ghetto residents "to the east" (as went the Nazi euphemism) have commenced, although the ghetto policemen, along with the also Nazi-created Judenrat (Jewish Council), have been assured that they, their wives, and their children will be spared deportation. On the morning of 19 August, Perechodnik and the other ghetto policemen help round up eight thousand of their fellow Jews, forcing those selected by the ss into railway cars. At the end of the day, the ss order the policemen to march away from their own wives and children. Perechodnik watches in horror as his wife, Anka, and two-year-old daughter, Alinka, climb into the fourth car from the locomotive. He subsequently learns that their destination is the Treblinka death camp (Perechodnik 1996).[1]

This incident in the Otwock ghetto telescopes the unambiguous trauma and terror of the Holocaust that we rarely confront because it impinges on our own historical consciousness (Lewin 1993:312) and cries out for closure because of our positivist temptation to avoid that which appears "indeterminate, elusive and opaque" (Friedlander 1992:52). While state-sponsored violence, suffering, and terror undeniably constitute brutal facts of human existence, anthropology has paid little attention to such "evil" because it has regarded "wholeness" and the absence of suffering as the cultural norm (Hastrup 1993:727).[2] Two things are required if we, as anthropologists, seek to reject muteness on evil such as that epitomized in the Nazi genocide. We need to jettison the idea that this genocide was an aberration or failure, rather than a product of modernity (Bauman 1989:12). We also require two interwoven ethnographies, that of the state and that of the individual, to come up with an ethnography of terror which can "realize the state in all its sublime horror" as it brutally destroys everyday lives and sensibilities (Desjarlais and Kleinman 1994:9).[3]

There are numerous limits to the representation of Nazism and the Holocaust. Our received imagery is overwhelmingly that of the death factories—Auschwitz, Treblinka, and others—with endless cattle cars, piles of corpses, and pitiful survivors at the end of the war. The power of this imagery cannot, and should not, be obliterated, but we must not neglect other facets of the genocide that permit us to approach its vortex and a clearer understanding of genocidal intentionality and implementation. A significant and retrievable phase in the Holocaust is the internment and isolation of the Jews in ghettos created by the Nazis in Eastern Europe. Ghettos were improvised social fields in which both perpetrators and victims coexisted, sometimes very briefly as a short phase in the murder of the Jews, while at other times almost until the end of the war. This improvised social field was one in which roles and symbolic constructs were imposed on the Jews, who had no recourse but to attempt to create a facsimile (however distorted) of a social system based upon social contracts as they understood them.

The Judenrate, or Jewish Councils, consciously created by the Nazis to administer the ghettos, were a key node in the social, political, and economic motivations and machinations of the genocide. The forced participation of the Judenrate in what became the subjugation and destruction of their own people highlights the pathogenesis of the Holocaust. Degradation and persecution framed the accommodative attempts of the Judenrate as they were sucked into the Nazi-created illusion of order, reliability, and legality (Fein 1979:126). As will be seen in the examples of three ghettos, competitive relations between the components of the German war/genocide machine fed into the miscalculation by the Judenrate of mutuality in moral calculi, thus conspiring to bring about a fully determined genocide. In the depiction of ghettos below, we see how the negotiation of reality and social relationships under escalating conditions of terror was marked by alternations of denial and acceptance, of acquiescence and resistance, of despair and hope among the Judenrate and other ghetto residents. As terror and death increasingly became routinized, cognitive dissonance and moral nihilism compromised attempts to approach a mimesis of ordinary life and ordinary discourse. In all ghettos, ultimately, the ruse was finished for both victims and perpetrators. The life histories of ghettos indicate foremost that there was "a method to the madness" in which the state was "ordering the disorder" (Desjarlais and Kleinman 1994:11), notably in the Nazi-created illusion that the labor of the Jews would postpone their annihilation. This is clear in the reading both of the bureaucratic development by the Germans of the so-called "Final Solution" and of the depiction of Jewish attempts, recorded in diaries, chronicles, and memoirs, to define and redefine everyday life under extraordinary circumstances in which any remnant of wishfulness for normality irrevocably collapsed into despair.

Nazi Intentionality

In their exploration of the determination of the Nazi Final Solution with regard to the Jews, scholars have presented two poles of explanation, the "functionalist" and the "intentionalist." The former asserts that there was neither motivational logic nor consistency in Nazi policy, that it was arrived at incrementally, shifting in response to changing circumstances. "Intentionalists," on the other hand, propose that very early on the Nazis had clear notions as to the fate of Jewry under the eventual domination of Europe. More recently, it has been suggested that neither approach is entirely adequate and that the Final Solution was an unfolding plan, a combination of functionalism and intentionalism (Browning 1992:30). This newer approach is explored in this essay, which focuses on Poland and Lithuania, and, more particularly, the ghettos of Lodz, Warsaw, and Vilna. Here the Nazis had the problem of what to do about the Jews in the newly conquered territories, Poland in 1939 and Lithuania in 1941. Ghettoization had been raised as a possibility by Goering (the dominant figure in the war economy) as early as 1938 (Yahil 1991: 164). By the time of the invasion of Poland in September 1939, there were plans to reorganize demographically the conquered territories by concentrating Jews in urban centers. Heydrich (ss Reich leader Himmler's chief deputy) gave orders to dissolve Jewish communities of less than five hundred, transferring the populace to urban "concentration centers" located on rail lines. Instructions on setting up Jewish Councils as a means of creating order also were included. At this early point, competitive relations developed between the ss and the civil governor general, Hans Frank, and between the ss and Goering, which had a profound effect on the life history and fate of the ghettos in Poland.

As the point of departure for Nazi bio-racial policy, Poland was regarded by Hitler, Himmler, and Heydrich as a locus for the resettlement of Jews from Western Europe and attendant "racial cleansing." The ensuing struggle for power between the elements of German bureau-

cracy became determining factors in the eventual process of extermination (Scheffler 1985:35). Put simply, the conflict grew between
those with escalating genocidal intentions and those who wanted to exploit the Jews as slave laborers until such time when Poland would be
"cleansed" for the purpose of future German settlement. There was, at
first, no true consensus of policy; indeed, Hitler encouraged a de-
centralized system of regional autonomy that fomented competition
and rivalry (Headland 1992:179).

By February 1940, the ghettoization process in the large cities of
Poland commenced, with Lodz as the first systematically fashioned
ghetto, while the Warsaw ghetto was formed in October. But ghettos at
that point were regarded as interim measures. During the first half of
1940, Nazi leadership pursued the so-called Madagascar Plan with the
idea that the island would pass from French hands and European Jews
would be settled there under a mandate. There is some debate as to the
seriousness with which this plan was pursued (Breitman 1991:121).
Whatever the case, impending war with the Soviet Union and the fore-
seen problem of transporting the Jews to Madagascar led to the abandonment of the plan. By the summer of 1940, ghettoization, which had
slowed down temporarily, once again picked up speed.

The implementation of the Final Solution at this juncture rested on a
predicted high rate of attrition under conditions of starvation and
forced labor in ghettos; meanwhile, economic profit and contribution
to the war economy would be affected (Breitman 1991:136). Given the
problems of food shortages and the creation of viable ghetto economies, the struggle between the "productionists" and the "attritionists"
in Lodz, Warsaw, and other ghettos in Poland, intensified (Browning
1992:30), although the Germans put in charge of the ghettos at that
time had no premeditated plans for mass murder (Browning 1992:54).
Raul Hilberg's attempt to straddle the controversy between "intentionalist" and "functionalist" arguments, characterizes what ultimately
became the Final Solution: the Holocaust was "not so much a product of
laws and commands as it was a matter of spirit, of shared comprehen-
sions, of consonance and synchronization" (Hilberg 1985:54–55). This
is the context in which ghettoization first proceeded, one in which
components of German bureaucracy were somewhat at odds with regard to the Jews. The conflict over the economic needs of the war effort versus the genocidal endeavor was never fully resolved (Headland
1992:90) and greatly influenced Jewish leadership in the ghettos. Little

did the Jews know, however, that by at least early 1941, Hitler fully intended to annihilate them, although the overall plan remained malleable until the summer of 1941 when the Soviet Union was invaded (Breitman 1991:206). Along with this invasion, the special task forces of Einsatzgruppen, set up by Himmler and Heydrich, entered the scene, unleashing the genocidal program in the Russian territories, ultimately killing two million Jews by shootings or in mobile gas vans. By the time the Vilna ghetto was established in September 1941, these mobile killing units had killed thousands in Lithuania.[4] Here again, conflict between the elements of the German bureaucracy prevailed in the form of antagonism between the Einsatzgruppen on the one hand and, on the other, the civil administration and the Wehrmacht (the German army) as recruiters of Jewish labor. Thus, a report by the commander of Einsatzgruppen Unit Three in Lithuania dated 1 December 1941: "I wanted to eliminate the working Jews and their families as well, but the Civil Administration (Reichskommissar) and the Wehrmacht attacked me most sharply and issued a prohibition against having those Jews and their families shot" (cited in Arad, Gutman, and Margaliot 1981).

The crossfire between productionists and attritionists helped shape the perceptions and structure the reactions of ghetto Jews during the step-by-step genocidal process. In the end, however, in both Poland and Lithuania, ultimate ss control, along with the anti-Semitism of the local populace, conspired to seal the fate of the Jews (Fein 1979:82).

Establishment of Ghettos and Judenrate

Ghettoization began as an interim measure to effect demographic policies in the occupied territories, an expedient to round up Jews until it could be figured out what to do with them. Meanwhile, property could be confiscated and labor exploited. The Lodz ghetto was created when a plan to expel the Lodz Jews to Lublin fell through and the Madagascar Plan collapsed (Browning 1992:32). Warsaw was ghettoized in fits and starts, taking a full year in a process highly affected by concern over typhus, which became the final rationale for sealing the ghetto (Roland 1992:23). By the time the Vilna ghetto was set up, direct genocide was in full swing. Ghettoization was an important move in the extermination process, as it isolated the Jews and cut them off from potential sources of outside help, however meager these were. Looking at all of Nazi-dominated Europe, isolation and the degree of anti-Semitism in the local populace emerged as the most highly linked variables leading to the most intense victimization; simultaneously, Judenrate accompanied the highest degree of segregation (Fein 1979:127). Ghettos and Judenrate combined in Eastern Europe to create the most effective killing field in the Holocaust.

In establishing the Judenrate, the Nazis seized control by taking advantage of a long tradition of Jewish communal organizations (Yahil 1991:238). What had been indigenous welfare organizations known as Kehillot, which had served the social service and cultural needs of local Jewish populations, were transformed into structures that would serve to deflect hostility away from the Germans and turn it inward (Trunk 1972:261). In conjunction with the increasing isolation of the ghettos, the Jewish Councils grew into ramified administrative apparatuses, supplementing social welfare with new tasks created by the Nazis. These included the provision of municipal services, food rationing, taxation, and ransom payments to the Germans, as well as the supplying of forced labor, and, eventually, the victims of deportation and annihilation. There was some "haphazardness" in the "bizarre formation" of the Judenrate (Trunk 1972:25). What is clear, however, is that the Nazis constructed a divide-and-rule policy in which the Jews were forced into a complicity of repression. In creating the Judenrate, the Germans aroused hostility between Jews in order to offset unity; they tended, for example, not to intervene in strikes and demonstrations by ghetto residents against the Judenrate (Friedman 1980:148). That the Judenrate and the associated ghetto police were excused from forced labor and received more food rations increased hostility as the labor supply and food situation deteriorated.

There was some evolutionary quality to the establishment of Judenrate in Eastern Europe. In both Poland and Lithuania, many of the Jewish elite left for the Soviet Union or Western Europe just before and just after the Nazi invasion, affecting potential membership in the Judenrate. From the beginning, there was a rapid turnover of council members, and, in the long run, about 80 percent were killed or committed suicide (Trunk 1972:328). About one-half of the first council leaders in Poland were executed very early on by the Nazis; three quarters of these had refused to cooperate in the escalating deportations (Fein 1979:136–37). It is difficult to generalize about the Judenrate, although Isaiah Trunk's (1972:30–33) statistical survey on the Eastern European Judenrate membership indicates the following:

90 percent had families with children

40 percent had higher education (and knew German)

26 percent were professionals

67 percent were Zionist; few were communist or socialist

43 percent were previous members of Kehillot or municipal organizations

very few were religiously orthodox

Since the tendency was toward political conservatism, nonorthodox religiosity, and a higher socioeconomic status in the Judenrate (Friedman 1980:145), members could not be representative of all social sectors in large ghettos such as Lodz, Warsaw, and Vilna. This factor looms large in the issue of the Judenrate's attitude toward a resistance against the Germans that was dominated by the young and the politically more adventuresome. In smaller ghettos, on the other hand, resistance was more accommodated by the Judenrate; there was less dissonance and debate because of greater social homogeneity and closer ties between the council members and the populace (Yahil 1991:475). In the larger ghettos, political factionalism and class issues compromised resistance efforts.

Before examining the specific Jewish leadership in Lodz, Warsaw, and Vilna, it is worth emphasizing just what the Judenrate were up against. Cramming the Jews into crowded quarters with woefully inadequate municipal services (water, sewage, and so forth) and under conditions of unrelenting hunger, the forced creation of the Judenrate provided the Germans with a convenient alibi in the form of a "local leadership" which covered up the lawlessness of the civilian and military occupation authorities (Trunk 1972:28). While the Judenrate were by design left mostly to themselves in terms of everyday organization, they were wholly dependent on the Germans who deceived them into believing that the rational thing to do was to work within the German-defined system (Fein 1979:126). Much of the success of the Nazi plot was in the fraud and deceit that hid what actually was going on. The Jews were kept in the dark as to what "resettlement" was all about. After each deportation "to the east," the Germans would assure the councils that there would be no further round-ups (Trunk 1972:418). In addition, the Judenrate were put in charge of deploying the food-rationing system, which became a growing problem as the war ground on. Another nefarious component of the Nazi scheme was the promulgation of the "rescue through work" strategy that lulled the Judenrate (and the ghetto police) into the belief that if they provided the labor of others, they, their families, and the remainder of the populace would escape "resettlement." Given that the councils were threatened continually with incremental liquidation of the ghetto if they refused to obey orders, they felt they had to participate in the mass-employment strategy, even though the ultimate effect was only to slow down but not stop the extermination process (Trunk 1972:412). Crucial to the slowing-down process on the part of the councils in Lodz, Warsaw, and Vilna, was to take advantage of competition between the civilian and military labor circles that desired slave labor and the ss and police orders who were bent on the physical extermination of the Jews. Simultaneously, however, disease and starvation decimated the ranks of those capable of maintaining the Jewish labor force. Unsurprisingly, graft, corruption, speculation, and profiteering developed in the ghettos as means of coping with starvation and avoiding labor and deportation.

The experiences of the Lodz, Warsaw, and Vilna ghettos point to a perceptual failure of the ghetto residents that was born out of a cognitive dissonance created by conscious Nazi policy and the more chaotic elements of Nazi rule. The pattern was one in which the Judenrate initially believed they could better the situation through competent administration and pursuit of the "rescue through work" strategy. As the genocidal machinery geared up at a frightening pace, the Judenrate degenerated into "fatal oligarchies or dictatorships" (Friedman 1980:551), unable to engage in the social responsibility they had attempted to exercise at the inception of the ghettos. The problem was that the Judenrate had become convinced that they could not reverse the process of destruction and that the imposition of forced labor remained the only lifeline to survival (Hilberg 1992:114).

Lodz Ghetto

Before the war, about two hundred thousand Jews lived in the industrial city of Lodz and made up one-third of its population. Lodz ghetto was the first systematically organized large ghetto; it also was the longest-lived, existing from the spring of 1940 until liquidation in August 1944. At its height, the ghetto housed from three to four hundred thousand, including Lodz natives, Jews from the surrounding district and from the Reich, as well as five thousand Gypsies. The history of the Lodz ghetto is framed by two major cycles of selection and deportation, the first between January and the fall of 1942 and the second in August 1944. The interim period focused on forced labor within the hermetically sealed ghetto, with the "rescue through work" stratagem increasingly perceived as the only key to survival (Bauer 1989:37). In fact, it was Chaim Rumkowski, the Nazi-appointed head of the Judenrat, who convinced the Germans that the ghetto was economically exploitable (Yahil 1991:211). Early on, before the deportations began, the German manager of the ghetto made the case that starvation had to be attenuated in order to expand this exploitation (Browning 1992:47).

Motivated by power, honor, and historical mission, Rumkowski was a "pseudo-savior" who believed he would become the redeemer of the Jews after the war (Friedman 1980:336). He has been regarded by many as a megalomaniac tool of the Nazis (Peck 1987:349; Trunk 1972:432).[5] While he might have believed he could develop a policy of accommodation by providing financial profit to the Germans, what he interpreted as "autonomy" the Germans saw as "partnership" in the destruction of the Jews (Peck 1987:351). "Rescue through work" increasingly became "extermination through work," the logic being that those who could not work ought not be fed (Browning 1988:165).

Extermination was driven by a food pyramid of ration cards established by the Germans and based on labor potential; this system sped up attrition through starvation and selection for deportation, first to Chelmno, and later to Auschwitz. Class upheaval exacerbated the effect of the food pyramid with the inclusion of twenty thousand Jews from Western Europe, largely upper- and middle-class people who could not adjust to an economy based on skilled labor in the industrial workshops of the ghetto (Peck 1987:348). While they could use their material assets for ransom and bribery, their elite status was inappropriate to the needs of the ghetto. Social structure in Lodz was dominated by Rumkowski, the council, and the ghetto police, all of whom were exempted, along with their families, from deportation; skilled workers occupied the middle; nonworking people were at the vulnerable bottom.

Whatever his motives, Rumkowski appears as an autocratic leader who handed over Jews, including children, even after he knew that resettlement meant transport to death camps (Bauer 1989:423). Contingent on the "rescue through work" stratagem was the notion of sacrificing some to save others (Trunk 1972:423). In a speech on 4 September 1942 in which Rumkowski tells the ghetto residents that a quota of children under the age of ten will be deported, he also says that he has convinced the Nazis to exempt children older than ten. "I must perform this bloody operation," he explains, "I must cut off limbs in order to save the body itself" (cited in Adelson and Lapides 1989:328). Consequently, opposition, particularly by communists and socialists, grew against Rumkowski. Earlier there had been food riots, strikes, and demonstrations. But, with the support of the Germans, Rumkowski's centralized rule prevailed. He was so intent on controlling the economy that he strictly prevented the smuggling of food into the ghetto, and the food situation worsened (Trunk 1972:97). Clearly, the "redeemer" role of Rumkowski was encouraged by the Germans granting him authority in order to provide labor for the workshops and implement deportations (Trunk 1972:97). By the fall of 1942, however, the illusion of the autonomy of Rumkowski's regime was completely broken. Lodz became nothing more than a slave labor camp in which his powers were severely curtailed and the administrative apparatus of the Judenrat reduced (Yahil 1991:449). After a "quiet" period from 1943 to 1944, during which the ghetto survived because of its industrial importance, Rumkowski and his family were sent to their death at Auschwitz when liquidation occurred in August 1944. The irony is that Rumkowski was not altogether wrong in his pursuit of "rescue through work"; seventy thousand Jews remained just prior to the Auschwitz deportations when the Russians stopped their advance only seventy-five miles away. However, when Lodz was liberated by the Red Army in January 1945, only nine hundred Jews had survived.

It was not the Jews, but the Nazis, who raised Rumkowski to prominence. He had been a petty civil servant who "emerged from obscurity and whispers of corruption to become dictator of the Lodz ghetto" (Ezorsky 1984:75), and who was convinced that he had a role to play in the fate of modern Jewry (Trunk 1972:431). At the very least, he was instrumental in the Nazi scheme that focused first on the ghetto as a containment center for Jews until a policy could be fully formulated, then next as a work ghetto providing goods for the Wehrmacht, and finally as an embarkation point for deportation and death. The Nazi plan required that leaders like Rumkowski be transformed into accomplices by ensnaring them in a web of deception in order to lull the population into submission (Braham 1989:263). Rumkowski appears to have been the right man for the job, as he was able to contain opposition from ghetto residents as long as the Germans were willing to back him, and he maintained the illusion that "rescue through work" was the only key to survival.

Warsaw Ghetto

In 1939, one-third of Warsaw's population of 1.2 million consisted of Jews. The fate of Warsaw ghetto, fully established by November 1940, was determined in part by competition among the civilian administration under Hans Frank, the Wehrmacht who were intent on economic potential, and the SS who desired to control and decimate the Jews. Whereas the Gestapo was always very much in control in Lodz, in Warsaw both SS and German civilian authorities prevailed, often engaged in feud and contradiction (Gutman 1989:97). Until Himmler ordered massive deportations to Treblinka in the summer of 1942, the productionists held sway due to need for supplies for the war with Russia (Yahil 1991:331). As in Lodz, a food pyramid was enforced, and famine and disease began to decimate the ghetto at a furious pace.[6] By mid-1941, there were close to 150,000 deportees from Western Europe in Warsaw ghetto who died off quickly, unable, as in Lodz, to adapt to the economy (Roland 1992:18). Despite these similarities, there were some differences between the two ghettos. Lodz was a very tightly controlled economy, sealed off from the gentile part of the city, while Warsaw ghetto was more of a "free enterprise" system from the German standpoint (Browning 1992:50), with some permeability between the ghetto and the rest of Warsaw. Trade and smuggling continued between Jews and gentiles, with little interference from the Judenrat; whereas, in Lodz, Rumkowski came down hard on such activities (Trunk 1972:97).

The social organization and political economy of Warsaw ghetto created different death risks every day; survival depended on one's place in a class order rewarding those able to serve the Germans (Fein 1979:319). The mediator of this social order was Adam Czerniakow, an experienced leader in the Jewish community who was appointed in October 1939, prior to the set-up of the ghetto, as head of the Judenrat. In his role as chairman in the ghetto, Czerniakow spent his time scurrying between various German offices to deal with escalating and frequently contradictory decrees, as civilian officials and the SS competed for control over Warsaw (Yahil 1991:170). Feeling it was his obligation to allay misfortune by saving those who could be saved, Czerniakow willingly, although ambivalently, assumed his role (Fein 1979:138). Developing the ideal of the "passive martyr," he contrasted with Rumkow-ski, the "paternalistic autocrat" (Fein 1979:223). While he may have had personal courage, Czerniakow presided over a largely corrupt and inef-ficient Judenrat (Bauer 1989:164) and was beleaguered by constant de-mands from the Germans for extortion and labor. While there was some opposition to Czerniakow and the council due to their handling of the forced labor mobilization (Gutman 1989:24), there were no large-scale strikes and demonstrations as in Lodz (Trunk 1972:543). It may be that in more "liberal" Warsaw, with its greater array of political factions, the Judenrat had to listen to other prestigious groups—Zionist, communist, and socialist, of all sorts—and to their many underground newspapers, while in Lodz, Rumkowski held greater control over the press and other political activities (Trunk 1972:545). Nonetheless, as the middleman between the ghetto and the Germans, the Judenrat in Warsaw became the object of displaced rage and hostility as physical survival became increasingly difficult (Gutman 1989:38).

In July 1942, Himmler ordered the liquidation of all Jews in Poland. About 350,000 remained in Warsaw on the eve of deportations. It was believed in the ghetto that "resettlement" to labor camps in the east was at hand; however, by September, two-thirds of the ghetto populace had been sent to their death in Treblinka. Czerniakow continued in his role as mediator when deportations began and raced between his German contacts to chase down rumors and barter for smaller quotas of de-portees. When it became clear to him what actually was going on and, further, that children were to be handed over, Czerniakow committed suicide. There are various assessments of the possibly symbolic value of this suicide. Those in the underground resistance decried his failure to inform the ghetto of the true nature of the deportations (Fein 1979:249), while Yitzhak Zuckerman, one of the few survivors of the resistance, cannot forgive Czerniakow for choosing to die as "a private person" (Zuckerman 1993:195). Even though Czerniakow was liked and re-spected despite the unpopularity of the Judenrat, another survivor of the ghetto felt that the suicide constituted desertion, not leadership (Donat 1978:60).[7] In any case, the result of the suicide and the ongoing deporta-tions was chaos, as the Judenrat lost control to the ghetto police who frantically continued the roundups in order to save themselves and their families. At the final deportation, sixty-five thousand remained in the ghetto and another eight thousand managed to steal over to gentile

Warsaw (Yahil 1991:380). Like Lodz, Warsaw ghetto became nothing more than a slave labor camp.

Now, organized Jewish resistance finally coalesced when the ZOB (or Jewish fighting organization), a coalition of several political factions, stepped up contacts with the Polish underground and scrambled to obtain weapons. It was as if rebellion could not be organized until the authority of the Judenrat had been destroyed (Fein 1979:318). By January 1943, the ZOB, not the Judenrat, was in control of the ghetto (Roland 1992:214). The resistance executed some 300 of the 2,600 ghetto police remaining, but it was emotionally difficult, given that the Germans were the true enemy (Zuckerman 1993:210). Fines were imposed on economic collaborators and Judenrat members, a step aimed deliberately at humiliating them and emphasizing the authority of the ZOB, as well as providing a means to obtain weapons (Zuckerman 1993:332). The Warsaw Uprising, the first mass revolt in Nazi-occupied Europe, broke out in April 1943 and lasted several weeks but resulted in the destruction of the ghetto. Those remaining in the defeated and burned-out ghetto, unable to escape to the gentile side of Warsaw, were killed outright or sent to either labor camps or death camps. The Red Army did not arrive until two years later in April 1945.

Despite differences in the nature of leadership in the Judenrate of Lodz and Warsaw, important parallels mark the responses to Nazi steps to annihilate the Jews. In both ghettos the Judenrate and, more so, the populace were kept in the dark as to what "resettlement" really meant; all were encouraged to subscribe to the "rescue through work" stratagem. They also were encouraged by the Germans to believe that only certain sectors (deportees from Western Europe, for example) would be expelled and that able workers would be exempted. Resignation to the idea that dispossession of part of the population might secure the safety of the remainder was accompanied by the assumption, also fomented by the Germans, that resistance would make matters worse (Gutman 1989:227). In a third setting, Vilna ghetto, similar responses informed the reactions of the Jews to the Nazi genocidal scheme.

Vilna Ghetto

About sixty thousand Jews, making up 30 percent of the population, lived in Vilna when the Germans attacked the Soviet Union in June 1941.

Einsatzgruppen actions commenced in Vilna in July, and by the time the ghetto was set up in September, twenty thousand Jews had been slaughtered by the mobile killing units. As in Lodz and Warsaw, the competitive needs of the Germans helped shape the fate of the ghetto. While the military sought to protect the slave labor supply, since Vilna was an important railway hub and airbase at the rear of the eastern front, the Einsatzgruppen snatched men off the streets and took them to the nearby Ponary forest to be shot (Arad 1982:69). The skilled Jewish labor force was used in labor camps outside the ghetto, not in workshops within the ghetto as in Lodz and Warsaw. Leaving the camp to work facilitated the smuggling of food (Trunk 1972:86). Indeed, this source of food, as well as a lower incidence of disease, resulted in less "natural" attrition in Vilna than in Lodz and Warsaw (Trunk 1972:545).

The first Judenrat, made up of established community leaders, was liquidated by the Nazis almost immediately. Under a new Judenrat, the chief of police, Jacob Gens, a former officer in the Lithuanian army, rose to prominence as the titular head of the ghetto. Gens was not a native of Vilna; moreover, he was married to a gentile Lithuanian and probably could have hidden outside the ghetto. Why he accepted his position of authority remains a mystery (Friedman 1980:366). By the end of December 1941 when the shootings at Ponary had more or less ceased, thousands had perished and slave labor reigned. By July 1942, the Judenrat was deemed "too democratic" by the Germans and essentially was dismantled; all authority was vested in Gens (Friedman 1980:367). In an address on 15 July, Gens emphasized that the existence of the ghetto depended on work, discipline, and order, and, indeed, for fifteen months the "rescue through work" policy prevailed, favoring the young and the healthy (Hilberg 1992:180). Supporting the theory that some would have to perish in order to save others, Gens tried to quash rumors about what was going on in the Ponary forest (Hilberg 1992:180). When the Germans started deportations to work camps in Estonia, Gens ordered people to sign up or he would revoke the employment and ration cards that were the key to survival for workers and their families (Trunk 1972:403). Moreover, Gens helped force people into the trains headed for Estonia: "He got drunk, ran back and forth with his stick, beating and prodding Jews who refused to enter the transport cars" (Friedman 1980:377).

But Gens never surrendered children, as did Rumkowski, nor did he have the same monopoly of power as did Rumkowski (Hilberg 1992:147). Gens had to consider the attitudes of influential political factions in the ghetto (Friedman 1980:370). Resistance activities became highly organized early on in Vilna, in part because of knowledge gained about the deportations taking place in Warsaw. Moreover, there was more social homogeneity in Vilna than in the larger ghettos of Lodz and Warsaw (Trunk 1972:546), thus facilitating the organization of resistance. In January 1942, the FPO (United Partisans Organization) had been formed, a coalition of youth movements and political parties, including Zionists, communists, and other previously competitive groups (Arad 1982:234). From that point on, there was a struggle between Gens and the resistance over whether or not the ghetto should support the smuggling in of arms and the escape of young resistance members into the forests to join up with Soviet partisans. Gens's justification for nonsupport was his fear of eroding the labor force and the well-substantiated fear of collective reprisals (Hilberg 1992:176). In June 1943, in a speech to the ghetto police, Gens explained: "We may all maintain that escape to the forest is for the good of the ghetto. This may be so. But my task is to guard a loyal ghetto as long as it exists, so that nobody reprimands me" (cited in Trunk 1972:470). Gens's attitude toward the FPO was "vague and inconsistent from the start" (Friedman 1980:373), an attitude shared by many ghetto residents, especially toward the end of the life of the ghetto when it was believed that liberation by the Soviets was at hand (Trunk 1972:375). Due to continuing reprisals and deportations, the ghetto was deeply ambivalent about the resistance, hoping that liquidation could be postponed by buying time (Trunk 1972:467).

In the summer of 1943, Himmler pressed for the annihilation of the Lithuanian ghettos because of the deteriorating situation on the Russian front and the strengthening of the partisan groups in the forests (Yahil 1991:444). Dispatching Vilna workers to Estonia and Latvia was a part of his plan, as were escalating selections for killing. By the time Vilna ghetto was liquidated in September 1943, there were only about four thousand Jews left, half of them hiding in underground bunkers in the ghetto (Yahil 1991:446). Unable to muster an uprising, FPO members escaped to the forests to join with the partisans. Remaining ghetto residents were used to dig up the graves in Ponary in order to hide the evidence of the massacre; more than fifty thousand bodies were cremated (Arad 1982:445). Those remaining in the Vilna ghetto were killed in July 1944, just prior to liberation at the hands of the Soviets and the Jewish partisans who had fled to the forests.

As for Jacob Gens, he was shot by the Gestapo one week before the liquidation of the ghetto, accused, ironically, of aiding the resistance (Trunk 1972:470). Opinions of Gens are mixed. He may have been "a genuine collaborator" (Fein 1979:138), or a "misguided soul" who "possessed an arrogant faith in his special mission," but he had become a victim of the Nazi terror in which there was "no room for normal moral perceptions" (Friedman 1980:378). In 1964, the President of Israel, Zalman Shazar, argued that Gens's advocacy of sacrificing some in order to save others was correct (Trunk 1972:436). Conversely, my father-in-law, a survivor of Vilna ghetto who had escaped several labor camps and joined up with the partisans, today characterizes Gens as a traitor, conceding, nonetheless, that Gens was trapped in a bind created by the Germans that left him few options.

Rationality and Ambivalence

This reconstruction of an important phase in the Nazi genocide is based on historical documents and interpretations, as well as immediate rec-ollections (diaries) and less immediate, reconstituted narratives (mem-oirs). The problematics of the role of memory and our post hoc evalua-tions inform the attempt to reconstruct what occurred in the Holocaust. We are confronted with difficulties expressed in the equivocation about "reality" and "truth" articulated in some postmodern discourses. The irony is that while postmodernism presents an ethical challenge in its seeming rejection of identifying an ultimate reality, it also reminds us that there is an "opaqueness," or limit of understanding, in even the most precise renditions of the Holocaust (Friedlander 1992:5). Just as genocide questions conventional historical narrative, so does it chal-lenge the ethnographic attempt to delineate its social fields and struc-tures. In the case of the Nazi ghettos, our paradigmatic assumptions appear inadequate to a social system that so forcefully constricts human creativity and negates human existence, reminding us again of the limits of language and the elusiveness of representation. And yet, what is perturbing to our ethnographic (and moral) sensibilities is some recog-nition of "ordinary" life in our reading of the ghettos. Thus, a conscious divide-and-rule policy in Nazi rule is reminiscent of the colonial backgrounds of so many traditional ethnographic settings. The social organizations and value assumptions operative in the ghettos seem like echoes of "normality," twisted in bizarre ways to become cruel mimicries of the familiar. Thus, we learn that the children in Warsaw ghetto continued to play games in the street, even as they were starving to death; a favorite game was known as "tickling a corpse" (Ringelbaum 1974:174). A dialectical combination of uniqueness and normality, in which the Holocaust became the outcome of a weird encounter between "ordinary" and "common" factors (Bauman 1989:xiii), strains our ethnographic capabilities. It is no wonder we consistently run into irony in our retrievals of the routinization of terror. As Linda Green observes in contemporary Guatemala, it is routinization that "allows people to live in a chronic state of fear with a facade of normalcy, while that terror, at the same time, permeates and shreds the social fabric" (1994:231).

When we look at the transactional space in which the Nazi genocide was played out, themes of rationality (and irrationality), ambivalence, denial, and resistance emerge. Despite the facts that the success of the Holocaust rested on the Jews having become "a cognitive incongruence," placed outside "the universe of obligation," thereby abrogating social morality (Bauman 1989:27), and that the ghetto administration consciously insulated interaction between the perpetrators and the victims, there was some operational necessity for face-to-face encounters. The diary of Avraham Tory, the deputy secretary of the Jewish council in Kovno ghetto (Lithuania), illustrates this transactional space. In it, Tory recounts a number of encounters he had in 1943 with the ghetto commander, Lieutenant Miller.

In explaining Miller's communication style, Tory says that he "understands" the "accepted practice" whereby Miller uses a "domineering and commanding" voice when other Germans are present. Otherwise, says Tory, "I often speak to Miller one on one: on such occasions our conversation is polite and to the point" (Tory 1990:178). Even so, he describes a January meeting with Miller that is "quite theatrical": "The Germans speak with us as humans quite often, but when they suddenly realize that the person they are talking to is simply a Jew, they raise their voices" (181). After another meeting Tory describes how the permanent state of nervous tension in the ghetto is encouraged by the Nazi policy of secrecy and ambiguity. Thus, he says, "we are to remain always in a state of anticipation without understanding what is going on around us. . . . This is always the way with the Germans. They do not tell you things clearly, except when they curse you and scream at you. It is therefore imperative to assess their mood properly before they open their mouths" (209). At a meeting the following day, Tory discusses food rations with Miller. Tory is taken aback when Miller speaks "like a logical human being," referring to "equality of rights" with respect to the Jews. But then Tory realizes that this equality is all "relative," and that Miller has been having problems with the non-Jewish Lithuanian labor force also needed for the war effort, and that he has just gotten news of the setback at Stalingrad (214).

In April, Tory confronts Miller about the slaughter of five thousand Jews from Vilna who were supposed to have been transported to Kovno but instead were taken to Ponary and killed. Tory wants "an open, human conversation"; he knows that when Miller "is not angry, and is alone with me in the room, he is capable of speaking as one human being to another." Miller is elusive, but, when pressed by Tory, he shifts the responsibility for the slaughter of the Vilna group to the Gestapo. Tory reads this as an "unspoken admission" and concludes that "under his Nazi uniform there is some spark of humanity." Miller continues "with eyes cast downward" and reassures Tory that nothing will happen to Kovno ghetto: "I give you my promise" (285–86). Fifteen months later, Kovno ghetto is liquidated.

A number of things stand out in this report of dialogue in the context of the ghetto. Evident is the need for the Jews to read the intentions of the Germans. In an encounter with a member of the civilian administration, Tory is "anxiously following not only the drift of his questions but the tone of his voice, his facial expression, and his gaze" (176). Trying to anticipate Nazi behavior, the Judenrate were allowed "just enough social normality" to "nurture the illusion that they could act in furtherance of their own survival" (Diner 1992:133–34). Perceptual failure stemmed from the Nazi policy of deceit but also from an ambivalence, on both sides, evidenced in the dialogues between Tory and Miller. The Judenrate ended up adopting an impossible compromise between placating the Nazis and trying to save their own community (Yahil 1991:334). One result was that the Judenrate, like the Nazis, did not always tell the truth to their constituencies about their own intentions (Gottlieb 1990:340). Belief in the "rescue through work" stratagem depended on what amounted to collusion between the Judenrate and the Nazis on what "resettlement" really meant.

While the options for the Jews were limited and uncertain, choices and decisions did occur (Lang 1990:65) and were made within "the web of meanings and activities" that constituted the culture of the ghetto (Marrus 1987:118). Ultimately, the "competitive incentive structure" based on the labor stratagem led the Judenrate to the judgment that it was rational to work within the Nazi-defined system (Fein 1979:126). One of the reasons social science has neglected the Holocaust is that it upsets the received notion of the progressive rationalization of social life (Bauman 1989:176). When historians judge Nazism in terms of customary criteria of rationality, they often disqualify it as "irrational," thereby relegating Nazi behavior as unamenable to rational insight (Diner 1992:130). But if we look at it from the perspective of the Judenrate, the Nazi system was neither rational nor irrational, but rather counterrational (133). That is, the Judenrate operated on the premise that labor would take precedence over annihilation, because they assumed the Germans were guided by utilitarian motives and the civilizing logic of "*Homo Economicus*" (137).[8] Culturally indebted to the criterion of rationality, the Judenrate were using unsuitable forms of thought and action, given that their oppressors had engendered a reversal of the value-ethics of ends and means, and the Judenrate ended up directing this reversal against their own people (140). In this sense, they were engaging in unconscious complicity (Gottlieb 1990:342), although in a framework in which the Nazis appear to have buried logic as well as people.[9]

A further example of how different systems of logic functioned is in the persistence of organized educational, cultural, and religious activities in long-term ghettos like Lodz, Warsaw, and Vilna. The Jews regarded these as signs of stabilization and as a means of combating demoralization; nowadays, they often are interpreted as significant forms of resistance (Roskies 1984). From the German perspective, however, a policy of permitting such activities in a space of isolation and dissimilation (Dobroszycki 1980:225) was rather a means by which the "otherness" of the Jews could be highlighted.

Yet another example of contrary logic was the use of the ghetto police to help round up Jews, first for labor brigades and later for deportation. From the German standpoint, this was a way to get the Jews to do their dirty work for them. The Judenrate, on the other hand, early on felt that it would be more orderly and humane to have their own police round up labor. When it became clear that people were being rounded up not for labor but for extermination, Czerniakow committed suicide in Warsaw, but Rumkowski in Lodz and Gens in Vilna never changed their minds about this use of the ghetto police (Trunk 1972:508).

The social field occupied by the Jews and the Nazis was characterized by a fundamental dissonance in norms, values, and mental models with which to construct reality. While rationality of choice is always delimited by the fact that aspects of reality are only selectively noticed and used as a basis for reasoning about action, the ghetto was clearly a caricature of "normal" social life as the reality became one of increasing terror. The utter dependence of the Judenrate on the Germans, along with their anticipation of protection and survival, forced them into the strategy of "buying time" to which everything else became subordinate (Diner 1992:139).

If we realize that the Jews and the Germans were operating under antagonistic and contradictory premises, we can retreat from the dichotomies of acquiescence and resistance that have dominated much thinking about the Holocaust (Marrus 1987:121). The Judenrate were engaging not so much in collaboration as cooperation that, given their Nazi-appointed task, was unavoidable (Trunk 1972:572). Weighing their limited alternatives, the Judenrate chose the "rational" device of taking advantage of the competition and friction between the productionists and the attritionists. The Nazis induced the Jews to adopt such a "rational" mode, leading them to believe that their conduct did matter and that something could be saved, even though the choice was not between good and evil but between greater and lesser evil (Bauman 1989:130). Is it ex post facto to blame the Judenrate for their blindness, as do Hannah Arendt (1963) and Raul Hilberg (1985; see also Browning 1986), because we now know the outcome (Ezorsky 1984:76)? Aside from the fact that singular normative standards cannot relate to behavior under conditions of unrelenting stress and terror, it is naive to adopt a paradigm in which victims must be both innocent and uninvolved in the system (Fein 1979:142). Indeed, the most cunning thing about the Nazi genocide was that it created the ghetto as a bizarre mixture of self-government and isolation, making the Jews a part of the social system that destroyed them (Bauman 1989:122). Acting against both the group and the individual, the Nazi program set out to destroy the bond between the self as individual and the self as a member of the group (Lang 1990:77).

Conclusion

Invigorated by the Nazi system, denial shaped the Jewish reaction to the genocidal endeavor and compromised the ability to conceptualize resistance. Denial won out even after the true Nazi intention was realized. The conflict and struggle that raged in Vilna and Warsaw between the Judenrate and the resistance came about from the Judenrate's perception that resistance threatened their position and also the survival of the ghetto (Yahil 1991:463). Reconstructing what went on in this struggle rests on the two planes on which memory plays: "the historical and the rhetorical, the way it was, and its verbal reformation, or deformation, by later commentators" (Langer 1993:39). The rhetorical shield of heroism surrounding the Warsaw Uprising, most notably, cannot cancel out the reality that the uprising essentially was futile and that the ghetto was doomed (Langer 1993:86–87). It was neither individual courage nor complicity that sealed the fate of the Jews. Helen Fein (1979), testing Hannah Arendt's (1963) thesis of a causal link between the extent of genocide and the cooperation of the Judenrate, found that isolation and a lack of outside help were more immediate causes of mass destruction. By the time of the Warsaw Uprising, so very late in the process, the motive of the resisters was more that of revenge than an attempt to save themselves and their already decimated community. "The struggle was a hopeless one as it could neither bring rescue nor offer a way out" (Yahil 1991:463). It was too little too late.

The contradictions, ambiguities, and discontinuities characterizing the ghetto settings of the Holocaust indicate that the Jews had no choice but to improvise a social order out of chaos and, consequently, our usual ethnographic sensibilities appear inadequate to fully retrieve these improvisations. In part, our need for redemptive closure leads us to link up these altered conditions and altered lives to ordinariness and familiarity. Thus, we can understand the dearth of active resistance by young people who hesitated to smuggle in arms or leave the ghetto because they feared abandoning their families to fully anticipated reprisals. An equally relevant piece of reality was the wider context of abandonment in which Jewish resisters had enormous difficulty obtaining arms and were rejected or even killed by anti-Semitic partisans or underground groups if they left the ghetto. If resistance is a free act in the sense that "to resist is also to recognize the possibility of engaging in alternative acts which are not resistance" (Gottlieb 1990:330), then our usual modes of understanding resistance are sorely tried under such intentional genocidal conditions. Nonetheless, it is clear that the ambivalences and ambiguities of resistance emanate in part from "the intricate webs of articulation and disarticulation" between the dominant and the dominated (Ortner 1995:190). This helps explain why ambivalence marks the assessment of Jewish leadership by both ghetto residents and latter-day commentators.

Without diminishing the uniqueness of the Holocaust, there is continuity between the "rescue through work" stratagem in the ghettos and other fascist endeavors. Thus, Robert Gordon in this volume speaks of how the regulation of labor in Namibia (formerly German South West Africa) served as an instrument of pacification not only of the colonized but also of the colonizers. As their work became fetishized as the ordinary while social fields became killing fields, self-delusion set in. The signs over the entries to the labor camps and death camps in the Holocaust read "Arbeit Macht Frei" ("Work Shall Set You Free"). What we regard as a cruel attempt at cynicism also may have been a signifier of normalization, a reminder to perpetrators and victims alike, that structure is achieved and power is made manifest through order and discipline. As unwitting participants with limited strategic possibilities, the Judenrate were caught up in the workings of a fascist imagination that cleverly took advantage of a subversion of usual understandings of the meaning of labor. What had been an ordinary component of social life, so important to self-realization and the actualization of social structure, became an extraordinary means of control and annihilation. As depicted in the film Schindler's List, the ghettos and the Judenrate had the misfortune to participate in an inversion in which the killing mode surpassed the labor mode and in which the terrifyingly extraordinary became just ordinary in the Holocaust.

Notes

Kay Warren and my dear colleague, Rob Gordon, have been most generous with their interest in my essay; they have my gratitude. I have been inspired over the last several years by the annual Raul Hilberg lecturers at the University of Vermont, most notably, Christopher Browning, Yehuda Bauer, and Saul Friedlander, who, along with Hilberg, are foremost historians of the Holocaust.

1. The diary recounting these events was compiled by Perechodnik in gentile Warsaw, where he hid in a bunker prior to his death (probably from typhus) in July 1944.

2. Other anthropologists who also address this issue include Christian Krohn-Hansen (1994) and Linda Green (1994). Their call to anthropology is not to ignore the harsh realities of everyday life, but rather to confront violence and cultures of fear and terror with all the ethnographic sensibilities we can muster. At the same time, we must be aware of the risk of overtheorizing the suffering of others lest we unintentionally add "abstraction to injury" (Benthall 1997:2).

3. That is, in Desjarlais and Kleinman's (1994) terms, there are two ethnographies that, of course, are disparate, but might combine to form an "ethnography of terror." In the case of the Holocaust, historiography provides the ethnography of the state: narratives in diaries, chronicles, and memoirs, the ethnography of the individual. Any retrieval of the Holocaust is surrounded by hermeneutical issues in both historiography and narrative, but the limits of language and the elusiveness of representation, as Carol Greenhouse indicates in her introduction to this volume, are problems for both ourselves and those whose lives we depict. Interestingly, some historians of the Holocaust now are calling for the depiction of "everyday life" during the Holocaust and a focus on people's "difficult decisions, vacillations, and problems" (Ofer 1995:66). A convergence between historiography and ethnography is suggestive of more nuanced and less stereotypical accounts of the Nazi terror.

4. In the very early days of the occupation of Lithuania, pogroms were encouraged by the Nazis. A report submitted by the head of an Einsatzgruppen explained how "local anti-Semitic elements were induced to engage in pogroms against the Jews, without letting on the German involvement. . . . The impression had to be created that the local population itself had taken the first steps of its own accord as a natural reaction to decades of oppression by the Jews and the more recent horror exerted by the Communists" (cited in Klee, Dressen, and Riess 1991:24).

5. A survivor from Lodz, Perec Zylberberg, who was fourteen years old at the establishment of the ghetto, has this recollection of Rumkowski: "He used to claim indirectly the title of King of the Lodz ghetto. He boasted about his grand designs for making the ghetto tick like a watch. His manner of dress was one of an affront to the poor, impoverished ghetto people. He wore long, shiny boots and spotless clothes. He just made the bystanders feel, or he wanted to make them feel, inferior and powerless. In his mannerisms he copied the German style. So did his cronies, crawlers, and henchmen" (cited in Gilbert 1996:79).

6. Food rations were allocated to families according to type of employment. The severe inadequacy of caloric intake and the speedy decline of health in the ghetto is well documented in Roland (1992).

7. Ambivalence about Czerniakow also suffuses the diary and chronicle of Emmanuel Ringelbaum (1974). In September 1940, he recounts: "Heard that the president of the Jewish Council of Warsaw, Adam Czerniakow, was kept standing in a German office for eight hours and not offered a chair. There are some who consider him a martyr who is honestly fulfilling his duty. 'He is picking up the smell of the Gestapo,' said an elderly community worker. The influence of the environment"

(53). When Czerniakow kills himself, Ringelbaum tersely notes: "The suicide of Czerniakow—too late, a sign of weakness—should have called for resistance—a weak man" (316).

8. Ghetto residents consistently subscribed to this logic. Calel Perechodnik (1996) records in his diary: "Jews were probably not as happy when they received the Ten Commandments as when they received the permit to open workshops, especially now wagonloads of rags that are to be washed have now arrived in Otwock. Great happiness reigns: There are workshops, there are rags, we will work, we'll remain in place" (20). A survivor of Kovno ghetto remembers that those who received work certificates referred to the permits as "Licenses to Live" (Faitelson 1996:53).

9. Judy Rosenthal's essay in this volume describes how the agendas of Vodu worshippers and colonial authorities did not function within the same logical framework, reiterating this point about the relationship between the dominated and the dominators.

Robert J. Gordon

Unsettled Settlers: Internal

Pacification and Vagrancy in Namibia

The laws alone remove us from the condition of the savages.—J. Fenimore Cooper, *The Pioneers*

At five o'clock one green dawn, when the stars were paling and the pea-fowl were screaming from the thickets across the tracks, another man and I waited to be picked up from a railway station in upper South-West Africa. . . . Seeing that I was a stranger, he talked in a grand way about his farm. "When I get a new boy," he said, "the first thing I do is walk over to him and twist his ear." With a terrible thumb and forefinger he showed me how he walked across to a new labourer, took hold of the man's ear, and screwed it around.

"But doesn't that humiliate them?" I asked. "Sometimes I make them cry." "Don't they ever try to hit back?" "Sometimes a Herrero [*sic*] will. They've too damn much cheek; two words for every one of yours." "What do you do then?" "All you've got to do is guard your head. They fight with sticks. They'd kill you, when they get mad—so you go for them." He had grown up, he said, in the Karoo, fighting with nigger boys. And he knew stick fighting. "After a minute or so I always get the stick away from them . . . and then I let them have it! I make them understand I'm *baas.* Then we get along fine." Then he added: "But I always tell them why—why I—twisted their ear . . . you see, I always find some good excuse for it." "Sort of make them see reason?" I suggested. "That's it. You've got it!" he said. "Exactly!"—Negley Farson, *Behind God's Back*

What is it that states find so threatening about people whom they believe have no fixed address? This is a question that has vexed scholars for a long time. In this essay, I pursue both particularities and implications of Hannah Arendt's (1971) well-known and controversial thesis that the origins of German totalitarianism lay in the colonial experience—not in colonial treatment of "natives" per se, but of those officially defined as vagabonds.

Vagrancy is a topic of vital importance to those whom the colonizers have labeled "Bushmen." For the last number of years I have been engaged in a project documenting "Bushmen" as an impoverished rural underclass—indeed constituting the most brutalized people in southern Africa's bloody history. The German colonial officials who imposed their state upon the estate that later became known as Namibia made a distinction between *Eingeborenen* (indigenes) and "Vagabond Bushmen." In the ethnography of "Bushmen" within the colonial context, it is striking how much effort—both administrative and emotional—colonizers invested in controlling people of no fixed address: vagabonds, vagrants, "Bushmen," and the like.

My central claim in this chapter is that in order to understand the nature of the relationships between Bushmen and colonizers one must analyze the colonial state's efforts to control the movement of indigenes.[1] My question is not about how colonizers used law in consolidating a newly transforming and reconstructing settler state or in ensuring a stable labor supply, but rather how lawmaking—vagrancy legislation—was shaped by the psychological demands of what Vincent Crapanzano (1985) calls "waiting," that moment when the privileged expect the inevitable invasion of the Barbarian other. In particular, I focus on how people in a position of domination, suffering the unbearable powerlessness of waiting, anesthetize their situation with the magical use of law. Settlement entails not only physical movement but also a psychic domain: Angst and other anxieties have to be allayed for settlers to be settled. Law is crucial in this operation, creating what Jürgen Habermas (1971) terms "facticity."

My analysis is set in the early years of South African overrule of the territory of South West Africa, a parcel of land annexed by Germany in 1884 and designated a *Schutzgebiet* (protectorate). As part of its contribution to the Allied war effort during the Great War, South Africa successfully invaded the territory. In 1920 the League of Nations granted South Africa a mandate to administer the territory as if it were an integral part of that country. Faced with a variety of internal problems not least of which was that of "Poor Whites" (Afrikaner peasants driven from the land) coupled with the need to develop a strong settler presence in Namibia to underline South African claims to sovereignty, the South African administration embarked on a policy of encouraging white colonization.

Colonization, as Frederick Cooper (1994) reminds us, involves control of both space and time. One of the first legal documents the South Africans issued when they were granted the mandate over the former

German South West Africa was the Vagrancy Proclamation of 1920, which, according to its preamble, was intended to *suppress both trespass and idleness.* It would thus appear to be a key piece of colonial carceral legislation, yet most scholars, building on Karl Marx's horrific descriptions of "primitive accumulation" (1977: section 8), have taken it to be only a tool to promote labor supply since it provided that a first offender be placed in a term of service on public works or with a private person (Wellington 1967:282–83; Mbuende 1986:82; Moleah 1983:56). The proclamation extended beyond protecting private property from trespass. The person accused of trespassing had to demonstrate "visible lawful means of support." And this was rather arbitrarily fixed at a herd of either ten cattle or fifty small stock, leading Lord Lugard, the eminent British colonial administrator and member of the Permanent Mandates Commission (PMC), to complain that this meant that all Bushmen were de facto vagrants (PMC Minutes 1923:61, 293)!

As a strategy for inducing labor, the legislation was by no means unique. Similar situations were found in many parts of the world (Nye 1984; Huggins 1985), yet vagrancy laws have not been subject to thorough analysis in the making of the colonial state. Indeed, given the centrality of private property and the institutions that circled around it in the key Western intellectual notion of civilization, especially in the 1920s, it is surprising that vagrancy is so underresearched.

In Namibia indigenes experienced the state most directly in its efforts to regulate labor markets and in its steady elaboration of a panoply of legislation that was part of the same ideological package as the Vagrancy Proclamation. Native policy rested on a "system of reserves, pass regulations, and more or less compulsory labor service enforced through Master and Servant and Vagrancy laws under the general supervision of magistrates and police" (Swanson 1967:659). The emphasis on the instrumentality of vagrancy legislation has diverted attention from the contradictions inherent in it. In particular the cultural and moral meanings of this legislation have been ignored.[2] I argue that vagrancy legislation was more important on a symbolic level for the settlers than a crass instrumentalist interpretation would allow. There were important contradictions between agency and structures in this process of what Anthony Giddens (1985) terms internal pacification, not only of the colonized but, more important for this discussion, of the colonizers as well.

Law not only regulates sociocultural life, it represents it as well. As an ideology, law contributes to the social construction of the world by creating images of specific relationships as natural and fair (Merry 1992). In Namibia, law emerged out of complex factors; settler society was rarely homogenous in its legal needs. Legislation was generally a compromise measure designed to satisfy the needs of several factions of settlers in both Namibia and South Africa as well as for the international audience at the Permanent Mandates Commission of the League of Nations to which the South West African administration had to submit annual reports for oversight and advice.

Locating the Vagrancy Proclamation within the Legal Panoply

The Vagrancy Proclamation must be read in conjunction with other legislation from this period, and, in such a context, the argument that this overlapping battery of laws served to provide cheap labor for settlers seems eminently reasonable. Already by 1923 it was clear to the Permanent Mandates Commission that settler farmers, as well as the administrator, thought natives existed chiefly to serve as labor for Europeans (PMC Minutes 1923:120).

In 1921, one of the first tasks the new administration undertook was the establishment of a Native Reserves Commission to "establish certainty for the whites as to the permanent abode of the natives" and to "combat vagrancy and idleness" (Olivier 1961:94). As a working principle, the commission decided, not surprisingly, to adopt the general principle of segregation based on the South African model, and thus it created reserves—the location of which had nothing to do with ancestral lands or ethnic heritage but everything to do with providing each magisterial district with a "holding tank" for surplus and redundant labor.[3]

In addition to the Vagrancy Proclamation, the key proclamations that served to bind indigenes to workplaces while at the same time promoting their movement away from other abodes included the Masters and Servants Proclamation (34/1920) that, while based on civil contracts, allowed for criminal penalties of incarceration and corporal punishment for offenses like "withholding full effort," "desertion," "unauthorized absence from work," disobedience, nonobservance of work rules, and "intentional or unlawful acts or omissions which actually or potentially damage persons or property." It provided punishments of up to three pounds or two months Imprisonment with Hard Labor for a variety of offenses like willful breach or neglect of duty or drunkenness or, for a herdsman, failing to report the death or loss of stock or "fail[ing] to preserve part of the carcass of the animals he alleges to have died." Lesser penalties were applicable for infringements like lateness or absence from work, refusing to obey a lawful command, and "impertinence and the like" (Raedel 1947:432–33).

Along with the establishment of reserves, the Native Administration Proclamation of 1922 provided for "passes." All natives (defined as "every male over fourteen years of age one of whose parents is a member of some aboriginal race or tribe of Africa") except those specially exempted were required to carry passes when traveling beyond the confines of the location or reserve where they resided. Passes could be demanded of natives by police, municipal or railway officials, "or any landowner or lessee." Failure to produce such a pass on demand resulted in arrest by such official or landowner. These passes could be issued by employers, magistrates, or a number of other authorized officials; employers could refuse to issue passes if the employee had not completed his contract. In 1927, Proclamation 11/1927 further tightened access to passes. An employed native could obtain a pass only from his employer.[4] Should his employer refuse such a pass the worker had the option of either deserting or staying on. Workers could, but rarely did, take grievances to the magistrate. The same proclamation amended the Masters and Servants Proclamation by doubling the severity of punishment for servants. Fines went from three to seven pounds, imprisonment was similarly extended, and whipping was introduced. When asked about this, the administrator explained—to the incomprehension of some members of the Permanent Mandates Commission—that the increased penalties "had been designed to make it worth [the farmers'] while" to lay charges against servants (PMC Minutes 1923:67–68).

If conditions were bad in the reserves, they were even worse in the towns. Here, Lord Lugard observed, regulations amounted to "extremely drastic class legislation. It was, for example, laid down that natives might not make a noise at night, that they might be expelled without appeal to the courts, and that in the case of Swakopmund they were not allowed to walk on the pavements, etc." Administrator Hofmeyr replied that such legislation "was necessary to ensure the peace of the white man" (PMC Minutes 1924:79).

The baselines of native policy were shaped by the Native Reserves Commission that reported in June 1921 and underwrote the principles of segregation by arguing for reserves. Its professed aims were to secure the contentment and welfare of indigenes "as far as possible" while ensuring a permanent labor supply for settlers. A concurrent aim was to "tighten up Native Administration in order to prevent vagrancy and idleness" (South Africa 1921:13). And this aim periodically re-emerges in the official discourses. It comes out succinctly at the hearings of the Permanent Mandates Commission. For example, "it was entirely in the interests of the natives. The natives, if allowed to live with the white people, eventually parted with their land and became *vagrants and a source of danger*" (my emphasis). And, in justifying the pass regulations, advocates explained that they were "intended to prevent vagrancy. The European population was continually complaining of the large numbers of vagrants, who had no means of subsistence and who stole stock from the farmers. To meet these complaints, the pass system had been invented by the Germans. It acted as a protection for the natives, who, so long as they had a pass, could not be arrested" (PMC Minutes 1923:104, 105).

Enforcing the Proclamations

The world the Germans imposed was considerably weakened with the establishment of the mandate. The same basic organizational structure persisted but in a much diluted condition. In April 1919, the German population stood at some 12,300, of whom the South Africans deported 6,384, including 1,226 civil officials, 1,619 military personnel, and 873 police (Wellington 1967:272). The South Africans engaged in considerable downsizing. In 1923, the administrator noted that his staff consisted of only 311 officials of whom 212 were hired on a temporary basis with large anomalies in pay, allowances, and local privileges that eventually led to problems of demoralization (PMC Minutes 1923:48).

In addition to the 19,714 whites enumerated in the first census in 1921, there were approximately 200,000 "natives" (Goldblatt 1971:265) who fell under the control of native administration. Native administration in Namibia was always a shoestring operation. In 1939 it consisted of one part-time (ex officio) chief native commissioner (the secretary for South West Africa, who until 1928 was also police commissioner) supported by two native commissioners, twelve clerks, and ten reserve superintendents. In addition each magisterial district was in charge of a magistrate who doubled as a native commissioner. These whites were in turn supported by some 18 native constable/messengers, 46 chiefs/headmen, 70 reserve councilors, 54 native clerk/interpreters, and 3 guards (South Africa 1939:6). At the same time it was decided that for financial and other reasons there was no justification for personnel expansion. Since magistrates were primarily officials in the Department of Justice, they tended to give native administration a low priority, usually delegating such matters to a junior clerk who would then oversee the reserve superintendents. Magistrates were recruited from the South African Department of Justice on a rotating basis, and a usual posting lasted for less than four years (South Africa 1939:6).

There was no requirement of professional experience or skills for either the magistrates or Department of Native Affairs officials. An attempt was made to reward the study of local languages and customs with a cash bonus, but after a few years and general lack of interest this fell into abeyance. Indeed it was argued that most of the settler population knew something of native customs and languages in any case, and thus no special training was deemed necessary (PMC Minutes 1931:61; 1938:77).

In effect then, native administration within the police zone was carried out by ordinary magistrates in the course of their functions as administrative and judicial representatives of the government at the local level. Typically they were transferred in from South Africa on a two-year tour of duty. As they were also the police commanders until 1928, it was the police together with the junior clerks in the magistrate's offices who carried out routine as well as penal aspects of day-to-day native affairs.

Given the low organizational density in which these officials operated, it was obviously difficult to audit their performances. This meant that they had considerable informal power. Nowhere is this better illustrated than among the superintendents. Each reserve was under a superintendent who had to "know every native, prevent idleness," limit excessive livestock, and see that the reserves were used as retirement centers for the older people (Olivier 1961:102). They were responsible for all reserve development work, the collection of grazing fees, the allocation of grazing and habitional areas, and had an important say in admission. Moreover they had to approve the appointment of the reserve's headmen and councilors and could overrule them almost at will. About the superintendents, Lord Hailey, the prominent expert on colonial affairs remarked:

> The post . . . is of great importance. . . . But these officers are not . . . on the regular cadre of the Native Affairs Department; they may be-

fore appointment have little experience of Native Affairs; and they have not the same incentive to study the language and custom of the people. . . . At present, their initial pay is as a rule below that which would be drawn by junior officers of the Department. (Hailey n.d.:97)

Superintendents were frequently "relieved" by local policemen, which indicates that they were easily replaced and that the police played a crucial role in the general administration of the territory.

The military constabulary that had been the prime means of internal pacification ceased to exist at the end of 1919 and was replaced by the South West Africa Police which in addition to line officers also had a small criminal investigation department, a police training depot, and a herd of some four hundred camels. It drew most of its recruits from the old military constabulary but had "great difficulty" obtaining suitable recruits, the "principal defect being lack of education." Complaints about the lack of suitable recruits were to be a near constant refrain (South Africa 1920, 1936).

Despite settler demands for increased policing, abatement was the norm. Until 1939, the general pattern was for a consistent decrease in authorized strength and a constant undermanning as actual strength never matched the authorized members. Indeed, when the administration was forced to retrench personnel during the Depression, the largest single block of retrenchments, 81 Europeans and 114 natives, came from the police force (South Africa 1931). Downsizing occurred not only in raw numbers but also in terms of distribution. While the Germans had operated 113 police stations, this number decreased to 39 under the South Africans (PMC Minutes 1924:44).

Gradually, however, the number of outstations increased, but not for the purpose of directly policing vagrants and pass-law offenders. In 1923, for example, four new outstations were opened to control the movement of infected livestock from the north. In 1925 and 1927 another three outstations were commissioned, but their purpose appears to have been largely to prevent the theft of diamonds. The major expansion of the police force occurred in April 1939 when the South West Africa Police was combined with the South African Police. This occurred not because of rebellious natives or recalcitrant workers, but because the South Africans feared a putsch by the local German settler minority.

The business of the police, at least in popular police folklore, was patrolling (Swanepoel 1972). Typically they would undertake three-week camel patrols. It was only in 1939 that their camels and horses were replaced by twenty vehicles. Premechanized patrolling could not have been very effective, if only because of the 20 to 30 percent annual mortality rate of their patrol animals.

Given the paucity of officials, the role of the constable devolved into that of general administrative factotum. The 1939 report lists over thirty-three "extraneous" duties that the police were required to shoulder. These included the following tasks: administration and prosecution under the Motor Vehicle Ordinance (including roadworthiness and driver testing), prosecuting, pass issuance, branding native stock, preparing voters rolls, relieving reserve superintendents, agricultural census, examining sheep and goats for scab, land board inspections, compiling lists of school children, representing the meat trade control board, inoculating cattle, and serving as subreceivers of revenue and as postal agents (South Africa 1934:37).

Such a situation was not conducive to formal policing, and this was acknowledged by the administration:

Laws have been provided to deal with this aspect of native administration, but in a country of vast distances . . . it is impossible to provide ready means for enforcing them unless of course the Police Force is greatly increased and this means additional taxation. Persons living at great distances from the nearest magistracy prefer to put up with impudent conduct on the part of their natives rather than undertake long journeys for the purpose of putting the law in motion and risk the possible loss of their servants, to say nothing of the delay and expense and thus no special training was deemed necessary. (PMC Minutes 1931:61)

"Lumping it" (Galanter 1974) or "redressive self-help" were apparently common settler strategies on the outlying farms as accounts by Wilhelm Mattenklodt, Raif, and other settlers attest. Indeed, this was reflected in a subgenre of German colonial literature epitomized most notably by Hans Grimm, author of the influential Nazi-era best seller *Volk Ohne Raum* (People without space). In a series of books, Grimm (for example, 1970, 1973) meticulously documented the plight of German farmers who remained in the mandate of South West Africa and were forced by state inaction to "take the law into their own hands"—leading him to the inevitable conclusion that "a piece of New Germany in Africa is a burning necessity" (1970:338).

Similarly, workers could often evade the law as well. For example, in 1926, only 33 of 1,174 reported workers who deserted in the first eight months were apprehended by the police despite the circulation of their names to "traditional authorities." This practice continued more or less unabated through the period under review. Efforts to control desertion included the development of enclosed compounds with a central entrance away from the white parts of town; thus, movement could be easily controlled.

Given the quality of this enforcement system, statistics should be treated with more than average suspicion. But, while they are problematic, they do provide pointers with respect to the main emphases and relationships of the enforcement system. A more specific problem in examining statistics entails classification. Official statistics classify offenses as being against the state, public order, public peace, administration of justice, persons, property, statutory offenses, and offenses against revenue. Vagrancy is officially classified as an offense against the public order, a category into which fall "a curious assortment of crimes, such as bigamy, soliciting, illicit sexual relations between Africans and Europeans, various religious offenses, cruelty to animals, . . . and the unlawful possession at night of housebreaking implements" (Simons 1949:86).[5]

Like their colleagues in other mandated territories, the constabulary achieved exceptionally high conviction rates ranging from 79 to 91 percent. If one examines the ratio of the number of cases sent to court per policeman, the ratio increases from 19 to 1 in 1924 to 43 in 1937, and peaks at 50 in 1938 before declining to 29 with the infusion of South African Police in 1939. This suggests that a number of factors are at work: ranging from increasing police efficiency, increasing lawlessness or, more simply and more importantly, increasing bureaucratic expansionism epitomized by increasing the number of offense categories.[6]

By examining the categories under which charges were laid, it is striking how comparatively unimportant vagrancy is as a category while charges under the Masters and Servants Proclamation show a progressive increase, although still less than expected.[7] From a labor instrumentalist point of view, the Vagrancy Proclamation was ineffective. Workers recruited by this means simply deserted again! The draconian amendment in 1927 (Proclamation 32/1927), whereby the maximum period of imprisonment was increased from three to twelve months (including the option of three months in solitary with a spare diet) and the maximum fine skyrocketed from two pounds to one hundred pounds, can be read as a signal of defeat.[8]

What conclusions can be drawn from this brief discussion? Despite the extravagant lengths the administration went to, including its usurpation of vast powers, it is quite clear that the settler state lacked the logistical and personnel capacity to derive maximum benefits from the laws so clearly loaded in favor of them. Could there be a correlation between administrative incompetence and incapacity and excessive laws?

The Nature of the Settler State

Contemporary social theory places great emphasis on the knowledge/power equation in state formation (see Foucault 1980).[9] The state's documentation creates and normalizes a vast amount of information that forms the basis of the capacity to govern (Cohn 1988). Yet as anyone who has extensively used the Namibian archives will attest, one of the most obvious changes accompanying the insertion of the South African administration is the massive decline in administrative documentation. The scribal culture was not well developed among the South African administrators. Records, reports, and routine data collection became increasingly problematic. Unlike their British counterparts who proudly saw themselves as the cream, emphasizing their "Oxbridge" tradition, the South Africans made do with minimal education requirements. Indeed some of their most famous native commissioners did not complete their high school educations. Evidently South Africans did not feel the need for such knowledge. An incentive bonus to officials who studied a native language was withdrawn because of the disappointing response (South Africa 1937:144). Instead, when justifying themselves to the external world like the PMC, the administration argued that white South Africans did not require education or knowledge as they had an inherent understanding of natives that was derived from long experience, a claim they would repeat on numerous occasions (Pienaar 1987:127).

Nor was there any keen interest in amateur ethnography. The Journal of the South West Africa Scientific Society, when compared to its colonial counterparts, is remarkable for its lack of ethnographic observations. The only significant colonial publication was the book The Native Tribes of South West Africa (1928) written by a commissioner (Hahn), a missionary (Vedder), and a medical doctor (Fourie). While well received by the Permanent Mandates Commission of the League of Nations, the book did not enjoy wide distribution in the territory itself. In retrospect, it is clear that it was used to establish South Africa's credentials for administering the territory more than for any practical use. This book was claimed to be so definitive that it was held up as a rationale for discouraging research in these areas. Indeed as late as 1980 the United Nations Institute for Namibia still regarded this text as definitive (UNIN 1980:199)!

Idlers on the Land

After the First World War, the League of Nations required a moral justification for colonization. Specifically, such justifications had to satisfy the audience at the Permanent Mandates Committee. The discourses colonial powers presented here were largely accepted because they fitted the dominant discourses of the era. One of the constant refrains in annual reports and in accounts justifying colonial policies is the notion of the need to work in order to "progress":

> Civilisation will never be developed on idleness, and education of the native does not consist of teaching him the alphabet or the Bible only. . . . Left to himself he will simply sit in the sun and dream about women and cattle. A good harvest results in liberal brewing of beer, heavy drinking and tribal disorders. Work brings him in contact with civilisation and therefore necessarily assists the process of civilising him. (South Africa 1926:98)

Such discourse has to be contextualized. In particular, the notion that "idleness is sin" was well grounded in social science theory at the time as well as in the dominant Christian and evolutionary notions of progress through "hard work." The administration emphasized the importance of "work" as development strategy. Labor and poverty were held to be simple polar opposites, and increasing the one would reduce the other.[10]

Generally the administration believed that the natives were happy to have whites run their affairs for them. Any problems were readily ascribed to "contamination" by "outside agitators" (PMC Minutes 1923:67–68). And in 1931 the PMC was satisfied with the explanation the administration gave for prohibiting trade unions because of the danger of "agitators" who would revive old feuds and intertribal conflict. This also meant that in the event of trouble the administration, in order to maintain its belief in the "peaceful natives," focused on finding the "ringleaders." Such a stance not only reinforced the overall belief that "the natives are dumb," but it also enabled the colonizers to continue production. More importantly, since the identification of the ringleaders was arbitrary and hence largely unpredictable, it served as a useful terrorization strategy.[11]

Overall such rhetoric also served to justify the colonial presence. Writing after a period in which he served as a public relations officer in the South African Native Affairs Department, Oliver Walker reflected: "The longer you charge the African with ignorance, laziness and stupidity, the longer you require the services of a Native Affairs Department and the safer are the jobs of the people in it" (1949:102).

Administration rhetoric consistently used the phrase "idle and disorderly." Work and order, in short, were cognitively connected. Indeed one could make a reasonable case that the rhetoric of "idleness and the nobility of work" was shaped for the international audience, who might have looked askance at any rhetoric featuring "insecurity" or settler fears. In terms of a Millsian "Grammar of Motives," the South Africans had boxed themselves in with their claim to inborn expertise on natives. At the same time constructions of settler masculinity also had an impact: Real men don't show fear (see Dawson 1994). Instead, the rhetoric of civilization and its inherent need for controlling labor enabled colonials to control the situation, not in the name of fear, but in the name of the desire to civilize.

Unsettled Settlers: Fear and Loathing in Namibia

Yet, if one examines the nooks and crannies of documentation generated by settlers of that era—like debris floating around Luderitz harbor—arresting references to fear and insecurity are found. Indeed, the dominating characteristic of Namibian settler society immediately after the First World War was one of great apprehension fueled by postwar inflation and constant rumors of native uprisings. These rumors peaked with the Bondelswarts Rebellion. As the administrator observed:

> Previous to that, every three or six months we had rumours of risings, resulting in farmers leaving their farms and running into the towns for protection. The natives found these rumours profitable—an opportunity for looting and theft of stock—and naturally repeated the exercise. There is ground for suspecting that certain white people

had encouraged these rumours, probably with the object of pre-cipitating conflicts between us and the natives. Every time such a rumour was set on foot Europeans all over the territory would clam-our for police protection, and it was difficult, without having police on every farm, to keep the occupants there; moreover, a sudden increase of police is always dangerous, especially where untrained men have to be enlisted. (PMC Minutes 1923:48)

The major settler newspaper, the *Windhoek Advertiser*, substantiated the administrator's remarks. In May 1921 it reported that there had been widespread rumors of unrest but that the authorities had investigated and found "no cause for anxiety" (7 May 1921). A contributor, using the pseudonym "Settler," undoubtedly wrote for the majority of his con-freres when he called for more stringent application of the native pass and taxation laws to "effectively overcome the complication of veld kaffer and bushmen who are directly responsible for a large percentage of stock thefts" (11 May 1921). A month later the administrator felt compelled to address a Windhoek settler audience to confront the issue and claimed to have begun an investigation into who started the rumors which had "caused unsettlement throughout the country and extreme anguish of mind to the farming community on lonely farms. . . . [And] moreover suggest[ed] to the native ideas which might prove dangerous in the future . . ." (11 June 1921). Such was settler paranoia about black mobility that settlers even presented the administrator with a petition protesting "with alarm" the issuing of motor vehicle drivers licenses to "non-Europeans," and in this they were supported by the Automobile Associa-tion and a strongly worded editorial (*Windhoek Advertiser*, 20 Aug. 1921).

Isolated murders of white farmers like Mrs. Coleman in Aus (18 Feb. 1922) led to the formation of Settler Rifle Associations (25 Feb. 1922). And settlers in Gibeon demanded an investigation into the behavior of the local police detachment who took rumors of a native uprising so seriously that they panicked, fortified themselves in their barracks, and ignored the other settlers in the town and districts (22 April 1922). The Bondelswarts Rebellion in late May, suppressed by machine gun and air-plane, was an international cause célèbre. The July 1922 assassination of Gobabis Magistrate van Ryneveld by a Bushman (Gordon 1992:92–98) further exacerbated matters. By December 1922, rumors that Hereros in the north were going to revolt were so strong that the administration felt compelled to send rifles and ammunition to the area.

Editorializing on "Native Unrest," the *Windhoek Advertiser*, on 15 December 1922, shrewdly noted the psychological and imaginative dimension of the problem:

> In lonely country-sides anything in the nature of truculence on the part of a single native may be construed as a symptom of native unrest. . . . The constant anxiety of people who feel that they have no proper protection is productive of a state of mind, which in itself constitutes one of the gravest menaces to peace. If the native is constantly reminded that his slightest act is followed by a general panic amongst whites, he will inevitably, in due time, conceive a contempt for the people who have him in subjection.[12]

This situation should hardly be surprising. In his careful examination of demographics, David Courtwright suggests that rumors are especially apt to generate insecurity in contexts where there are large numbers of single, unattached men (1996:174). In Namibia, settlers were thinly scattered on the ground, and the country in general was notorious for its low population density. Like settlers everywhere, whites in Namibia believed that the natives were lazy, yet, unlike other colonies, and especially British settler colonies, the Namibian settler community had a distinctive demographic profile. Not only were they sparse on the ground, but they were also split into several German and English and Afrikaans factions which mitigated the effect of community efforts designed to reinforce their spirit and status.

If there is one thing Catholics, anthropologists, and neo-Marxists agree on, it concerns the crucial role ritual plays in both coping with uncertainty and insecurity on an individual level and state formation on a collective level. This insight was clearly discerned by Sir Herbert Spencer:

> The earliest kind of government, the most general kind of government, and the government that is ever spontaneously recommencing, is the government of ceremonial observances. More may be said. This kind of government, besides preceding other kinds, and besides having in all places and at all times approached nearer to universality of influence, has ever had, and continues to have, the largest share in regulating men's lives. (quoted in Goffman 1971: preface)

Many anthropologists have argued that the inculcation of awe and respect by the colonized was more important than force as a means of ruling. In this regard, "invented traditions" like commemorative events were especially important. Certainly, rituals were deployed for such purposes in Namibia, but given the fractured and politically divisive nature of the Namibian settler community, such commemorative events further fragmented the fragile settler solidarity.[13] Thus when they did occur they were generally small-scale, scattered, and, in most cases, segregated (Schmidt-Lauber 1998). Instead, the focus was on the day-to-day rituals. Indeed these were the contexts in which natives experienced the states.[14]

Given the lack of personnel to enforce compliance, interaction ritual in the form of exaggerated etiquette between colonizer and colonized took on added importance. According to Albert Memmi, "Formalism is the cyst into which colonial society shuts itself and hardens, degrading its own life in order to save it. It is a spontaneous action of self-defense, a means of safeguarding the collective consciousness" (Memmi 1967:101). A few examples follow:

In 1919 Captain Bowker, the Windhoek Location Superintendent went to Orumbo reserve to deal with Herero land claims. Rather than mention land claims, he instructed them to stand and doff their hats: "Now on this first day of the new Government this is the first lesson I will have you learn. When your officer leaves his house to open his office you will rise and greet him" (cited in Emmett 1985:96).

Dealing with the 1922 Bondelswarts Rebellion, the administrator, Hofmeyr, with no previous military experience, proclaimed himself colonel. Previously, during the 1916 Mandume expedition, Captains Manning and Fairlie were given temporary appointments as majors when they went up to Ovamboland "as this would give them the necessary standing for carrying out their duties" (Kotze 1984:32). Such exaggerations of rank suggest that the affirmations of "standing" were directed to the officers themselves—perhaps a self-confidence trick?

The two most famous native commissioners of the interwar years were sticklers for etiquette. According to Reverend Tobias:

Hahn and Eades are very much on a pedestal and keep aloof and speak through an interpreter—they are very anxious for me to speak just as they do. . . . The Bishop came to me before he left and said that Hahn wanted to speak to me [about] my attitude to the natives. "Speak to them" he said, "like a Sergeant Major, give orders and never hold a conversation and do not be friendly." Hahn also said "Always speak with authority as to a child who is rather in disgrace."

Hahn is on excellent footing with the people . . . but his attitude is "I have spoken—there the matter ends." (Mallory 1971:29–30)[15]

More generally, legalism is a prominent feature in South Africa. In addition to its instrumental uses, legalism connoted important symbolic values; indeed, compliance with laws was taken as the criterion by which "civilization" was demarcated. As the *Windhoek Advertiser*, on 3 January 1925, editorialized on native policy:

> Not only are the natives beginning to lose respect for their European masters but *they are beginning to lose that respect for the law which is the fundamental basis of civilizations.* . . . There is an atmosphere most unhealthy to our safety in the local locations. Organized meetings are held in broad daylight and at night the uproar and noise testify to the absolute lack of control existing due to no fault of any official in charge of native affairs. . . . *Let the native once flaunt the laws of the white man and the crisis is here.* (my emphasis)

There is a further aspect of the symbolic dimension. In order to ensure compliance and intragroup cohesion, the ethnic state must exercise power legally. In practice, authorization or legality replaces legitimacy as the administrator's key concern. In such circumstances "divorced from substantive ideals with universal content, normative regularity becomes a reified faith in procedures" (Adam 1971:48). As Eiselen, pioneer *volkekundige* (ethnologist) and "architect of apartheid" put it: "Once any measure becomes law, it is the duty of every citizen . . . to obey that law. [Anything else is] nothing less than bare-faced incitement and thus a matter for the police" (cited in Evans 1986:265).

In Namibia, as in South Africa, oppression occurred not so much by terror per se as by the routinization of terror in day-to-day interaction. Settlers allayed their own terrors in part by ritualizing law, as well as by broadening their definitions of legal agency. The Vagrancy Proclamation was strikingly vague in its criteria as to what was entailed in "wandering over any farm, in, or loitering near, any dwelling house, shop, store, stable, outhouse, garden, vineyard, kraal or other enclosed place." The potency of the proclamation lay not in its penalties but in Section 8, which effectively allowed any settler or anyone acting under a settler's orders to apprehend—with or without a warrant—any person declared to be idle and disorderly. "Idle and disorderly" entailed more than nonwork: any "person found in any street or road . . . or place of public resort or in view thereof, respectively, without sufficient clothing for purposes of decency, is [also] liable to the penalty prescribed." Other proclamations, like Proclamation 43/1929, were to reinforce this potency as they allowed any European—not just officers and constables of the South West Africa Police—to enter any native residence to ascertain the number of natives residing there. Even the key provision of showing "visible means of support" empowered settlers in their daily interactions with indigenes. The proclamation authorized any settler to stop and interrogate any person driving livestock and, if given an unsatisfactory account, to conduct "said livestock and the person . . . to the nearest public prison or police station, so that such persons may be detained . . . until the next sitting of the magistrate." In addition, at the grassroots level, the situation conspired to promote complex European empowerment. Police salaries were notoriously low. Indeed, they were so low that in addition to high turnover, they occasioned a number of letters of complaint in the press from farmers who objected to having to provide patrolling policemen with sustenance. At the same time, an extremely important element of police power came from their nonpolicing duties, since a major source of power was in the control of access to valued goods and services. Structurally, the situation was conducive to a cozy relationship between settler-farmer and patrolling policeman, in which the latter would frequently overlook indiscretions of the former and vice versa.

The weak administrative state survived by franchising its legal use of violence to its settlers.[16] At the same time, shadow knowledge of the law provided an explanation for why things were the way they were, and it allowed moral agency to be shifted away from individual settlers who could engage in a process of self-moralizing in which the threat of "taking the law into their own hands" was the ultimate illusory opiate.[17]

Conclusion

One of the most sensitive observers of the colonial situation, Albert Memmi (1967) notes the profound ambivalence permeating the colonial project: How could the colonizer look after his workers while periodically gunning down a crowd of the colonized? For the colonizer, to think about the contradictions inherent in colonialism was to undermine it. The panoply of legislation was a mechanism for the colonizers to grant themselves self-absolution. This legislation and the interaction rituals it sustained established a moral and psychological palliative for the needs and insecurities of the colonizers, it did not directly control the colonized. The laws' effectiveness lay less in their implementation than in the reassurance they provided settlers against their worst fantasies.

Law was a massive local anesthetic that sedated the contradictions and the necessity of thinking. As Habermas would say, it successfully "fettered the imagination" (1971).[18] It certainly was an instrument of internal pacification, but more of the colonizers than the colonized. This type of power called not for increased knowledge as Giddens, Foucault, and others argue, but rather for what James Scott calls a "knee-haltered knowledge"—a shadow knowledge for which law provided the silhouette and the complexity of which was left as a unidimensional monochromatic blank.[19] Sustaining interaction on the colonizer-colonized interface called for actions based not on deep or dense knowledge but on a shadow or shallow stereotypical erudition. Settler society depended on information derived from "events which are *atypical*, present[ed] . . . in a *stereotypical* fashion, . . . contrast[ed] against a backcloth of normality which is *overtypical*" (Hannerz 1981:33). Berger and Luckmann write: "He who has the bigger stick has the better chance of imposing his definition upon reality" (1967:11). Knowledge may be power under some circumstances, but, in others, power rests on denial and studied displacement.

This image of a smoothly functioning social order lends itself to the creation of the capacity for fascist self-delusion. As Erving Goffman noted in *The Presentation of Self in Everyday Life*:

> A performer may be taken in by his own act, convinced at the moment that the impression of reality which he fosters is the one and only reality. In such cases the performer comes to be his own audience; he comes to be performer and observer of the same show. Presumably he intracepts or incorporates the standards he attempts to maintain in the presence of others so that his conscience requires him to act in a socially proper way. It will have been necessary for the individual in his performing capacity to conceal from himself in his audience capacity the discreditable facts he has had to learn about the performance; in everyday terms, there will be things he knows, or has known, that he will not be able to tell himself. (1959:80–81)

The spread of fascism depended on a set of everyday social practices, the fetishism of the ordinary, as Dean MacCannell convincingly argues.

The capacity for self-delusion enabled settlers to suppress or gloss over the obvious in order to normalize a terrible event, "cooly re-inscribing the event into the realm of the ordinary" (1992:208). As Foucault points out, power is based on the repression of conflict. Power works from the bottom up—not only from the top down—and the "paramount concern, in fact, should be with the point where power surmounts the rules of right . . . and extends beyond them, invests itself in institutions, be-comes embodied in techniques, and equips itself with instruments and even violent means of material intervention" (1980:107). From this per-spective, power is the disciplining of men, just as technology disciplines nature as the Farson epigraph shows. Frederick Cooper's (1994) axiom-atic conditions for colonization—namely the requirement to control both time and space—must be modified by the addition of a third condi-tion. The long-term success of colonization also requires that the con-trollers or colonizers maintain the often delusory "proper attitude" to colonize themselves, too. In inculcating this attitude, laws like the Va-grancy Proclamation played a major role.

Notes

Some of the material in this chapter first appeared in my "Vagrancy, Law and 'Shadow Knowledge' " M. P. Hayes et al. 1998 *Namibia Under South African Rule*. Ox-ford: James Currey.

1. In developing a framework to deal with the issue, I want to invoke Max Gluckman, who, in his devastating critique of Malinowski's "Theories of Culture Change" (1945), faulted the latter for a lack of appreciation of the dynamism and diversity of white interests. As a counter model, Gluckman proposed that analysis start by ob-serving that Africans and their interactions were an integral part of the modern world system (1963:213). In short, to understand the meaning of "vagrancy" one must "study up" (Nader 1974). That colonization unleashes a vortex of instability and unpredictability upon the colonized is well established (Fanon 1967). But what is the impact and psychic cost of domination not on those at the receiving end but on those who (ostensibly) dominate? As anthropologists widen their focus and take in the larger context the question of the culture of colonialism has been pushed to the fore (Thomas 1994; Dirks 1992; Cooper and Stoler 1997). A trail-blazing effort in this regard was Vincent Crapanzano's (1985) study on whites in apartheid South Africa.

2. Corrigan and Sayer (1985) describe how the British state was constructed as a repertoire of rituals and routines of rule which legitimized the state's power to control its subjects' activities, demonstrating how strong the "idle poor" was as a moral category.

3. Segregation had more to it than simply ensuring an equitable labor supply for settlers:

> After providing for domestic and similar essential services at European centres, it is undesirable to allow surplus natives of various races to crowd into municipal locations . . . where, even under the best of control, they are liable to contract, or infect others with diseases . . . and in any case they generally deteriorate physically and morally, besides embarrassing the white population in regard to the use of commonage and water. (South Africa Annual Report 1923:13)

See also generally the South Africa Annual Reports. Titles vary: *Report of the Administrator, Territory of South West Africa*, Pretoria, 1919–1925; *Report of the Government of South Africa on South West Africa*, Pretoria, 1926–1928; *Report Presented by the Government of the Union of South Africa to the Council of the League of Nations concerning the Administration of South West Africa*, Pretoria, 1929–1940; *Report by the Government of the Union of South Africa on the Administration of South West Africa for the Year 1946*. Hereafter these reports are cited in the text as "South Africa [date]," with the date corresponding to the year of the annual report.

4. Male-gender language is used exclusively in the legislation.

5. Moreover, it is difficult to draw a clear distinction between these categories since vagrancy can be accounted for under multiple headings: against public order (trespassing on nonprivate property); against the person (i.e. owner of the farm or shop); against property (i.e. trespassing on the property); and probably also statutory offenses that include the largest and most varied grab bag of offenses including those against the liquor, pass, labor, and health acts.

6. Given the unreliability of official statistics, I compared them to my own field statistics from the Grootfontein District. They support the general tenor of the official record. It is only after the Second World War that pass/vagrancy and masters and servants offenses show a dramatic increase.

7. Noting this increase the administrator commented:

> Although the offences under the M&S Law appears to be on the increase, it must not be lost sight of that in recent years farmers are more and more employing recruited labour. These boys are mostly "raw"—untrained, and undisciplined—and consequently give cause for being brought before the Courts on various trivial charges. As stated above the sentences imposed are lenient (7 days IHL [Imprisonment and Hard Labor] or a 5 shilling fine)—very often involving merely a reprimand or a warning, and, it may be added, the offenders very soon learn to adapt themselves to the changed conditions of civilisation and to avoid transgressing the law. (South Africa 1939:8–9)

8. Another practice was to use prison labor despite League of Nations discomfort with such practices. In 1920 the territory boasted eleven jails and three lock-ups controlled by magistrates and sixteen by police; the average daily number of prisoners was more than 270. For a number of years, settler demand for prison labor exceeded supply. In the allocation of prison labor, administration requirements were given preference, and then labor was allocated to municipalities at a rate of one shilling per unit while private individuals had to pay one and a half shillings (South Africa 1924: para.275). Prison labor statistics are scanty; nevertheless, the following emerges: Assuming that prisoners worked for three hundred days per year, the number of prison workers per day increased from just over 60 for the whole territory in 1920 to more than 120 in 1927—hardly an unlimited source of cheap labor.

9. Thus Giddens argues that a key component of the exercise of power is "surveillance activities." These, he says:

> refer to two connected phenomena. First, to the accumulation of "information"— symbolic materials that can be stored by an agency or collectivity. Second, to the supervision of the activities of subordinates by their superiors within any collectivity. It is important to distinguish these as it is to emphasize the potential connections between them. The garnering and storage of information is a prime source of time-space distanciation and therefore of the generation of power. Power is also generated by the supervisory activities of superordinates, since supervision is one medium of co-ordinating. . . . (Giddens 1981:169)

10. Or as another official document put it:

> It was felt absolutely necessary to make provision for the better control of natives in urban areas in the interests of the natives as well as Europeans. Experience has shown that there is a strong tendency for natives, both men and women, to drift into urban locations where in both cases they neither want nor seek employment. As they simply loaf and do not earn money honestly they resort to illicit liquor selling, prostitution, gambling and other means to obtain it and generally degenerate. Under the new law a proper system of registration is provided for, and the Administration will be able to exercise effective control and keep urban locations clear of loafers. (South Africa 1924: para.98; South Africa 1925: para.100)

The administration's theoretical paradigm is obvious from the following quotations:

> Can one wonder if the natives, whom we have been trying to persuade to abandon the doctrine of the survival of the fittest, became sceptical (by the white nations plunging into war)? (Administrator Hofmeyr in PMC 1923:48)
>
> As has been mentioned in previous reports, the natives of this territory, with the exception of the Ovambos, are purely pastoral people: agriculture has never been practised by them owing to the greatest part of the country being entirely unsuitable for such pursuits, and their only concern was for the care of their herds. Progress amongst such a population has always been much slower than in the case of agriculturalists and it is only to be expected that there would be little evidence of any real progress. (South Africa 1926:29)

11. How notions of masculinity permeate law is seen in the treatment of indigenous women. Women were legislatively invisible. The ever alert Lugard picked this up in 1923 when he observed that native females were excluded from the legal definition of who was a native. Herbst, the Secretary for SWA, circuitously explained that this was because women were excluded from the pass regulations and that as women and children were exempt from the pass laws they were "free to move and were allowed on the farms with the native men." While men had to show a visible means of subsistence, there was no law compelling women to work, and it thus appears that women were exempt from the vagrancy proclamation.

While some of the labor laws were rhetorically justified in terms of protecting the indigenous family, at other times they aimed at preventing couples from living together. Thus the restriction on wives accompanying migrant workers was rationalized with the explanation that as there was "no suitable accommodation," and this would "encourage immorality among the native women" (South Africa 1927:129).

Frequently people did not know the laws, and they were encouraged in their ignorance. Thus the "Consolidated Instructions" advised:

> The definition of a "native" contained in Proc. 11/1922 excludes a native female who is thus NOT subject to the provisions of that Proclamation. Nevertheless the majority of native women are under the impression that they are required to carry passes and in the interest of control, they should *not* be disabused of this idea and travelling passes should continue to be issued to them. It would however be remembered that a native female cannot lawfully be convicted of failing to carry a pass in terms of the provisions of Proc. 11/1922.

Space does not permit an analysis of the exclusion of women from this legislation. Such an analysis would have to include an analysis of women's resistance to pass legislation in South Africa, which obviously shaped the male administration's attitude (see e.g., Wells 1986). In practice exclusions generally meant increasing men's rights over women.

12. The administration responded with its Burgher Law of 1923 that allowed for the drafting of settlers into civilian defense units, but the actual functioning of these units drew much derision from the settler press.

13. For example, the usual rituals of solidarity typically celebrate "victories." Yet any victory celebration in settler Namibia was bound to offend some settler segment. For example, the Great War was between Germans and English, and Afrikaners supported both sides. Similarly, rituals involving extensive liquor would offend the Afrikaner Calvinists.

14. It was Goffman's sagacity to realize that everyday life is the site of the only truly significant drama. It is in social interaction that "most of the world's work gets done" and on the basis of such mundane performances that character, dignity, and competency are assigned. Indeed, verbal communication plays a very small part in such assignments. Social order is fragile, impermanent, full of unexpected loop-

Unsettled Settlers   83

holes, and in need of constant repair. It depends on a "veneer of consensus" in which each individual conceals his "own wants behind statements which assert values to which everyone present feels obliged to give lip service" (1959:9).

15. The initial supplies for an administrative presence in Ovamboland also included a large number of khaki messenger uniforms.

16. Indeed even in the eighties, when the South West Africa People's Organization (SWAPO) was engaged in a low-intensity guerrilla war against the South African overrulers, the Vagrancy Proclamation was amended to provide heavier penalties for "terrorist" activities, but again no actual prosecutions were made under it as far as I am aware, underlying once again its magical and symbolic qualities.

17. As "Constant Reader" (*Windhoek Advertiser* 24 Dec. 1925) put it:

> The farmers have been defied now for a number of years and all appeals to Police and magistrates result in the same answer, namely that they cannot do anything because their hands are tied. . . .
>
> In no part of South Africa has the white population had to submit to more indignities and humiliations from the natives than they have to in this country and it speaks volumes for the forbearance and their loyalty to the Administration that they have not taken the law into their own hands long ago.
>
> The serious financial position of a number of farmers in this country to a large extent is due to the laziness, dishonesty, malingering and thieving propensities of the natives. . . .

18. Its impact permeated other domains of settler society as well and would be a major factor in explaining the excruciatingly dull settler literature of that era. See, for example, Haarhoff 1991.

19. In *Seeing Like a State* (1998), James Scott also attempts to answer the question of what impels the state to sedentarize its subjects. He wound up looking at social engineering projects and concluded that these projects failed because they made use of a shallow, simplified knowledge to administratively order society and nature based on a high modernist ideology with authoritarian overtones coupled to a "prostrate civil society" which lacked the capacity to resist these plans. Similar elements are present to varying degrees in the Namibian situation. It is also clear however that aspects of Scott's provocative argument need to be amended. Rather than shallow knowledge leading to failure of high modernist projects, the Namibian colonial case clearly suggests the situation is more complicated: ignorance clearly has its virtues in governance as well.

Howard J. De Nike

Judges Without Courts:

The Legal Culture of German Reunification

Law commonly provides a symbolic arena in which ideas about history, property, and law itself are disputed.[1] German unification involves precisely this role for law. After forty years of separation, there is now an intense public effort to establish (or re-establish) a common narrative of German history and political culture. That effort relies on law for both its means and ends. Using legal means to redefine the meanings of citizenship, Germany is re-inscribing citizenship with new attributes and powers, and the new definition of citizenship simultaneously entails homogenization and differentiation. Indeed, as part of this process, the courts have disenfranchised the former judges and lawyers of the German Democratic Republic (GDR). Formerly powerful at the bench and bar, they are now faced with the challenge of defending their professional licenses and personal reputations. In the new German narrative, they have been placed in what Karl Llewellyn and E. Adamson Hoebel (1941) termed the crucible of litigation.

In his writings about the production of intersubjective meaning, Jürgen Habermas describes how new understandings result from the substitution of fresh "presuppositions" for old (1990). Habermas's insights are not only a means for analyzing what is occurring in the context of the clash of ideas about German history and citizenship in which the ex-GDR jurists are embroiled, but are also a justification for an ethnographic approach which privileges the "voices" of others. In such a fine-grained examination, identification and analysis of interests and the means for advancing them become possible. With this method "fragments of an epoch . . . of a cultural field" are redeemed (Comaroff and Comaroff 1992:16), and agency is appropriately lodged in individuals.

By interviewing GDR jurists, I collected their professional life stories and learned about their present situations. In focusing attention on individual GDR jurists and their understandings of their pasts and their present experiences, I intend to contribute some much-needed nuance to the standard picture of law's relation to the nation. Nation is not a concept built only around the "unifying" ideas of citizenship and ethnicity (compare Hobsbawm 1990). Through the instrumentality of law, nation also becomes a "differentiating" principle (Verdery 1993:38). In the developments I explore in this essay, the nation enters the controversy over the ex-GDR jurists by systematically producing symbols and practices of delegitimation and exclusion. These in turn define specific concepts of history and political participation for the benefit of the eastern population. In this process, the reviewing and prosecuting authorities have adopted a strategy that minimally calls into question, and, at times, arguably abandons, the cultural achievements of the *Rechtsstaat*, or "state of law," itself (see De Nike 1997).

The first level of confrontation for the former GDR jurists arrived with the moment of legal unification, on 3 October 1990. The numbers are not difficult to ascertain: 1,493 judges and 1,237 prosecutors were in office in the final year of the GDR (Statistisches Jahrbuch der DDR 1989:448). According to the terms of the Unification Agreement, all GDR judges and prosecutors were ousted in one manner or another from their official positions upon legal unification. The (re)constitution of the German nation as a single juridical and political entity—from the West German perspective at least—called for a thoroughgoing *Delegitimierung* (delegitimation) of the GDR. As the months after unification unfolded, this increasingly meant designating the GDR as an *Unrechtsstaat* (a state without law), in contrast to the Federal Republic of Germany (FRG) *Rechtsstaat*. Judges, prosecutors, and law professors who served the GDR's "socialist legality" were reviewed to determine their suitability to serve in the united *rechtsstaatlichen Regime* (government of laws). Within Berlin and throughout the five new federal states, commissions of jurists, led by West Germans, set procedures for deciding the futures of applicants. The process contained an implicit message: a new regime, one already established in the West, was capable of unifying the German polity and acting as guarantor of the benefits of German citizenship. Within and against the semantic space of those various procedures, the affected GDR jurists "construct and represent themselves . . . and hence their societies and histories" in terms of opposing "signs and practices" (Comaroff and Comaroff 1992:27).

Hard on the heels of the judicial *Ueberpruefungen* (official reviews) came a second wave of assault, a series of criminal prosecutions against the former GDR judges and prosecutors—usually for *Rechtsbeugung* (law bending or perversion). The gravamen of Rechtsbeugung is that a defendant judge or prosecutor acted officially in a manner contrary to his or her conscientious understanding of the law. This offense, virtually unknown in West Germany before the *Wende*[2] and unheard of in Anglo-American jurisprudence, wraps judicial decision-making in intense moral rhetoric. In doing so, the prosecuting authorities exploit the unique characteristics of German legal history from Weimar through the cold war. No understanding of the power of these charges is possible without a grasp of German jural history, that is, how it acts as a template for contemporary legal arguments. Moreover, the contradictions inherent in this prosecutorial strategy in turn create the career-saving, pension-protecting, prestige-shielding discursive possibilities of resistance among those experiencing the force of these attempts to discipline and punish—to borrow Michel Foucault's phrase.

As noted, the western legal forum stands as an arena where opposed ideas of law are at times contested. Edward Thompson observes that a legal system that advertises itself as fair must in fact (at least occasionally) be fair (1975:263). It is not simply an expression of prevailing superstructure. The Rechtsstaat possesses history, internal logic, and traditions that open discursive opportunities for the prosecutors' targets. After unification the "GDR trials" assumed critical importance, not only as a site where careers hung in the balance, but where understandings of the past—its meanings—were constructed and expressed in opposition to the normalizing capacities of the *Bundesrepublik*'s dominant unification narratives.

The core of the Federal Republic's unification narrative was its equating of the communist GDR and the Third Reich. The different scales of legal injustice under German communists compared to the Nazis, and the different nature of the GDR's break with German legal history versus that of the National Socialists, count little against the new narrative which equates oppression practiced by each regime against the better nature of decent Germans. Indeed, since the Wende, the West has sought to promote a unifying continuity and identity of experience between East and West populations who were subjected to tyranny first at the hands of Nazis and later by Stalinists. The trials of GDR judges whose courts are described explicitly by contemporary prosecutors as linear descendants of the Nazi *Volksgerichtshof* (people's court)[3] publicly buttress this association. The strategy of this argument rests in its challenge to the self-professed "founding ethos" of the GDR that had held that the GDR, not the FRG, was the authentic antifascist postwar German state.

The Field of Dispossession

The professional dispossession suffered in the GDR merely reflects the latest of several legal transformations in Germany in the twentieth century. Following World War I, the Weimar Republic introduced a flawed democratic regime for all of Germany. Thirteen years later in 1933, a fascist dictatorship assumed control, remaining in power until 1945. After 1945, separate governments prevailed in the East and West—one socialist economically and dictatorial politically, the other capitalist economically and democratic politically (see Schoeneburg 1995:25–36). This ideological taxonomy of German constitutions and politics, though perhaps helpful conceptually in making comparisons between eras, sheds only partial light upon the shocks and traumas to lives lived within what Carol Greenhouse, in the introduction to this volume, terms "the operations of legalities and politics . . . where social fields are in disarray." My ethnographic goal in Germany was to identify and study these "operations of legalities," in particular using the case method pioneered by Llewellyn and Hoebel, while probing the histories of individual "legal lives" of the GDR's former jurists.

The impact of the fall 1990 dismissal of GDR legal officials was felt most heavily in East Berlin, which contained roughly 25 percent of the country's judges and prosecutors. Unlike the five newly created states in the territory of the former GDR, all judges and prosecutors in East Berlin who wished to continue their careers were required to apply affirmatively for professional acceptance in the unified city. In the remaining states, judges and prosecutors were for the most part allowed to hold their positions while retention was under formal consideration (Hutt 1993:94–96). Given these contrasting approaches, only a small number in East Berlin submitted themselves to the procedures set up for gaining acceptance, and only a small fraction of this group was eventually retained for future service. In contrast, approximately 50 percent of the same categories of officials were retained in the new states (*Der Spiegel* 1992(1):44). The procedure determining acceptance usually involved commissions headed by West German judges inspecting pre-1989 court records in search of incriminating "political" decisions—for example, where lawyers or judges had been involved in cases of individuals convicted for "unauthorized attempts to depart the GDR."

For the most part, the reviewing period lasted twelve months (November 1990 through October 1991), although some unresolved cases languished for many months afterward. The process raised broad issues of historical interpretation, among them the capacity of West German jurists on short notice to "frame" more than forty years of legal events in the East. Even with goodwill the task would have been daunting; without it the results might be appalling. How could outsiders appropriately judge a legal culture they had never experienced?

The post-Wende world of the GDR legal profession involved endless difficulties, not least because the lives and experiences of the GDR's jurists became common property, no longer their own to interpret and express. Now they were exposed to external (that is, West German) forces that often eluded their ability even to object effectively. But change was everywhere. As Habermas observes: "Every instance of problem solving and every interpretation depend on a web of myriad presuppositions. . . ." (1990:10). When presuppositions are torn away, destroyed, jumbled, or otherwise negated, the ability to grasp symbolic content, dependent on almost intuitive pre-understandings of context, is likewise undermined or uprooted entirely. A small incident observed in 1993 in former East Berlin brought home how pervasive the invasion is felt to be. One morning a young clerk at the counter greeted a customer in the neighborhood bakery. He asked for a certain pastry but drew only a blank expression. He then gestured toward the desired item in the display case. This produced a look of recognition, and the clerk said, "Oh, you mean *Eierschecke*," using a local designation. He replied somewhat confused and irritated: "Of course I know they're Eierschecke, so why do you have that sign there calling them something else?" Rolling her eyes, the clerk responded: "Oh, don't pay any attention to that—the new manager's from Bavaria." In such contexts, individuals have limited freedom to translate their formerly unproblematic background knowledge into explicit new knowledge. The difficulties may be as innocuous as learning new bakery terminology or as weighty as the penal measures familiar to Foucault's students of modern punishment.

Major shifts of power dominated the landscape, producing a demand for replacement of an entire value system: from party centralism to elective bodies; from a socialist to a capitalist economy; from pressures favoring collectivism to those promoting individualism, and so forth. Moreover, abrupt substitution, over a brief span of time, caused a kind of "value vacuum" as old primacies disintegrated and new ones had not yet taken hold. In her analysis of post-Ceausescu Romania, Katherine Verdery has written about this kind of situation as a "phantom limb" phenomenon, wherein former socialist institutions and solutions were appealed to despite their absence or inappropriateness (1992). How individuals and groups become torn between what they are used to and the demands and attractions of the new must be linked ethnographically and critically to specific circumstances and interests.

The forty-year period of the GDR was long enough for a generation of East Germans to have known no other life, while for many unsympathetic West Germans it proved sufficiently fleeting that they could dismiss its reality. Several pervasive crises have recently emerged in the East, provoking humiliation and shock over (1) the depth and extent to which corrupt governmental practices existed in the state-party, (2) the breadth and abuses of the informer system, (3) the extent of privileges accorded party leaders, and (4) the despoliation of the environment by expedient agricultural and mining practices. Each of these scandals produced sensational revelations bannered in thick headlines and paraded on nightly television newscasts as reporters plunged into unexplored party records and government files. And worse, such disclosures stood in stark contrast to the ideals preached in the socialist system and used constantly to justify the Socialist Unity Party's (SED) "leading position." A Canadian criminologist attempting to explain the rise of crime in the former GDR asked whether the aftermath of postunification scandals was "a state of normlessness, of lawlessness, of anomie, where nothing is sacred, where nobody is clean, where anything goes?" (Fattah 1994:46).

In the East, after a period of initial optimism, the shock of economic disillusionment quickly appeared. As in the Russian situation studied by Ries in this volume, the strength of the West German economy was supposed to create a cornucopia of goods that flowed directly into the GDR and enriched its citizens. Years of exposure to scenes (in telecasts from the West) depicting lives of comfort and luxury compared to those on the other side of the Wall whetted this expectation. The dominance of the deutsche mark against GDR currency and the prompt payment of DM100 "welcome money" to each easterner who trekked briefly across the line in late 1989 further increased people's hopes. However realistic or unrealistic expectations of East/West financial partnership and prosperity for the former GDR may be in the long run, these visions proved exceedingly barren in the short haul. Instead of prosperity, unemployment ravaged families, hitting women especially hard. In the East, jobless figures moved quickly from an initial 0.1 percent in January 1990, to

12 percent by July 1991, and 59 percent of the unemployed were women.[4] Unification also brought vendors of costly appliances, home furnishings, automobiles, job-training courses, stereophonic equipment, holiday packages, fashionable apparel, and merchandised sex. What at first seemed so attractive and necessary turned rapidly to ashes as monthly credit payments mounted. An immediate consequence was the gradual eclipsing of the Christian Democratic Union (CDU) in almost every election in the East after December 1990, when Helmut Kohl had managed to retain his chancellorship on the strength of promises of easy union and economic reward.

Given socialism's austerity and uniformity that obviated wide gaps in wealth, extreme feelings of material deprivation had previously been largely absent. In contrast, today's abundance of goods lying beyond the means of the majority in the East gradually transforms an embrace of the new system into varieties of resentment. Scarcity brought modest aims. Goals were realistic. Frustration began to appear in the East with the painful realization that not everyone can afford the new goods. After unification, eastern Germany witnessed an escalation of violent crime and an eruption of skinhead and neo-Nazi movements that produced further shockwaves. A weary refrain emerged to the effect that, without the intense government programs aimed at the socialization of GDR youth, little else could be expected. The former jurists of the GDR were not immune to these pressures, compounding their distress. Along with family members, they faced the prospect of unemployment. Like many others they succumbed to the blandishments of high-pressure salesmen. And, their teenagers began to adopt what they saw as the jarring clothes, hair, and music fashions of West Berlin youth.

With the accelerated collapse of the Socialist Unity Party in 1989 and its absence as a forceful participant in the unification negotiations, GDR officials lost their claim to professional legitimacy, parting the way for thousands of West German civil servants to serve as the importers and implementers of new rules, regulations, and policies. Men and women from the highest echelons of GDR law faculties were reduced to mere assistants. Their lack of West German legal knowledge transformed experts into unskilled novices operating under the authority of "on loan" western civil servants. And the prestige of high judicial office gave way to the ignominy of criminal accusation.

GDR law was enlisted as a site for production of "law about law" and as an overarching paradigm of delegitimation. Prosecutions against

GDR judges and prosecutors for the offense of Rechtsbeugung served as the centerpiece in this delegitimation process (and concomitant legitimation of FRG law). Though the number of these cases was at first relatively small—fewer than one hundred were either in progress or completed in mid-1995—thousands of accusations were under investigation, including many where subpoenas had already been issued or were pending (*Berliner Zeitung* 1995). Moreover, whether or not a former judge or prosecutor was actually a defendant or target of an investigation, the charges tainted the entire GDR legal profession.

A historical backdrop is needed to appreciate the Rechtsbeugung accusation. After World War II in West Germany, the majority of jurists who served during the Nazi era were either reinstalled as judges or allowed to pursue careers as lawyers. Ingo Mueller (1989) details the postwar Federal Republic's record, which contains not a single criminal judgment against anyone for judicial crime, despite thousands of Nazi-era cases of court-ordered euthanasia, enforcement of racial purity laws, and death sentences decreed for petty acts characterized as wartime treason. Though these same officials took part in the creation of the West German Rechtsstaat, the unredressed record of the Nazi jurists remained a scandal, rankling many of the current generation of West German judges and prosecutors entering the profession as part of the 1960s "more moral" generation that was determined not to allow the atrocities of the Nazi past to be forgotten (see Craig 1982:170–89). By the 1990s death and infirmity had claimed the Nazi-era judges and legal apologists, but the GDR jurists seemingly offered fitting surrogates. In addition, a conflation of Nazi and GDR jurists as a rationale to discipline and punish not only delegitimizes the forty years of East German socialism, it fences the GDR's reconstituted state-party, the Party of Democratic Socialism (PDS), out of contemporary political discourse.

The career destruction confronting GDR legal professionals at the time of unification represented the loss of a lifetime investment. After the founding of the GDR in 1949, legal careers entailed three to four years of specialized education (the *Studium*), followed by several additional years as assistant judges and prosecutors (usually somewhere outside Berlin), involvement with one or more legal-professional organizations, advancement through the ranks of government assignments, and so forth—all in a formal manner not unlike the modern profession as it has developed from the mid-nineteenth century in most other European settings (see Siegrist 1994). Naturally, assaults on long-established, prestigious careers produced widespread devastation among a majority of those judges and lawyers. This was less the case for younger members, but they too commonly expressed deep resentments about their treatment.

Almost daily exposure to sensational accusations against lawyers and judges aggravated the uncertainty about future income and loss of stature. In early 1992, for example, two former military prosecutors were indicted for Rechtsbeugung for failing in 1984 to bring charges against a *Stasi* (state security) officer who shot two men to death in a dispute at a bus stop.[5] In another instance, a labor court judge, Dr. R., was criminally charged based on his rejection of the petition of a GDR schoolteacher who had been fired from her job after seeking in 1985 to emigrate from the GDR.[6] In July 1993 the Berlin Lawyers' Chamber moved to expel an ex-GDR attorney exposed for informing against his own clients to the GDR Ministry of State Security (*Berliner Zeitung* 1993b).

Considering the effects of these new state boundaries reminds us that here "the state" itself may lack the ethnically primordial character that the modern nation-state usually ascribes to itself. To the extent Bonn's program of unification ignores the differences between eastern and western experiences by wrongly imputing a common East and West German history, it produces an ersatz German nation, one fraught with contradictions and a spurious community of citizens. The primary "national question" for the eastern jurists is this: What was the experience of the legal profession and how does it now compare with that of the West?

The answer is complex since both continuities and discontinuities predominate. Immediately after the Wende, that is, during the period between the fall of the Wall in November 1989 until mid-1990, there was a prevailing belief—ultimately quite quixotic—that the union of the two German polities would include at least a partial melding of legal histories and ideas, a *Rechtsangleichung* (legal adjustment). That expectation is traceable in part to East-West exchanges taking place during the Willy Brandt-inspired *Ostpolitik* (Eastern Policy) initiated in the early 1970s and sustained by each of his successors. Deep disappointment—even betrayal—stands forth, especially among legal scholars who had been warmly greeted in the 1980s when they were members of delegations in touch with Western jurists (including West Germans). In that context,

West Germans treated them as confreres, expressing genuine interest in the operation of socialist law. After unification, GDR jurists suddenly became pariahs, functionaries of an Unrechtsstaat.

A time of confusion followed. Many sought both to meet individual culpability and secure a degree of professional union by publicly coping with the past, or, as the process was termed in German, engaging in *Vergangenheitsbewaeltigung* (Wolff 1990). Rather than proclaiming the positive features of socialist legality, this process emphasized a reduction of legal obfuscation, a willingness to seek broad rather than piecemeal solutions, attempts to embrace rehabilitative instead of punitive penal sentences, and guarantees of fundamental health, education, and social services (Quigley 1990), and the lawyers and judges of the GDR retreated into an examination of the role law and its functionaries played in the achievement of the single-party state's goals. If their western counterparts would not greet them as brethren, perhaps confession and contrition would be effective. This approach soon proved unworkable; fumbling efforts were swiftly abandoned as indictments and disbarments commanded increasing attention. The GDR bar's *Vereinigung demokratischer Juristen* (Association of Democratic Lawyers), a mass organization of seven thousand judges, state prosecutors, lawyers, notaries, and justiciaries, lost any semblance of purpose and effectiveness and promptly crumbled to a membership of four hundred.[7]

The *Gauck-Behoerde*,[8] which controlled roughly six million "files" amassed during the four decades of the GDR's *Ministerium fuer Staatssicherheit* (Ministry for State Security), was a critical factor, both in the overall delegitimation campaign and the post-Wende disorganization of the GDR jurists. Its manila folders and computer disks contained the names of hundreds of thousands of Germans, both East and West, who served as official Stasi agents or more commonly as *informellen Mitarbeiter* (informal collaborators or IMs) who, usually without monetary compensation, provided information, sometimes about friends and neighbors, to the state security agency (Die Zeit, "Deutschland, deine Denunziatianten," 10 Sept. 1993).

Anyone whose name reached the public nearly always faced calamitous prospects. Teachers lost positions, lawyers were disbarred, diplomats were sacked, and politicians were humiliated. To the thinking of many people in the former GDR as well as in the old federal states, those who suffered in the post-Wende period deserved their pillorying. No apologies were needed if "occasional excesses" occurred. In their eyes, the record of civil and human rights abuses over the forty years of the single-party state more than justified the subsequent downfall of the legal functionaries and others who benefited from or accommodated themselves to its rule (see Furian 1992).

Professional dispossession involved more than personal costs. Politicians most likely to provide continuity of leadership in the East have faced enormous roadblocks. Manfred Stolpe is a case in point. Stolpe had been elected prime minister of Brandenburg as a Social Democrat on the strength of his legal representation of the Protestant opposition in the time of the GDR. By early 1992, his reputation had fallen under a pall of suspicion. He acknowledged "1,000 meetings with the security police" in the course of his legal work (*Week in Germany*, 28 Feb. 1992, 2). The Stasi, however, considered Stolpe an *informellen Mitarbeiter* (perhaps, ironically, because of the reliability of his information—normally an essential ingredient of effective legal representation). Stolpe denied the IM appellation, declaring that any listings credited to him had been made without his knowledge. With controversy still raging about him, Stolpe fought the accusation and managed to survive in office.

Gerhard Riege, a Party of Democratic Socialism deputy to the Bundestag, took a different course when it came to light that he had been a "contact person for the security police thirty-two years earlier, from 1954 to 1960" (*Week in Germany*, 28 Feb. 1992, 2). In the foreword to a book coauthored with Riege, Uwe-Jens Heuer sets out a portion of the last letter his friend and colleague wrote before Riege took his own life:

> The power to fight and to live fails me. It has been taken from me under the new freedom. I fear the publicity that the media will produce and against which I cannot defend myself. I fear the hatred which will be lashed upon me in the Bundestag from the mouths, eyes, and attitudes of people, who perhaps never imagine how immoral and merciless is the system to which they have devoted themselves. (Heuer and Riege 1992:5)

Two years later the vilification had barely diminished. Lawyer Gregor Gysi, the chairperson of the PDS parliamentary group, was the target of IM accusations to the effect that he had communicated with the Ministry of State Security while serving as counsel for the GDR critic Robert Havemann in 1979 (*Berliner Zeitung* 1994).

Under these circumstances, the sensible choice for more than a few GDR jurists was "early retirement," and, recognizing the glut of workers produced by unification, Bonn extended monetary inducements to leave. Though the Federal Republic was ill equipped to sustain such a costly remedy that eventually produced widespread resentment among tax-payers in the western states, the Bundestag considered premature retirement preferable to the chaos anticipated when tens of thousands of GDR enterprises began closing their doors. Idle fifty-five- to sixty-year-old prosecutors and judges, who would otherwise have been at the pinnacle of their careers, now had mornings, afternoons, and evenings free for interview sessions and such pastimes as reading three or four news-papers, walking dogs, and writing irate letters. Shattered and outraged, they railed against the "unfair treatment" of being categorized *regierungs-nah*, that is, "close to the government." Until a decision was reached in March 1994 by the Supreme Social Court in Kassel, regierungsnahe GDR functionaries received substantially reduced pensions and unemployment stipends. However, this was declared "unlawfully punitive" by the court. But the ruling was a rare bright spot in a terrain more often clouded by a host of legal difficulties. And even this victory faced another review and additional legislative hurdles (*Berliner Zeitung* 1993a).

An Ethnographic Approach

During periods of extreme social instability and far-reaching change such as witnessed in the formerly socialist world, the ordinary pitfalls of fieldwork are increased manyfold. After 3 October 1990, with but a single exception concerning the conditions permitting early pregnancy termination, the statutory law of the FRG replaced that of the GDR. However, this categoric statement is a bit misleading as the *Einigungsver-trag* (Unification Treaty) directs that past GDR judgments and applications of law are to be honored by the Federal Republic, at least insofar as they are not inconsistent with fundamental human rights. The false starts seen in the expectation of a Rechtsangleichung, followed by transitory concern over the need for Vergangenheitsbewaeltigung, expose the vulnerability of the GDR jurists. The factors distinguishing each individual's professional circumstances, for example, age, occupation (judge, professor, prosecutor), family relationships, retirement options, targeting for prosecution, and so forth, were the focus of my interviews. Out of this matrix emerges the distinctive processes of post-unification legal culture. My goal was to identify a "genealogy of knowledge" revealing the "relations that characterize the temporality of discursive foundations" (Foucault 1972:167). Each fieldwork encounter is uniquely capable of illuminating an individual actor's state of mind, whether it be well reasoned or clouded.

In the field, I collected "legal life histories" of disbarred judges and prosecutors in an effort to understand the patterns and uniqueness in individual experiences. I found that life histories yielded three generations of East German jurists: Generation 1, whose careers began in the immediate postwar period (1945–61); Generation 2, whose legal training occurred after the erection of the Berlin Wall and as East Germany's economy improved but also worked during the suppression of the "Prague Spring" (1962–74); and, Generation 3, the last GDR generation, whose law careers covered the flowering of West German Ostpolitik, the GDR's membership in the United Nations, and rapprochement between the East and the West (1975–89).[9] A first level in the creation of social cohesion is generational: common experiences result in shared tropes that are woven into master narratives uniting, at least loosely, and at the same time demarcating, generational groupings. Individual lives may then be said to possess a "protypicality," embodying a narrative's "generative logic" for an identifiable age cohort (Borneman 1992:47).[10]

As in several contexts considered by this volume's contributors, varied strains of nationalism produce tensions that affect people's sense of themselves as individuals and as members of society. The tensions of nationalism at play in German history manifest themselves in the habitus of the three "generations" of GDR jurists and in the administrative and prosecutorial initiatives taken against them. The three generations of GDR lawyers and judges in a sense recapitulate the phases of German national development. Their responses to current conditions in turn mirror the differences in experience and circumstance produced by the distinct temporal placement of each generation. Generation 1 was dominated by personal awareness of the horrors of World War II, a knowledge of Nazi atrocities, and the experiences of the cold war—in particular, the repressions directed against the adherents of communism in the West, the intensities of the U.S.-Soviet confrontation (including the possibility of nuclear annihilation), the depth of hostility between the FRG and the GDR with its antagonistic praxis of spying and counterspying, and a staunch conviction that the likelihood of nuclear war could be lessened by the continued existence of a vital German communist state. The first generation's proximity to the most extreme era of German ethnonationalism results in the greatest post-unification animus being directed against them. If the first generation in the East unceremoniously purged Nazi judges, that led to the need to install a generation of jurists who were unsuitable by virtue of their lack of independence. Now, using eastern surrogates, the West seeks to atone for its acceptance of jurists with Nazi histories.

Generation 2's consolidation of statutory codification under the influence of heightened economic performance corresponds to the "conservative middle phase" in the development of German nationalism with the founding of Bismarck's Reich in 1871. The number of judges accused of Rechtsbeugung from Generation 2 does not yet match those criminally charged from Generation 1. Law professors, those with expertise in socialist statutory schema of all types, however, were heavily represented in Generation 2. This generation has thus been hit hard by faculty expulsions and also has been rejected while pursuing the continuation of judicial careers. While they have been damaged by loss of income and prestige, their situation is thus not nearly as dire as the pensioners of Generation 1, who are often impoverished as a consequence of Bonn's discriminatory policies against those who "participated in judgments against the principles of legality and humanity." It is this generation who is seen at colleagues' trials and heard in rancorous disagreement with the verdicts of the courts.

The last of the three legal generations in the East, trained after the advent of Ostpolitik and the Basic Treaties between the FRG and the GDR in 1972, was the generation with the least investment in combating the Nazi past, and the one that chafed most under the yoke of SED authority over judicial administration. It is also the age group that has received the most benign treatment at the hands of prosecutors and administrative officials. Before the end of the GDR, this generation no longer troubled itself with strident demands for prosecution of aged Nazis in the West. Its young judges were inexpert in the internecine ways of the SED's manipulation of law. It was also the generation likely poised to engage in reformation of the foundations of legality—that had never been entirely torn away—in the existing, albeit deeply flawed, framework of GDR judicial administration.[11]

For the ethnographer in former East Germany, as in any context of dramatic change, the problem of defining generations is complex: delineating the novel sets of presuppositions experienced by individuals while they actively respond to the array of previously unfamiliar "communicative actions." The situation presents a constantly shifting field of meanings. The post-Wende discursive habitus of the GDR jurist has been ruled by the rationales for the actions taken against them. These rationales are the debate's legitimating halo. Abstracting from published sources and ethnographic interviews, the chief justifications can be summarized as follows:

1. GDR law must be publicly examined in order to establish an accurate historical record

2. The jurists responsible must be punished for their abuses, that is, those who caused injustice under the GDR legal system should suffer retribution

3. The "German character" suffers from a propensity to adhere unquestioningly to all authority, and thus the opportunity to condemn and thereby cure this flaw should not be bypassed

4. Condemnation of the SED's legal regime forewarns the eastern population against a renewal of antidemocratic policies, particularly those urged by the PDS

5. Prosecution of GDR jurists fulfills four decades of FRG government policy commitments and sacrifice by West German democrats

6. Making examples of responsible individuals and purging the thinking underlying the former system is needed to build a legal system in the East committed to a contrasting set of values

7. Establishing responsibility for GDR legal misdeeds provides a basis for reducing the pensions of the culpable individuals and thereby the monetary costs of unification

8. The exclusion of unworthy individuals opens eastern territory to western jurists capable of instilling democratic values and erecting a new legal infrastructure in the most rapid manner possible

9. Focusing on the legal injustices of the past will draw the attention of the eastern populace away from an unhealthy obsession with the loss of socialism's "iron ricebowl" (that is, guaranteed housing, employment, education, health care, retirement, and so forth)

10. Punishment of responsible jurists "makes whole" the victims of judicial injustice

11. And, finally (perhaps most importantly) the entire process is a demonstration of the power and effectiveness of the new legal culture.

Both within and beyond these rationales, we find examples of Sally Falk Moore's (1978) "models of agency" and "counterprocess," Thompson's (1975) "contested legal discourses," and Emile Durkheim's (1983) "social norms"—at times sharply and satisfyingly delineated, at others only vaguely hinted at. That elusiveness, always evident, but most particularly in periods of sudden, accelerated, profound, and widespread change, leads Clifford Geertz to declare that the "grand categories of comparative ethnography seem blunt and ill-made" (1995:16). The ethnographer senses "all the really critical things seem just to have happened yesterday and just about to happen tomorrow . . . (that he came) too late and arrived too early . . . [at] a pause between the right times, between a turbulence somehow got through and another one obscurely looming" (Geertz 1995:4). The solution to this "after-the-fact . . . life-trailing nature of consciousness" is, for Geertz, a "continual effort to devise systems of discourse that can keep up, more or less, with what, perhaps, is going on" (1995:19). Without denying the value of statistics, graphs, and data to "dress interpretation," Geertz no longer sees any whole but merely "assemblage"; no longer part but "pieces"; "it is no longer possible for even the most methodological anthropologist, eyes fixed on shape and coherence, to tell that kind of story now" (1995:16).

Geertz's observations are profoundly apt in the aftermath of German unification. Whether the lives of East Germans today are "half-full" (of the yet unrealized promises of market-capitalism) or "half-empty" (of the lost sureties of state-socialism), their unsettled states are no less palpable. As seen in Oliver Sacks's socioneurological description of the blind man whose life-long cataracts are removed for the first time in his late forties, the acquisition of vision can have deeply disturbing, even destructive, effects (1995:108–52).

Normative Conversion

New norms become generally teachable and publicly defendable through subsumation of an agreed upon "logic of practical discourse" (Baier and Gert in Habermas 1990:62). The continuing problem is whether—in the context of mores, customs, habits, and tradition—reasons can be mobilized for obedience to a norm, reasons that are sufficient to make the norm's "claim to validity" appear justified. In searching for a foundation of universal normative imperatives, Habermas downplays the notion that a universal norm must exist in "what *each* can will without contradiction to be a general law," but rather insists it must be "what *all* can will in agreement to be a universal norm"

(McCarthy 1978 in Habermas 1990:67; my emphasis). Only an intersubjective process is needed to produce a consensus among the participants to an ethical discourse before they will be morally convinced of something. Each party must be willing to submit his or her position to discursive testing by the other concerning its universality. That testing process amounts to inviting each person, in what Habermas terms "the last court of appeal," to judge whether one's claim is or is not in that other persons' best interests (1990:67). Such an invitation, however, must be accompanied by an awareness that needs and interests are interpreted in the light of cultural values, including the terms used to describe those interests. In Habermas's words: "Since cultural values are always components of intersubjectively shared traditions, the revision of the values used to interpret needs and wants cannot be a matter for individuals to handle monologically" (1990:67–68). Experiencing the legal actions mounted against them, it is precisely the eastern jurists' sense of the failure of the prosecuting authorities to engage in such a process of "mutual submission" that informs their production of eastern legal culture.

Habermas's abstract formulation suggests that "moral argumentation" takes place around a negotiating table—and, surely, at times it does occur on a relatively even playing field. However, in practice conditions are more often noteworthy for their unevenness. Every relatively minor discrepancy in the sociology of knowledge hints at massive accumulations of divergence across a multitude of contexts in eastern Germany. For more than forty years German culture developed along separate, often starkly contrasting pathways in the East and West zones. West Germans at the Wende recognized no special obligation to take that gap into account in their dealings with easterners. To the contrary, the tendency was to mock the easterner as the bumpkin seen in the popular television sitcom *Motzki* (*Newsweek*, 22 Feb. 1993, 55). Certainly there was little or no evidence of interest among West Berliners in learning the outmoded lexicon of the easterner. Had the two former zones been more equivalent in their respective positions of power—economic, legal, and social—there might have been sufficient trade-offs along the fault lines where normative consensus-building occurs, but this was seldom the case.

The "framing" concept developed by Erving Goffman (1974) sheds light on the easterners' difficulties. At one end of the spectrum a problem can appear rather harmless (as in the bakery incident); at the other end of the spectrum, a problem may assume major importance, as when the appropriate "frame" is breached in the course of criminal proceedings.[12] In post-unification courthouses, West German jurists rendered decisions turning on their view of how the law of the German Democratic Republic was interpreted, or in their judgment how either would or should have been interpreted. Since the West Germans could not perform this feat inside a GDR court, nor within the broader outlines of the GDR's "real existing socialism," how, the GDR jurists asked, could the FRG courts provide the necessary "frame" to give their judgments contextual validity?

For example, in August 1992, a Berlin criminal court had to decide whether a previous ruling by a GDR *Arbeitsgericht* (labor court) had been correctly rendered. The question turned on whether the Arbeitsgericht had properly upheld the termination of an electrical foreman who lost his job because he had been expelled from the SED. The Berlin court (three years after the GDR court's original ruling) upheld the earlier East German decision by citing general language drawn from a resolution of the 10th SED Congress. It was hardly the kind of firm precedent one might have desired to support the judgment of the Arbeitsgericht (see De Nike 1994:103). The problem was not so much whether the Berlin criminal court's opinion was correct. (It was subsequently affirmed in a decision by the higher *Bundesgerichtshof* [Federal Supreme Court].) Rather, the court dealt clumsily with the framing issue in judging its former socialist adversary. In case after case West German judges purport to determine whether judicial behavior, occurring sometimes as long as forty years earlier, conformed to the then applicable GDR law. This process usually takes place with full knowledge that during the often lengthy intervening periods no GDR court ever lifted a finger to disturb the earlier decisions. Daunting as this assignment may be, German judges thus far have performed it with alacrity. The result has sometimes been decisions "on behalf of" GDR courts, which apply doctrines unfounded in GDR precedent.

Invocation of "self-executing" treaties is an example. Application of self-executing treaties hinges upon whether a treaty becomes effective as part of the organic law of a state *when* it is signed by the national executive or only *after* implementing legislation is adopted. The courts in the GDR held that the country's treaties (for example, the Helsinki Agreements bearing on international migration) were not self-executing, that is, implementing laws were needed for the treaty contents to become enforceable as the nation's law. That stance mirrored the approach taken by both the Federal Republic of Germany and the United States. Today, however, the courts of the FRG enforce the GDR's international agreements as if they had been part of its organic law, despite a complete absence of necessary legislation adopted during the life of the GDR. In the pivotal 1993 decision by the Federal Supreme Court that affirmed the conviction of border guards who on 5 February 1989 shot the last person to die at the Wall, the following language appears: "The described state practice, which included the deliberate killing of fleeing persons by firearms, is considered the same as the conditions which were the object of the *Senat* judgment from 3 November 1992. . . : Because of obvious, intolerable violation of basic standards of justice and against human rights, the protection of which the GDR had committed itself as a treaty-state to the International Covenant on Civil and Political Rights of 19 December 1966 . . . , the interpretation of section 27 of the GDR border-statute, which characterized such state practice, can provide no justifying effect."[13] Needless to say, no GDR court had ever accorded such effect to the covenant, since it was not considered self-executing.

That and other discontinuities in the East-West dialogue fall within the class of "statements" which Habermas designates "validity claims . . . contested in moral argument" (1990:52). The moral truth of validity claims, or "normative statements," he cautions, is not to be confused with the truth or falsity of "descriptive statements" (1990:52), a problem seldom seeming to trouble the courts now hastening to graft FRG constitutionalism onto the East.

The GDR jurists grapple with the capacity of law to transform the normative content of validity claims into the truth of descriptive statements—what Habermas also terms the "assimilation of normative descriptive propositions" (1990:52). Hence, a legal-political ethnography of German unification owes particular attention to the "voices," that is, those who must deal with these claims. Concentration upon voices meets what Geertz terms contemporary anthropology's "nervousness about speaking for others" (1995:129), while also taking pains to present and analyze the significance of responsive social actions for those who enact them and the creative institutions and practices which lend those enactments their significance.

Conclusion

German nationalism was a relative latecomer compared to other European states, especially neighboring France. A "liberal phase" culminating in the short-lived revolution of 1848 advocated a democratic transformation against a vestigial feudal order. An "official nationalism" emerged after 1871 with the founding of the German Reich, in which "traditional elites used national rhetoric to express political opposition . . . while fostering military aggression" (Joppke 1995:219). And, finally, in the Nazi movement, the "nation" of *Blut und Boden* (blood and soil) became a cudgel in the hands of the extreme right against the democratic experimentation of the Weimar Republic.

After World War II, both German nations attempted to separate themselves from the immediate Nazi past. Without such a break, no moral or political renewal was possible. The West recollected the Reich of 1871 and attempted to revive the democratic foundations unveiled during Weimar. The East espoused a radical break and an embrace of utopianism: "[T]he task of confronting the past . . . was elevated to the central program of state and society" (Joppke 1995:221). A consequence of this eastern radical break, however, was a form of exculpation. As the survivors of the murderous Nazi campaigns, the communist leadership of the GDR readily eschewed the shouldering of moral responsibility, and the entire eastern populace was effectively absolved. On the other hand, western "continuity" led to the "permanent suspicion (in the East) that the Nazi past was not really over" in the Federal Republic (Joppke 1995:222).

Generational cleavages among the GDR's jurists are unmistakable. The vocational investment, from Studium to profession of Generation 3, is too great to cast off casually. They do not balk, however, at identifying the oppressiveness of the SED—one referred derisively to "passing out red armbands"—as a major source of pre- and post-Wende discontent. Yet they also recognize the values vacuum accompanying the collapse of socialist institutions which, to their expressed dismay, have been filled by political chaos and an alluring but concomitantly repellent materialism. As members of the postwar cohort they are naturally less willing to accept blame for excesses of the Ulbricht era of state formation. Educated and socialized after the advent of Brandt's Ostpolitik and for the most part enjoying the self-image and confidence of Berliners, they saw themselves—even before the date of the Wende—as approaching a future where the two Germanys would stand in increasing rapprochement. By the same token, the younger individuals have better managed to survive—even professionally. Berlin's cultural vitality and promise as Germany's future capital and trade gateway to Eastern Europe create many openings for legal professionals to shift laterally—to insurance, taxation, real property fields—when they are precluded from retaining their former positions. Not feeling the prosecutor's lash directly and thinking no doubt about the wisdom of measured responses in the face of ongoing investigations, they tend to be more muted in their criticisms of *Rechtsbeugung* charges than their older colleagues.

Drawing on Habermas's model, my purpose in this essay has been not to discover universal norms or general laws, but rather to search for the processes producing knowledge of moral convictions by collecting life histories of jurists disbarred in the context of German reunification. Intersubjective ideas, values, claims, and the like, must be tested for universality—by the other; anyone's propositions regarding universality are contingent on relations with other people and their interests. Each person judges the other's claim, not in terms of the framework of his or her own values, but rather in the context of the other's interests. Thus, capturing the perspective of East German lawyers and judges—in the manner urged by Habermas—is among the ethnographer's tasks. Listening to the voices of GDR jurists and examining the new juridical cosmography where they have been so suddenly projected, one finds individual and collective phenomena seeming at once to confirm and undermine the analytical utility of Habermas's behavioral and dialogic model of "intersubjectively shared traditions" of "cultural values" (1990:67–68). The difficulties arise, however, not in contravention of Habermas's prescriptions, but because, as he acknowledges, different "speech acts," including those of legal proceedings, may contain competing claims to validity that are reflections of unequal power and disparate histories (136). As a consequence, the ethnographic landscape is not limited to consensus and tradition but also includes opposition, self-interest, and at times outright confusion.

The rallying cry of "victor's justice" rings out from those who experience the brunt of the Rechtsbeugung accusations. The erstwhile legal functionaries often find themselves placed in the uncomfortable position of defending a legal system with which they were in many ways constitutionally at odds. The origins of the GDR's institutions of law— its judicial offices, prosecutorial processes, its bar—were historically consistent in much of their form and content with the rise of bourgeois legal professionalism elsewhere in Europe. Hence the easterners challenge Unrechtsstaat charges, though few know the defects of the GDR legal regime better than they, who dealt daily with its mechanisms of control.

The general shock of unification within the eastern populace is exacerbated for the judges and law professors who are treated as outcasts, fit only for dismissal from the bench and their university posts. Being willing, ready, and able to learn the new system is meaningless in the face of accusations of service to the Unrechtsstaat. Those jurists now pay dearly for the GDR's decades of self-congratulation over its founding ethos. In the eyes of the West, the life-experiences of World War II fail to justify the choices made, however insistent the jurists may be about being guided by a spirit of antifascism. That message is especially distasteful to them, since their antifascism came wrapped in the noble glosses of socialism. That "real existing socialism" may also have been consistently understood as a masquerade (see Burawoy and Lukács 1992) does not dispel its egalitarian idealism—what Eric Bentley called "the great hope of our era: the hope of Socialist humanism" (1971:944). The revolution may indeed have "dismissed its children" (Leonhard 1979), and, at its core, the GDR may have been an Unrechtsstaat. But this does not obviate espousal, at least tactically, of socialism's vision for a better humanity. However welcome the Rechtsstaat might be to judges and lawyers, who institutionally and professionally stand to profit enormously from modern expansion of law, it is difficult to embrace it unreservedly as it goes about establishing a post-Wende definition of German citizenship by vilifying one's past. The clash of interests seen in the cases against the GDR legal functionaries reflects Habermas's opposed validity claims embedded in the separate histories, ideologies, and traditions of two cultures. The legal forum, however, comes preset with its own maxims, procedures, and ways of doing things, and the rules of the Rechtsstaat delimit the means for legally condemning past injustices. The GDR's former jurists invoke those constraints today as they are being simultaneously stretched to serve the legal-political interests of the West's prosecutors and political parties. This politicization of the law, together with its historical anomalies, does not go unrecognized. Rather, it produces alternative definitions of citizenship and discursive modes for reflecting upon East-West power disparities and the loss of eastern self-determination.

Moore posited a legal universe in which individual agents operate either according to rule-congruent, regular patterns, or according to discretionary, manipulative actions (1978:253–56). For every rule, a political counterprocess may be expected. The ethnographic imperative becomes clear. Indeed, I found that without actual voices, "legitimation," "normative elements," and "the role of the state" were vague abstractions—fertile ground for cool, distanced debate but divorced from the cluttered social history of individuals and groups at particular moments in time and space. Found in the context of the surrounding legal culture, "normative legitimation," "counterprocesses," and strategies of "manipulation" are the everyday expressions and behavior of what Sacks calls "the irreducible uniqueness of the individual" (1995:165).

Making one's way through the ethnographic topos of judges and prosecutors and observing the intensity of the assault upon their ambitions and careers, the picture at times appears terribly out of focus. On one hand West Germans spoke with conviction about the evils of the GDR Unrechtsstaat, the pervasive SED mechanisms "to control the administration of justice," and the unsuitability of GDR judges; on the other stood jurists who saw themselves at worst as history's pawns, or at best as men and women who had "struggled to uphold a rule of law." Meanwhile, judicial decisions made thirty or more years before were being disinterred, stripped of context, and made the subject of new charges. When, they asked, did the Rechtsstaat, which now sat in judgment of them, take into account the cold war? The nuclear confrontation between the United States and the Soviet Union? The forty-year occupation by Soviet troops? The invasions of Prague and Budapest? The GDR's antifascist ideals? The internal reforms periodically initiated within the GDR's constraining orthodoxies? The "dirty hands" of the Federal Republic with its ex-Nazi judges? To the eastern jurists, those and a host of other questions were ignored as the investigations, prosecutions, reviews, and disbarments proceeded apace. Within such problematics one finds the "incommensurabilities" to which Greenhouse refers in her introduction to this volume as she urges a redefinition and rethinking of "structure and agency" and "hegemony and resistance." In the earnest desire to give a voice to the subaltern, does the ethnographer "discover" not only the structural order of a Radcliffe-Brown but also a dubious cultural grammar overflowing with resistance? As Duncan Kennedy might caution, "interstitial resistance" can have a "dark (collaborative) side" (1993:205).

Notes

1. See Thompson 1975:266; Humphreys 1985:251; and also chapters by Gordon and Ries in this volume.

2. The term *Wende*, or "turning," signifies the moment when East Germany moved toward unification with West Germany following the opening of the Berlin Wall.

3. The root of *Volksgerichtshof*—*das Volk*—carries a strong connotation of ethnic German identity, which does not translate well as "the people's," as, for instance, in "People's Republic of China."

4. Sources: Central Labor Administration of the GDR and the Press Service of the Federal Labor Department.

5. The Stasi officer was charged and sentenced to ten years in prison following the Fall of the Wall, while the derelict prosecutors were convicted for their nonfeasance and placed on probation, respectively, for nine and twelve months (*Berliner Zeitung*, 30 April 1992).

6. Personal communication, 19 May 1994, Dr. R. In March 1995, I was informed by Erich Buchholz, lawyer for Dr. R., that this case resulted in *Freispruch* (acquittal) for his client.

7. Personal communication, 28 June 1993, Dr. Evelyn Kenzler, President, Vereinigung demokratischer Juristen.

8. Literally "Gauck authority," named after its director, Joachim Gauck, an East German Protestant pastor active in the antigovernment citizens' movement before the Wende.

9. See Ash 1993:28–47.

10. Using "generation" as an analytical device has the built-in advantage of historical, or political-chronological emplotment. It is a rough categorization, however, for some individuals may not "belong" to their generation, that is, they may be atypical of an age cohort.

11. Taking generations as heuristic devices draws out the significance of the law in shared responses, that is, intersubjective interpretations of the conditions, problems, and opportunities that jurists confronted and continue to confront. In reacting to their circumstances, the significance of generation emerges in the way the members of each group see themselves in relation to the performance of their "law roles," and in the ways they are viewed by the officials who hold the power to determine their post-unification professional fates. Since each generation except the first overlapped with its predecessors(s), earlier, unique periods provide the basis for generationally differentiated understandings of the legal eras which followed. Any cultural artifact can be considered both a meaningful expression of what Habermas terms "an observable event" and "an understandable objectification of meaning" (1990:23). As a conscious human creation, law possesses the same qualities. It is communicative action imbued with meaning, capable of being misunderstood, of being used oppressively, of producing reactive resistance, and so forth.

12. Erving Goffman recognized the problem of framing in the courtroom, citing the example of Lenny Bruce's protestations when a San Francisco police officer tried to replicate his comedic routine from the witness stand (with less than hilarious results) (1974:68–69). Quips that had drawn laughter in the nightclub fell flat, producing startled gasps from the judge and courtroom.

13. Original text:

> Fuer die geschilderte Staatspraxis, die die vorsaetzliche Toetung von Fluecht-lingen durch Schusswaffen einschloss, gilt dasselbe wie fuer die Verhaeltnisse, die Gegenstand des Senatsurteils vom 3.11.92 (NJW 1993, 14) waren: Wegen offensichtlichen, unertraeglichen Verstosses gegen elementare Gebote der Gerechtigkeit und gegen die Menschenrechte, die zu schuetzen sich die DDR als Vertragsstaat des Internationalen Paktes ueber buergerliche und politische Rechte vom 19.12.1966 (DDR-GBl II 1973, 1533) verpflichtet hatte, konnte abs. 27 DDR-GrenzG in der Auslegung, die durch eine solche Staatspraxis gekenn-zeichnet war, keine rechtfertigende Wirkung entfalten. (Bundesgerichtshof Urt. v. 25.3.93–5 StR 418/92) (30 *Neue Juristische Woche* 1932, 1935)

Part Two

Ethnographies of Agency in the Fissures of the State

Stacia E. Zabusky

Ethnography in/of Transnational Processes: Following Gyres in the Worlds of Big Science and European Integration

Although this essay concerns scientists and citizens in Europe, I begin not with physics, politics, or polemics but with poetry, specifically these lines from William Butler Yeats's "The Second Coming":

> Turning and turning in the widening gyre
> The falcon cannot hear the falconer;
> Things fall apart; the center cannot hold;
> Mere anarchy is loosed upon the world

It is not Yeats's theory of the end of Christendom and the coming of some "rough beast slouching towards Bethlehem" (or, in my case, Brussels) that concerns me here. I want instead to call attention to the image of the "widening gyre" with its constant, shifting movement, pulling apart a center that becomes more attenuated with every turn of the falcon's wings, a dissipating center over which the falconer has lost all control.

I will suggest here that when doing ethnography in moments and contexts of political reconstruction and instability, we—ethnographers and participants alike—confront and move not through "social fields" but "widening gyres" in which "the center cannot hold." In such contexts, centers displace other centers, peripheries mutate into centers, and centers and peripheries pile atop one another, now dissolving the distinctions, now recreating them in another place. No one is in control of this ongoing "gyration," this making and unmaking of centers—people stumble through these gyres, improvising some place to stand for a moment, a place where they try to get something done.

What are the implications for ethnography if we recognize social spaces delimited not by fields but instead by gyres? What, more particularly, are the implications for the ethnography of the privileged and the powerful, if these gyres simultaneously generate and displace centers? These are the questions I will address here through a consideration of what we might call a "happy case" of reconstruction and instability: space-science mission development in Western Europe.[1] I call this a happy case because the situation I address differs in significant respects from those addressed by many of the other contributors to this volume. Their essays discuss more painful and tragic cases as they confront instabilities arising out of war, violence, dislocation, and poverty.

Space science in Europe seems, by contrast, to take shape in a context of remarkable stability and comparative calm as its participants are able to pursue technical activities undisturbed by such massive traumas as urban poverty or genocide. Space science in Europe is in fact a domain of activity characterized by tremendous productivity; every year, scientists and engineers in Europe are involved in the launch of new missions, including such projects as the orbiting Hubble Space Telescope (in which the Europeans are active and integral partners with NASA), the Giotto space probe (launched by the European Space Agency in 1985 to observe Halley's comet at close range), and the Huygens space probe (a European Space Agency mission launched in the fall of 1997 to study Titan, one of Saturn's moons). These missions have been, even with inevitable and much publicized flaws, successful in innumerable ways: they return data to scientists that result in discoveries and publications; they push the boundaries of technological capabilities for engineers; they fuel high-tech industries with multimillion dollar contracts; and they contribute to the political viability and existential reality of the European Union. I will argue, however, that it is not political or professional *stability* that leads to this productivity; instead productivity emerges from the participants' ongoing *struggle* to find and make stability while engaged in the daily work of European cooperation in space science. It is a struggle because participants find themselves working at the intersection of two powerful transnational processes: European integration and big science. These processes continually destabilize productions as varied as satellites, individual careers, and government organizations, making it difficult to identify any one domain as the centralized locus of decision and activity. Thus, for participants, productivity is achieved through what they experience as instability and uncertainty, as they improvise moments of clarity in which work can get done and lives can be lived.

This is no easy task. Participants struggle to construct missions that meet their professional or intellectual needs in the face of constant shifts in political priorities, organizational policies, and economic reallocations over which they have little or no control. Those involved in mission development thus often recognize their achievements only in the past tense; in the present moment, and in the future that stretches before them as so many technical "milestones" to be reached, they can see only a barrage of impediments, as the fluid circumstances of European integration and big science engulf them in endless gyrations, unsettling them at every turn. This constant upheaval engenders experiences of frustration, alienation, and cynicism, as participants see themselves as unable to control core resources or direct those activities necessary to complete their work. Such experiences are countered, however, by the excitement that comes from improvising in the spaces of power, where participants make use of the cultural materials provided by science and state in an oscillating dynamic of domination and resistance that ultimately leads to production.

In what follows, I tell a story about how I came to notice these improvisations in the context of space-science mission development in Europe. The story begins with the problems I encountered when conceptualizing how to frame or conduct an ethnographic project in the transnational arenas of European integration and big science. It moves on to consider how I realized that there were neither clear-cut normative communities (for example, the international scientific community or even the European Community) nor definitive social fields (for example, bounded nation-states and organizations) in which I could pursue fieldwork in any traditional sense; there were, instead, widening gyres and constant improvisations. In the course of such realizations, I found the problem of power increasingly complicated and complicating.

Context: Transnational Processes Reviewed

When I began to plan my project in 1987, intent on conducting fieldwork in a more or less traditional vein, the prospect of studying the large-scale transnational processes of European integration and big science from inside seemed daunting, to say the least. These were momentous and gargantuan undertakings, characterized as much, if not more, by institutional and bureaucratic maneuverings of grand proportions as by any set of local, intimate practices more amenable to ethnographic analysis. Moreover, both these processes seemed defined more by constant change than by definitive structures; at every moment, political, economic, and organizational realities shifted, challenging my ability to hone in on a place I could call "the field."

I had to consider, in the first place, the larger political-economic context of reconstruction that defines European integration. Coming on the heels of the devastation wrought by World War II, this "regional impulse" (Twitchett 1980:7) seeks to produce a new and permanent set of political arrangements among the states of Europe. European integration is an attempt to forge a unified Europe, to turn multiple nation-states into a superstate with a new, singular "center." It is a project that operates at the level and borders of nation-states, where national economies, political parties, and social welfare policies dominate analysis and action. Although this integration takes place in multiple venues, the primary symbolic and institutional locus of this project is the European Union or EU (known at the time of my research as the European Community or EC).

To date, this movement toward integration has been highly successful. Institutions, treaties, laws, and contracts have established increasing connections across state boundaries; common standards for industry and manufacturing have been developed and put into practice; national economies are coordinated in the European Monetary System; borders have been demolished as people show their common red passport identifying them as co-citizens of this new superstate (see Bull 1993, Twitchett 1980, Varenne 1993). Thus, since its inception, integration as a project is one that has been constantly on the move; however, it is not always forward moving. It has been challenged repeatedly by problems of both identity and control.

The identity problem is in part definitional, as member states of the European Union ponder just what criteria (beyond economic health) are necessary and sufficient for extending membership to applicant nation-states. Who can be considered part of a unified "Europe"? For a long while, the primary question was whether the Scandinavian states and the traditionally neutral states of Switzerland and Austria would be interested in joining or would be welcomed by this common European market. Another vexing question was whether Turkey, eager to join in and already a member of NATO, could really be considered "western" enough to fit in to a European alliance. These questions of belonging, of who and what was culturally, properly, and legitimately European, have been challenged anew with the advent of perestroika and glasnost in the Soviet Union in the late 1980s and the fall of the Berlin Wall in 1989. Along with the restructuring of economies, politics, and social policies in the countries of the former Eastern Bloc, have come new applications from the countries of central and eastern Europe to join what had been a purely "western" European endeavor.[2] The identity of the evolving superstate has been in constant flux, as voters and leaders consider who can be now and in the future definitively European.

The issues promoting instability in European integration concern more than identity and belonging, however, and address the ever-thorny issue of control. In the political arena, the transnational process of integration requires individual states to give up sovereignty in at least some arenas in return for increased collective power on a world stage. It is no easy matter, however, to demand that states give up power or redefine their centers, any more than it is an easy matter to identify citizens of these different states only as "Europeans," passports not-withstanding. Some "peripheral" groups have seen in this movement a liberating potential: women's groups, peace groups, environmental groups, and ethnic groups all have begun to take their cases and their issues directly to this new, growing center, in an effort to bypass those state structures which have silenced them for so long. Such groups seek incorporation and inclusion for all the diverse "peoples" of Europe (for example, see Darian-Smith this volume; Galtung 1989; Stephens 1993). Many others see in this new center a threat to their independence and identities, and, indeed, there have been frequent paroxysms of resistance to this project, whether in the form of Britain's refusal to join in the beginning and again under Margaret Thatcher, or in Charles de Gaulle's refusal to let Britain join when it finally wanted in, or in the withdrawal of Britain from the European Monetary System—or, on a more local level, the violent protests by French farmers and fishermen, and the referendum in which Danish citizens rejected the Maastricht Treaty (only ultimately to vote to accept it). These independent movements, these denials and objections to increasing union are all part of the inexorable trend toward integration (see also Gerlach and Radcliffe 1979), themselves an expression of the profound "reconstruction" that is underway as Europe seeks to redefine its center(s).

Besides European integration, there were also the complex dynamics of big science to consider as I developed a fieldwork project. Big science, too, represents a form of transnational reconstruction, albeit an ongoing, temporary one, in that it challenges the defined and fixed boundaries of nation-states in order to reach the desired end. Historically, scientists have long respected and insisted on the value of cooperating across state boundaries; in the familiar rhetoric of science, all practitioners are accorded membership in an "international scientific community" which extends its citizenship to all scientists regardless of nationality (Zabusky n.d.).[3] Accordingly, in the interests of pursuing their research scientists have always seemed particularly able to move about the world with ease, taking up residence now in this country, now in that, regardless of their countries of origin. As scientific interests became realizable only within more and more complex technologies, states and industrial capital became enmeshed in the development of these monumental, "disinterested" projects (see, for example, Galison and Hevly 1992). The idea of international cooperation is now glorified not only by scientists but also by states and industries, as they undertake big science in a context of global capitalism. Such projects by definition depend on transnational flows of people, technology, and capital for the production of functioning artifacts, whether they are the Channel Tunnel, the Ariane rocket, or the particle accelerator at the European Center for Nuclear Research (CERN).

Space science in Europe developed in a context of superpower rivalry; the "space race" between the former Soviet Union and the United States left the Europeans in a small, virtually invisible position to begin their own space pursuits. Their efforts required the formation of alliances among states, the infusion of capital into new central locations, and the conscription of human participants focusing on the myriad technical, economic, and social details that together constitute a larger, integrated artifact (Zabusky 1995). These arrangements introduced, and continue to introduce, "instability" into state goals, particular institutions, and individual lives. States continue to shift, or manipulate, national interests to meet international goals of cooperation, accommodating other centers in an effort to retain some power for themselves. The infusion of capital leads to the establishment of joint institutions that then take on lives of their own, becoming new "centers" which have to be accommodated. And people must move, accommodating themselves not only to the pressures of cooperation on the microlevel but to the pressures of reconstructing homes and selves in foreign lands (see Zabusky 1996).

These transnational processes of European integration and big science, with their mammoth proportions and rationalizing tendencies, conjure up many of the dreams and terrors of modernity including those of centralized states and technological utopias (or dystopias). At the time that I was planning my research project, such nightmares did not constitute a typical domain for inquiry in cultural anthropology; although, in the wake of the cultural studies movement, anthropologists have increasingly turned an eye toward such nightmares (or fantasies, depending on one's point of view). Nonetheless, it was out of this contradictory and constantly changing maelstrom of state-building and science that I attempted to construct a field to which I could go to conduct an ethnographic research project.

Conceptualizing Fieldwork: Theoretical Difficulties

I faced a series of conceptual problems when imagining my ethnographic project. A major problem was that, for a lone anthropologist interested in the grounded, lived experiences of real people working out the myriad details of daily life, it was difficult to conceptualize a "cultural" study of such macro-level, large-scale, encompassing phenomena as "international scientific cooperation" or "big science" or "European integration." These transnational domains seemed to be empty of people, defined instead, as I have briefly described here, by the political-economic and practical-technical goals of states, organizations, and technology. Without people, it seemed that there could be no ethnography. Or perhaps the problem really was that the only people who were there—making policy, signing memoranda of understanding, connecting wires, studying electronic signals—were people who had "culture" squeezed out of them by their involvement in the rational, instrumental, and technical practices of state, bureaucracy, and science. Bureaucrats, technocrats, scientists, and engineers often seemed to revel in their rationality rather than their culturality; Sharon Traweek (1988) described this phenomenon, in the case of American high-energy physicists, as "the culture of no culture."

This sense that people engaged in such activities are themselves empty of culture prevented anthropologists from turning their attention to these remarkable social processes for a long time, even after anthropologists began ethnographic study of Western societies.[4] In part this resulted from the historical legacy of the divide between sociology and anthropology, in which sociology claimed as its disciplinary territory the study of modern, complex (western) societies and their attendant institutions (such as organizations, professions, and science), while anthropology turned its disciplinary attention to the "non-Western world." (All this was rather like the way the superpowers divided up the globe into delimiting spheres of influence.) This division of labor itself, however, led to or at least reflected a particular facet of anthropology's worldview, namely, its preoccupation with and glorification of the exotic. As so many scholars have reminded us in recent years, cultural anthropology's fascination with the primitive, the marginal, and the peripheral, caused us to construct the Other in a particular way, in a way that fed our own needs and interests (see Clifford and Marcus 1986; Taussig 1987). Simultaneously, by taking the Others as objects of cultural study, we made it possible to ignore or forget that we, too, had culture. Only those Others out there, with strange customs, bizarre rituals, and mystical beliefs, all of which required explication and analysis in rational terms, had culture.

That perspective derives in part from the ideology of rationality on which modernity depends. The ideology itself defines rationality in opposition to culture, and, as Traweek's notion of the "culture of no culture" suggests, this is the point of view to which technocrats, scientists, and engineers of all kinds subscribe. Those involved in the work of organizations and technology insist that they transcend the petty preoccupations and contaminating influences of politics, identity, and emotion in their everyday working lives, if not their personal lives, although the boundary is drawn blurrily if at all. If, then, there were no culture in the processes of bureaucracy, technology, and science, then there was also no reason for anthropologists to pay any attention to those activities, organizations, or those involved in them, since anthropologists are supposed to study culture almost by definition.[5]

In this way, anthropologists have long been seduced by the ideology of rationality that we also endeavor to critique, embracing the exotic objects of our inquiry out of a conviction that they, alone, continued to live in worlds enchanted by culture. Even with the erosion and loss brought about by imperialism, colonialism, state-building, capitalism, and increasing tourism, it has transpired that only those Others retain and contain the comforts and excitements of culture, while we (educated, bourgeois, professional), on the other hand, have been rendered bland and dull by modernity—"no culture here," we might say, whether approvingly or in lament. As Charles Taylor (1989) has written, to many of us in the contemporary world, it appears that life at the center is fundamentally "disenchanted."

That sense of emptiness haunted my initial efforts to imagine a cultural study of scientists and engineers at work on European space science missions, especially because at this time there were virtually no such studies to emulate. What could there possibly be to look at that would interest an anthropologist? Perhaps such studies should be left to our colleagues in other disciplines, with their highly developed analytic tools for examining rational choice, decision-making, institution-building, and the like.[6] I remained convinced, nonetheless, that there were people with culture, even here, in the midst of bureaucracies and high technology, people whose lives we needed to understand ethnographically if we were to have a complete picture of the impact of modernity on ordinary lives in the Western world. Modernity, after all, was a cultural space and not simply a rational space, even if ideologies of rationality characterized its culture. Ethnography as a method of inquiry offered an opportunity to understand peoples' experiences of modernity, in its apparently new transnational incarnation, from "the natives' point of view"—which still seems to me to be the hallmark of an anthropological approach, the problematic status of that native notwithstanding.

Conceptualizing Fieldwork: Practical Difficulties

Theoretical convictions aside, my knowing that people doing the work of modernity also had culture that needed to be studied ethnographically did not solve a second, more practical problem: to learn about living cultural processes, I had to go do fieldwork somewhere. Indeed, the explicit rules and regulations of dissertation approval and grant writing insisted that I establish an "area" and a "site" in which to do fieldwork. Moreover, the implicit rules of the discipline of anthropology mandated that I be an ethnographer, one known primarily by my geographic area and published and hired in terms of it. My interests in transnational processes, however, made such defining difficult. Most Europeanists, after all, went to particular villages or towns in particular nation-states, and funding opportunities were typically constructed according to such criteria. Where, though, was "Europe" (as opposed to its constituent nation-states)? Where was "the international scientific community" since it was, by definition, everywhere?

The existing ethnographic literature did not provide much guidance in this regard. Europeanist studies in anthropology had by and large focused on rural villages (Cole 1977; Ennew 1980) or perhaps urban enclaves and neighborhoods (Belmonte 1979; Kenny and Kertzer 1983). There was a decided lack of interest in the high-level, political machinations to produce a united Europe; this was a topic for political scientists to study. Cultural anthropologists found it difficult even to consider turning their attention to "Europe." The only way, it seemed, for anthropologists to attack the problem of "Europe" was at the village level, where analysis could show how European integration was irrelevant to, imposed on, or resisted by local people.[7]

The literature in science studies, too, did not afford much support. There was a plethora of studies in the international dimensions of science, but these were historical, economic, and political in orientation (for example, Ben-David 1971, Merton 1973). There was a burgeoning literature in the ethnography of scientific work, led by the pioneering laboratory study of Bruno Latour and Steve Woolgar (1979), that claimed to use an anthropological approach to the study of science. However, the majority of such "laboratory ethnographies" were ensconced in the sociology of knowledge tradition, and their arguments were developed and carried out in opposition to a nonempirical philosophy of science (for example, Lynch 1985, Knorr-Cetina and Mulkay 1983). As such, these ethnographies, while using participant-observation techniques, were not framed in the universe of cultural questions typically posed by anthropologists. More problematic from the point of view of conceptualizing a fieldwork study of big science, such small-scale, micro-oriented studies of science created a cleanly bounded social space for ethnographic work; from these studies, it was difficult to know whether there were transnational processes that established or affected such laboratories, or whether there was any structure at all beyond the microinteractions around a laboratory bench (Hagendijk 1990). All context had been radically excised, precisely the kind of context that interested me. These were not studies of how, for instance, international scientific cooperation actually worked; these were instead studies of the epistemological processes and problems confronted by generic scientists—how they knew what they knew, not how they did what they did.[8]

Villages and laboratories, then, did not provide me with a solution of how to conceptualize an ethnographic study of the massive reconstructions accompanying European integration and big science. Moreover, these transnational processes made it difficult to identify any one space or site where the productive work got done. Yet, I had to identify some bounded site that provided a home for the people who made up the amorphous international communities of science and of Europe, a place where I could pursue ethnographic inquiry. In the end, I decided quite self-consciously to conceptualize my study in terms of "semi-autonomous social fields," which are, as Sally Falk Moore (1978:55) has written, the "most suitable way of defining areas for social anthropological study in complex societies." Social fields generate their own internal rules and customs, yet are simultaneously "vulnerable to rules and decisions and other forces *emanating from the larger world by which* [*they are*] *surrounded*" (emphasis mine). Thus defined, the image of the social field was of ever-widening concentric circles, in which interior social fields were embedded.[9]

I slowly narrowed my focus from the widest concentric circles of "European integration" and "scientific cooperation," until I found a circle small enough to do fieldwork in. The social field I first identified was the European Space Agency (ESA). Founded out of two progenitor organizations in 1974, ESA was dedicated to the production of space technology to benefit European commercial and intellectual life. At the same time, it proclaimed itself proudly to be (and was regarded as) a participant in the political efforts to forge a united Europe. For instance, Helmut Kohl, chancellor of Germany, stated during an address at the jubilee celebration marking ESA's twenty-fifth anniversary that "the joint European conquest and utilisation of space also strengthens the European identity, and this makes ESA's activities a major factor in building Europe as a political entity" (European Space Agency 1989:20). ESA appeared, thus, as just the kind of "semi-autonomous social field" Moore had in mind: a definable social, political, and economic organization embedded in the larger fields of European integration and international big science. But selecting the ESA did not immediately solve the fieldwork problem. The organization presented formidable methodological challenges since it was made up of many smaller establishments spread throughout Europe; the four primary ones included the headquarters in Paris, a telemetry center near Frankfurt, an archives and computation center near Rome, and the research and development center near Amsterdam, along with numerous subsidiary locations in Nice, Cologne, Madrid, Redu in Belgium, Sweden, and so on. Where to go?

I chose the European Space Research and Technology Center (ES-TEC), the main research and technology center located in the Netherlands, where most of the technical and scientific work was carried out. In order to find a manageable social field in which to do my fieldwork, I narrowed my focus even further to a particular department in this institution—the Space Science Department (SSD). Here, ESA staff scientists were charged with the responsibility of coordinating the efforts of other scientists, engineers, and technicians from across Europe in designing, developing, and manufacturing ESA space-science missions. This was where I eventually took up residence to carry out ethnographic field-work from 1988 to 1989.[10] In the time-honored manner of participant-observers since Malinowski, I spent my days watching and listening to the European professionals who worked together daily. My informants were engaged in their own magical and practical tasks: designing and testing spacecraft and instruments such as mass spectrometers, tele-scopes, and imagers; convening, attending, and complaining about meetings; and gathering data and dreaming about magnetic fields, cos-mic radiation, stars, galaxies, and the solar wind. It was this work, this quotidian, technical, focused work, that turned out to be the stuff of transnationalism. This was where it all happened—transnational forces were produced in the turn of a screw, the click of a mouse, an argument in the corridor. Indeed, without the ordinary routines and decisions worked out here at this confluence of transnational streams, there would be no ESA, no European integration, no international sci-entific community.[11]

Executing Fieldwork: Ethnographic Challenges

I settled into a daily fieldwork routine at SSD to explore the contours of this social field. Overtly, my daily experience was straightforward and clear. There I was, undeniably in some *place* watching people design and develop some *thing*. Everyday, I traveled by bus to ESTEC, located by a small coastal village near the Hague, where scientists, engineers, com-puter specialists, technicians, statisticians, lawyers, and accountants from thirteen different European countries worked together to produce space missions for ESA. The physical plant occupied thirty-five beau-tifully landscaped hectares and included several multistory buildings of wood, concrete, metal, and glass. Inside the buildings, there was a pro-liferation of technical equipment: computer terminals in every office, huge laboratory facilities filled with instruments, and in-production satellites that protruded wires, antennae, and the shimmering blue panels of power-generating solar arrays. Inside the buildings, I ob-served countless meetings of teams, working groups, and departments, yawned during tedious sessions in the laboratories as technicians and engineers tested equipment, listened to arguments, and participated in conversations about frustrations and dreams.

It all seemed quite solid. I had found a clearly defined social field where work got done, a social field circumscribed by and embedded in larger, contextualizing fields, and a semiautonomous social field party inventing its own rules, partly dependent on the rules emanating toward it from some exterior, more encompassing, circle. Yet I was plagued by a vague sense that SSD was not far enough inside, that I needed to move in closer to a circle that was more relevant, more defined and confined than that of SSD. One reason for my unease was that, despite the presence of many technological artifacts, most of those relevant to space-science missions rarely, if ever, made a physical appearance at ESTEC.[12] Most of the time, spacecraft, instruments, and telescopes for space-science missions were simply *represented*, visually in models, photographs, blueprints, and computer-generated designs, and in talk about specifications, delays, and testing.

Not only were the technological components not in evidence, but more and more it appeared that, organizational charts notwithstanding, neither was SSD. This administrative unit held little or no experiential significance for the scientists who worked at ESTEC. No one except upper management conceived of SSD as a meaningful social entity. Indicative of this lack was the fact that staff members routinely experienced tremendous difficulty in organizing department-wide activities. (For instance, the year that I was there, the SSD Christmas holiday party was canceled due to insufficient interest.) Moreover, people never referred to themselves as members of SSD but instead identified themselves by their profession or discipline (technician, engineer, astronomer, plasma physicist) or by the particular missions on which they were working (the Hubble Space Telescope, the Infrared Space Observatory, and so forth).

Eventually I realized that SSD was not a relevant or recognized, perhaps not even a genuine, social field for European scientists; rather, missions were what really mattered to people. Instead of caring about or orienting themselves toward the activities of others in SSD, SSD scientists focused on the activities of the teams and working groups of professionals in diverse disciplines, departments, organizations, and countries who were involved in making the mission a reality. These teams and working groups comprised networks of people in different locations but all working toward a common goal—the production of a particular spacecraft. In this way, missions served as, or perhaps produced, a significant kind of semiautonomous social field, even though they did not exist in any single physical space but rather came to exist through the work of collaboration. The spacecraft in particular, with their technological components, scientific specifications, and data generation, seemed to focus everyone's attention inward to the kind of bounded space that constituted a clearly delineated field site at the heart of the powerful transnational processes I was trying to understand.

For this reason, after my initial exploration of the SSD environment, I decided instead to focus on space-science missions as the relevant social field of ethnographic inquiry. But this final, narrowing step, made in an effort to get to the inside of these concentric circles of social fields, proved to be my undoing. The further inside I got—the closer to the careful working out of such details as mass budgets, payload configuration, ground system planning, and the like—the less and less it seemed as if I were inside anything at all. In the day-to-day routines of SSD, I felt, as did participants, that the walls were dissolving.[13] Mission work carried people off in different directions and oriented them toward other people and places even as they sat at their desks.

All around me, people were acting not as if they were at the interior of anything, not of SSD, nor ESTEC, nor even ESA. Instead, they treated such entities as opportunities, as resources, as gyres upon which they could hitch a temporary ride, only to get off again when other needs arose. They did this by literally breaching the walls of ESTEC: by traveling, phoning, faxing, and e-mailing. They did this symbolically, as they manipulated, constructed, and unraveled reams of documentation and the objects that these represented. Indeed, the visual and discursive representations of the technological artifacts that consumed participants' constant attention condensed and resonated with the participation of multiple professionals from multiple sites (institutions, countries, disciplines), making it impossible to think of myself as being inside a field in which I might either harvest or do ethnography; fields were too definite, places where things grow inside clearly marked boundaries. What could be considered boundaries here? The staff scientists were in constant contact with all kinds of "outsiders": other ESA staff members at other establishments, engineers in industry, scientists in European organizations, scientists in the United States, yet these were only "outsiders" to a social field called SSD. From the perspective of the social field called a "mission," these others were intimate and integral participants in the ongoing process of space-science mission development. Their work, moreover, created independent sites (or gyres) of mission-related activity. Missions depended on a process that could not be confined in or defined by any single organization, any more than the people who worked at that particular physical plant could be singularly identified with it. Every detail—from what materials to use, to what temperature to test them at, to where to buy them, to how many to include—required consideration and manipulation of social connections, alliances, and allegiances outside the offices of SSD, through the walls of ESTEC, beyond the limits of ESA, past even the borders of European states.

This was transnationalism in action. The process of space-science mission development contains no clear-cut interior or exterior; instead, every social field cuts across other social fields, creating areas of overlap at the moments and points at which they intersect. Overlapping is not embedding. This is not a series of regular concentric circles but instead is a wild ride on a gyre. To put it another way, instead of marking the limits and describing the interior features of some bounded field—with hedges, trees, rows of plants—enclosed within yet other territorial borders, I found myself standing in a field that was being inundated by streams of water flowing from multiple unseen points, washing away all trace of boundaries. The experience was not of "doing fieldwork" but of trying to "stem the tide" that seemed to sweep away any physical or even discursive evidence of solid physical or social worlds. This is, as Emily Martin (1994) writes, the only experience possible in the "complex systems" which characterize the contemporary world. She argues that "the complexly interconnected world in which we now live seems to say that . . . the current nature of reality . . . [is one in which all] is in flux, order is transient, nothing is independent, everything relates to everything else, and no one subsystem is ever necessarily continuously in charge" (250). Productivity, in such a maelstrom of interconnections, is vulnerable to even the smallest fluctuations in the most distant reaches of the system; thus, "the enormity of the 'management' task . . . becomes overwhelming. Who will manage all this? Is anyone in control?" (122).

Participants in ESA space-science mission development, too, recognized and articulated this experience of vulnerability, where the possibility of "catastrophic collapse" (Martin 1994:130) looms menacingly. As one ESA scientist said to me about the mission he was working on: "This mission is one of the most complicated things ever put together by mankind. It has lots of bells and whistles; it is really a big technological experiment which represents the limits of what humanity can handle. That's why no one knows everything about it, and there are always problems lying in corners waiting to be stumbled on." One person's corner often turned out to be another person's center, and there was no falconer to call anyone back from the spiraling gyres, no one to say, definitively, that this was it, the center, the source, the eye overseeing it all. In the dynamic currents of European integration, big science, and international scientific cooperation, technological components and human participants were swept along without regard to such social or physical boundaries as organizations or countries or corners.

This experience repeated itself over and over during my stay in SSD and posed significant challenges to the ethnographic endeavor. For instance, after I had been at ESTEC for some months and had made the transition to a focus on missions rather than the department, I finally felt that I had figured out all the important players and groups and technologies. But once again I had the familiar sensation of vertigo during an interview with an ESA scientist, Ian (a pseudonym), at SSD. Ian was responsible for coordinating the scientific aspects of an instrument that ESA was providing to a mission being sponsored by another European national space agency. In our conversation, Ian told me about the process of building this instrument, which included a prototype design that had been created in SSD, but which could be built in industry. The work on the electronics for this instrument had to be "contracted out," which meant that an industrial firm had to be hired to do the work. Selecting this firm was not in the hands of the scientists and engineers in SSD, however, but was rather in the hands of an international review board that was charged with the responsibility of ensuring that ESA distributed its contracts in a geographically fair manner: the principle of *juste retour* stipulated that the member states of ESA receive a "fair return" in proportion to their contributions to the agency's operating budget in the form of contracts for national industrial firms. This board, consisting primarily of industrial policy experts, reviewed documents provided by the scientists and engineers, who prepared these documents with the assistance of an ESA contracts officer; its decisions were primarily based on "bottom-line" issues. This board set up yet another review board under its auspices to review both the financial and the technical and quality control issues on which the scientists and engineers also reported. This board was known to be "fussy about format" and could conceivably ignore scientific or technical issues in favor of geography and/or budget.

I had never heard about these review boards before, even though this configuration of people, capital, artifacts, and services was quite significant in determining the current arrangements that I saw around me, since together these boards made all decisions about major contract allocations for components or other technological development costing more than U.S. $800,000. I could not have encountered these boards earlier as they did not exist anywhere in particular but appeared only at the moment when called into being by a set of rules and regulations and by ongoing practices of participants. Only at that moment would the members of these boards, scattered in different countries throughout Europe, appear as "the board," a social group as ephemeral as the meeting they would hold, not scientists versed in the intimate details of astronomy and detectors, yet powerful in determining the outcome of Ian's request. As I sat in that office talking to Ian, I had the sensation that a hole was forming in the office wall, and through that hole I could see an entire world that had been invisible to me, but where Ian entered and circulated with ease. This was no field; this was a gyre, and the acceleration of that widening arc threatened to catapult me through that hole and into some strange, new land. I struggled with that force, trying to decide whether to let go and follow Ian or whether to hold on tight, and try to keep the boundaries around this field intact.

My methodological and ethnographic efforts to limit, confine, and contain people in this or that community or to confine them or their artifacts to this or that field was thus rendered impossible as participants transcended, breached, or crossed such boundaries at every moment. Doing ethnography of the transnational, then, required not just identifying a "site" in the sense of a social field where I could settle down to do fieldwork; doing ethnography of the transnational meant instead being poised for movement, sensitive to flows and trajectories, to instability and reconstruction, to disruptions and re-orientations. I had to be prepared to ride the ongoing currents of capital, people, and services, and to see that what was significant was not the organizations, the communities, or even the artifacts, but instead the practices that created all of these things. There was, in the end, no single, paramount place from which to observe these processes, no moment in time, no edifice, no organization that would provide the definitive view. Instead, I had to improvise my way through and to ethnographic research.

Practices of Transnationalism: Improvisation and Cynicism

My efforts to discover the appropriate social fields for ethnographic inquiry in the complex transnational arenas of European integration and big science had led me to search for my own "village" deep inside more powerful forces. In the process, I made solid and structured the organization of ESA (and with it the establishment that was ESTEC and the department that was SSD). In the end, however, these entities turned out to have less experiential reality for participants than those villages of the proverbial "community studies" that were once the mainstay of ethnographic research in Europe. Indeed, physical edifices and the strictures of bureaucratic rules and regulations aside, in the day to day process of working together, ESA appeared almost as a mirage, constantly disappearing in the swirling currents. These currents created, recreated, and dissolved ESA over and over again. In response, everyone had to keep improvising some common ground on which to stand.

STRUCTURE AND PRACTICE

Before I explore the intricate dance of improvisation, I want briefly to turn my attention to structure, which certainly played a role both in the production and the ethnography of space-science missions. Structure, as the "outcome" and "medium" of ongoing practices (Giddens 1984), is reflected, for instance, in the accumulation of capital in certain places where "gyres" overlap (often instantiated as organizations and institutions). It was also apparent in the credentials and status accumulated by those who moved among various institutional and social networks. These credentials and status, often instantiated as titles like Project Manager or Principal Investigator or as academic degrees like Ph.D., signified access to capital and other resources. For instance, it was senior scientists with Ph.D.s and high titles in university or research laboratories who served on ESA Science Teams; their status reflected their ability to control social and financial resources not available to those with less status or to those from poorer or marginal countries or institutions.

Despite the undeniable significance of such structural aspects of this mode of production, it is not enough to demarcate such structures and then to assume stability in production. These are, after all, complex systems in which multiple networks and institutional structures are at work. No matter how much status participating scientists might have accrued in one institutional domain (for example, as department head of a national research laboratory) or social network (for example, as leading scientist in the field of infrared astronomy), this status did not translate into power or even influence in the arenas through which these same scientists moved to produce a particular mission (for example, the Infrared Space Observatory Project managed by an ESA engineer and in which the scientists' role was advisory not supervisory).

Even in the local, day-to-day work on ESA space-science missions, participants felt this structural tension in their positions acutely. Although these were "scientific" missions, scientists were not in control of the development process. In concrete terms, this lack of control manifested itself in the fact that the budgets for space-science mission development were controlled by senior engineers (project managers) rather than scientists. During the course of development, scientists and engineers repeatedly found themselves pitted against each other in the ongoing negotiation of fund allocation that characterized the development process. Funds were always scarce, and unanticipated delays or errors in design or manufacture could drain the budget rapidly. Scientists routinely complained that all project managers wanted to do when faced with rising costs was to "descope the payload," that is, to cut down on the number and size of the scientific experiments that could be carried on board the satellite. These instruments were critical to the interests of the scientists since it was the instruments, rather than the satellite itself, that would collect and transmit the data that the scientists depended on for their research. Scientists thus complained that the engineers' efforts to save payload costs would in the end result in the launch of a "pointed brick," a hunk of metal incapable of detecting or imaging anything, even though it could be "pointed" at distant stars or galaxies. There was, thus, a structural tension at the core of this mode of production, a tension that was in part responsible for the dynamism of the process of space-science mission development.

IMPROVISATION

Despite these significant structural constraints—of status, time, money, and personnel—"in the end of the day," as one of the scientists I knew was fond of saying to me, the scientists could nonetheless be proud of the first-rate missions that they produced. They produced them, however, not because of the structures that determined their positions in various networks and flows of capital, goods, and services, but rather almost in spite of them. They produced them by exploiting the multiple structures, with concomitant contradictions and tensions, that constituted their domain of practice.[14] Thus, just as my own ethnographic technique had turned out to depend on split-second decisions to leap onto other gyres or to ride out the trajectories I was on, so too did ESA mission participants' practices take shape as an endless series of ongoing improvisations, across dangerously flooded terrain, in which fields lay submerged beneath currents of uncertainty.

In certain respects, then, the participants' primary challenges were to establish some stability in the midst of this complexity so that they could get things done and move their projects forward. Participants resorted to various strategies for defining, even momentarily, some stability, as they tried to create spaces and moments where and when people could put their feet down. For instance, participants made every effort to construct discursive representations of stable social networks, in large part for the purpose of getting work done. Once constructed, they would step into them, or define themselves in relation to them, even if in the next moment these entities would evaporate. An example of this can be found in the way that the staff scientists in SSD, those who were the focus of my ethnographic inquiry, acknowledged their responsibility to "glue together a community." They talked about how "part of our work is to be out and about," meeting with scientists in other institutions and engineers in industry. This made sense to them "because the [scientific] community is all over the place, [so] you have to keep talking." By being "out and about," they demonstrated the ephemerality of ESTEC, despite its physical presence. It is not location with definable "insides" and "outsides" that determines a social field then, but rather "talk," at least in this case. In fact, as one participant said, "the only thing to do is to keep talking" if you want to get anything done. Thus, any community they attempted to forge could exist only in the moment, convened in talk to solve a particular problem, or to produce a specific result. "Community," said one SSD scientist, "is only the guys you know, sitting around a table, working together"; once "the guys" went off to their own offices, departments, institutes, or countries, whatever social group had appeared in that social space no longer existed.[15]

In their ongoing efforts to make sense, to make connections, and to make stability, participants manipulated and asserted their commitment to various ideas and ideals, only to undermine their own assertions in the next moment. Nothing ever seemed secure. Instead of the rational practices ideologically associated with bureaucracy, state, science, and technology, in which conscripts harmoniously follow rules and enact regulations in the instrumental interests of efficiency and orderliness, there was instead constant argument, negotiation, and the bending of rules as people struggled, with politics, with scarcity, with emotional unpredictabilities, to produce artifacts that worked. Their struggles were carried out in terms of organizations (ESA, the European Union), of communities (the international scientific community and various national communities), and of other artifacts (detectors, computers, cryostats), but these solid structures did not define their practices, could not contain them, could not dictate them. They provided the terms in which argument, negotiation, and rule-bending occurred; they provided the resources with which people could do their arguing, negotiating, and manipulating; they appeared as the outcomes of these same practices (Giddens 1984)—but they were not the practices themselves.

In practice, people took these materials of power and improvised with them. These improvisations appeared as contradictory orientations in the practices and discourses of participants. For example, at some moments, SSD scientists and their colleagues would argue that nationality did not matter in the intense concentration required to design and build scientific instruments that would permit their users to discover the secrets of nature. ("When we get together in a meeting . . . it's not a question of being British, French, or whatever; we're just a group of scientists doing a job," said one SSD scientist.) In this gyre, science and technology defined a powerful center, the source of a widening spiral that pushed aside nations, people, politics, and money.

At other moments, these same scientists would describe their endeavors in terms of national differences, ascribing successes, failures, and strategies to different national customs or to different state interests. ("Italians are good at a lot of things, but not at making decisions," said one ESA engineer, while another SSD scientist opined that "if you think of German efficiency, Dr. Schmidt is it" [Zabusky 1996].) In this gyre, nation-states and their attendant "mentalities" defined a powerful center, the source of a widening spiral that pushed science, technology, and nature into the margins. Sometimes, these same scientists would describe themselves as those who safeguard ESA's interests in the face of constant demands from naive scientists in the academic world, from the excesses and incompetencies of industrial firms, from the parochial concerns of separate European states (see Zabusky 1992). In this gyre, ESA defined a powerful center, the source of a widening spiral that pushed science and state to the edges. In still other moments, these same scientists would insist that industrial firms determined the missions selected and developed and that neither science, nor technology, nor national interests had much to do with it. In this gyre, capital defined a powerful center, the source of a widening spiral that pushed national pride, scientific interest, and bureaucratic mandates into the margins.

It is such protean discourses of identity and difference that are the improvisations through which participants cleared out spaces in which to do their work. At every moment, different gyres carried participants away from one center, making them more peripheral the further they followed its path. Every turn called up another improvisation, and, as multiple gyres spun out of control, participants found themselves traveling from one to another, maintaining balance only by moving with the flows.[16]

CYNICISM

It is no wonder, given the participants' sense of shifting and unstable centers, that participants also insisted that power was always somewhere else. Indeed, a critical part of life and work in the intersection of transnational flows is the overwhelming sense that the center—that place from which power emanates, dictating rules and actions—is always under someone else's control. Yet this sense that participants had of being out of control may seem paradoxical, or even hypocritical, given that the scientists and engineers who were the focus of my study worked for or at an organization that clearly appeared to be a source of power. In concrete, physical terms, this status was manifest at ESTEC in the chain-link security fence that surrounded the entire site, by the security policy that required visitors to leave their passports at the guardhouse, and by the multitude of BMWs, Mercedes, and Cadillacs found parked in its parking lots.

ESA is an undeniably wealthy organization—its budget in 1988, at the time of my fieldwork, was almost two billion dollars, amassed from the contributions made by its thirteen member states, and much of it was disbursed in turn to national industrial firms (Longdon 1989). It is also undeniably an organization run by and dedicated to the interests of the elite—a site for science research and high technology production, "inhabited" by scientists, engineers, and lawyers who oversee the work of less powerful personnel such as technicians and custodians, and oriented toward producing competitive technologies to help national industries compete in a global marketplace. It is also undeniably a dominant political player—its governing body is made up of high-level national politicians whose presence underscores ESA's role in the construction of a new European union. In all these ways, ESA seems to exist exclusively to further the interests of capital and state.

Nonetheless, the SSD scientists in particular often felt at odds with ESA, and they made great efforts to distinguish themselves from its powerful grip. They articulated their resistance to such interests often in terms of "science" (versus politics) and sometimes in terms of "community" (versus bureaucracy). Throughout, they struggled for legitimacy and control of a technical process in which they were integral and crucial participants yet, from their perspective, undervalued and marginalized.

The public rhetoric of ESA officials certainly made science seem significant in the overall scope of the agency's activities. A most eloquent statement of science's role in the agency was made by Reimar Lüst, director general of ESA during the time of my fieldwork, in a 1987 address:

> To me, European space is a living vibrant entity, and like all living things it has a heart. For European space, that heart is the Space Science Programme [the ESA directorate responsible for space-science missions]. It pumps out the blood of new ideas, fresh challenges, and technical innovation to the limbs of the application programmes. (5)

As a living entity, it needed "oxygen," which could only be provided by more data produced by more missions that demanded more funds. This was not, in the history of the agency, easy to obtain. ESA had been established in 1964 at the instigation of scientists who, in Lüst's words, "jogged the political elbow" (2) to get a regional European space organization started. Lüst remarked that "in the beginning there was some doubt that the enthusiasm of the scientists could be turned into a political reality" (2), but he went on to describe the many successes of the early incarnation of ESA (then the European Space Research Organisation). By 1974, however, member states had grown restless, tired of expensive missions that did not produce a clear benefit to them in terms of improved industry or increased capital. As a result, they lobbied for the creation of a new organization that would focus on "applications missions," in other words, missions with commercial application, and out of this "revolt" came ESA (Russo 1993). The tension between missions dedicated to "pure" scientific research and "applied" commercial ventures remains within ESA; member states and industrial concerns do not see science as the lifeblood of the agency but as a drain on the agency's potentially more lucrative undertakings, and they still prefer to put their frames, marks, and pounds toward "useful" and "practical" missions such as heavy launchers (rockets), meteorological satellites, and communications satellites. For many years, indeed, the budget of the Science Programme did not increase with inflation; even in 1987, despite Lüst's impassioned rhetoric, science missions accounted for only 10 percent of ESA's overall budget (Longdon 1989).

This state of affairs—the disjunction between official rhetoric and actual conditions—generated feelings of alienation among the scientists I knew. Some non-ESA scientists talked about ESA as a "black cloud" that hung over their heads as they endeavored to make an instrument for a space-science satellite. One SSD scientist grumbled about the way science was treated as "a jewel in the crown" for ESA, an ornament that the organization used to legitimate its choices and its expenditures as being "for the good of human kind," without matching such rhetorical emphasis with significant resources. In more cynical terms, another SSD scientist complained to me that ESA was "just a money laundering scheme for government and industry," such that it was the needs of national industries that drove decisions about scientific missions rather than the needs of scientists.

For the scientists, this sense of not being where the power was, yet at the same time being called on to legitimate the capital expenditures of ESA and European states, engendered cynicism in spades. Cynicism appeared in various guises. Often, it appeared as complaints, whether about daily work practices such as those concerning the "pointed brick," or about the disparity between rhetoric and circumstances; these complaints were tempered by a shrug of shoulders, a knowing glance, a remark made to the naive ethnographer that "of course" this is the way it has always been: "I'm forty, so I'm more cynical," an SSD scientist commented wryly during an interview. At other times, it appeared as a kind of disengagement, as an inability to believe in or even dream of possibilities, whether technical, political, or cultural. For instance, one ESA publication made much of the fact that:

> The Agency itself, with its staff and committees made up of representatives of the Member States, constitutes one of the melting pots for the material from which Europe is gradually being forged, and in which nationalist preoccupations have to give way to wider, more promising vision. All who contribute to the life of the Agency have a sense of belonging to a European unity. . . . (Longdon and Guyenne 1984:229)

Such romantic imagery was easily and often countered by SSD scientists, who talked about the internecine conflict between the various member states and their representatives in the agency. There were stories about French politicians putting pressure on French scientists to vote for the selection of French-led missions. There was laughter about the insistence of Germany on having German treated as a third official language (the two official languages of ESA are French and English); several scientists remarked to me that the presence of multiple languages was evidence of political maneuverings and not of technical cooperation, where one language would not only do, but one was in fact necessary for successful working together. These were not stories of "more promising visions" but the weary remarks of embattled participants whose ability to determine what really mattered was severely restricted.

Discourses of cynicism can be understood as cultural expressions of the contradictions inherent in transnational processes, contradictions that arise as centers are continually undermined and power seems always to impinge on people from somewhere else as they travel in directions not of their own making. The scientists I watched had created elaborate space missions that produced transnational flows when they were first dreamed up as mission scenarios. However, once these missions entered into the development process, once put in motion, the scientists no longer directed the flows themselves, any more than the falconer directs the falcon how to fly. Instead, they were caught up in powerful forces over which they had no control, and they struggled, improvised, and complained their way to some stable center.

Dreaming of Freedom in the Iron Cage

The shifting centers that accompany the transnational processes of big science and European integration produce not only improvisation and cynicism but dreams and domination as well. As participants slip from the grip of one source of power, they often—perhaps inadvertently—assume the mantle of power over yet another momentary collection of people, people who in turn evade this manifestation of power. The result is that everyone feels out of control, pushed and dominated by forces that they cannot see and over which they have no control. For this reason, scientists working on ESA space-science missions dreamed of freedom all the time. Their dreams of freedom often took the form of appeals to "science" to help them clear out a space where they could get something done. These appeals depicted a clean and pure science that needed to be unfettered and free if it were to lead all humanity to the truth. Scientists insisted on science's power to transcend the petty and confining details of national, political, economic, bureaucratic, and industrial interests. This idea of science at times insinuated itself as ideology, as a discourse of power that enabled participants to dominate others.[17] Yet, at the same time, this idea of science subverted the power of others and served instead as a discourse of resistance that enabled SSD scientists to withstand domination from others. In this way, the interests of capital and state—which science was supposed to serve—were carried along by the transnational processes of big science and European integration and were transformed from materials of power to cultural resources that participants used to resist those same interests. Thus, these improvisations provided participants with a measure of freedom.

Nonetheless, the participant's experience was not of freedom but of struggle and confinement. Although they appeared to be working in a privileged world, full of money, power, and limitless possibilities, SSD scientists talked endlessly of constraints, obstacles, and impediments to their dreams. For them, the forces of big science and European integration seemed, on the one hand, to make their work possible and, on the other, to lock them in prisons—silencing, inhibiting, and oppressive. Why, then, continue to work within them? Because the scientists at SSD, as professionals everywhere, were called to their vocation with "passionate devotion" (Weber 1946). Most of the scientists I knew in SSD desperately wanted to *be* scientists, to work in their calling, to discover truth, to work for the social good. To be a scientist was not a choice but a duty; indeed, as Weber remarked, "The Puritan wanted to work in a calling; we are forced to do so" (1958:181). The hegemony of modernity thus forces all of us who work in the modern age to want to work, even to *need* to work, if we are to have any identity, any authenticity, at all. The scientists were, thus, trapped by their own desires, an outcome Weber saw clearly when he wrote that the "cosmos of the modern economic order . . . determine[s] the lives of all the individuals who are born into [it], with irresistible force" (1958:181). The scientists in SSD struggled every day to find the key to unlock this "iron cage" of modernity in which they felt themselves trapped, dreaming, as do all of us who are so caught, for freedom—from constraints, from contamination, from need, from power.

REFLECTING

Doing ethnography in the space of the transnational brings one to a confrontation with power. How to read that power, however, or where to locate it comes down, in the end, to a matter of taste or perhaps political preferences—which, in Pierre Bourdieu's (1984) terms, amounts to the same thing. In this project I found myself unable to exercise the kind of critique of power that seemed called for by other scholarly study, in part because I could find no steady field in which to stand and from which to exercise such a critique.

Anthropologists today call for reflexivity and show how studies of the Other—the subaltern, marginal, non-Western—can and must provoke us to reflect on ourselves, our own aims, the consequences of our actions. In doing so, many of these writers seem to claim for themselves a moral status built on suffering, a suffering they have not themselves endured, but which those they study or work with have endured.[18] I cannot lay claim to such moral authority. The people among whom I pursued my studies are privileged and powerful compared to the typical subjects of ethnographic inquiry—just as I am. Indeed, although at times I felt uncomfortable conducting ethnographic research among such an elite stratum of an already privileged world, and I wanted to distance myself from the seductions of power and the complicity of privilege,[19] most of the time I felt a kind of familiarity. I felt, indeed, that I was looking at myself. My informants' dreams were my dreams; their desires, my desires; their cynicism, my cynicism. As I rode the gyres with these scientists, watching them make their satellites (which fly higher than any falcon ever dreamed of flying), I realized that I was trapped as well, trapped in an iron cage of my own making, but from which, nonetheless, there could be no escape.

Confronting this reality was profoundly disturbing. By doing ethnography among people like me—participants in and producers of the transnational flows of modernity—I was forced to the kind of reflexivity for which anthropologists of non-Western people have argued. In the process, I learned that hegemony works on all of us, poor and privileged alike, propelling us to think its thoughts, to work for its goals—its goals become our goals; this is its power. Yet my experience was not only of unremitting power and privilege, secure at the center overseeing and controlling all that went on. As did the scientists, I, too, longed to resist those forces that pushed me, willy-nilly, against or even along with my will. Hegemony, whether or not it is in our interests, engenders a desire to escape, to be free. The paradox is that even our dreams (of liberation, of equality, and of diversity) are formed in the images of this power. Hegemony works just so, by making us all desire what it claims. The iron cage closes in on us more tightly. And yet there are those gyres, those unending spirals, catching us up and whisking us away to another space. There are those improvisations, that playfulness, that cynicism which dissolves the bars of the prison, even if for just a moment. Acknowledging that the center has vanished affects ethnographic choices. No fields exist but rather something less sure, less stable. In the end, at work among scientists and engineers in Europe, I recognized that there were places and moments when moral demands and aspirations emerged from the interstices of transnational processes and privileges and connected us through what we hoped for rather than through what we resisted. These are the gyres I prefer to follow in the improvisational flight that is ethnography in/of transnationalism.

Notes

1. The data on which this paper is based were collected from 1988 to 1989 at the European Space Agency's main research and technology institute (ESTEC), located in Noordwijk, the Netherlands. See Zabusky 1995 for a full treatment of these data.
2. Since 1998, the European Union has been exploring the possibility of enlargement in negotiations with thirteen countries: ten countries of the former Eastern Block (Bulgaria, the Czech Republic, Estonia, Hungary, Latvia, Lithuania, Poland, Romania, the Slovak Republic, Slovenia), as well as Cyprus, Malta, and Turkey. The

negotiations, which involve representatives of each EU member state and each candidate state, are lengthy, complex, and sometimes controversial. Moreover, because each candidate country moves at its own pace to satisfy the criteria in thirty-one areas of discussion, progress toward "accession" is variable. As of fall 2001, none of the applicants had negotiated agreements in all of the areas required for complete membership in the EU.

3. At the twenty-fifth anniversary celebration for ESA, Carlo Rubbia, director general of CERN, the European Center for Nuclear Research, expressed this view, simultaneously evoking an image of nonpartisan scientists cooperating in the interests of "humanity" and the superiority of European scientists long at the forefront of such endeavors: "Science is nothing if it is not international. . . . [Its] truths become firmly rooted, irreversible, inalienable, and enter into the common stock of property, so to speak, owned by the whole of humanity. This self-evident fact has always spurred 'men of science' to cooperation across national frontiers. From the birth—in Europe, let us not forget—of modern science, from the days of Galileo, Descartes or Newton, the free exchange of ideas was always the natural way . . ." (European Space Agency 1989:14).

4. Anthropologists have been studying Western societies almost from the beginning, of course (e.g., Arensberg's 1937 classic study of Ireland), but such ethnographies were considered marginal in the discipline. Michael Herzfeld (1987) offers an insightful analysis of the reasons for this marginalization of ethnographic studies of European societies.

5. For instance, in Robin Horton's (1967) classic discussion of the open and closed systems of African magical thought versus western scientific thought, Horton derived his analysis of magic from close ethnographic study of African society. His argument regarding western science, however, was built entirely on philosophical speculation by scholars such as Karl Popper and not on commensurate ethnographic study of scientific "thought" or even work among western practitioners. Even after the revolution in science studies spawned by Thomas Kuhn's (1970) *The Structure of Scientific Revolutions* and, from a radically different perspective, by Paul Feyerabend's (1975) *Against Method*, it was primarily sociologists who undertook fieldwork-based ethnographic studies of scientific work. It was not until the mid-1980s that cultural anthropologists began to turn their gaze on science; the preeminent work signaling this shift in direction was Sharon Traweek's (1988) ethnography on high-energy particle physicists from a cultural perspective. For a discussion of anthropology's role in science studies, see Hess 1992. For two provocative ethnographic examinations of the culture of rationality, see Cohn 1987 and Herzfeld 1992.

6. In this way, our definitions and ideologies about Self and Other, about Rationality and Enchantment, have led anthropologists largely to leave the study of such powerful but apparently meaningless phenomena as states, international collaboration, organizations, and science to our colleagues in political science, economics, organizational behavior, engineering, and science policy. Ironically, I believe that in this

way, anthropologists have contributed to their own marginalization within universities and government institutions. Political scientists, economists, and organizational sociologists acquired greater power, or at least influence, through their studies
of powerful institutions and processes. I am not denying the importance of anthropology's mission to bring to the centers of power the voices of those who have been
oppressed, silenced, and marginalized in the machinations of global capitalism.
However, these voices seldom are heard by those ensconced in the centers of power
because of anthropology's own marginal position.

7. For example, one of the first books to address European integration from an
ethnographic perspective, *Cultural Change and the New Europe: Perspectives on the European
Community* (Wilson and Smith 1993), contained papers that took a primarily "local"
perspective on Europe, from the point of view of villages or communities. This
emphasis reflected the history and bias of Europeanist anthropology. Increasingly,
however, anthropologists have turned to issues in Europe which demand attention
beyond a narrowly-defined local level. Such studies examine the power of the state to
influence identities and not just incite resistance (for example, Borneman 1992;
Herzfeld 1992), the institutions and discourse of this "New Europe" (for example,
Abélès 1992; Bellier and Wilson 2000; Borneman and Fowler 1997; Holmes 2000;
McDonald 1996; Shore 2000), and experiences in transnational modernity (for example, Marcus 1993; Darian-Smith 1999).

8. An exception to this mode of inquiry can be found in the sociology of organizations, where ethnographic studies of scientific and technical work (as opposed to
knowledge) have been carried out. See, for instance, Van Maanen and Barley 1984
and Barley and Orr 1997. For an interesting critique of this type of micro-oriented
laboratory study from within the sociology of knowledge, see Fuchs 1992.

9. Interestingly, the concept of the semiautonomous social field identifies a new
metaphor for the "center." The usual anthropological conceit of "center" was as a
place of power. The center was rarely where anthropologists did their field studies
(although it was often where they were raised or trained); instead, anthropologists
traveled out to the "periphery" or to the social "margins" to do fieldwork. Thus, the
"center-as-power" metaphor was defined by designating different global spaces or
social groups in terms of a spatial and social topography in which power sat at the
center of some designated whole (country, class system, etc.). The center was a place
of control from which decisions, wealth, and ideas snaked out in long sinewy arms,
seizing hold of the smaller, poorer, devalued peripheries, possessing them, and
squeezing out of them their own wealth, ideas, or autonomy. The idea of the semi-
autonomous social field, by contrast, changes the topographical map. Here, the
"center" is inside, encompassed by a "larger world" which directs it (even if only
imperfectly). Thus, the center in this metaphor of power is more impinged on than
impinging, and power has been transferred (conceptually) to largely unseen external
"forces" that act in much the same way as do the sinewy arms of power emanating

from that other kind of center discussed above. In both cases, power is never where the ethnographer has settled down to study. In this essay I use the idea of the "center" (in gyres, or elsewhere) to refer to the first topography noted here, of a powerful center controlling and dominating geographic, social, or cultural peripheries. I use the idea of "interior" to refer to the surveying procedure used to identify social fields.

10. My effort to narrow in on a clearly delineated site was motivated not only by a particular conception of fieldwork (namely, "the field") but was necessitated, too, by my structural position in the academic research system of which I was a part. When I conducted my study of ESA, I was a graduate student without the credentials or status to command either the economic or human resources to pursue every research avenue. For instance, the grant that funded my fieldwork provided me a monthly stipend half that of even the lowest paid research fellow at ESTEC. Thus, I lacked the funding to travel as frequently as did the ESA scientists on their constant trips to meetings at universities or at industrial firms, even though I knew that these sites and meetings were as significant to the production of space-science missions as was SSD. I also had no colleagues or staff or students to work with. In a team approach we would be able to cover a wider terrain, visit different sites, and become connected to different social networks than could I alone. As a solo student researcher, I was thus unable to pursue the tantalizing richness of the complexity that I was observing around me. A useful contrast to the limitations I faced when trying to conduct fieldwork amid the gyres of modern complexity is supplied by recent work done by Emily Martin (1994) in her research on the complex and intersecting structures that surround AIDS research and public health in the United States. As Martin became aware of the multiple forces at work in her research area, she had at her disposal, as a tenured professor at a prestigious U.S. university, a cadre of graduate students whom she could dispatch to pursue fieldwork in different locations (both physical and social). Her ability to marshal these human resources was made possible by her command of financial resources (in the form, minimally, of a "generous" grant from a philanthropic foundation [Martin 1994:xx]), which derived in part from her already accumulated professional capital. Thus, while many ethnographers perceive the importance of studying the multiply connected systems that characterize modernity, and while all may insist that we not restrict our fieldwork purview too narrowly, the fact remains that the outcomes (e.g., the comprehensiveness of our research, and the concomitant depth of the findings we arrive at in our finished writings) are directly affected by our place in established structures and our position in these structures.

11. Ulf Hannerz and Orvar Löfgren (1994) make a similar observation when they write that "people, simply by going about their daily lives, and observing and commenting on one another, set in motion a massive, although largely undeliberate and decentered, flow of meaning, through a variety of institutions and contexts" (200).

12. ESTEC provides testing facilities for all the missions undertaken by ESA, not just the space science ones, and also offers other agencies the use of its testing facilities for non-ESA missions. Hence, many of the technological artifacts that I saw in clean rooms and testing bays were not part of the Science Programme's missions.

13. Anthropologist Emily Martin (1994), writing about her experience "tracking immunity in American culture" in the 1980s, similarly notes that "I was never simply inside or simply outside any one group" (xv). Everyone—scientists, AIDS activists, government policy makers, working-class residents of Baltimore neighborhoods, as well as university researchers—was equally affected by a common "set of organizing ideas with similar potential implications" (16).

14. Rather than feeling trapped in established positions and places, participants' experiences were often the opposite: too many positions and places and policies pushed and pulled them in contrary ways. Indeed, the lack of a single, overarching, definitive structure often gave every participant in ESA space-science missions a feeling of what Martin (1994), in another context, calls "empowered powerlessness" (122) as "individuals lose a sense of agency in the face of the systemic forces that appear to be overwhelmingly and inexorably playing themselves out" (125). Improvisation thus appears as a core technique of agency.

15. Certainly, repeated interactions led to enduring friendships and extended collaborations over time; the point is, again, that such enduring structures did not *define* practices, in part because these were not the only structures impinging on and affecting peoples' practices. People were enmeshed in multiple structures, leading to the experience of instability and constant flux that generated improvisation as a key mode of practice.

16. This constant shifting of centers—an interchange of position in which participants oscillate between being marginal and central to the process as a whole—is reminiscent of the "border crossings" among the Ewe practitioners of vodu in Togo, which are described by Rosenthal in this volume. The Ewe resist the imposition of centers and of power through mystical practices, assuming in trance the identities of others with whom they exist in complex relations of historical power and subordination. For the scientists and engineers in Europe, such resistance takes place not through trance but through the everyday practice of rationality, whose unsettling consequences contradict the ideology that provides the resources for such practice. This constant movement also evokes the new cultural trope of "flexibility" which permeates public life in the United States, whether in corporations, universities, hospitals, or in the rhetoric of government and Madison Avenue (see Martin 1994).

17. This has been, indeed, the analysis offered of the Mertonian norms of science (as first set out in Merton 1973) by other sociologists of science (e.g., Mulkay 1975, Restivo 1988). For another cultural analysis of this rhetoric of purity, see Zabusky 1995:196–219 and Zabusky 2000.

18. The valorization of suffering also characterizes Russian discourse, according to Ries (this volume and 1997). In the Russian version, it is "mystical poverty" that gives Russians their soul and makes them better—in an ethical and moral sense—than other wealthier individuals or states. In the academic version, scholars who are not themselves the products of poverty or oppression but of privilege, acquire a certain moral superiority from their apparently selfless act of serving the subaltern and oppressed by giving space and sound to their voices. See Sangren (1988) for an interesting discussion of the effects of postmodern calls for reflexivity and "polyphony" in ethnographic texts.

19. This sense of unease stems partly from contemporary circumstances in academia, where, as Maryon McDonald (1993:222) has argued, the cultural categories of "Europe" and "the West" "have become important metaphors of blame or of self-castigation." More so, however, this unease results from the dilemma facing all anthropologists who attempt to study societal elites, whether western or non-western, with ethnography. In an analysis of the "normative dimension" of elite research, George Marcus (1983) discusses the problems of fieldwork facing the researcher who embarks on such a project:

> Normally anthropologists are empathetic with their subjects and become increasingly so the longer they are involved with them. However, as members of Western liberal society, ethnographers of elites may have difficulty in developing such a natural working empathy. . . . Working empathy for one's subjects can be misconstrued as ideological sympathy; ideological distancing from one's subjects, to the point of disapproval, is a difficult condition of work in an ethnographic style of research . . . ; and ambivalence or silence in judgment on subjects makes the ethnographer's research equally vulnerable to a charge of elitism, or conversely to its use in a polemical condemnation of elites. (23)

This construction of the problem facing fieldworkers among society's privileged members suggests two things: first, that the fieldworkers are not themselves members of the elite, a questionable assumption; and two, that the central ethical dilemma for ethnographers is simultaneously a methodological one. Without "rapport," one might ask, can there be effective fieldwork? I would argue that in fieldwork, there must be rapport (or "working empathy," as Marcus calls it), however awkwardly constructed, however imperfectly achieved; this remains, in my view, a critical tool for the anthropologist interested in the "emic" perspective. The problem of rapport is more difficult, it seems to me, among those whose views anthropologists consider explicitly reprehensible (e.g., among bigots of all kinds) rather than among those who may have power and/or privilege (and whose own reproduction of, for instance, institutional racism, is systemic rather than overt). Such views, especially when espoused by members of those societies in which we ourselves live, do not seem to warrant the culturally relativist stand anthropologists normally take, and thus make any possibility of rapport unthinkable. Douglas Holmes (1993 and 2000) has confronted this problem directly in his studies of neo-Nazi, right-wing, and nationalist groups in Europe.

Phillip C. Parnell

The Composite State: The Poor and the Nation in Manila

It is August 1987 in Manila. I have just arrived from the United States
and am buying newspapers in Makati, the wealthiest of the city's business districts. Manila's free presses analyze a recent armed coup attempt against President Corazon Aquino and warn that there could be
attacks on the city by the New People's Army, the military wing of the
Philippine Communist Party. Contradicting the brawling state of morning editions, Makati's towering office buildings and luxury hotels suggest a well-anchored national order, one newly freed from dictatorship
by a snap election and the People Power Revolution of 1986. More
contrasts appear when I visit an urban squatter settlement. It feels like
the rural mountain villages in Mexico where I lived and studied for two
years. In the midst of poverty's brutality, I sense one of its paradoxes.
For the first time, I feel the presence of community rather than the
contests of an embattled state.

Within a few days I have been invited by an urban poor organization
to move into a single-room shanty within a family compound in one
of metropolitan Manila's largest squatter settlements. The region is
known as Payatas Estate. This is my first foray into mapless urban
ethnography. I don't know how and whether disputes over the state's
future take form or find succor here. Therefore, with little to lose, I
place my time in the hands of my neighbors, and their lives become my
agenda. Some have been spinners of discourse on the Western mind;
they know me better than I know them. As we look up from the settlement together, they teach me lessons of disorder.

■

*Perhaps it is instinctive for me to look up for the state, as do most social scientists in
post-Spanish colonial societies who follow the gold-plated threads of clientelism to
the states as a source of economic patronage or to the ideological goals of grassroots
hegemonic movements. But an ethnographic ghost excites my intuition: While
conducting long-term ethnographic research in rural Mexico, I experience undissolv-
able secular fear and uncertainty upon realizing there is no higher authority to
which I can appeal, not even within anthropology: it is just me, the villagers, and
a very tough walk through the mountains to the end of an undependable dirt road*

(see Parnell 1988). Now, in the Payatas settlement with my immortal emotion, I have a troubling realization: Several different sources of patronage claim or distribute the same land in Payatas Estate for different, sometimes the same, clients. The apparent absence of a higher authority that could resolve contradictions and establish a rational notion of private and public property bothers me much more than it appears to bother residents of the land.

Throughout much of my research in Payatas, I conduct two ethnographies, a conscious ethnography of what is apparently present, and a less determined ethnography of what is absent as I rummage haphazardly through my own cultural reasoning. I am trying to understand how the abundance of organization in Payatas, from homeowners' associations to multileveled networks of corporate land syndicates, gives me a sense of profound disorder and uncertainty. I discover that my rationalities and logics of bureaucratic universalism and imagined forms of liberal constitutional democracy are ersatz knowledge that transforms the land on which I live in Payatas Estate into a mirror for the sky.

■

The columnist Richard Grayson observes that the significance of the state of New Jersey has been magnified by journalists' frequent use of the state to describe other geographic locations, citing, among others, this example from the *Los Angeles Times:* "Galileo's cameras also caught Jupiter's sulfurous moon Io in the act of spewing out a 60-mile-high bluish plume, probably glowing sulfur dioxide gas. The outburst rises from an area called Ra Patera—the size of New Jersey—that has been completely resurfaced by volcanic eruptions since the Voyager fly-by 17 years ago" (1997:21). For those who cannot approximate the actual size of New Jersey, or who know it as one-fourth to one-half inch long, depending on the size of the map, the comparison allows a self-referential relativity indicating what Ra Patera is not; it is neither the size of a house nor the size of the United States.

The blueprint of the Western state drawn by Max Weber (1946) may be the ethnographer's New Jersey. The Western-type state as a form of calibration frequently stands proxy for what we don't know about the contexts of national life, a conceptual "Are-the-blanks-filled-in?" context for the present and future that takes the place of an unknowable indigenous past and the unknown of an indigenous present. Winichakul Thongchai, studying the discourse of nationhood in Thailand, observes: "One of the major questions yet haunting the historians of early Southeast Asia concerns the formation of states. To be more specific, how one can talk about a state's formation without taking for granted what a state is—the criteria usually prescribed by social scientists, not by the early Southeast Asian peoples themselves. Thus historians sometimes doubt that the state qualifies as a state at all" (1994:14).

Conflicts that grow out of the disorganization of multiple ownership of the land in Payatas Estate will reveal a composite rather than a Western state, one that unfolds in disputes spreading across the sprawling settlements of Payatas and up into institutions of the official Philippine state. Disputes activate alliances that range across a broad spectrum of societal institutions and unite various components of the Philippine state in debate over national issues and through the rhetorics of kinship, community, and morality rather than that of centralized political authority. Payatas Estate is thus not a distorted reflection of the Western state, but the vessel of a people seeking their nation.

Don Mariano San Pedro's Bewildering Legacy

I have traveled with members of one of Payatas Estate's largest urban poor organizations across Manila in the back of a large pickup truck to attend a dance held by allies in another settlement. As we arrive and take our seats around a basketball court, the tone is unusually quiet and formal, almost stiff and cautious. I wonder if there is danger, but then music of the tango bounces across the court, and couples in this celebratory colonial collage assume a dignified posture, then a dip and twist. As I follow disputes over Payatas land, I search for their colonial scripts in provincial and state courts.

■

Cultivation of Payatas Estate as a national resource began in 1894, when the Spanish government in the Philippines granted to Don Mariano San Pedro y Esteban property title number 4136, which his heirs claim covers all of the land of metropolitan Manila and vast regions within neighboring provinces. The estate is today popularly known through two of its larger portions called Commonwealth and Payatas, both located in the national capital of Quezon City, which is part of the seldom interrupted concrete flow of metropolitan Manila. Carved out of these two regions is the National Government Center (NGC), home of the Philippine Congress (Batasan Pambasa) and several official state bureaucracies.

In October 1970, the Court of First Instance of the Province of Bulacan concluded that 4136 was a bona fide title. Such titles were recognized in the Treaty of Paris of 10 December 1898, in which the sovereignty of Spain over the Philippines was transferred to the United States. Although the Philippine government had contested the title's authenticity, by 1996 courts had not decided what amount of land was covered by 4136, who were the rightful heirs of Don Mariano San Pedro y Esteban, and whether the title was part of his estate. Nevertheless, throughout the twentieth century, numerous administrators were appointed to account for and dispose of the estate's land, and numerous legal titles for regions of the estate were issued. One legal title (Torrens title) to land allegedly covered by 4136, known as OCT 333, mothered many of the titles the Philippine government purchased to form the National Government Center.

Following World War II and the Philippines' administrative independence from the United States in 1946, Republic of the Philippines President Ramon Magsaysay, in a memorandum addressed to "All Concerned" and dated 23 December 1953, named Prudencio Falcis as the estate's administrator:

> Effective immediately you are hereby designated and appointed as *Administrator-Plenipotentiary-Extraordinary,* over a property subject for Expropriation now in the Lower and Upper House. This property is known as the *Estate of Don Mariano San Pedro y Esteban,* covered by Titulo de Propiedad No. 4136 dated 25 April 1894. You are further instructed to investigate and look into the legal heirs of said property of which portion is now being sponsored for expropriation by our government. Furtherly advise to report from time to time any results of your activities to me or to my Technical Assistants concerning thereof confidentially.

Seven years later, in August 1960, President Ferdinand Marcos sent the following memo to Falcis:

> I hereby concur with the herewith attached MEMO of late President Ramon Magsaysay, dated December 23, 1954, [sic] to pursue his undying endeavors in defending the landless, the poor and the oppressed through your capacity as an ADMINISTRATOR-OVER-SEER and close relative of late Don Mariano San Pedro y Esteban. Re: TITULO DE PROPIEDAD NO. 4136, dated April 25, 1894, hence this instruction to carry this mission.

In 1946, following World War II, Philippine veterans began moving onto land in Commonwealth and Payatas, where some had once been stationed. Other veterans arrived in Payatas in the 1950s when the armed anti-landlord Hukbalahap (Hukbong Magpapaylaya ng Bayan: People's Army of the Philippines) insurrection was moving through the region. The government offered Payatas land to retired soldiers so they would live there and resist the Huks; however, the soldiers never received titles to the land.

Legal Fission

I am at Veterans headquarters in Payatas attending a birthday party for Don Ignacio San Pedro, self-proclaimed heir of Don Mariano San Pedro y Esteban and leader of one of metropolitan Manila's largest land syndicates. I feel out of place, for most of the guests have arrived in military jeeps wearing uniforms and carrying rifles. A chief of police is there along with several Quezon City lawyers. Walls of this office of Don Ignacio are plastered with copies of court memoranda, all bearing his name. Don Ignacio says they are proof of his ownership of Payatas, but I know that no court has found him heir to Titulo 4136. On the basis of these court documents, clients purchase from Don Ignacio large tracts of Manila's land. I think the documents could say anything; Don Ignacio would be able to turn them into land titles. What is the source of his contractual magic?

■

In December 1971, Don Ignacio San Pedro, who claimed he fought as a guerrilla for the government against the Huks, made the Philippine judicial system an ever-present player in disputes over land in Payatas Estate by petitioning the Court of First Instance of Bulacan. Don Ignacio argued that Don Mariano San Pedro died intestate during the Philippine-American War and that his estate needed to be administered and adjudicated to Don Ignacio and other heirs whose names followed on the petition. In February 1972 the court appointed Don Ignacio San Pedro administrator of the estate (without mentioning Falcis) and in March authorized him to relocate and survey all of the estate's real property.

Several other would-be-heir-administrators would also petition the court, and some, over the years, replaced Don Ignacio on a growing list of court-appointed administrators of the San Pedro Estate. Many, along with Falcis, sold portions of the estate and settled other portions with the urban poor who turned the region into an ever-expanding squatter settlement. Among the poor were police and military, some of them members of unofficial groups already formed within federal military organizations. Some settlers believed they were acquiring title to the land from its rightful heirs, others merely paid rent to the heir-claimants who promised legal protection against demolition of their houses by the city, federal government, or private developers. Several of the heir-claimants, including Don Ignacio, would become known as leaders of large urban land syndicates, all developing networks of appropriately registered corporations linked to lawyers, governmental officials, educators, police, and military groups.

As these syndicate leaders formed urban poor settlers into homeowners' associations and linked the associations to corporations, they also created alliances with other groups present in Payatas, including those formed from World War II veterans and their descendants. Another type of syndicate, operating out of the federal Bureau of Lands, sold private titles to the same occupied land in Payatas. At the same time, captains of units of local governance known as *barangays* settled new arrivals from among the urban poor on the land and charged the settlers rent. With both false titles and legal titles that may have been derived from false titles, private real estate corporations and syndicates developed middle-class subdivisions that rose like castles near the squatters' shanties. In a 1981 speech President Marcos called on his audience of future administrators to "fight against well-entrenched oligarchs who with the connivance of crooked government officials managed to acquire Torrens titles to vast tracts of land" (Bureau of Forestry Development 1981). The words had little effect, for during the Marcos regime "oligarchs" flourished and multiplied while gaining control of large portions of Commonwealth, Payatas, and the National Government Center.

The Bureau of Forestry Development (BFD) challenged all who claimed title within Payatas and Commonwealth by arguing the land was unclassified public forest and therefore could not be legally titled through the Bureau of Lands. In 1983, the BFD issued Residential Use Permits to applicants in Payatas and other regions who qualified on the basis of land occupancy and improvements made to the land prior to 31 December 1981. Although the Minister of Natural Resources discontinued permit issuance in 1984, their holders had turned them into land sales and a city-wide organization called CONSEP (Confederation of the Settlers of the Philippines) that would seek their revalidation as the answer to metropolitan Manila's urban poor housing problems.

Commonwealth, Payatas, and the National Government Center (NGC) became a bustling region of households, commerce, and politics stretching from well-developed, middle-class suburbs at the one end, across densely populated urban poor shanty and concrete block home residential areas in the NGC, the multistory Philippine Congress, open spaces and clustered settlements of squatters and veterans and some well-to-do syndicate clients in Payatas, to the Marikina River and two of metropolitan Manila's largest fume-spewing garbage dumps. It seemed to matter little that the entire area was supposed to fall under the control of local barangay governance and Quezon City, with the possible exception of the National Government Center, also divided into barangays.

Although squatter residents may have been beholden to barangay captains for rent and some benefits in exchange for political support and cooperation, each association of residents looked up to a local leader outside of local government, and that leader linked them to someone more powerful, a syndicate lieutenant or head, a governmental bureaucrat, a city official, a court employee or judge, or a city-wide association or coalition. Those linkages were imbued with allies and opponents, policies and philosophies, locations on social and cultural maps that sprang from a shanty or concrete-block house in a neighborhood of Payatas Estate. Each land-acquiring group offered a path of opportunities along which innovation trumped fuzzy legality.

God and Law

Now, in 1987, as I explore squatter organizations from my very small and windowless tin-roofed shanty (an oven) in a family compound in Commonwealth, it is not yet clear to me how and whether the myriad possible passages out of poverty cross; equally unclear are highly contested urban and national governmental contexts of Payatas Estate, contexts I cannot take for granted or typify. Newspaper headlines speak of new coup attempts and plotters and of the shootings of U.S. servicemen on the streets of Manila. Unidentified dead bodies in plastic bags are discarded into the settlement as if the place is marked by its smoke spewing dumps rather than its Congress now freed from the handshake of authoritarian rule.

■

Syndicate organization appears to offer a philosophical template for many other groups. One of the more powerful syndicate leaders who resides in Payatas, Don Emiliano Pasero, claims 250 organizations and corporations within his larger umbrella corporation known as McManagement, which employs twenty-seven lawyers. Pasero also claims five million beneficiaries throughout the Philippines who can rally at the nearby Batasan Pambasa on his behalf. The influential sixty-nine-year-old leader speaks of his role in the Philippines:

> We don't have Philippine law now, we still have American law. So there is no law. The law of twenty years of Marcos is cosmetic. We can consider it cosmetic because Aquino has removed it. We can't now determine if the law of Aquino is cosmetic because we don't know if it will be adopted by the people. Part of Marcos's law was that of the dictator, but many unauthorized persons signed on his behalf and set up the dictatorship. . . . The presidential staff made the laws. The cart pulled the *carabao.*
>
> I tried to handle some of the problems of land reform, but the law is crooked, so how can I help when those helping are not recognized because of the cronies, some of whom hired guns to cause trouble. . . . That's why my work of allotting land, in any Philippine province where I can allot land, is being disturbed. I can allot the land alone, I can do it by myself. I have my 250 corporations, and if I think the people of the corporation are good I will give them a big area for them to distribute to the poor at minimal cost or fee.
>
> If the government always disposes the land without our consent, when another president enters all of the laws will be erased again and the land will come back to me. I am now amenable. . . . I would give the government 27 per cent of what I own, but I don't. They distribute my property. They are stupid. They don't understand us. Congressmen borrow money from the United States for themselves, not for the people, so they can make the poor their slaves. . . .
>
> All things found in this world belong to God. I'm just temporary, or administrator. So we help people to make villages where they can make their children live comfortable lives. If I create villages, I create churches. . . . All members and beneficiaries of our association should also give 10 percent to the church. . . . The voice of the people is the voice of God, *vox populi—vox Dei.* The welfare of the people is the supreme law.

God and Bureaucracy

It is 3:00 A.M. in the NGC, and I am summoned from my shanty by women leaders of Sama-Sama, the settlement's largest and most powerful squatter organization. Sleepy, unbathed, unshaven, and dressed in the forever-dirty clothes of the rainy season, I join them in a jeepney that travels across Manila to one of the city's richer neighborhoods. We are inside the house of the head of the federal Housing and Urban Development Coordinating Council singing "Happy Birthday" to his wife who, in her bathrobe, looks embarrassed. I find out that she and the women of Sama-Sama's Ten-Man Committee are members of a Catholic organization called Kriska. But why am I here? They know I can't sing.

■

Those who worked in the name of God stirred settlement organization in various ways. In the late 1970s and early 1980s, seeds that would grow into one of the most powerful people's organizations in the Philippines were sown in Commonwealth by the Catholic church through small prayer groups known as Kriska (*Kristiyanong Kapitbahay*), or Christian Neighbors. The prayer groups would quickly change form as their members came together to form a larger association known as Sama-Sama (*Samahang Maralita para sa Makatao at Makatarungang Paninirahan*). As Sama-Sama grew, the ties of its members to other groups would weaken or break.

Sama-Sama's first powerful squatter leader, Mrs. Vargas, spoke of the organization's genesis:

> At the beginning we were a church group. We had prayer meetings at home. We had Kriska. . . . Share and Care Apostolates for Poor Settlers also started here. They gave seminars, talking about forming community groups. . . . But it is too boring. It's very boring for me. It goes like that every week. There's no action. That's why I suggested we form an organization to help the people with their land problem. There were prayers and prayers but no action. It helps people in getting together, but the real objective is lost. So by October 1981 we had a symposium. It was about the condition of the land, that we needed to unite, that we needed an organization to fight for on-site development.

In 1982, Community of the Philippine Enterprise (COPE), a group of community organizers linked to the Catholic church, began work in

Commonwealth through championing the spread of Sama-Sama; they were soon followed by Father Gintaba, a new priest at the major Catholic church in Commonwealth and an influential Catholic educator and leader in Manila. Some called Father Gintaba "the priest of the urban poor." With the help of COPE and father Gintaba, Sama-Sama, led by women squatters, spread its chapters throughout the NGC, recruiting members from other organizations, including those linked to syndicates. They rallied the urban poor at Quezon City Hall and the National Housing Authority (NHA), and drew over 2,500 people to demonstrate at the Batasan Pambasa on behalf of a bill proposing "As Is Where Is" for the NGC's squatters. But events would overtake Mrs. Vargas's leadership and create a lasting rift within Sama-Sama. Mrs. Vargas was linked to the National Housing Authority that, in turn, was popularly linked to Ferdinand and Imelda Marcos, squatter demolitions, and impotence in developing housing for the poor.

"The People Were All Angry"

It is February 1986 in Bloomington, Indiana, where I am watching a courageous people's dramatic cry for freedom as it spreads throughout the world. Filipinos have moved from their homes onto Manila's Epifanio de los Santos Avenue to face down the tanks of their dictator, Ferdinand Marcos. Marcos blinks, and Philippine democracy is reborn. I wonder if the effervescence of social participation spawned in the People Power Revolution will affect the Philippines' many intergroup disputes. This question transports me to Payatas.

■

Two events of 1983 opened doors to Sama-Sama's future as what some would later designate the most successful people's organization in the Philippines and Southeast Asia. Benigno Aquino, a popular Marcos opponent, was assassinated at Manila International Airport, launching a growing public outcry against Marcos's dictatorship and kleptocracy. In April 1983, women of Sama-Sama placed their bodies in the paths of Quezon City bulldozers attempting to demolish homes in an area of Commonwealth. Some of the women were shot, but they decided, even though most had children, to return to the barricades and risk their lives for rights to the land.

With these events the opposition of COPE and Father Gintaba to Mrs. Vargas strengthened. Vargas then concentrated her organizing within two separate organizations, one a housing cooperative and the other a coalition of groups within Commonwealth. In a 1995 election that she would contest for years to come, Vargas was replaced as president of Sama-Sama by Aling Chit Herrera. Vargas was painted as a secret betrayer, along with the NHA, of on-site development with maximum retention of land and housing and minimum relocation of squatters living in the NGC.

Facing growing opposition across the Philippines, President Marcos called a snap election for February 1986. Sama-Sama campaigned for his opponent Corazon Aquino who, in January, visited Commonwealth and promised that her victory would lead to squatter acquisition of NGC land. Aling Tess Mendoza, a Sama-Sama chapter leader who supported herself by selling gasoline in bottles to passenger scooter drivers, described Sama-Sama's involvement in the snap election:

> We had several meetings in the area and we asked the people if they were willing to support Aquino versus Marcos. . . . We met with the people in respective chapters, and they tried to change the administration of President Marcos and were willing to campaign among neighbors. . . . Our tactics were house-to-house campaigning for President Aquino. Then the people volunteered to watch the ballots with NAMFREL [National Citizens' Movement for Free Elections].
>
> During the election, when they were counting, we used to stay overnight. The head of COMELEC [Commission on Elections] told us the box would go to city hall, and all of the members assigned to the balloting accompanied the ballots to city hall. And they stayed with the ballot box until it arrived at the right place. The trick of some of the followers of Marcos was to switch ballot boxes. We stayed a week at city hall. . . . After city hall we went to the Batasan Pambasa.
>
> Annette saw a ballot box with blood on it. We stayed at the Batasan Pambasa one week. On that spot we united—Atom, Bandila, Bisig [NGO coalitions], priests and nuns, the rich and poor. We united as one because we wanted to change the administration. The rich people supplied the food and the poor watched the ballots. . . . When we were there we prayed. It was very solemn.
>
> The people were all angry when they knew Marcos was winning and when the speaker of the house announced Marcos had won. Then the chapter leaders of Sama-Sama had a meeting because President Marcos was winning. The result of our meeting was to have a

barricade at the entrance to the Batasang Pambasa and have a Mass officiated by Father Gintaba. Aquino announced we would have civil disobedience. It was on Monday, February 19. We also blocked the road to Fairview. That was our plan before Aquino declared civil disobedience. When we were going to do those things [General] Enrile already had things going at EDSA [Epifanio de los Santos Avenue, main site of the People Power Revolution]. Then we met again, and we agreed to go to EDSA and Radio Veritas and other places to help Enrile and [General] Ramos. We stayed day and night at EDSA for four days.

And then Marcos left the Philippines. Corazon Aquino became president and moved into Malacañang Palace, the presidential home and offices.

Constructing a Processual Infrastructure

A few days before Christmas 1987, my shanty in the family compound is broken into, and my clothes, sheets, and pillows are stolen. The compound has several chained dogs, their tracheas crushed, that squeal at all intruders; perhaps the thief is familiar. My intuition tells me not to report the theft to local authorities; that could lead to retaliation. Sama-Sama, using its contacts, quickly locates the culprit and massages kinship ties to gain me his acceptance. I join long Christmas lines at shopping malls to replace the stolen items, and my neighbors express delight as a more colorful wardrobe takes the place of my lost wash-and-wear grays.

■

Through Aquino's new administrative appointments, the alliance of Sama-Sama, COPE, and Father Gintaba reached into the new national Housing and Urban Development Coordinating Council (HUDCC), Aquino's cabinet, and Malacañang. Sama-Sama acted on two fronts. Through its all-female Ten-Man Committee, it negotiated with governmental agencies for NGC land and a housing project that would be planned and implemented through a partnership between the residents of the NGC and the national government. Within the NGC, Sama-Sama chapter leaders recruited new members, sought input and support for Sama-Sama's negotiations with governmental agencies, developed physical infrastructure, and championed new day-care centers and schools. They employed PROS (Planning Resources and Operations

Systems), an international development firm of architects and planners located in Manila, where they met with governmental officials to construct strategies for acquiring NGC land from the federal government.

A member of the Ten-Man Committee describes Sama-Sama strategies:

> We have a preparation before negotiations. We have for example one member who will be [a representative of the government] . . . and we will tell our demands to him and we practice what will be our answer, and if we know we are right we don't have to give in. We have to recess and assess if their proposals are not good for the urban poor. We have briefings where we practice, role play. . . . One member plays the government. For example, one said this land is for the government, and you have no rights to the land. We said the government must share the land and segregate some land for the urban poor. We are not grabbing land, we just ask for some land, for the government to budget some for poor people. . . . We take government proposals to the people and ask them what they think. The people are the ones to say, and we take it to the government. Another standard operating procedure is never commit the organization. We have to take it to the people. . . .
>
> In negotiating, if a person is someone we don't know we try to find a friend of theirs and ask them for a favor. We call that *palaka-san*—to ask a favor of someone through a mutual friend. For a fellow at DPWH [Department of Public Works and Highways], [we talked with] a friend of PROS in DPWH who talked with him. So before the election and at rallies for Aquino we made friends and now they have positions.

Within chapters, Sama-Sama leaders and supporters play the roles of both local government and extended family, as one member explained:

> People come to me with problems, family problems; they ask me to help. When a deep well is not functioning we collect a little from members to pay to fix it. I know about places they can go with problems; I know institutions and agencies. Husbands and wives who are quarreling come to me, and I advise them to try to understand each other and advise them to reconcile. . . . Sometimes children are beaten by policemen. The most common problem is . . . with the dead, every time a member of the family dies. They go to the

[Sama-Sama] chapter head, and she signs a paper endorsing she is a member and she collects money for her for a funeral. . . . If somebody is sick and can't afford to pay a private hospital, I accompany them to hospitals where there are free services or medicine. They have no money so we go to a radio station and the announcer announces over the radio this person from Commonwealth is sick. [there is] no money, so they send in pledges. . . . Sama-Sama does brokerage for sick or pregnant women.

Ironic Growth and Parity

Some of my Manila acquaintances outside the settlement, including academics and civic leaders, tell me that Sama-Sama will never succeed. Ironically, Sama-Sama, as it seeks partnership with the government in creating a housing project, also argues that the government has never been able to complete a housing project for the poor. Each day I am troubled by a question that only time can answer: Should the project fail, against what scale can one measure the costs and benefits of social participation?

■

Sama-Sama's services, recruitment efforts, and vertical organization appeared to be working. On 11 August 1987, President Aquino, through Proclamation Number 137, sets aside 150 hectares (370 acres) of the 440 hectare (1,087 acres) National Government Center for a housing development and acquisition by NGC residents. On 27 January 1988, through Memorandum Order Number 151, Aquino creates the National Government Center Housing Committee, recognizes Sama-Sama as representative of the residents of the NGC, and proclaims, "The organization of beneficiaries, SAMA-SAMA, shall be given equal voting rights as all the government agencies in policy decisions affecting the project. In case no consensus is reached, the Chairman of the Committee shall have the authority to make the final decision." Governmental agencies on the committee combined have one vote, and Sama-Sama has one vote.

Sama-Sama estimates the total population of the NGC at 150,000 people, who now have to be squeezed from 440 hectares into 150 hectares. To deal with possible overflow problems, Sama-Sama, COPE, and HUDCC expand their organizational efforts into Payatas, where they attempt to replicate the NGC project through bringing existing groups of residents into a coalition. Plans for Payatas soon mushroom into a relocation site for all of metropolitan Manila's estimated two million squatters.[1] HUDCC is also fostering projects patterned after Sama-Sama's in other regions of metropolitan Manila.

Disputing Up New Alliances

In 1987 the journalist James Fallows publishes an article featuring photographs of squatter settlements in which he labels the Philippines a "damaged culture," a phrase not out of synch with anthropological accounts of problems inherent to postcolonial societies. The article is widely discussed in Manila. Citing Filipino loyalty to family, schoolmates, compadres, and tribe, Fallows argues, "The tradition of political corruption and cronyism, the extremes of wealth and poverty, the tribal fragmentation, the local elite's willingness to make a separate profitable peace with colonial powers—all reflect a feeble sense of nationalism and a contempt for the public good" (1987:57). Fallows doesn't know the urban poor; he knows only that they are poor. I am troubled by his mistakes; in Payatas, conflict is coalescence. Fallows should jump into the schisms to discover the state and nation.

■

Payatas differs from the NGC where Sama-Sama has incrementally built support and a large organization. Payatas squatters fall within at least one and most often more vertical organizations through home-owners associations linked to syndicates, elaborated barangay organization, the Bureau of Lands (through residential use permits), veterans' associations, and many other groups. Existing organizations resist Sama-Sama's expansion.

Sama-Sama confronts two additional major problems. President Aquino names as beneficiaries of the NGC Housing Project all who lived within the NGC prior to the 1986 snap elections. However, Sama-Sama, Quezon City, and the national government cannot control the influx of urban poor into the region. Syndicates and barangay captains continue to sell and rent NGC land. In addition, Mrs. Vargas has challenged the 1985 Sama-Sama elections within the Home Insurance Guarantee Corporation (HIGC), which oversees urban poor "homeowner" associations. HIGC chooses not to recognize the 1985 elections and calls for new ones. With her defeat nullified, Mrs. Vargas could resume leadership of Sama-Sama and fill its seat on the National Government Center Housing Committee (NGCHC). Sama-Sama is not willing to tolerate an ally of Marcos's National Housing authority on the NGCHC. Sama-Sama increases its recruitment efforts within the NGC with HUDCC sponsored rallies and information campaigns.

Mrs. Vargas and other groups have been growing a coalition to oppose Sama-Sama within the NGC and Payatas, one that includes a wide range of powerful organizations previously unassociated except through some overlapping membership. Mrs. Vargas has established alliances with syndicate leaders Don Santiago Pasero and Don Ignacio San Pedro. She agrees to purchase land for her housing cooperative from a real estate developer who is purchasing the land from Pasero and who had run against the mayor of Quezon City in the last election. The same land is owned by a real estate firm associated with both a powerful Philippine congressman and a powerful general. As Mrs. Vargas builds her alliances she adds new enemies to a list that already includes influential Aquino appointees and Catholic leaders.

Mrs. Vargas moves cooperative members onto the newly acquired land that is covered with concrete-block houses previously abandoned before they were finished by a subdivision developer who had run into legal problems. Soon after this move, Quezon City forces supported by Philippine Marines and a federal SWAT team bomb the office of Mrs. Vargas's real estate benefactor, which is located among the new homes of her cooperative. Those homes are soon demolished. Perhaps emboldened by the armed attack against Mrs. Vargas, an HUDCC official pursues plans to put together a large armed force headed by a respected Philippine general to put an end to new arrivals within the NGC and Payatas.

The force, if organized, would face powerful opposition including that from members of the armed forces and police who have settled on the land. They would also face unarmed but powerfully committed opposition from organizations such as those headed by Boy Biag and Mrs. Dolores Marimante, who are part of the growing confederation opposing Sama-Sama.

Society as Autonomy

Philippine society is often criticized for producing a weak state, one that lacks the autonomy necessary to produce "a unified channel for people's passions," (Villacorte 1994:69; see also Neher 1985). Noting the absence of a nation prior to colonization and no colonial attempt to produce one, Wilfrido Villacorte argues democratization produced a process through which the elite furthered personal rather than national interests. Drawing on Temario Rivera (1991), he attributes the absence of a highly rationalized state bureaucracy to oligarchical control of politics and the economy, authoritarian-clientelistic political leadership, popular opposition movements, and dependence on foreign resources. I wonder why individuals without state resources can turn disputes into society and develop the land while the official state cannot.

■

Boy Biag leads a residents' association within the NGC that is allied with the Bureau of Lands through CONSEP. He is also leader in Payatas of approximately four thousand members of a nationwide organization headed by former Hukbalahap leader Luis Taruc. He has recently formed a ten-group Payatas coalition that claims seven thousand members. Biag believes Torrens titles to land in Payatas are either counterfeit or based on illegally issued titles. He explains his opposition to Sama-Sama:

> I oppose Sama-Sama in Payatas. When we went to PCUP [Presidential Commission on the Urban Poor], [Commissioner] Belaso told us Sama-Sama was representative of four barangays in the NGC. We said, "Who gave them the authority?" . . . I know Father Gintaba is behind that matter. His influence is in Malacañang, and what he says is always followed by the secretary of Aquino. . . .
>
> CONSEP will be the organization to challenge Sama-Sama. I am an officer in that organization, and that is our stand. . . . Leaders in Payatas are convincing us . . . that they and we stand and oppose Sama-Sama. My aim in being a leader is collective leadership. . . . I am interested in my people and tenure of this place.

Biag's philosophy concerning the land is similar to that of syndicate leaders:

> The government will define our situation here. I don't know what will happen, but I believe in laws if the law will be implemented equally and in the right situation, because we have complete papers and the law can say if our papers are genuine and complete.
>
> I am not against the government but against who runs the government. They are all vested interests. I have already been through five

presidents of the people, but until now I am still a squatter. Where is the government? There is no true government. My father is sixty-nine, and he is also still a squatter. If you say there are problems with the government, they will say you are a communist. If there are any laws being made, even the Constitution, the implementation is not right. The government is just like a building that is good, but it becomes bad through the people who are running it. The corruption is grave. . . . During the Magsaysay administration we said those who have less in life must have more in law. But now, even if you are not guilty, you will be "salvaged" [murdered by agents of the state for political reasons] and put in the garbage.

Mrs. Dolores Marimante controls an area known as Manila Remnants, about twenty-one hectares of land within walking distance of the Philippine Congress that is the home of an estimated three hundred families. She has enclosed the land with a fence and five outposts for guards to control "squatters" and "crime." She opposes Sama-Sama, which has been recruiting members from her group known as Madya-As Confederation, Inc. Mrs. Marimante has contracts to control the land with the Bureau of Forestry Development through a residential use permit, with a lieutenant of Don Ignacio San Pedro, and with P&L Reality, which claims title to the land and has an unfunded contract with Quezon City to develop it for city-employee housing. P&L's title is derived from a title being contested in court by the Philippine government. Mrs. Marimante has developed within her area a four-room elementary school and a priestless Catholic chapel for *rosarios*. She has a long-standing dispute with the barangay, which has attempted to take over the school and place it under the Ministry of Education and Culture.

Mrs. Marimante is one of P&L Realty's two employees, an active member of CONSEP, the PTA, the National Conference of Farmer's Organizations, and the Federation of Land Reform Farmers, and she is Payatas president of the Visayan Confederation that "has seven thousand members in Quezon City." (The Visayas is a region of the Philippine Islands.) Her husband is a member of the Philippine Constabulary, as are some Remnants residents. She moved to Payatas from the provinces in 1981. Various corporations that have claimed ownership of the land attempted demolitions between 1981 and 1985. Marimante sought court injunctions against all of them. She is involved in numerous land disputes. She explains:

I have had twelve complaints against me. I was the only one who developed the area and improved the roads. It was only me, and my husband and my brother. We developed the area without help from the people. . . . I have received three letters of death threats this year . . . telling me to vacate the place or else. They have misunderstood me regarding development of the area.

If we have to wait for the government to develop the area that will be a long time because of the economic setbacks now. I am afraid we will be ejected without resettlement. The back of my site is claimed by Veterans . . . they [i.e. their homes] were demolished by Filinvest [a rest estate firm with contested titles]. The Veterans had RUP's [Residential Use Permits]. We also could have the same problem. Why were our cases decided in favor of the landowners when we have letters [from the Bureau of Forestry Development] saying the land is unclassified? There were eight attempts at demolition. . . . There were also military men residing in the place willing to defend the area. And I would also have to call the press if they went ahead. . . . I will run for barangay captain in the coming election because I also want to protect my men. . . . My only project now is for members to have a piece of land they can call their own, and then after that a livelihood. . . . I don't want to fight any more because you need bullets to fight and bullets cost money.

The director of P&L Realty, whom Mrs. Marimante supports, hopes to locate three thousand city employees in Remnants. He will allot one hectare of the land for members of Madya-As and plant a "buffer zone" between the employees and the "settlers" so that the employees will not be able to see their neighbors. He plans to develop livelihood projects for the former squatters explaining, "It seems that I'm putting up a factory wherein settlers in one hectare of property are my workers." Sama-Sama, on the other hand, has promised residents of Marimante's land that they will eventually have on-site development and will be able to purchase titles to the land from the government. It appears Mrs. Marimante does not know that Mrs. Vargas has recently purchased a portion of her land from Don Ignacio San Pedro for her housing cooperative.

As I leave the Philippines in August of 1988, Sama-Sama's president has taken her place on the National Government Center Housing Committee. Mrs. Vargas's case against Sama-Sama continues at the Home Insurance Guarantee Corporation as her coalition enters into public protests against Sama-Sama at governmental agencies. A new syndicate, one of Don Ignacio's rival heir-claimants for title 4136, has just opened offices near the Batasan Pambasa to sell NGC land. Other syndicates have placed "For Sale" signs along Commonwealth Avenue to lure prospective buyers of the NGC. A long-time leader of CONSEP, a lawyer at the Bureau of Forestry Development, has started working for Don Ignacio. A bomb explosion and subsequent fires have gutted at least two upper floors of the Quezon City municipal building. The fires, in addition to destroying court documents and evidence, burn around half a million land titles in the office of the registrar of deeds.

The Morality of Family, State, and Termite

I return to the Philippines during the summer of 1994 and head for Commonwealth. Not far from the National Government Center my jeepney passes an enormous multistory enclosed shopping mall that covers an area at least as large as a football field. The director of Development and Planning for Quezon City tells me it went up without a building permit. Arriving in Commonwealth, I am immediately whisked into a dispute that has spread across metropolitan Manila. Father Gintaba has broken with Sama-Sama and COPE and has formed a new organization that is recruiting members in the NGC to oppose Sama-Sama for its seat on the National Government Center Housing Committee. The division repeats a pattern, but I am surprised by the opposition. In the past, such disputes have led to peaceful expansion of horizontal and vertical coalitions, increasing local influence over official state policies related to Payatas. But will this schism doom the nation that arises from Payatas society and give the land over to office buildings and shopping malls?

■

The settlement appears much as it did before but now has significant infrastructure development in roads and legal electricity. Many patchwork shanties have been rebuilt in concrete blocks. The government estimates the settlement has grown from 18,000 to 60,000 families since 1988, but COPE's estimate of 30,000 appears more realistic. Philippine President Fidel Ramos has extended the cut-off date for beneficiaries of the NGC Housing Project, moving it from the 1986 snap election to include all residing in the NGC prior to 28 March 1992. He has appointed a presidential task force for the development of Payatas, and it has issued the "Payatas Special Area Development Plan"; Quezon

City has issued "Payatas 2000" by the Payatas 2000 Special Development Committee, a title that draws upon President Ramos's political slogan "The Philippines in the Year 2000."

The syndicates of Don Santiago Pasero, Don Ignacio San Pedro, and others are still settling and selling land they may or may not own, and Mrs. Vargas's cooperative is still facing problems purchasing land titles. Sama-Sama's coalition in Payatas has made little progress, as Sama-Sama predicted, under the direction of the National Housing Authority. Subdivisions are making inroads in Payatas even as they confront resistance from settler groups.

In a ten-hectare pilot project area of Commonwealth, several five-story concrete-block buildings have risen, and more are being constructed under the direction of PROS (Planning Resources and Operations Systems). The "medium-rise buildings" (MRBs) will house thirty-six to forty-five families, and each family will have about twenty square meters [215 square feet] of open living space in one-room apartments that face onto a common hallway and include no access to land. There are to be fifty-seven MRBs in the pilot project alone. This is not "As Is Where Is"; these are not houses that respond to the Philippine family. Their use outside the pilot project area is opposed by Sama-Sama, which has developed the PHASE-LAD Program (Peoples' Housing Alternative for Social Empowerment and Land Acquisition Development Program) in which about one hundred contiguous households are formed into an association that purchases the land on which the houses stand. Twenty neighborhoods in the NGC are already participating.

Sama-Sama explains the program:

> Agreements are signed with the government—a memorandum of understanding about the roles of NGCHC, the local government, and the area association. Then a contract to sell is signed. This is a legal document, the first step in the titling process. The association begins its development construction with its own money or with government money. Finally a mother title is made and individual titles awarded.

In defending the PHASE-LAD program, Sama-Sama writes:

> It has succeeded in distributing some land to almost every family in 20 areas covering about 2,000 families. A limit of 110 square meters is in force and all land that families have above that limit is

given to renters. If the government would make sure the generated lots [land above 110 square meters] went to renters, and took over the large parcels of land still held by private people [some as large as 2.5 hectares], and gave priority in the MRB to renters there will be a decent solution for all—90 percent of all families would have a piece of land. . . .

In this plan no family will be displaced, since it is basically an acceptance of the situation as it is. Other plans require large scale destruction of houses and shifting of people. The plan also has the great advantage of leaving neighborhoods intact. These neighborhoods where people have learned to live and work together—for example, in implementing this PHASE plan and solving their problems—are the lifeblood of the whole NGC. They will execute the upgrading and development plans and make sure the present bad living conditions in the NGC come to an end and attractive healthy communities develop. . . . Only a solution that leaves most people in place, preserves neighborhoods, and minimizes relocation will succeed, and only that makes political sense. . . . Any other plan will have to be carried out by the police and will be fiercely opposed by people.

■

I am standing in the pilot project area in front of two new homes: the first is a well-finished, two-story concrete-block home with balconies; its neighbor is a leaning one-story shanty with hole-ridden patchwork and a tin roof that doesn't fit. I am deeply moved and tears fill my eyes. In achieving this juxtaposition, Sama-Sama has prevented the NGC Housing Project from creating a ghetto of the very poor. As the people rise, they can stay and return resources to the community. Others will rise through them. But what of the very poor who will not fit onto the NGC land? If the wealthy of Manila are not willing to share land with the poor, why should poor families have to reduce the sizes of their plots and houses, hard-won resources, to make room for others? Is this question a moral cop-out?

■

Father Gintaba is in dispute with Sama-Sama and COPE over maximum lot size. He believes a family of six should be allotted thirty-six square meters, but, in exceptional circumstances, he is willing to allow a family that already has seventy-four square meters to keep that amount. Sama-Sama, fighting for a maximum of 110 square meters, believes a lower limit will lead to substantial demolition of homes, creating a massive backlash against Sama-Sama within the NGC. To the NGC family, this issue is significant. Mrs. Vargas explains: "If they say thirty-five square meters I will have to slice my house into three, and I will not like that. In the Philippines we keep our families together, children do not leave at eighteen, we will not put our grandmothers in old folks' homes. I have two new grandchildren now."

A second issue deepening the schism is the role of people's organizations in decision-making processes. As a result of various actions taken by Father Gintaba, this issue has spread the dispute into the hierarchy of the Catholic church, PROS, appointed officials of the Ramos government, and a newly-formed coalition of some of the Philippines' most powerful nongovernmental organizations, which has issued a lengthy argument in support of Sama-Sama's position.

A director of COPE explains what happened:

> Last October a new Presidential Proclamation said everybody living in the NGC as of [28 March] 1992 is a beneficiary. That doubled the beneficiaries. It said, because of the number of families, we must look to vertical rather than horizontal development. The assumption of this is everyone comes over to the left side [location of the 150 hectares] and all live in high-rises. That's how Sama-Sama interpreted the proclamation with the advice of [HUDCC] and PROS. So Sama-Sama had a demonstration of seven thousand people against it, the biggest demonstration ever of the urban poor in Manila. Father Gintaba disagreed, and this is the history of the break.
>
> Then, after the demonstration, everything was decided by the government in Sama-Sama's favor: the Sama-Sama PHASE program, Sama-Sama as the unique representative of the people, the right side as recipients of the Presidential Proclamation, no vertical development except on the 10.5 hectares area agreed upon—the pilot project. Then [came] the fight over the maximum lot size. In December of 1993 a committee was set up on the problem and anybody could participate in the committee, any organizations. [This] task force met and met and in April adopted 110 as the maximum.
>
> Then Father Gintaba reacted violently and went to Mayor Mathay [of Quezon City and a member of the NGCHC], and Mathay and Father Gintaba went to the head of HUDCC, and a month later they steamrolled through making seventy-four [square meters] the maximum. The NGCHC adopted this. . . . The whole idea of people's

participation was thrown out the window. The new head of HUDCC gave orders down the line and HUDCC changed to fifty-four as a maximum lot size and seventy-four if there is a building, a real house, on the lot.

■

Before, the disputes of Payatas were about the poor and the land. Now they are about broader human rights. Are these rights available to be invoked at all times in a way that will inspire people from all walks of life across a vast city to take action in defense of their beliefs, or must human rights be stirred into existence at different times in different places by those who have proven they will sacrifice everything for a chance at equality?

■

Father Gintaba explains his position:

> At the maximum lot size of 110, that's where I came in and messed up everything. . . . [T]he 110 square meters looked to me to be excessive for owners looking for land in a socialized housing site, for the concept of socialized housing is to provide for the bottom 30 percent of the urban poor. . . . If we allot 110 then we knock out two beneficiaries, and a precedent would be set by which the urban poor would be demanding 110 square meters for their houses. . . .
>
> For me, in our fight for structural reform and legislation we have always held ourselves consistently to the human right to human shelter. A human being should have what is necessary to live humanely and legally in our society. We have asserted this right against those who claim ownership to property. Our position has been the human right to shelter trumps the ownership right. . . .
>
> So, the norms regulating socialized housing sites are not yet defined, and what the human being has a right to is not yet defined. We went into laws and building codes and general United Nations norms on building and have concluded that, given this legislation and United Nations norms, the right to shelter includes 6 square meters per person or 14 cubic meters per person in a family. So, if the average Philippine family is 6, the human right to shelter would be operationalized to 36 square meters to a family. . . .
>
> I have been contributing to organizing a group in the NGC that's more representative of the people. We are looking for a new

organizational concept. How do you get everybody represented? Sama-Sama's claim that they have a broad consensus in the area is certainly not true. The people don't all know what Sama-Sama is doing. . . . So we might as well face the diversity of the area. If we take the easy way of dealing with small groups, then implementation will be a disaster. We are still dealing with an elite. We don't have a democratic process.

■

After following this expanding dispute from shanties to corporate skyscrapers, I return to the family compound where I lived in Commonwealth and, sitting under a plywood awning in front of the home of Mang Noli, the compound's founder, I confront an old nemesis. In front of me stands a termite mound as tall as I am. I ask once again why the termite mound has not been destroyed and receive a familiar reply: "If you don't disturb the main termite, source of all of the other termites, the termites will live well with you. Because there is a leader, I don't disturb the termite mound. There is a large hole under or within the ocean that connects the oceans of the Philippines, such as the Cebu Sea, with the Pacific around Los Angeles, so that the water that enters here comes out there. There are also holes in the earth, like the one inside the termite mound. These are like lines of communication through interconnection. We are all interconnected."

Mang Noli knew all along that to find the world's medium in Commonwealth he need only look down.

■

The Composite State

The view from Payatas Estate and Commonwealth follows Philippine squatter networks to patrons with documents from state bureaucracies and corporations; Sama-Sama's networks wind through the Catholic church and NGOs into the leadership of national agencies. Mary Hollnsteiner's (1963) analysis of the dynamics of power in the Philippines describes accumulation of individual power through the allegiances of alliance networks structured by kinship, ritual kinship, reciprocity, and associational ties. Analyses of inefficient nation-states of Spanish postcolonial societies and Southeast Asia frequently attribute the personalistic and particularistic behavior of bureaucrats and politicians to ladders of such dyadic contracts (Foster 1963) that link basic social units including the family, town, or cultural region to bureaucrats in social structures that have the outward appearance of Western bureaucracies. In these analyses, ties of personal loyalty and support wind among bureaucrats and politicians of the state and choke off their rationality.

The hierarchical logic of clientelism is commonly viewed as both the enemy of equality within highly centralized state systems and constitutional liberal democracies and the friend of those who must subscribe to pragmatic norms (Fallers 1969) while negotiating social and cultural change and diversity and constructing the mechanisms of collective action.[2] The individualism of modern society grows a far-reaching structural logic in clientelism that is reinforced by cultural history and the continuity of highly adaptive institutions that antedate "modern" society.

A dominant theme of studies that juxtapose clientelism and modernity is measurement of the value, sometimes moral value, of patron-client relations as if clientelism were a simulacrum of the Western state form—moreover, a form it does not truly inhabit. L. M. Hanks (1975:197), in contrast, analyzes patterns of social relations that emerge from pervasive patron-client ties in Thailand without reference to existing nation-state models, thus avoiding "the implication that some societies are more 'advanced' than others by dint of greater specialization and differentiation." Searching for a "style of social construction," Hanks finds that Thai clients are part of a multifunctonal "entourage" through common personal loyalty to a patron. The entourage can be activated more broadly as a "circle" consisting of a patron's clients and the clients of these clients.

Circles, as autonomous monopolies, extend a wide range of services to their clients and can expand those services through deals with some circles while at the same time competing with others. Hanks finds: "No universals order all the people, and no special economic apparatus supplies the consuming public. Indeed, there are no publics, no masses, nor even a proletariat; instead of these, segments of the population are provided for more or less adequately according to the circle of their affiliation" (1975:207). The Thai state functions as a series of circles, a "collection of self-sufficient units" (197), as the monopolies of some stable circles approximate the functions of a Western state. Hanks constructs a social image: "The social order of Thailand is like a bundle of fine golden chains of varying lengths, with only occasional cross-connections. Pulled taut from the end, the chains resist or move as one, but a finger passes easily between the strands" (1968:146).

Unlike Thailand, the Philippines is a postcolonial society, having been the United States' only official colony after more than four centuries of Spanish rule. The official Philippine state is by intention a constitutional democracy with an elected president, senate and house of representatives, and national bureaucracies; the infrastructure of the Western state is in place, and goals of a Western-style state play a large symbolic role in popular political discourse. Christopher Clapham assigns three essential features to real states: (1) a "hierarchically structured organization, composed primarily of permanent officials though directed by a potentially changeable group of leaders"; (2) a "territorial scope, such that virtually all land areas of the world fall under the jurisdiction of one state, and virtually none under that of more than one"; and (3) "state monopoly over some forms of control and allocation including the use of force, regulation, and taxation established in law" (1982b:18).

The view from Payatas and Commonwealth suggests that the official Philippine state satisfies none of those three criteria. And this is not because it doesn't try, as is common within many squatter areas of the "third word" (Gugler 1988), for the official Philippine state is deeply involved in the National Government Center and several areas that surround it. The official state in the Philippines is, rather, a component of a larger, less-hierarchical state organization responsive to the processes and priorities of Philippine social order. I refer to this organization as the composite state. Although the model of the Western state is constantly channeled into the composite state through discourse over official Philippine national governance, it is actually the maintenance of basic social units (from family to bureaucracy) that appears to be the goal of its participants, rather than the realization of a Western state as described by Weber. H. G. Koenigsberger describes early modern European monarchies as "composite, rather than unitary or national, states" (1989:135); and, following his lead, J. C. D. Clark (1991) claims the United Kingdom of Great Britain and Ireland was and still is a composite state. Koenigsberger explains, "the constituent parts of composite monarchies always antedated their unions. They therefore had different laws, rights, privileges, and traditions." From Koenigsberger's perspective, sovereignty within the composite state was shared with its larger units. Although I use the term composite state to describe a different form of political order, residues of the Philippine colonial past contribute to formation of its governing parts that share, at various points in time, sovereignty over its regions. The colonial composite state may contribute to its postcolonial form.

The official Philippine state accepts shared sovereignty within Payatas Estate as the organizational reality of plural governance. Although centralized law is the source of the Weberian state's autonomy, in Payatas Estate and Commonwealth the official state is a source of legal fiction, the maintainer and writer of a script from which various legitimate forms of legality can be constructed. Don Pasero and Don Ignacio, like Villacorte (1994), recognize law's malleability and its past use to further the economic and political interests of powerful Philippine families. Don Pasero's and Don Ignacio's control and practices within rural and urban regions has remained steady across changing presidencies representing oligarchical control.

Through the law, Payatas syndicate leaders invoke and construct a colonial past that they connect to contemporary official state policies in order to rationalize autonomous urban regions that defy presidential decrees and usurp control over segments of national police and military. At the same time, these leaders bring families as household units and compounds into networks linked to the official state, both ideologically and socially, rather than to those who would overthrow it. The syndicates are legally generated components of the composite state. Their patrons are the courts, the multiple forms of living legalities that have accumulated within the composite state.

Other components, such as those of Boy Biag and Mrs. Marimante, find their charters within abandoned policies of various official state bureaucracies. The enforceability of these policies is unimportant, for unlike patron-client relations in which resources flow down in exchange for allegiance, loyalty, and support, bureaucratic policies provide existing groups with fictional links to the official state rather than material resources. Group-organized loyalties do not flow along these links to individuals with access to official state resources, which are scarce indeed; rather, these links are realized as horizontal coalitions, such as CONSEP, within an array of vertical ties to religious, political, "criminal," and voluntary associations that are sources of information, publicity, opportunity, and protection.

Like syndicates, groups acting autonomously while linking their primary charters to governmental bureaucracies generate and share knowledge of the fractured, changing, and sometimes ineffectual nature of the official state and federal and municipal bureaucracies. Biag claims "there is no true government," while at the same time arguing that the law will solve his problems. Although Mrs. Marimante seeks links to the city, she fights against her school becoming a part of it. She assumes militaristic opposition to infringements on her land while seeking land-sharing within a proposed municipal development.

The members of Sama-Sama, dedicated to notions of modern constitutional democracy, do not believe it is achievable through the Philippine simulacra of the Western state. They also believe, as the legal theorist Roberto Unger (1976) might suggest, that Western influences on the Philippine state could undermine efforts toward equality (Parnell 1992). Several Philippine governments, they argue, have not addressed the problems of poverty—by all estimates much more than half the Philippine population lives below the poverty line—whereas the Philippine poor have constructed mechanisms of survival and the infrastructures of communities. Tied also to church institutions linked to the state, Sama-Sama members sometimes voice a romantic notion of the precolonial indigenous past that establishes Filipino ownership of Philippine land. Within the group's public discourse, members of Sama-Sama seek land as a link between their families and participation in the capitalist economy.

Like the organizations of Pasero and Don Ignacio, Sama-Sama seeks autonomous control of the land but recognizes, as do the syndicates, that autonomy within the official state can be achieved only through linkages to the official state. All organizations seek to be in the state but not of it—in a manner strikingly similar to Philippine participation in Catholicism without conversion during the early period of Spanish colonization (Rafael 1993). All organizations, when they become components of group networks, use their disputes to organize components of the official state, national religious organizations and, to a lesser extent, private enterprise. Sama-Sama, through its disputes, has brought coordination to some federal housing policies and influenced, through its larger networks, the contents and passing of the Urban Development and Housing Act of 1992. Representatives of the official state also become members of Payatas groups, including agents of control and discipline within the legal system, military, and police.

These various components become a state as participants in intergroup networks with overlapping membership engage each other in disputes that express and generate segmentary opposition,[3] what Michael Herzfeld (1987:141) calls "the conceptual matrix of social relativity." Of segmentation, Herzfeld says it is "the relative deployment of political alliances according to genealogical or other criteria of social distance between the parties to a dispute. Anthropologists most commonly treat it in conceptual contrast to state-like formations, and hence as irrelevant to the study of occidental political life" (156).

Within the Philippines, as viewed from Payatas Estate, the deployment and creation of political alliances on terms relative to particular intergroup disputes repeatedly interlinks and organizes components of the state, including the official state, which is, as a result, encapsulated by a segmentary system of shifting intergroup alliances and oppositions. Like the patron-client networks of Thailand, those of the Philippines are linked vertically, but unlike those of Thailand they are also interlinked horizontally through a segmentary system that has a leveling or balancing effect on political, as opposed to purely economic, power.

The schism between Sama-Sama and Mrs. Vargas, who originally led a very small group of followers in the National Government Center, generated within Sama-Sama and among high-ranking leaders within bureaucracies of the official government a pervasive preoccupation with the power and threat of Mrs. Vargas. This opposition energized Sama-Sama's intergroup network and its expansion within the NGC and into Payatas. In response, Mrs. Vargas, in collaboration with other Payatas and NGC leaders, united disparate groups, from those of barangay captains to syndicate affiliates, into a confederation that sought additional, official state charters for its members and increased their shared memberships and alliances. The discourses of varied groups over land and the state, such as those of Pasero, Boy Biag, and Sama-Sama, though they shared many ideological components along with opposition to official state control of the land, had been directed to different audiences. Through dispute, these discourses became united in a mutually beneficial opposition and formed a common parlance. All sides sought maximum retention and minimum relocation but disagreed on the mixture of means—legal, bureaucratic, religious—through which the official state should be involved in keeping the official state and developers at bay. Enactment of this dispute secured the presence of both land reform in Payatas Estate and the issue of people's participation in national discourse about urban land reform, poverty, and social housing.

The NGC Housing Project, through which Sama-Sama enacted its partnership with governmental agencies, progressed only slowly over several years. However, by constructing medium-rise buildings the NGC took what Sama-Sama and other Commonwealth and Payatas groups had predicted was the only route the official state could approve: a Western-style project, one of high-rise, concrete-block buildings and rooms that effaced reference to the Philippine family. Renewal of the dispute between Sama-Sama and agencies of the official state, symbolized by the schism between Father Gintaba and Sama-Sama, rejuvenated the formation of relativistic alliances and oppositions within the NGC and Payatas.

The National Disorder

Payatas Estate is a landscape of the legal and bureaucratic vicissitudes of the colonial and imagined precolonial past and the highly personalized centralized state. Overlapping claims to the same land between groups with similar goals generate oppositions and alliances that express uncoordinated policies and rulings of governmental, legal, and political institutions that respond, as Villacorte (1994) might claim, to disputes within the mechanisms of an oligarchical state control rife with regionalism and familism. Disputes between Payatas groups concerned with family housing, land tenure, survival, and the contexts in which they can be achieved, unite their powerful allies and opponents in peaceful debates about the national roles of families and communities, human rights, and political morality rather than a quixotic quest for an instant Western state that has never planted roots from the top down.

The weaknesses or instabilities of the official state allow the land of Payatas, Commonwealth, and the NGC to become a palimpsest for residents' challenges to poverty that bring institutions of the official state into a national discourse over moral issues. As Herzfeld (1987) noted in Greece, the disputes are not over absolutes derived from the top. In Payatas, they unite individuals, groups, and institutions in the construction of forms of housing that symbolize a nationalistic endeavor grounded in what Partha Chatterjee labels *vertu*, "that sense of community, which is not prior to the establishment of political authority but coeval with it, which nevertheless regards itself as having an identity distinct from that of political authority" (1993:229).

Examining the creation in India and elsewhere of modern national culture that is not Western, Chatterjee calls for a theoretical language that allows us to talk about community and state at the same time (11). Through the composite state, residents of Payatas have created the spaces if not the theory where individuals as participants in communities engulf the official state in prolonged widespread dispute over who should control government land, the community or the state, and the morality of thirty-six-square-meter homes versus those of one hundred square meters. In this sense, segmentation as praxis creates Michel Foucault's (1980) insurrection of subjugated knowledges as well as the moral ground of a nation within processes that address the problems of most citizens as members of families and communities rather than those of imagined modern states.

When analysts such as Fallows (1987) and Villacorte (1994) look up for the Philippine state, they see what is missing. I would describe what I and, perhaps, the residents of Payatas Estate see when we looked up as what ethnographer Stacia Zabusky—evoking W. B. Yeats—describes in this volume as her experience of space-science mission development in Western Europe: a "widening gyre . . . pulling apart . . . a dissipating center." In the Philippines, the construction of the dissipated or missing center is replaced by the creation of social and cultural systems and spaces in which components of a decentered state explore the spiritual and moral realms that, like Payatas Estate, can be the breeding grounds of a nation.

Notes

This research was funded by a Fulbright Senior Research Scholar Award and by Indiana University through a Research Supplement Award. I am very grateful for the skilled research assistance of Connie Bascug and the advice of faculty and staff at the Institute of Philippine Culture, Ateneo de Manila.
1. Census data gathered about squatters tend to be unreliable partially as a result of squatter fears of demolition.
2. See Landé 1965, 1977; Scott and Kerkvliet 1977; Hart 1977; Clapham 1982a; Roniger and Gunes-Ayata 1994.
3. See Fortes and Evans-Pritchard 1940; Evans-Pritchard 1940; Waterbury 1970; Karp and Maynard 1983; Dresch 1986; Herzfeld 1987.

Elizabeth Faier

Domestic Matters: Feminism and

Activism among Palestinian Women in Israel

We can't be like the Jews because they are so Western. And, since we live together, we are afraid [to be like] them. But some of us think [that] we are very backward. We are from a traditional society but we want to be somewhere in the middle—not Jewish and not traditional.—Reem, Palestinian feminist activist

In 1993 I went to Haifa to learn whether Palestinian nongovernmental organizations afforded women new forms of power.[1] Recent studies of the Middle East describe how women contest, subvert, and negotiate power, calling into question older but still prevailing theoretical distinctions between public and private domains as separate spheres of power and authority.[2] This newer literature on women's activities in grassroots and nationalist movements suggests that women may successfully carve out new leadership roles for themselves but nonetheless remain subjugated, since traditional ideas of gender roles are inscribed within nationalist ideologies and state politics.[3] Accordingly, I expected to find nongovernmental organizations (in Hebrew, amutot; s. amuta) functioning as bridges between distinctly male and female spheres of interaction, enabling women to transfer power from one realm to the other without challenging underlying concepts of gender.

But the situation that unfolded during my two years in Haifa was a different one. The women with whom I worked faced a double dilemma in that they see themselves as both Palestinians marginalized within a Jewish state and as women dominated by men and masculinist discourses of gender. Women activists' critiques of what they regard as traditional gender hierarchy implicates more than male-female relations; it encompasses all social relations—among individuals as well as between state and nation. For these women, domestic matters extend far beyond simplistic dichotomies of public and private spheres. For them, gender figures in their intimate roles to be sure, but their personal reworkings of family and friendship are integral to the way they understand multiple dimensions of their belonging—from citizenship to modernity itself.

In this essay, I examine the gendered aspects of Palestinian women activists' discourses of activism, culture, modernity, and nation. Palestinian activism entails more than matters of gender equality or the ability of women to define the parameters of a specifically feminist or nationalistic activism. It involves gendering a national struggle and simultaneously reconfiguring gender, anchoring both (in theory and practice) firmly to domesticity, where women can live their ideas of nationalism and feminism in Palestinian terms. Those ideas and their effects are not limited to domestic spaces, but their wider impact is not along an unbroken horizon, given women's unpredictable success in disrupting public discourses that marginalize them.

Accordingly, feminist and nationalist women undertake to refashion the discourses that are central to Palestinian activism—land, family, and honor. In so doing, they must confront Palestinian men even while expressing their solidarity with the nationalist cause. The fact is that men, not women, control these discourses. Women do control other discourses (for example, discourses of feminism, individual choice, mutual trust among women, and self-help)—though they sometimes pay a high price for this discursive space, as I shall explain. Female activists occupy a difficult position between espousing their fantasies of an equitable future and living the violent realities of their lives. Reflexivity (for Palestinian female activists and for ethnographers) does not always make a clear path for change but highlights the conflicts between activists and their own communities. Still—as I suggest in my concluding section—Palestinian women's activist discourses show the extent to which feminism opens up political space outside the state.

Organizations, Activism, and Feminism in Haifa

Today, 850,000 Palestinians live in Israel, constituting 19 percent of Israel's total population and 13 percent of the global Palestinian population (Statistical Abstract of Israel 1995; Center for Policy Analysis on Palestine 1992:5). Although some of the problems of Palestinians living in the Occupied Territories may be familiar to Western audiences, Palestinians in Israel have unique political, cultural, and social dilemmas arising from the fact that they are *Palestinian* in terms of national and cultural identification and *Israeli* in terms of state citizenship. Complicating matters further for activists—and especially women activists, given the gendered implications of "culture" and "tradition" for Palestinians—the stakes in the question of what constitutes Palestinian culture loom large. On one hand, activists (again, especially women) reflexively critique Palestinian traditions as antithetical to modernity, yet, on the other hand, they invoke these same traditions (reworked according to their ideas of progress) as cultural markers of identity.

Thus, for activists, the paradox of being both Palestinian and Israeli complicates daily life in very immediate ways.[4] Overt and covert discrimination distances Palestinians from the state in a number of different ways: Palestinians do not serve in the military, village communities and schools receive proportionally less government funds than Jewish areas, and Jews view Palestinians as potential enemies.[5] Furthermore, while Palestinians in Israel reside in the geographic and mnemonic spaces of Palestine-past, the political reality of Israel temporally, politically, and socially displaces them from what many people globally and locally consider the authentic Palestinian national body. For many Palestinians, especially those originally from destroyed villages and confiscated lands, Palestine exists only through mnemonic devices such as stories of village life and visits to the sites of former villages. It is in this way that space transcends physical boundaries to be located in collective, familial, and individual memory.

On both practical and ideological levels, the leaders of nongovernmental organizations have to deal with considerable obstacles in reconciling their ideals with the realities of Palestinian society in Israel; this is doubly so for women who face marginalization both as women and Palestinians. As I will demonstrate, women activists explain their own roles in terms of this dualism—and in this, they are well aware of cultural stereotypes from outside of their own milieu. In fact, they argue that they must emphasize stereotypes of inequality and hierarchy to demonstrate that they understand local problems and global constructions of Arab society.[6]

Increasingly, young Palestinians (especially women) like Reem (quoted in the opening epigraph) are turning to amutot to address Palestinians' structural problems within Israel—to express their criticisms of traditional Palestinian culture and society and to voice their own feelings of displacement.[7] Nearly all Palestinian amutot work explicitly on social and economic problems such as land rights and domestic violence, addressing needs that have previously gone largely unattended by traditional Palestinian village leaders (in Arabic, mukhtars), political parties, and state bureaucrats. Consequently, a majority of organizations are direct service providers, running programs such as rape crisis hotlines, youth camps, and women's leadership programs; other amutot concentrate on community building, political lobbying, lectures, and public information projects.

Nearly all Palestinian amutot formed within the past decade. In 1993 Israel listed approximately one hundred registered Palestinian amutot; by 1995 the number of organizations operating within the Palestinian sector had increased to four hundred (Abraham Fund 1992; Neu 1993).[8] In March 2000, an amuta leader told me that over one thousand organizations exist and more register every day.[9] Through what I consider "postpolitical" activism, amutot are supplanting political parties and circumventing the state by placing, through activism, the building blocks of civil society that emphasize national over civic identity. Political parties such as Labor, Hadash (Communist Party), and the Arab Democratic Party have elected Palestinian members to the Knesset, but the efficacy of Palestinian MKs (members of the Knesset) advancing Palestinian concerns has been negligible—partly because Palestinian politicians must often participate on the fringes of Israeli politics (see Lustick 1982; Peretz and Doron 1997; Peretz and Smooha 1989). Hanan, an activist in an educational committee, told me that she no longer voted in state elections because: "I don't believe that the Knesset can be one's goal if one wants to develop the Arab community. In Israel, Arabs are just potential voters for Knesset lists. That is all." Other activists echoed Hanan's comments, rejecting political activism as ineffective and arguing instead that social activism charts the way forward.

My use of the category "social activist" (or, interchangeably, "activist") includes individuals who are active participants, and often leaders, in amutot. In this category, I also include individuals who are not associated with any specific amuta but who participate in activism through demonstrations, symposia, and social networks.[10] Together, these two groups constitute what I term the "activist community." Most female activists are between twenty-five and forty years old, having grown up after Israeli authorities lifted the internal military administration that governed Palestinian movement in the state in 1966. Activists in Haifa are usually not from Haifa but Western Galilee and Northern Districts.[11] Many women told me that they initially moved to Haifa for higher education or employment—both of these being situations in which families usually support unmarried women living away from home.[12] All female activists from villages told me that they *stayed* in Haifa partly because of these reasons but more because the city offered them greater measures of anonymity, privacy, and individual opportunity than villages.

Activists debate the distinction between who is and is not an activist. "I am an activist," Jamila said. "So is Suhad, Selwa, Rawia. We're all public figures, too. I think there are others, some of the ones you know. The people who work at all the amutot here [are activists]. Not the ones who use the amutot [but] those who work."[13] Umm Khalil, a member of the activist community and mother of an amuta director, explains her interest in activism as a difference between herself and other women in her community:

> I'm different from the ordinary Palestinian woman because I don't go from house to house, visiting people, talking, and gossiping [*darwIn faDi*]. Educated people don't have time for this—to sit around a drink, a cup of coffee, and make up stories about people. Well, we talk but not as much as those in the house. I used to sew clothes for Palestinian prisoners with the Democratic Women [women's organization of the Communist Party] but now with work, I don't have time. If I had more time, I would volunteer at an organization, maybe in education or children's rights. I think it is good to do something for Palestinian people. I'm not like the rest; I like to be active.

Part of the ambiguity surrounding who is inside or outside the activist community arises from women activists' differing responses to family pressures against their activities.[14] Women often told me that their families worried that their activism would hurt their future chances for employment and divert them from the "normal" life developments of marriage and raising children.[15] Although most activists marry and raise families like other Palestinians, they do so later in life, with women marrying from the mid- to late twenties and men from the early thirties and upward.[16] Most women I knew married between twenty-five and thirty, and all called attention to their late age of marriage as something special. Because I was twenty-eight years old and single when I began fieldwork, many women wanted to know my opinions on gender and marriage; in turn, they told me their narratives of romance lost on account of their commitments to activism and feminism. One woman, Wafa, explained that being unmarried was difficult because of constant family and societal pressure to marry:

> My mom thinks that I don't have much time for myself anymore. My dad, he doesn't say and he won't say, but I know. He is afraid because I am involved in politics. And in CEGAS [an amuta]. My father is like all parents. Live your own life. Find a guy. Live comfortable. Have a family. These are all the things he likes. I do suffer sometimes from my schedule. When I tell my mom that I want to grow [by working], she says "why?" I'm ready for children but not marriage. I mean, something happened this year because I really want children. I don't think I am ready for marriage though. Living with someone you love . . . that's it. A lot less freedom to do what I want. This is not what I am looking for and I know there is less possibility for freedom when there's children involved.

For Wafa, being single affords a measure of independence away from her family and this pleases her; for other women, being unmarried and living in Haifa is more difficult. Near my apartment, three female activists from the Galilee lived together while they worked and finished their education; two of them often spoke with me about being unmarried. Fatina, an optometry student in her mid-twenties, told me that she wanted to finish her education before she thought about marriage. Nasreen though was decidedly unhappy with her situation. She spent less time in amutot than her sisters, and told me she wanted to meet a man, preferably a foreign man, because she said they are more liberal in relation to gender equality. Later, when I visited these women in 2000, they were still unmarried; for the first time, I heard them express concern that they might never marry. Nasreen claimed that men their age did not want to marry women like them—educated, activist, and older. Other unmarried activists expressed similar complaints that Palestinian men did not want to marry women who had spent time developing themselves by furthering national causes. One woman told me that while the concept of marriage was important to her when she was in her early twenties, now that she had her own profession, it was important to find the right individual for marriage; marriage took secondary status to her desire for self-development. Importantly, the women I knew linked personal and national development as two modalities of their feminist activism.

For women like Wafa, Fatina, and Nasreen, living in Haifa within the activist community affords opportunities to live life according to their personal interests. However, negotiating the intimate levels of urban modernity—dating, marriage, autonomy—is problematic. Although activists stress their claims to freedom in choosing their own ideas, they also acknowledge their sense of isolation in relation to popular understandings and ideologies of gender, culture, tradition, and community. Rawia, an activist from Haifa, explains that because of activism, her personal priorities have shifted:

> I have friends from high school, and that kind of relationship is very important to me . . . but I wouldn't choose them now as friends. My friends now—Jamila, Iman, Reem—those from my amuta, we're the ones with the same ideas. I used to not think that was important but now I know that it is—to have the same language and the same problems. I can speak to them frankly about anything. It's not even that we're feminists. We just understand each other.

Thus, women also stress the pleasure and novelty of their friendships within the activist communities of the city.

Through activism, like-minded women meet each other and form informal support networks. Rena, from Jerusalem, explains the importance of activist friendships:

> All of my friends in Haifa are very new friends. I mean, I didn't know any of them, *any* of them. I never met them before I came here, you see. I think it's not only these friends who have influenced me but also all the discussions I have had with other women. I don't know if it's direct influence, in a conscious way. I don't think so. You know, we talk about everything and we feel very related. But everyone has their own life, problems, lifestyle.

Every activist I knew told me that being able to entrust fellow activists with the intimate details of their lives was essential for maintaining a functional amuta. "I know that these women are not going to take my words and talk about them or me. . . . Or anything like that. And, well, I think that's important for me . . . especially because we have so much in common. This is why we work [well]," explained Jamila. Two activists who were not friends in 1995 said in 2000 that their relationship had become that of close confidantes, first developed through shared activities and then through mutual life concerns.

In addition to creating a community of like-minded individuals, activists insist that working with amutot empowers them because as they help other women, they learn about themselves.[17] Reem said, "Day by day, I get more confidence in myself and the things that I do. And the Rape Crisis Center gives you that power. It's a place that you can get all the power for life." Another activist explained: "The main question about feminism is how women can help other women on women's subjects like how to find her place in society. We need to ask women 'what are you afraid of?' In that situation, I can do something" (Rawia). For other women, the reaffirmation of a women's activist community is equally important:

> There's a good feeling you get when you help a person and the satisfaction you get when she is more relieved. It makes a lot of difference. And then, the relations here, between the women here— we weren't a lot of Arab women. So, it is nice to have relations when you're all of the same hand.[18] You know, we think about a lot of things in similar ways. It makes life easier. (Mary)

> When you're active, you know that you're doing a lot to change yourself and women. I do lectures for schools and teachers. I feel good about this because I can see the change. Maybe it's not going to be forever and maybe it's just for the money but my work does something for people. It's a good feeling this work . . . and to be with women together. I can go to work dressed like this and I don't care. I just don't care. And I don't hear any sexist words. Okay, maybe on the way to work I will hear some, but not in the amuta. I have done a lot of other work. But, the only place that I feel good is at the Rape Crisis Center. (So'ad)

As these statements indicate, women seek out activism as one way to reconcile at least temporarily the complications of gender, life in the city, and personal autonomy. Specifically, activism in Haifa opens up space for women to experiment with life choices from a position of relative autonomy as well to formulate alternate ideas of community that extend beyond village and family environments to urbanism and friendship. In part, they accomplish this by self-consciously retheorizing domesticity in their own distinctively feminist terms, and they also see this aspect of their project as divisive, especially in a political context that is increasingly dominated by extremist positions. Iman says:

You know, the political situation causes a lot of stress on the social life. The men feel it especially because we are here in the occupation. The whole people, the nation. But if we don't fight together as a nation, things will get worse. Right now, I think this political situation will soon become worse for all Palestinians because of right-wing movements. They are becoming stronger and stronger in Muslim and Jewish society. I think the whole problem with our [Palestinian] divisions began six or seven years ago [in the mid-1980s] when the Muslims' movement [Brotherhood] began to get strong. Many people now follow them and not the nationalists.

Wafa and Iman agree that Palestinians are at risk of becoming increasingly divided; however, Wafa thinks that the problem lies with people's misunderstanding that education and women's status are not personal issues but national problems. According to Wafa, Palestinians suffer from passivity that makes them unable to see that their personal problems are national problems, and that there is another way to live:

I am really sick of seeing people sit down, not doing anything, complaining of their personal problems, and not seeing the big picture. It's all of us, I mean. I never used to say anything. I watched Israeli TV, I studied in an Israeli educational system, and, through all these things, I heard the things that they wanted me to hear, the things they wanted me to see. It's like brainwashing. So, from one side, I can't blame people that don't know, but from the other side, it's people facing problems, personal problems. But, if they took the picture one step further, they would see that these [problems] are not personal problems but national problems. I get really mad. I am getting more and more [mad] every day. I have two choices. Maybe I shut my mouth and live my father's way or I live the other way. I say whatever I want, I do whatever I think I should do. I do it the whole way or I don't do it at all. There is not halfway. And I am not afraid. . . . This [activism] is what I live for.

Still, not everyone shares Iman's and Wafa's claim that activism is both the ideology and practice of nationalism. Reem told me that activists often present themselves as nationalists through false pretenses of intellectualism. Another activist, Sylvia, resists using the term nationalist because she feels that high-profile activists abuse nationalist rhetoric for personal and financial benefit, speaking only for the benefit of the media. She told me: "I am not a nationalist [Arabic: *waslli*]. I do work for my nation but not like those people. . . . They say they work for the nation, for the people. But what do they do? They work for themselves!" I found Sylvia's use of nationalism as a term of critique unique, and her comment underscores the reality that activists do not share singular conceptions of nationalism. Rather, they personalize their ideas of nationalism according to individual understandings of gender, culture, and politics.

In contrast, women activists discuss their confrontations as feminists in broadly shared terms—as modernizing "Arab society," Palestinian village traditions, or, through their own husbands or partners, reforming men one at a time. Sylvia identifies herself as a feminist activist for whom one tactic is to engage in "hard conversations" on topics like rape: "The people in our society like to feel that we don't have rape. But now, we [activists] publish articles in the newspapers. We write the stories and sometimes they publish them. But when they do, they present it as a very unusual thing." According to Sylvia, feminists must confront the objectification of women and the belief that women somehow invite rape. "We are not at the same point you are in the West, that women do not ask for this, that women are not objects. No, we think that only psychopaths do this. No one wants to hear that every man is a potential rapist." Reem told me that when women from the Rape Crisis Center give lectures to schools on the topic of rape, they often encounter resistance from the headmasters and teachers. She complained that the teachers do not want them lecturing in the schools because they find the activists too radical and too open in their challenge to tradition:

> The problem for us is that the old psychology—the traditions—they have the place of power in Arab society. These people are so old fashioned. They still think about virginity and the virgin bride. And they don't want us to speak about rape because society will know it. These people in the mission schools, they don't like us and they don't like our education.

Other women explained that being feminist—or even using the label—was difficult because most Palestinians associated it with something dirty or threatening. Denise told me that she was hesitant at first to tell people that she thought of herself as a feminist, but later became confident enough to do so:

At the beginning, I was afraid to say feminist because you know, here, feminists are whores. First time I met my husband, "You're not a feminist. You're just talking." But I said to him, "No, I'm not a feminist, you know I just care about women." But later I said not, it's not bad and I am like that.

Ismahan sees feminist activism as conflictual but freeing:

When I came to Haifa, I joined the Rape Crisis Center because I wanted to do something. For me, this type of activity is what it means to be free, to be a feminist, and do what I want to, when I want to. I want to be a feminist in my society, but most people do not agree. They think it is something dirty . . . or maybe nobody thought about this. But in the center, I can be a feminist. And we are doing something together; we are trying to change people.

Women who did not want to identify themselves as feminist told me that they considered feminism alien and too extreme for Palestinian society:

Feminism can only give us so much. I don't like everything they say. I mean, who can tell the Arab girls that it is okay to go from bed to bed without thinking. Yes, feminists do some good things, but a lot of what they say is too strong for us. It is too strong for me even though I like women's activities. (Umm Khalil)

Some of the things they [Westerners] want feminists to talk about are not suitable for me to talk about in my society. Yes, sometimes you need to be aggressive but not in their way. In my society, feminism makes people run away. Instead, you must find ways to talk and make people understand. They [traditional Palestinians] don't know that any Arabic movement is a political movement—a social movement—all of this. (Afnan)

Still, some women explained that it did not matter if women considered themselves feminist because, if they worked for women's advancement, then they were acting as feminists, whether consciously or not:

Not every woman who is active thinks of herself as a feminist, but I think that everyone who works for women is a feminist. It's like asking if I am a Palestinian or if I am an Arab—it's the same. I think it's me who decides, and that is sometimes very difficult. But I know that working in amutot is good for me because otherwise I don't have many people around who have the same ideas. (Mary)

Feminists recognize that the word "feminism" has a negative connotation in Palestinian society, and that it is not always the best route for working with other women. Rawia told me that once when she was giving a lecture in Nablus on sexuality, the women stopped her because they did not like her ideas:

And then the woman said, "Oh, you're too much of a feminist for us. We don't want to be like that in our women's group." But, I was thinking, you are feminists, too. They told me that "you're too much about revolution. Like, you want the girls to go out and sleep with the boys." They thought that being feminist was something sexual. It was a stigma to them. (Rawia)

Feminist activists lay claim to feminism as an ideology of difference, which implies a responsibility to challenge other Palestinians to think and act differently—even if such teachings conflict with normative understandings of women's behavior. The complications and risks in this task are richly and tragically illustrated in the case of Ichlas.

The Case of Ichlas: Contested Discourses of Honor

So far, we have seen that urban Palestinian women's efforts to contribute to the nationalist cause through activism commit them to helping other women.[19] These projects introduce them to new networks, new ideas of personal and family life, and specifically to an ideological commitment to personal autonomy as a means of creating a new Palestinian society outside of the dichotomy of Israeli and traditionalist male domination. For many women, then, feminism and nationalism are two sides of the same coin.[20] While activism for the most part means women acting among other women in the city, women I know are keenly aware of their natal village home as another cultural nexus that is both their own and not their own. They carry this disjunction with them whether they are in the city or in the village. Ordinarily, their discourse of culture, modern life, and tradition—and activism itself—bridges the incommensurate elements between their lives as feminists, activists, wives, and individuals in the city and their responsibilities as daughters and sisters in the villages. And, as I have shown, they are always aware that as

Palestinian feminist nationalists, their activism has two fronts. But, occasionally something happens that breaks this bridge, necessitating a crucial effort of rebuilding—personally, ideologically, and politically. This section is about one such episode. Women activists responded to an honor killing in ways that illuminate the complexities of women's political subjectivities and the extent to which their feminism and nationalism are directed to regendering the nationalist struggle and, with it, their own spaces of personal agency.

Anthropologists often treat honor as an overarching principle or discourse that structures relationships between men and women.[21] According to Richard Antoun, "a man or a woman without honor has forfeited his or her claim to act as a human being" (1989:202) because to live without honor undermines all social institutions from the ownership of property to religion. Usually Palestinians use "the honor of the family" as a conservative discourse to maintain communities and prevent the moral and social disorder (Arabic: fitna) judgment that arises from men's inability to control women's behavior. In colloquial Palestinian Arabic, sharaf and 'irD both translate to the English word honor, but activists self-consciously use these terms to differentiate types of honor. When discussing an individual's or family's honor, Palestinians use the word sharaf, which implies that honor can be lost or gained from people's actions. When talking about the Palestinian nation, Palestinians use 'irD.

Activists extend honor beyond these normative usages of "honor of the family," which equates men's honor with control over women's behavior and, especially, their sexuality. In personal and amutot discourses, in which activists suggest alternate ideas of family and gender, they reify the models of the family that they seek to unseat in their programs, deliberately calling into question what might be authentically "Palestinian." Activists perceive individual choices about gender and sexuality in the nuclear family to be the crux of their desired transition from the traditional to the modern, especially as Palestinians often associate the "tradition of honor" with the extended patrilineal group.[22] According to most activists, honor of the family should not be excluded from a new Palestinian cultural authenticity. Rather, activists argue that, especially in the context of modernity, Palestinians should concentrate on revising the notion of family honor within the domestic unit—that is, nuclear families in which men and women have equal power, authority, and opportunities. In that way, they say, ideas of the family, albeit different ideas, will still have meaning to Palestinian culture and society.

Activists reject the idea that honor belongs only to men. Instead, they argue that people must evaluate both men and women according to their social behavior and commitment to the nation, professing that honor lies not only in the community, but also within people's self-evaluations. For activists, then, discourses of honor emerge as a personal but still collective standard against which people evaluate their own behavior as well as that of other community members; honor is thereby a mode of judgment and self-amendment (compare Bourdieu 1974; Wood 1993).

In the context of honor, behaviors that might seem commonplace to Westerners—dressing fashionably, dating, and family planning—take on specific iconic meaning in communal and national contexts in relation to the tensions and alliances discussed above. Far from being trivial, these issues involve both the risk and reality of violence, as "systems of inequality and dominance generate relationships themselves capable of being violent in nature" (Nordstrom and Martin 1992:8). Women activists deliberately operate in this iconic realm of consumer choice, contending for example, that a woman should be free to wear miniskirts or go to parties without jeopardizing her honor or her life.

But women are not free to do these things. Sometimes they are killed for making choices their male relatives do not accept. Activists and anthropologists disagree amongst themselves as to why and where honor killings occur. Activists told me that sometimes women are killed because they have had sex, are pregnant, or are dressed provocatively. But killing is not a predictable consequence; activists were quick to point out that other women do these same things but do not die because of them. Despite the ways local media and villagers depict honor killings, they are neither isolated events nor simply expressions of boundary maintenance.[23] Rather, they are dependent on structures of power and prestige in Palestinian communities (Cohen 1989). The case of Ichlas demonstrates these complex interrelations as well as how honor killings emerge as a fulcrum in activists' discourses of honor, gender, and the nation.

Ichlas, a thirty-eight-year-old Druze woman, was killed on 10 July 1994 in the Galilee village of Rama'. This honor killing sparked debates, protests, and other activities throughout Israel over questions of honor,

Palestinian culture, and the family. Ichlas was originally from Rama' but had moved to the United States some years before. She was in Israel visiting her extended family—her parents lived in the United States—and finalizing plans to establish an orphanage in Rama'. During her visit, her younger brother, who was home on weekend leave from the army, shot her to death for purportedly violating the family's honor.

I had come to Rama' that same weekend with Reem to visit her Druze family as they prepared for the upcoming wedding of Reem's younger sister, Rana. In Rama', we first heard of Ichlas's murder as we were getting dressed for a wedding party. Two Christian women came upstairs and told us what they knew of the murder. Details were scant, and the family discussed possible reasons for her murder. Shaheira, an older unmarried woman in her fifties who was a close family friend, confirmed the rumor of an honor killing, explaining that she heard the news from a neighbor of the "dishonored" family who had visited her. In my fieldnotes, I wrote of the first news we heard:

> People were talking about how Ichlas was a prostitute and if that wasn't bad enough, she was so stupid to be with a man when her brother came home from the army for weekend leave. Afterwards he shot her twenty times with his automatic rifle. He then called the police and waited for them to arrive. People were saying what a shame that he did not also murder the other sister who was reputed to be a prostitute as well.

Throughout the weekend, at parties and coffee visits, neighbors speculated about what had happened. Almost all of the stories focused on what the woman could have done to deserve such a fate. Everyone assumed that she had violated the family's honor. Villagers also spoke about how they pitied Ichlas's brother. One young woman, also unmarried, said that it was a shame he would spend his life in jail because he was very handsome and good. Other villagers told me that they supported his action because families must do what they can to maintain honor and, thereby, the social solidarity of the community. Ichlas's family, the Bassams, neither condemned their son's act nor received condolence visits for the death of Ichlas, thus granting silent support to the killing. Of the people with whom I spoke, only Reem's parents and sister condemned the murder both in private conversations with me and social interactions with friends and neighbors. Even Reem's younger brother, about fifteen years her junior, disagreed with his family. As we walked home from a neighbor's house on the afternoon after the murder, he—as a male representative of the family—reprimanded Reem for talking so freely about women's rights. Reem ran after him, hitting him on his head, and told him that he had no control over her regardless!

URBAN-RURAL CONNECTIONS:
THE TRANSCENDENCE OF HONOR

Returning to Haifa, I found the murder no less a topic of conversation as people continued to talk about its cause. The rumors and theories were many and varied. One woman said that she had heard that Ichlas's brother was angry because Ichlas had worn a miniskirt. According to this woman, Ichlas had lost her sense of propriety about what clothing one wears in a village. Another activist explained that he thought the conflict arose from Ichlas's participation in American Jewish philanthropy. I also heard this rumor from a different activist who added that Ichlas wore a Jewish star and had thought about converting to Judaism. This activist claimed that Ichlas's parents, who lived in the United States, had conspired with her brother in the village to murder Ichlas when she returned. Conspiracy theories developed: Ichlas was a spy for the Mosad (the Israeli Intelligence Agency) and was having an affair with a Jewish Knesset member.

The media—English, Arabic, and Hebrew—had their own renditions of the story as well. According to an article in the *Jerusalem Post*, Ichlas's fatal mistake was that "she believed that she could have it all: a modern life as a liberated woman in New York, while maintaining emotional and philanthropic ties to her native village and the traditional Druze community she grew up in" (15 July 1994). While most villagers interviewed in the *Jerusalem Post* did not openly support the actual killing, almost everyone interviewed did maintain that honor killings serve a positive function, reinforcing Palestinian traditions. One man said: "It's forbidden to murder, but she stepped over the boundaries of what is acceptable," while another argued that: "This is treated inside the family. Inside Israel, we have tribes, inside of which there is the Levant code of honor."

Ichlas's killing became an activist cause. Activists expressed frustration over press coverage from all sides. Neither the Hebrew nor the Arabic press, they said, explicitly condemned the honor killing. Journalists from the Arabic press had interviewed Ichlas, on the evening of her murder, about her philanthropic plans for an orphanage. Still, according to activists, the tone of their articles supported the idea of honor killings. One activist told me it was ironic that the Hebrew media reinforced and deferred to Palestinian "culture" in their stories. In her opinion, Jews emphasize "authentic" Palestinian culture only in situations of violence, thereby reifying violence as something essential to Palestinians. I found that Palestinian activists also did this perhaps because of a tension between traditional men's authority over women and women activists' refusal of that sign as definitive of Palestinians.

Responses from the activist community condemned both the murder and the behavior of villagers. According to Nawal Assis, spokesperson for *al fanar*, a Palestinian feminist organization, what is important is not whether Ichlas was acting "Western." Rather, her death tells other Palestinian women about their opportunities for freedom, dignity, and security in Palestinian society:

> This [honor killing] happened not because she was behaving "Western." Not all Arab and Druze women are religious. This happened because she is a woman. . . . [E]very woman has the right to her life. This was a killing in cold blood of their own people. No Druze man has ever been killed because of this. They change their names, go out with Jews, and no one ever accuses them of dishonoring the family. This is a danger to all advanced women, to any woman who wants to be free. (*Jerusalem Post*, 15 July 1994)

Violence in a Demonstration against Violence

On the Saturday following the murder, activists from Haifa and Jerusalem scheduled a demonstration at the main entrance of Rama'. I traveled to the demonstration on the bus Haifa activists had chartered for the day. Before Saturday, activists talked about the demonstration, speculating about who would come and how Rama' villagers would receive them. Activists told me they expected trouble because they had heard rumors that Druze men in the village were conducting house-to-house visits, warning villagers not to participate, and making threats. Later, a Haifa feminist activist from Rama' confirmed this rumor.

The group traveling on the chartered bus met downtown on the morning of 16 July; other Haifa activists traveled by car to Rama'. When we arrived at the village, there were approximately sixty to seventy demonstrators, many handing out leaflets, holding up signs, and distributing placards. An example of one flyer from al fanar follows in full:

MURDERED . . . BECAUSE SHE'S A WOMAN

This regressive phenomenon that is called "family honor" has raised up another sacrifice. Ichlas is her name, Palestinian, Druze, thirty-eight years old, from the village of al-Ramah [Rama']. She was killed the eve of July 10th at the hands of her brother, the soldier, in a savage manner, unparalleled before.

Why was she murdered?

First, Ichlas was murdered because she's a woman!!

Second, because she possessed an elevated social consciousness in that she worked during her long years abroad in the United States to collect donations in order to establish charitable and development institutions in her locality [baladah] and in her society.

These factors in general, in addition to the manner of her dress, provoked the contempt of her brother, and his mother-in-law, who were influenced by these "legal opinions" which prevent Druze Palestinian women from wearing pants and driving cars, which are meant to ensure the submission of women and their world.

With her fall, Ichlas has been transformed into a martyr in a battle to struggle for her rights as a woman to equality.

We plead with the Palestinian leadership from all its sides and institutions to condemn and revile this crime and all who provoke its commission. Because, the continuation of these crimes ensures the impulses of regression within our society and will strengthen bigotry and tribalism and it will be nothing but a barrier upon the road to national independence and equality.

We plead also with the state of Israel, the minister of justice, and the state's attorney to classify the murder of women for the sake of maintaining men's superiority and "family honor" as a crime open to punishment by life imprisonment without the chance of pardon or parole.

We call upon all Palestinian and Israeli organizations for women's and human rights to aid our plea and to join our struggle. (al fanar, 16 July 1994)

Other activists used similar strategies for denouncing honor killings, stressing that honor killings are not about honor but the status of women. Salwa told me that activists write "the names of women that were killed by their husbands or their brothers" on flyers and placards and in newsletter articles to immortalize murdered women and further "dishonor" and "shame" of the family.[24]

The following is my eyewitness account of the event. Soon after protestors assembled by the side of the road, young men from the village, in their teens and early twenties, ran through the crowd, ripping placards and pushing people down. Violence quickly escalated from yelling to physical fights. One activist from Haifa, Theresa, actively engaged in a number of arguments as her husband stood to the side, holding their daughter away from the fighting. In the middle of the confusion, a jeep full of Druze police, dispatched from the police station at Karmiel, a nearby Jewish city, drove up to the crowd. They watched from their jeep—they did not break up the fighting.[25]

At this point, the demonstration had more than fifty participants, the legal number allowed without a permit. The police then began breaking up the crowd, despite arguments by demonstrators that they had se-cured a permit. Activists found out later that the police had revoked their permit under pressure from Druze men in the village who threatened violence if demonstrators assembled. Activists broke into two groups, each of fewer than fifty, and moved to either side of the village's en-trance. Fighting broke out everywhere, with the police in the middle. Other men from the village came down and joined the fighting while women from the village stood and watched from a distance. As the police intervened, the crowd also attacked them.[26] Moments later, Druze men from the village threatened to get their guns and fire at the protestors. When these men turned and started running to their houses, demonstrators fled from the scene. Some of the demonstrators had earlier told me that they were prepared to fight, as violence is routinized in almost all demonstrations, but not against people with guns. Several activists, though, continued to fight with Druze villagers. As police broke up these fights, demonstrators and Druze men continued to scuf-fle, and struck back, resulting in the police officers arresting both par-ties. A few activists confided to me that they were scared by the threat of guns—they worried that if the police did not defuse the violence more murder would occur in Rama'.

Demonstrators then proceeded to the police station in Karmiel, where police had taken those arrested. From an open window inside the station, those arrested yelled out to the demonstrators. In reply, those not arrested shouted slogans and words of support.[27] Druze men from

Rama' also came to the police station and waited outside to hear what would happen to the youth arrested from the village.

Again, fighting—this time verbal—broke out between the men from Rama' and some female activists from Haifa. An outspoken man from the village yelled that he agreed with the purge of Ichlas for family honor. He said that if a woman violates a family's honor then it is the duty of her father or brothers to kill her and thus restore honor. The following, from my fieldnotes, outlines the rest of the argument:

> A woman asked if she could then kill him for his sexual behavior, and he replied no because she was a woman. He said that a man could be an 'arse [pimp] and have ten whores but that his daughter could not date. Someone else made the comment that all whores should die and implied that the women from Haifa arrested were also whores.

Two of the men involved in this argument were later arrested. After questioning, police released everyone later that day.

RETURN TO HAIFA

I visited with activists during the following week, gathering their reactions to the murder and demonstration. Several women said that they found all honor killings sickening. Rena told me that she hated "tradition" because it kills and victimizes women. Similarly, several friends of Reem, the women whom I accompanied to Rama', informed me that they could not attend Rana's (Reem's sister's) wedding because they wanted to avoid the men from Rama'. "I can't face the eyes of those men . . . and at a wedding. There will be no happy times for me in Rama'."

Overall, it seemed to me that female activists were either angry or revolted, but not necessarily scared. However, in the days following Ichlas's death, one activist became increasingly alienated—from her friends and even from her own body. Soon after the killing, I noticed that Lila, a university student, began wearing layers of clothes on the lower half of her body. One afternoon I asked her why she was wearing a dress with leggings, athletic shorts, and casual shorts. She told me that she wanted to make sure that if her dress blew in the wind, she would not expose any of her body because "the men, they will come and kill me." The next day I saw Lila. She told me that she was soon going to die because she had worms in her stomach. She also explained that now, because of the worms, she had to wear more layers on her lower half.

I heard from Wafa that Lila was acting strangely in other ways as well. One night Iman and Basheer received a call from Lila from a hospital emergency room. She told them that the doctor said that she had cancer; she wanted them to come and pick her up. When Iman and Basheer reached the hospital, Lila had already left, and the attending medical staff told them that Lila had refused to be examined. Later that night, Wafa received a telephone call from Lila, now at a different hospital, who was hysterical because she claimed that after her examination she was no longer a virgin. Wafa went to the hospital and brought Lila home.

The next day Wafa told me she had spoken with Iman who had called the attending doctor from the night before. (Iman worked as a nurse at the same hospital as the doctor.) The doctor replied that he had not seen Lila, but, if he had, the examination would not have broken her hymen. Moreover, he said that doctors were especially careful with Palestinian women since they knew of the risks involved in an unmarried woman's loss of virginity. That night, Lila again went to different Haifa hospitals, calling Iman, Basheer, and Wafa from each one; each time they arrived at a hospital, Lila had already left.

On the following day, Wafa and Basheer told me that they were considering whether they should call Lila's father and inform him of the situation. Wafa and I said that might be a bad idea if Lila was worried about her honor; from the stories we put together, we wondered if she was pregnant or had been raped. After Lila's behavior became increasingly extreme, Wafa and Basheer spoke with her father who then brought her back to their village where she received psychiatric help.

Almost a year later, I went to Lila's village to see her and meet her family. Lila had returned to Haifa a few months earlier but spent little time in the activist community. At her parents' house, we watched videos from the weddings of her sister and cousin. Her father told me that while he loved Lila, he was worried that she would never get married and "lead a normal life." Her parents told me that some people in the village were gossiping about Lila because she lived alone in Haifa, had a boyfriend, and suffered psychological trauma during the previous summer. Before I left that day, Lila and I spoke of her breakdown. She said that she had been under enormous stress partly because her fiancé had ended their relationship and another man had started to call her, asking for sex. Lila cried that she felt that she had nowhere to turn because if she spoke about this man's requests, people would assume she was promiscuous.

From what activists told me, Lila's crisis is an example, albeit extreme, of the conflict women encounter when their subjective experiences clash with societal ideas about women and sexuality. Rena stated that activists feel they are fighting for both women and the nation but others treat them with disdain, as if they are the danger within. She explains:

> I went to the demonstration on Saturday in Rama'. I only heard about it fifteen minutes before it started. So, we went there. One man, he was walking with his little girl—she was maybe two years old. And he said: "See, they don't have anything to do with their lives so they come here and demonstrate."
>
> All of these killings make me, well, what can I say? Unfortunately, I don't know the words in English. Maybe, horrible. You know, *mukrif*, disgusting. Today I met some people from the Galilee and the village of Dhalyiat [Druze village near Haifa]. And I asked them what they thought about all this. And they say: "Yeah, poor guy. He was so proud for society and now he has to spend his life in jail. Poor guy, poor guy, poor guy." And I told them that *she* was the one who was killed. "What are you saying 'poor guy' "! You know what they said? "For girls like her, it is good that they are killed." I just couldn't look at them. I just turned around and went on my way. I just kept on going.
>
> You know, when we make a demonstration, I can see the way they look at us—like we're not worth anything. I can see this in their eyes. They can't accept that we are trying to do something. They always find a reason why she was guilty, not him.

According to Rena, such reactions are not unusual, especially when activists argue that "honor killings" are murders—femicides—in the name of Palestinian culture. Other activists charged that they regard honor killings as double examples of domestic violence—violence within the home against women and within the state against Palestinians (Adelman 1997; Badran 1991; Kandiyotti 1991).

Bringing It Home: The Politics and Place of Domestic Activism

Honor killings put women activists in acutely difficult personal and political spaces—between their personal desires and social risks, their own visions of Palestinian nationalism and others' ideas of Palestinian traditionalism, and urban centers of activism and personal ties to villages. Yet, within the context of activists' responses to honor killings and alternative discourses of activism, female activists display the greatest levels of activity through their words and their bodies. They challenge society's representation of women and the boundaries of women's participation in activism as a way to change society and nation; through amutot, they contest the state's power over civil society. Thus, in their struggles with "honor," "family," and "culture," activists argue that women are members of society, like men, who can possess and control their personal honor for the sake of their families and society.

Activists' attachment to honor is as an idiom of equality. They seek to reappropriate and supplant male discourses of family, nation, and order with feminine ones with the purpose of enabling all individuals, but especially women, opportunities to achieve greater personal liberties. While activists employ Orientalist stereotypes, they do so in ways that afford them opportunities to put forth their ideas as oppositional rhetoric, emphasizing that personal rights supersede tradition. "Honor" and "family" remain categories of authenticity but activism reconfigures the composition of these ideas to emphasize the individual, change, and modernity. Unlike what Souad Dajani (1993) describes in the Occupied Territories, where Palestinians use traditional ideas of the family (gender codes, honor, and so forth) to negotiate cultural identity, activists in Israel seek to unseat honor as the central discourse of family.

Although activists often associate the *place* of honor killings with villages because women's actions are easier to watch and control there, they are not simply rural phenomena, as they also affect women's constructions of self, gender, and nation in urban environments. As we saw earlier, activists consider the problems of Palestinian women in Haifa similar to those women face in villages; questions of honor touch women's lives in extremely deep ways from codes of behavior to threats of violence, as the case of Ichlas demonstrates.[28] While women advocate change and sexual freedom through amutot activities and support each other's decisions within activist friendships, they recognize that in order to make gains for society, their own lives must prove irreproachable to outside evaluation. I knew of a number of women who secretly lived with their boyfriends. One of these women explained, "If I want to work in this society, I have to be accepted by it. It's more important for me to change this society. I know it would be uncomfortable to live with someone in secret, but this is what I would have to pay to still have the chance to work in the community." In this situation, male discourses of sexuality and honor predominate; women's lives are not private but subject to moral judgments from family members and society at large.

This tension is especially evident in the ways activists attempt to protect their privacy while at the same time challenge distinctions between private and public discourses of honor that subjugate women according to terms of honor. One afternoon Wafa told me a story about a former boyfriend. She explained that she left him because she found his questions about her past romantic life intrusive: "One of my exes heard that I had a boyfriend before, and he didn't sleep for the whole night because he heard I had a boyfriend once, and he knew this boyfriend. And this boyfriend told him that he once had a girlfriend and he slept with her. And he thought it was me, and he didn't sleep the whole night." After he challenged her on something she considers "up to the woman to decide," she left him: "Bye-bye. It's none of his business. What's he asking something like that? I'm not interested to know if he's slept with someone. That's his business. You can't possibly come and control my past life. And not the present and not the future also." Sexual decisions are thus not simply matters of romance or love, but are expressions of autonomy, power, and individualism.

This is also evident in the ways female activists manipulate language when they describe themselves as individuals and as a collective group. Several women told me that they consciously try to blur the linguistic boundaries between public and private discourses about the connections between virginity and women's positions in society. Before marriage, Palestinians usually call women banAt, or "girls" (singular bint), which literally means "virgins." When a woman marries, people refer to her as a mara' (wife); however, mara' also translates as "nonvirgin." Many women activists said that they do not know what to call themselves because these terms, mara' and bint, which are commonly used, directly comment on a woman's virginity. Activists joked about what to call women of or past the common age of marriage, including unmarried women in their twenties. To call them banAt would be to use the word commonly associated with young girls, but to refer to them otherwise would be to comment on their virginity; activists reject the idea that virginity belongs to society and instead claim it for individuals. One woman, Rula, explained that this is a dilemma because there are few alternative terms in Arabic. She invests *nisat* with a certain feminist correctness—though nisat and niswan both mean "women" in Arabic (akin to *women* and *ladies* in English):

When I wasn't married, I used to call myself *mara'* not because I am a virgin or not a virgin but because I think *mara'* has no connection with sexuality. You know, niswan are married, too, but I hate this word, too, because it has kind of a meaning that implies a very, very typical woman. *Nisat* is a higher word than *niswan*.

Other activists, like Afnan, concur that "virginity—it is something of security or insurance [in Hebrew, *bitachon*] for women" in terms of how people "read" their value. Attitudes such as this reaffirm female virginity as something essential to a woman's value because, regardless, questions of virginity emerge as defining issues.

Still, activists hope that their personal examples of lifestyle, activism, and nationalism will empower all women to take control of their bodies, lives, and spaces and that this, in turn, will restructure the nation vis-à-vis gendered ideologies of nationalism and activism that stress equality. In practice though, when activists try to live out their ideals of modern everyday life, they risk critique from two sides: families and neighbors find them too modern and fellow activists may see them as too traditional. I believe that activists are seriously interested in finding ways for women to advance in Palestinian society; they identify personally with the agenda they espouse. It is not simply political or theoretical; many activists are young married women and, thus, face the often difficult question of how to practice at home what they say in amutot.

Women's agency is a salient concern for all activists, especially as many activists find that their activism—in terms of gender, not the nation—complicates relationships inside the family (Faier 1997). Usually this is the case when husbands support their wives' activities in amutot but object when their wives bring ideas of gender equality into the home. Sylvia told me about conflicts she has with her husband over what he perceives as her duties as a wife and mother and her interests in women's issues and activism:

He was very nervous and scared about the things I said. I was working at the [Rape Crisis] Center, and I had my own powers. I was thirty-three, something like that, and I was so independent of him. But, I was aware of this fact. All the time he was a good man, but it's not always good for the woman because this is also a form of power over you . . . to control you. I mean, he did everything for me like going to the bank. And when I said no, I want to do my own things, he said that he saw me as a grown child. He said to me that I can make my own career but that I have limits—I shouldn't forget about the family. So all the time we have to discuss things, and the people around us are talking about us. He doesn't give me all the freedom, but I think he makes it very easy for me. It is hard for him to do household chores and get the children ready. You know, I am a feminist, but in the house, it is different.

Sylvia's desire to speak out publicly comes with a price at home; there, she relinquishes her own quests for personal exploration of gender because of the limits set by discussions with her husband. By acting as a "wife"—taking care of the house and children—in ways that resonate with but do not reproduce social convention, Sylvia can express her ideas regardless of community gossip. And, she can, simultaneously, receive her husband's approval, thereby confirming his role in the family. Sylvia inhabits a contradiction here, but she recognizes this and accepts it; for her, what is important is that she is creating a place within the private-public structure in which women's activism can function.

Intimate Spaces

One commonly held assumption among Palestinians and scholars of the Middle East is that women are categorically less powerful than men, and that correspondingly, women's spaces (i.e., the literal and figurative spaces of domestic or private life) are less prestigious than the public realms associated with men. Activists reject this formula as a simplistic representation of the Middle East, but they also reproduce it in the distinctions they themselves draw between their own on-stage and off-stage performances. To be sure, their own distinctions are not bounded with the same bright lines as the reductionist portrayals they critique, but still, for activists, the self occupies a complex terrain defined by the public-private dichotomy they, too, assume to be synecdochic of the Middle East. Publicly, women activists fight for social change, and privately they are aware of their personal problems—such as physical abuse, gossip, and social isolation—as social and cultural problems.

As activists explore what gender means to them personally in their activist projects for the nation, and in relation to the state, they encounter conflict, inconsistency, and contradiction as they try to make the reality of their lives fit their ideals. Sylvia explained this conundrum in the following way: "I look modern but I do not think modern." Although Sylvia prides herself on breaking a number of established gender roles within her community—she has short hair, wears mini skirts, dresses casually, and avoids make-up and jewelry—she says, in practice, she cannot accept women who practice what she herself espouses with regard to sexuality. Still, Sylvia rebukes her son for displaying sexist behavior and sends her daughter to Jewish schools so that she can have different opportunities and greater social freedom than other Palestinian children. Like Sylvia, other activists acknowledge that they have internalized the very traditional ideas of the domestic that they want to discard. It is their self-awareness that confirms them as feminists, they say, since even if they limit their behavior, their reflexive examination of their own attitudes towards gender, honor, family, and tradition distinguishes them from those who accept tradition blindly. I suggest that in this situation, modern identity collapses new private-public distinctions resulting in the reflexive, dual presentation of the self. For example, as a lawyer, Wafa fights legal battles for Palestinian land and women's rights in the Israeli judicial system, but she explains that she subverts her education when she uses it for Palestinian causes, thereby challenging the state's control of her as a Palestinian and a woman. Similarly, feminists who hide live-in boyfriends from public gaze play with social mores, turning them into enabling structures that defy modernity-tradition dichotomies; they use urban and activist networks to conceal yet live out their private lives, and they pronounce their dedication to nationalist and feminist causes. For these feminist activists, the political and the personal are essentially dialectic by the sheer nature of conflict and fracture in their lives.

To the extent that activism opens up ideologies of nationalism for personal interpretation, feminism proves to be an equally problematic issue for female activists; realities of their lives often conflict with their fantasies for future equality. One woman, Selwa, told me, "we don't have a feminist community, only individual feminists who want to work for women but also themselves." All activists who work in women's organizations consider themselves feminists, but this is not the case for women who work in mixed male and female amutot. For example,

Umm Khalil argues that she is "working to help women" and that this is a woman's activity not a feminist activity (cf. Peteet 1991).

In interviews, I asked women what feminism meant to them. Many could not articulate it more than the idea of wanting equality and being different from both Jewish and typical Palestinian women. Others, however, expressed the desire to achieve the power to act freely without public or private censure. For example, Ismahan says that to be a feminist is to "do what I want to, when I want to." Other women said being a feminist is to have the freedom to engage in sexual activity without blame or fear for one's life and reputation.

Sylvia told me that she learned about feminism from volunteering at the Rape Crisis Center, especially when she compared her own ideas about sexuality with those of callers to the hotline. Still, Sylvia recognizes that what is best for her is not always best for other women:

> These women have very different lives from me. Sometimes I can't believe it can be like this because, well, I may say I am a feminist, but, in the home, I am not always. Look at us, I do all the women's work. But then I think who I am, what I believe. Sometimes I bring home "follow me" [call forwarding] from work. When it is a busy night, I think about what men want from women. You know, in the mornings, the lines are very busy. The girls call and they want information. And at night, we sometimes have two or three calls. I mean Arab calls. The girls they say that the woman, all the time, she is one who makes this [rape] happen. They are so very, very afraid not to be virgins. They must be virgins. This is what they think! So sometimes we go with them to the doctor and they make their examination, and they also perform the surgery [hymen reconstruction] so girls can be married.
>
> Stupid thing, this idea! I think if there is a man who believes it [new hymen] he has to lie [to himself]! I told one [woman] to lie to the man. And she says "no, I don't want to lie to the man that I am going to marry." So I told her, "look this [operation] is easier for your life." These things happen all the time. Those girls think that this is the way it has to be, getting operations like this.

Like most feminists working at the hotlines, Sylvia recommends to her callers that they accommodate traditional understandings of virginity and marriage because it will make their lives easier. Yet, activists, through amutot discourses, reject such traditional understandings and say that they are working toward the day when all women can make up their own minds and be free of patriarchy.

I asked Rawia if she thought it was hypocritical to suggest actions that activists themselves do not believe in. She explained that it was not so simple, despite what activists want to achieve in terms of changing women. All women, feminist or not, must face some type of disjuncture in everyday life. When we were talking about this, Rawia showed me an art project that she made while in university, explaining that the clay figures symbolized the difficult lives of Palestinian women. Her explanation of their symbolism is a fitting conclusion to this essay as it encapsulates the public and private nature of Palestinian feminism and activism.

> When I started the project, I thought it was about someone else, not me. Yeah, it's about me. It's about my father and the way he treats me. And my brother and the way he treats me. I mean my father treats me like I don't understand and that he shouldn't bother talking to me. You know, like I have no mind. And my brother treats me that way too. Like I am still a girl.
>
> I thought about the jarra [clay jars] as the typical Arab woman. The typical Arab woman is a very large woman, exactly like that, you know. I started thinking about the form of the pots, and I wanted something new. When a man describes a woman, he describes her like this. [She makes an outline of a curvaceous woman's form with her hands.] Okay, she has shape but I have shape too . . . and hands for raising and protesting. And then I said, I have to make the figures more sharp than soft.
>
> You see, no matter who you will be—the feminist or not—you still have this break, like the break in the pottery. The woman is broken, even those who remain standing. You see, the woman is broken from the inside because she had her own problems. I have my own problems with Farah's mother [her mother-in-law], with Rula [cousin], with Rena [cousin], with everybody. Okay but you see, if you touch this thing [jarra], it is very heavy. She's heavy because she is the center of the family. But she is also heavy because I don't like it when people expect a lot from her. Like you expect the woman to be well prepared and dressed, but I also want it so that I cannot be that way when you expect it from me.

I think my family, they were shocked when they saw this exhibition. Oh my God, my sister did this? I think it was tough on them because it was a critique of the family. But then again, from the other side, they said, well maybe she is right. I think that period of my life was very interesting—my relationships were very interesting. I don't know when, but there was a switch. That's when I started to call myself a feminist.

Notes

1. Throughout this chapter, I use the word "Palestinian" rather than "Israeli Arab" or "Arab Israeli." My usage reflects the ways activists identify themselves. This article is based on research conducted from December 1993 to December 1995, and in March 2000. Research was generously funded by the Indiana University Center for Philanthropy, Sigma Xi, Indiana University Research and University Graduate School Division, and the Aspen Institute Fund for Nonprofit Research. I owe special thanks to Carol Greenhouse for providing invaluable insight, guidance, and support for all phases of this project.

2. See Abu-Lughod 1998; Badran and Cooke 1990; Cowan 1991; Dubisch 1991; Hasso 1998; Herzfeld 1991; Kapchan 1994; Peteet 1991.

3. See Kandiyotti 1991; Moghadam 1993; Chatty and Rabo 1997; see also Aretxaga 1997 on Northern Ireland.

4. See Lustick 1982; Masalha 1993; Rekhess 1990; Sa'di 1996; Smooha 1990.

5. Sa'ar (1998) notes that by special petition, some Christian Palestinians do participate in the military. In March 2000, a Palestinian family won a unique court case after a Jewish residential community denied them the right to purchase a house there. However, this case is extremely unusual; Jewish sellers and landowners often refuse Palestinians petitions for housing in primarily Jewish areas. When it does occur, tensions often ensue (see Rabinowitz 1997).

6. See Breckenridge and van der Veer 1993 on internal orientalism.

7. All names in the text are pseudonyms. In some cases, when the activist is easily identifiable or because of social or political risk, I have altered other identifying markers. I have done this not to deceive the reader but to protect those who freely shared their thoughts and opinions with me.

8. My usage of "Israel's Palestinian sector" is not to denote a formalized sector within Israel. Rather, it is to highlight that Palestinian citizens often exist in separate economic, social, cultural, and political worlds than Jewish citizens; some of this separation is formal and structural such as the education system, family courts, and military service requirements.

9. In order to further the development of an autonomous Palestinian not-for-profit sector, *Itijaah*, a Palestinian umbrella organization, was formed at the end of 1995. It is unclear how Itijaah will impact programming, fundraising, or coalition building among Palestinian amutot. According to many activists, the Palestinian amutot sector is becoming increasingly divisive and competitive despite Itijaah.

10. See Faier 1999b on Palestinian activism in nongovernmental organizations.

11. Haifa is Israel's third largest city (population 250,000); Palestinians comprise approximately 12 percent of the city's population (Haifa Municipality Report 1994).

12. Nearly all activists, men and women, told me that they became active in committees during the years before or after their education. Many activists were also active within the Communist Youth.

13. I interviewed a number of individuals who only used amutot as service providers; they told me that they did not identify themselves as activists or consider themselves part of the activist community.

14. Volunteering carries almost no social capital outside the activist community although, within it, one can improve or develop a good reputation by volunteering for the nation. In the case of public gossip or a question of one's moral character involving an activist, the activist can appeal to their volunteer activities as collateral against a questionable reputation. They stress the "*méconnaissance*" (Bourdieu 1977) of the rumor by questioning how one could do such work for the common good if one is morally flawed. Usually this defuses the situation, but not always. I knew of two women who worried that rumors of their sexual behavior would jeopardize their family's approval of their living and working alone in Haifa. These women also expressed fear that they would lose their lives if they returned to their villages. In both cases, the women found solutions to their problems. One woman returned home, safely, for a period to prove that she was acting morally, and the other woman ceased her ties with the activist community except to participate in demonstrations.

15. Every activist I knew had participated, at one point or another, in demonstrations, which require a police permit if attendance will be greater than fifty individuals. Still, police intervention is common and fighting often erupts. Consequently, many activists anticipate the possibility of arrest and many have been arrested. Although regulations for many state jobs such as the educational systems have eased regulations on hiring individuals with arrest records, activists explain that having a record hinders their ability to secure some types of employment. See Faier 1999a, 1999b on demonstrations, violence, and activism.

16. According to activists, Palestinian women normally marry in their late teens or early twenties and men marry in their late twenties or early thirties, depending on their financial position.

17. In 1998, the Palestinian feminist organization Kayan (literally, "being") formed. In 2000 I found that most women activists I knew previously from Jewish-Palestinian feminist organizations and Palestinian amutot had left these organizations to work together as a collective in Kayan.

18. I heard a few people talking about being "of the same hand." This is a metaphor for unity and cooperation likening individuals to fingers and society to the hand as a structure. If all the fingers do not work together then the hand is useless.

19. See Faier 1999a on the relationship between nationalism, democratic ideologies of equality, and amutot discourses.

20. Frances Hasso (1998) documents that for Popular Front for the Liberation of Palestine (PFLP) activists in the Occupied Territories, women challenge the exclusivity of feminist and nationalist activities.

21. See Gilmore 1987; Ginat 1987; Herzfeld 1980; Peristiany 1974; Peters 1990.

22. Gideon Kressel argues that the concept of honor indicated by 'irD relates the honor of the patrilineal group with "the sex organs of its daughters" (1981:141).

23. See Cohen 1989; Glazer and Wahiba Abu Ras 1994; Kressel 1981; Wood 1993.

24. See Faier 1999b on the relationship between writing the names of women who have been murdered for family honor and the written display of destroyed Palestinian villages during Land Day celebrations. While writing the names of women challenges traditional linkages between honor and gender, writing the names of destroyed villages reaffirms linkages among nation, land, and honor. Concerning the latter example, one activist recited the proverb "al Ard mithl al 'irD" (the land is like honor). In both cases, activists explicitly described the connection between writing names and remembering people and places.

25. Activists later filed a complaint against the police, arguing that by sending Druze police to a village where the killing of a Druze woman had occurred, the police were conspiring with the villagers and creating an unsafe environment for the demonstration.

26. See Rattner 1994 and Zureik 1988 on Arab and Jewish attitudes toward police.

27. Fernea and Hocking (1992) note similar types of exchanges between Israeli political prisoners and their supporters outside jails.

28. See Shokheid (1980) on honor and capital in Israeli cities.

James M. Freeman and Nguyen Dinh Huu

"Best Interests" and the Repatriation of

Vietnamese Unaccompanied Minors

In this essay we discuss what happens to a vulnerable population, unaccompanied minors under the age of sixteen, when they are caught up in events that they cannot control but that profoundly affect their lives. The formative event affecting the children in this study occurred before most of them were born. On 30 April 1975, after thirty years of intermittent war, Saigon fell to the communists and came under the control of North Vietnam. The replacement of one state by another, and subsequent political and economic measures implemented to create a new socialist society in South Vietnam, prompted the exodus over the next twenty years of one to two million people seeking political asylum. About half who fled were children, and at least 5 percent of these were unaccompanied minors.

We focus on children who arrived in countries of first asylum after 16 June 1988 for Hong Kong and varying dates in March 1989 for Southeast Asian countries. These dates mark the beginning of a new region-wide policy of refugee status determination for Vietnamese asylum seekers. The Office of the United Nations High Commissioner for Refugees (UNHCR), countries of first asylum, and countries of resettlement created this policy titled the Comprehensive Plan of Action. At first, Vietnam refused to take back asylum seekers; later Vietnam allowed them to return provided they did so voluntarily and "with dignity." Many people who were denied refugee status refused to return to Vietnam. For several years they were allowed to remain in countries of first asylum and were housed in harsh detention camps unless they chose to repatriate voluntarily. Beginning in 1995 (or 1993 for unaccompanied minors) the policy regarding these asylum seekers changed. With the assent of Vietnam, they were forcibly repatriated to their homeland.

While residing in the detention camps, the children became part of a community without a territory, a violent and destructive arena where, in order to survive, they created a temporary social order vastly different from the world of children in Vietnam. Although often portrayed as victims, the children of the camps were not helpless. They soon learned that they would not be repatriated unless they chose to do so. Many opted not to be part of the "voluntary" process of repatriation and "reintegration" envisioned by those in positions of authority. The children, influenced by adults in the camps, devised forms of political resistance and adaptive strategies that disconcerted and embarrassed the officials and agencies entrusted with their protection and care who had tried to coerce nonrefugees to repatriate voluntarily.

The world of the children was disrupted again when they were forcibly repatriated to a homeland that had changed in the years they had been away. But they too had changed, causing concern for uneasy Vietnamese officials, social workers, and relatives who had to cope with them. Nordic Assistance for Repatriated Vietnamese (NARV), an international agency, was set up and given a contract by UNHCR to help the children "reintegrate" to Vietnam, with the expectation that these children would be remade along the lines of those who had never left. But, after years in the camps, the children have different experiences and expectations; their views and behaviors do not fit easily the social environment to which they have been returned. Many families sent out these children in the hopes that they would resettle and then be able to help their families in Vietnam. These children feel shame because they have failed their families. Some children are distrusted and shunned because they are viewed as having become tainted with outside, Western influences. These conflicts are not easily resolvable.

Since 1988 we have researched and provided assistance to unaccompanied minors who fled Vietnam and were incarcerated in detention camps. Some are orphans; others saw their parents killed during their flight; still others were separated from their parents or relatives during the escape; many were sent out alone while their families remained in Vietnam. Some children were resettled in countries such as the United States; more were repatriated to Vietnam. In addition to the United States and Vietnam, our studies have been conducted in Hong Kong, Singapore, Malaysia, the Philippines, Indonesia, and Thailand.

In 1988 we found that unaccompanied minors resettling in the United States were having a much more difficult time adjusting to their new country than had earlier arrivals. We also found that they were spending longer periods of time in refugee camps than their predecessors. This prompted us to found a nonprofit voluntary organization, Aid to Refugee Children Without Parents (ARCWP) to assist unaccompanied minors in refugee camps. In 1995 we extended our assistance activities to unaccompanied minors repatriated to Vietnam. Because they are not considered refugees, we changed the name of our organization to Aid to Children without Parents (ACWP). Our assistance activities have provided us entrée to the refugee camps and to Vietnam. They are therefore an indispensable part of our research and the basis of our advocacy views and critiques.

Refugee unaccompanied minors are considered to be especially vulnerable and in need of special protection. But governments and international organizations failed to protect Vietnamese unaccompanied minors. Political considerations prompted officials to disregard and deny indications that all was not well. Instead, they used terms such as "best interests," "durable solution," and "voluntary repatriation," to justify their actions. These terms are part of the language used by UNHCR in dealing with people seeking asylum.

The Office of the United Nations High Commissioner for Refugees was set up to provide protection and assistance to refugees and to seek permanent solutions to the problems of refugees (Goodwin-Gill 1983: 127–48; Holborn 1975:55–157; Loescher 1993). Sometimes, through the concept of "good offices," UNHCR assists persons who are not legally refugees (Holborn 1975:434–49). UNHCR also has become involved in activities that go beyond its original mandate set by the 1951 Convention on Refugees. Examples include tracing to facilitate family reunification and protection of unaccompanied minors (Muntarbhorn 1992:43–44). Both activities have provoked controversies when applied to the Vietnamese. UNHCR developed a narrow definition of family that focused only on parents and children, discounting the wider notions of extended family of Vietnamese asylum seekers. UNHCR then disregarded this view when it became expedient. This affected decisions related to determining the best interests of children. Similarly, UNHCR employed a contradictory notion of culture. At times this organization portrayed culture in essentialist terms to promote the policy that it is better to send people back to the culture with which they are familiar. At other times UNHCR emphasized that it is better to send people back because the culture had changed, was safer, and offered improved opportunities. UNHCR gave little consideration to the varying circumstances that returnees actually encountered.

The definitions of family and culture used by UNHCR are related to the concept of durable solution, which is intended to provide a humane and consistent principle for dealing with refugees. The durable solutions advocated by UNHCR are, in order of preference, voluntary repatriation to the country from which a refugee has fled, integration in a country of first asylum, and, finally, resettlement in a third country. The solution of voluntary repatriation is predicated on three principles. The first is that it is safe for the refugee to return, second that the refugee willingly chooses to return (forcible repatriation is illegal in international law), and, third that repatriation to one's own country of origin is always the best choice. If conditions are unfavorable for repatriation, then the next best choice is to integrate the refugee on the spot. To that end, assistance should be given to enable the refugee to become economically self-sufficient. If integration is not feasible or allowable, as has been the case with most Vietnamese refugees in countries of first asylum, the next best choice is resettlement elsewhere. W. Courtland Robinson has observed that from the start of the Indochinese exodus, UNHCR strongly favored repatriation (1998:24). In the case of Vietnamese children this has become source of bitter contention.

Vietnamese Refugees and the Comprehensive Plan of Action

After the fall of South Vietnam in 1975, the new government, later called the Socialist Republic of Vietnam, incarcerated hundreds of thousands of people in re-education or prison camps, relocated several million people to the countryside, nationalized major industries and businesses, confiscated much private property, issued new currency, and intruded into the family to bring about an allegiance to the new regime. During this same period, Vietnam failed to bring in adequate foreign assistance, suffered the American economic embargo that lasted until 1994, and became embroiled in a border clash with China and the war and eleven-year military occupation of Cambodia. The consequences were economic crises, chronic food shortages, widespread malnutrition, and the disruption of families. Millions of Vietnamese citizens, including supporters of socialism, became disenchanted with the new regime. The exodus of boat-people refugees began. About 150,000 refugees had fled previously when Saigon fell. Between 1978 and 1982, several hundred thousand people escaped to countries of first asylum. The exodus continued until the early 1990s. An estimated 10 percent perished along the way (Richardson 1979:34; Rumbaut 1995:238).

In the late 1970s, countries of first asylum, though initially reluctant, allowed refugees from Vietnam to remain temporarily until they were resettled in North America, Europe, and Australia. The expectation was that conditions would improve in Vietnam and refugee departures would decline. But boat people, including North Vietnamese, continued to flee (Zolberg, Suhrke, and Aguayo 1989:164–68). By the late 1980s, countries were less willing to accept the Vietnamese either temporarily or permanently. Up to this time, all Vietnamese escapees were automatically considered refugees. In 1988 Hong Kong instituted "screening" of new arrivals to determine whether they were refugees or simply "economic migrants" who should return to Vietnam.[1]

Faced with this situation, in 1989 UNHCR convened an international conference attended by seventy-seven nations. Fifty-one of them signed the Comprehensive Plan of Action, which instituted screening as of March 1989 to determine refugee status. The actual cutoff date in March varies in different countries. Over two hundred thousand asylum seekers landed in refugee camps after the 1989 cutoff date. Most were screened out and advised to repatriate, though the rates varied widely by country. By 1995, no country of first asylum would accept any new arrivals, and UNHCR was advocating the forcible repatriation of nonrefugees.[2]

Vitit Muntarbhorn describes the Comprehensive Plan of Action as "a package of measures interlinking the country of origin (Vietnam) with first-asylum countries and resettlement countries. The country of origin agreed to deter clandestine departures—for example, by means of a more extensive public information campaign—and to promote the Orderly Departure Program [legal emigration]. The first-asylum countries undertook to guarantee temporary refuge to those arriving in the region." The objectives of the Comprehensive Plan of Action were to prevent organized clandestine departures from Vietnam, encourage and promote regular and legal emigration from Vietnam, maintain guarantees of first asylum, establish consistent refugee status determination procedures throughout the countries of first asylum, continue the resettlement of long-staying as well as newly determined Vietnamese refugees, and to repatriate to Vietnam those asylum seekers who had been rejected as refugees (1992:48–49, 193–200).

Unaccompanied minors under the age of sixteen were assumed to be unable to articulate adequately their situation. UNHCR recommended that, instead of being subjected to an interview with an immigration officer of the country of first asylum, the child should be interviewed by a Special Committee including social workers and lawyers familiar with children's issues. UNHCR would provide advisors, including a "Durable Solutions Counselor," who is an expert in child development. The committee would determine the refugee status of the child and then, the durable solution in the child's best interests. For children sixteen to eighteen years of age, regular status determination procedures would be used, after which the Special Committee would consider their durable solution. Children were supposed to be identified on arrival, documentation compiled within the first few days, and decisions implemented expeditiously in the best interests of each unaccompanied minor.[3]

Different countries disagreed on how to set up Special Committees, refugee determination rates varied widely from about 10 percent in Hong Kong to over 40 percent in the Philippines, and in 1996 the Philippines finally decided not to repatriate their remaining screened-out asylum seekers. There were widespread complaints about flaws, bias, and corruption in the screening process of the Comprehensive Plan of Action. UNHCR has rejected allegations against it but admitted that they might have occurred with non-UNHCR employees.[4]

The most vexing problem was that of screened-out asylum seekers; many were unaccompanied minors. At first Vietnam refused to take them back, so they were stuck in camps even if they wanted to return. With the development of the Comprehensive Plan of Action, Vietnam agreed to accept them if they returned voluntarily and with dignity. But many refused to repatriate, fearing persecution as well as enforcement of Articles 88 and 89 of Vietnam's criminal code, which stipulated that illegal emigration was a crime punishable by incarceration in jail. Even when Vietnam announced that it would not retaliate against returnees, except for those who led the escapes, many people were distrustful of Vietnam's changing attitudes and still refused to repatriate.[5] Other screened-out asylum seekers remained in the camps in the hopes that a miracle would occur and they could be resettled. Many received letters and money from relatives living overseas who urged them not to repatriate. Some detainees intimidated others to prevent them from returning. Thousands of children remained in camps for five years or more.

Countries of first asylum delayed up to eighteen months the establishment of the special procedures for evaluating children. Christine Mougne of UNHCR explains that the procedures had never been field-tested nor even discussed at the field level before implementation. "Bureaucratic delays conspired with practical problems such as recruiting suitably qualified interviewers," with the consequence that the procedure got off to "a lamentably slow start." Because of this, there was a large backlog of cases. She concludes, "For me, the tragedy [of the delays] is that the unreasonably long time spent in camps has inevitably taken its toll on these children and young adults. After two, three, or more years separated from their families and exposed to the violent and lawless camp culture, the rate of delinquency and other disturbance is all too high. Reintegration in these circumstances is not going to be easy" (Nichols and White 1993:54–65). (The camps were sometimes violent but hardly lawless; many were controlled internally by gangs, who ran the camps according to various rules in conjunction with camp guards.)

Many unaccompanied minors had fled Vietnam not with their parents but with other relatives who were part of their extended family. Over the protests of critics who felt that the Vietnamese extended family was being disregarded, the UNHCR decided that "minors in camp without their parents would only be linked for the purposes of refugee status determination with adults who qualify as 'principal caregivers' in place of the parents." Alan Nichols and Paul White summarize UNHCR Officer Mougne's explanation: "This position . . . was reached, not out of any disrespect for the Vietnamese family traditions, but rather by the desire to protect each minor's options. To arbitrarily transfer a child to the guardianship of substitute parents for joint processing through the regular procedures would deprive him/her not only of having his/her own claim on refugee status considered but also of having a thorough examination into the durable solution in his/her best interest" (1993:55, emphasis in original).

As a consequence, many minor children were separated from their relatives and adult siblings who were given refugee status and were resettled; the children remained behind in the camps awaiting interview by the Special Committee. This led to heavy criticism of the UNHCR position, particularly when children were separated from relatives who had been their de facto parents for years. In 1995 UNHCR responded with a different justification, tacitly admitting that there were defects in the screening process, "Occasionally siblings were given different decisions. Such cases required careful handling at the appeals stage. UNHCR came to the difficult decision that unmeritorious positive decisions in the case of one sibling was not reason for UNHCR to support the case of another sibling on appeal."[6]

Mougne, representing UNHCR, also drew criticism for claiming that later Vietnamese unaccompanied minors were sent out as anchors so that they could later bring out other relatives. Since they were not refugees fleeing persecution, they should be returned to Vietnam. A major aim of UNHCR was to discourage the escape of children from Vietnam. Deterrence will only happen, she wrote, "when parents in Vietnam realize that sending their children out alone will no longer lead to their own resettlement" (Mougne 1989:37). To this, Anne Wagley Gow, a former UNHCR legal officer and harsh critic of UNHCR, responded:

> Attributing such motivations to Vietnamese parents is both culturally insensitive and erroneous. Multiple factors enter into a parent's decision to send a child to seek asylum, the most obvious of which is a desire for the child to be free from a future of persecution due to the family's social or political history. The decision is an agonizing one, and simplifying and generalizing the intentions of the parents does not contribute to an understanding of the situation of individual unaccompanied minors. (Gow 1991:30–32)

The decisions of the Special Committee to repatriate unaccompanied minors in their best interests contradicted the wishes of the parents who had sent the children out of Vietnam in the first place. Nichols and White ask, "What are the 'best interests' of the child? Who determines it?" Whether or not parents wanted to join their children later, the UNHCR emphasis on returning these children to their culture would thwart the parents' original wishes and cause anguish for the children in the camps, since they had failed to fulfill their parents' wishes (Nichols and White 1993:55–56).

Living in Detention

Because of bureaucratic delays and at the urging of parents and relatives, unaccompanied minors remained in the camps for years. They had a much harder time than children who had parents to protect and guide them. Unaccompanied minors endured harsh treatment by guards, overcrowding, inadequate food, physical violence, sexual abuse, little or no education or job training, and nothing to do. Theirs was an emotionally starved environment with little or no parental or adult guidance. The children were brutalized, depressed, lonely, and anxious over an uncertain future. Camp authorities and UNHCR pressed them to choose to return home, while their own families in Vietnam frequently urged them to remain in the camps. The children feared that they might be persecuted or mistreated if they voluntarily chose to return home. In their view, they had failed their families because they had been turned down for resettlement. After risking their lives to escape from Vietnam, they were particularly distressed that they might be forcibly repatriated. Many children chose to remain in the camps as a lesser evil than repatriation, hoping that they might be resettled at the last moment. The children responded to these stressful conditions in a variety of ways. A youth who had been jailed in the Chi Ma Wan camp, Hong Kong, for beating another child senseless, told us, "I simply lost control; I didn't care what would happen." He added, "This camp is divided into the 'haves,' who get money from relatives in other countries, and the 'have-nots' like me, who have no relatives or money. The 'haves' buy extra food; all I eat is the watery soup in which they throw MSG." Many children participated in mass protests against Vietnam and UNHCR. A boy in Palawan camp, the Philippines, said to us, "I won't go back; they'll have to carry me out." Others in the same camp hoped for a miracle, "I am doing very well in school, so maybe some country will give me refugee status." Many children were devastated by the camp experience. A girl in Hong Kong's violent Shek Kong camp said to us, "I am afraid but I do not know how to deal with my fear." A girl in Sikhiu camp, Thailand, spoke with despair, "My family does not want me, I have no relatives in the camp and I have nowhere to go. I just live day by day." In Palawan First Asylum Center in the Philippines, a boy confided to an American volunteer that "he sometimes prays to God that he will die in his sleep because he cannot commit suicide which is against his faith." In the same camp, a boy who was caught trying to run away was beaten with bamboo "because it leaves no marks; however the belt marks that remained on his neck could not be hidden" (Furcinitti 1993:12). A girl whom we talked with in Galang, Indonesia, subsequently burned herself to death when told to repatriate.[7]

UNHCR officials found themselves portrayed as the enemy and not the protector of refugees when, acting within the guidelines of the Comprehensive Plan of Action and the immigration policies of countries of first asylum, they advocated voluntary repatriation for screened-out asylum seekers (Mougne 1990:25). Those who were affected interpreted this as denying them protection from the communists and as favoring the Socialist Republic of Vietnam. Tens of thousands of screened-out adults and children, feeling betrayed by the organization that was supposed to protect them and disillusioned by what they considered to be inconsistent and unfair decisions on their refugee status, refused to be repatriated, preferring to remain in the camps despite terrible living conditions. As the situation of unaccompanied minors in these camps became known, criticism centered on UNHCR's failure to provide them with adequate protection and long delays in establishing Special Committees for their evaluation.

In desperation to show positive results, UNHCR intensified its efforts to persuade unaccompanied minors to repatriate by reducing their food rations, curtailing their schooling, badgering them to repatriate, and offering them money if they did so. In Hong Kong, with UNHCR approval, detainees were relocated from one camp to another so that they would have no feeling of "permanence." The detainees resisted; and this provoked a police raid on Whitehead Detention Center in 1994 in which hundreds of people were injured. Riots and protests occurred in other countries of first asylum.[8]

The longer the detainees refused to leave, the more they resolved to stay and resist camp authorities. Children were among the protesters, as we saw during our 1994 visit to Hong Kong's High Island Detention Center. We went there because we were establishing a children's shelter in Hue, central Vietnam, and many of the children came from that area. At first the children refused to speak. One youth brandished his fist and shouted, "I'm not telling you my name! I want you UNHCR to be as disturbed and embarrassed as possible for returning me!" Another youth commanded, "Don't talk to them! They're UNHCR. Why are you in that room? Stay away from them!" We assured them, "We are not UNHCR and we're not here to tell you what to do, but if you do go back to central Vietnam and need some assistance, we'll be there to help you." They calmed down and told us they feared forced repatriation, being returned to relatives who did not want them, and finding a Vietnam for which they were unprepared, since their schooling had been interrupted. Many were willing to return, but not on the basis of the vague promises of help offered by UNHCR; they were looking for very specific assistance; they knew what they wanted and needed.

UNHCR and other officials expressed grave concern about the children but the only solution they considered was repatriation. A high UNHCR official said to us, "The detention camps should be closed as soon as possible. It is not human." A high Hong Kong refugee official said, "I wouldn't want my daughter in that camp." A dispirited UNHCR officer, unable to protect the children in the camp where he worked, but widely liked by detainees for his efforts, told us, "I apologize profusely and say how embarrassed I am. These kids are in terrible condition, and there's nothing I can do." Six months later, he was no longer working in that camp.

Nowhere to Return

In Vietnam, specific cases of repatriated children were difficult to monitor. The Special Committees and UNHCR wrote reports claiming that the decisions on the children were in their "best interests," and Nordic Assistance to Repatriated Vietnamese (NARV), a Scandinavian agency under contract to UNHCR to help repatriated minors adjust to Vietnam, supported the UNHCR view with its own glowing reports. To question this view and show a less rosy reality required additional observers in the detention camps or in Vietnam who could contradict the official reports. Permission to visit camps was difficult to obtain. In Vietnam, the children were widely dispersed. To visit one child might require as much as two days of travel. Permission to visit them had to be secured first from the local provincial officials of the Department of Labor, Invalids, and Social Affairs (DELISA) and from NARV. Officials were uneasy about inquiries, and NARV wanted to protect its public image and contract with UNHCR. In the cases below, we visited the camps in which the children were detained, we had neutral observers in the camps who contradicted the official statements, and we visited the children after they had been repatriated.

James Freeman visited Vietnam in 1993, 1994, and 2000; Nguyen Dinh Huu observed children in Vietnam in 1991 and eight more times between 1993 and 2000. In 1993, we found a sixteen-year-old girl living on the floor of a coffee shop in Cholon, Ho Chi Minh City. We had first met her in Sikhiu, a grim detention camp in Thailand. Her stepfather had sent her out of Vietnam. She sobbed that she should never have left Sikhiu. Authorities had sent her back to her village in Vietnam; upon arrival, she found that her entire family had left the country. In that same year, we interviewed a twelve-year-old boy who had returned to Haiphong only to find that his mother had disappeared. His voice quavered, "If I had realized that I had no place to return to, I would not have left Whitehead. I would have never come back to Vietnam" (Nguyen and Freeman 1993).

Before children are repatriated, UNHCR claims that they locate relatives in Vietnam who can receive the children. The boy had been told that his mother was waiting for him, so he volunteered to return. NARV had not realized that the boy was on his own. After our interview, they searched for and found his mother in Ho Chi Minh City. They claimed that this case was an exception.

In August 1994 we returned to Vietnam to visit this boy and other children whom we had interviewed the previous year. The NARV office in Hanoi informed us that they kept records on a child for six months after the file was closed; then they sent the file to UNHCR. Once sent off, there was no way to follow up on a case unless the child or the child's relatives went to the NARV office for additional assistance. Even so, their earlier file was no longer available. NARV claimed that many people came to their office for help. The twelve-year-old boy from Haiphong was not one of them. We were never able to discover his whereabouts. At his last known address, people said he had simply disappeared.[9]

UNHCR and NARV claimed that most repatriated unaccompanied minors reintegrated well over time. We did interview children who seemed to have adjusted well. They had been returned to their biological parents. Children sent back to stepparents, other relatives, or to no one at all often suffered grievously.

Because many children refused to repatriate, in late June 1993, UNHCR, in cooperation with the Socialist Republic of Vietnam, began "Operation Family Reunion," later renamed the softer-sounding "Family Reunion Program." UNHCR justified their action as being "reaffirmed in the 1951 United Nations Convention Related to the Status of Refugees," and further stated, "UNHCR believes that family reunion is of paramount importance for each child separated from his or her family and living in detention. . . . A minor has fundamental rights which include a normal family environment."[10] Operation Family Reunion consisted of repatriating unaccompanied minors, often against their will, if a relative in Vietnam would accept them. NARV workers, accompanied by a Vietnamese official of DELISA, asked parents or relatives of the children to accept them in return for cash and other assistance. As one man explained to us, "I was very poor, but with officials telling me to take back my niece, how could I refuse?"

In doing this, UNHCR shifted the emphasis of two of its long-standing practices. They moved from voluntary repatriation to forced return. They justified this as in the best interests of a minor by getting a parent or relative to approve of it. Second, they abandoned the principle of reunification only with parents or "primary caregivers." UNHCR had used that principle in separating children in the camps from older siblings who had been their de facto parents because they were not "primary caregivers." Now, however, UNHCR claimed that it is best to send children back to their country of origin. Because some children had no parents, UNHCR sent unaccompanied minors to any relative who offered to be a caregiver. Distant relatives who had had little or no contact with these children, were designated as "primary caregivers." Not only did they receive cash assistance, they also were able to get hold of the repatriation allowances of the children, given to them to help them reintegrate. Many adults used the money for their own purposes (Freeman and Nguyen 1996:30).

UNHCR expected NARV to close cases quickly and call them "successes" and "happy endings." UNHCR was concerned that recommending resettlement in particular cases would give "false hope" to remaining screened-out asylum seekers, and this would encourage them not to return. But by recommending repatriation "in the best interests of the child," when it was clearly inhumane and harmful to the child, they hardened the resistance of asylum seekers, and provoked mass protests (Freeman and Nguyen 1996:28).

On 15 January 1994, Ngo Van Ha, a sixteen-year-old orphan, was removed from Hong Kong's Tai A Chau Detention Center in preparation for his repatriation to Vietnam. He was to be returned "in his best interest" even though an uncle who had allegedly abused him refused to take him back, his younger siblings had been thrown out of their house and were working as servants for nonrelatives, and a relative in the United States had offered to sponsor him. On Ha's behalf, more than two thousand Vietnamese detainees of Tai A Chau staged a mass demonstration, sit-in, and hunger strike which lasted three and half days. Newspapers throughout the world featured Ha's story with articles critical of the Hong Kong government and UNHCR. Human rights organizations urged humane treatment for Ha. Both Hong Kong and UNHCR officials admitted to us unofficially that the Ha case got out of hand, caused them much embarrassment, heightened the detainees' distrust of officials, and set back voluntary repatriation by several months. Faced with a continuous barrage of negative publicity, the Special Committee in Hong Kong recommended that Ha be resettled in the United States, where Ha now lives.[11]

Because his case provoked international attention, Ha was given a decision that is an exception to the rule but which falls within the UNHCR mandate. But what about other children who have not come to the attention of the public? NARV staff in the Mekong Delta took Freeman to visit a repatriated orphan whose parents had been killed by Thai pirates. The girl was withdrawn; she was wearing white medicinal patches on her temples to relieve a three-day-long headache. Her uncles had taken her repatriation allowance for their own use. Her grandmother said to Freeman, "I can protect her as long as I live, but what will happen to her after I die?" NARV staff were deeply concerned about the girl and wrote this in their reports.

An orphaned girl from Thua Thien Hue Province was lured back to Vietnam by the promise of assistance only to be denied it when she returned because there was a discrepancy in her case profile. Nguyen heard a NARV staff worker promise assistance to her uncle. The girl would not have returned and her uncle would not have agreed to accept her had they not been promised support (Nguyen and Freeman 1994).

Once a child returned to Vietnam, the responsibility for that child rested with Vietnamese authorities. But they were overwhelmed with the numbers of children, including orphans and street children, who were in dire need of assistance. We met many Vietnamese officials and social workers who had dedicated their lives to assisting children, but their resources fell far short of what they needed. In this situation, unaccompanied minors were particularly at risk.

Because NARV worked in Vietnam under a UNHCR contract, they were dependent on the directives and goodwill of UNHCR. When they were asked to help UNHCR persuade unaccompanied minors to repatriate, this affected the credibility of NARV in the detention camps. Officials and staff in many organizations, including UNHCR, told us that UNHCR did not want to hear about cases that failed in Vietnam and only cared that they were settled as quickly as possible. Whether true or not, this belief had a chilling effect on NARV field staff. They filed reports that were more positive than warranted by the situation.

In addition, some NARV staff told us that they did not agree with some of the home assessments that were conducted before unaccompanied minors were repatriated, but that UNHCR did not want to hear about failures, so they filed overly positive reports. One worker pointedly blamed UNHCR for this: "Children have been returned to relatives who said they could not take care of them, and to families where a parent is a drug addict. Those children should not have been brought back. But my superior said, 'do not recommend; just follow the orders of UNHCR.'"

While most of the NARV employees were dedicated and hardworking, their organization faced structural problems based on style of operation; these problems seriously interfered with their ability to function effectively in Vietnam. One worker said to us, "In 1994 we have a budget of $800,000 for staff and other expenses, and only $500,000 for unaccompanied minors." High salaries and expensive benefits paid to foreign staff and salaries to Vietnamese staff that were four to twelve times the salaries of ordinary Vietnamese workers caused resentment among other Vietnamese, and some Vietnamese officials were said to have obstructed projects because of this. Vietnamese officials in Hanoi told us they were concerned about the disruptive influence of certain foreign voluntary organizations and development projects which distributed large sums of money to families and communities, but that they had bowed to international pressure to allow NARV into Vietnam.

The most serious concern expressed by the NARV staff was that the job training the unaccompanied minors received did not lead to employment. One staff member said, "I know of no placement in jobs after the completion of training programs and the acquisition of job skills. This is a consequence of the bad economy in which jobs are not available."

In February 1994 the Fifth Steering Committee of the International Conference on Indochinese Refugees recommended that all unaccompanied minors be removed from the camps by the end of that year.[12] The NARV project was scheduled to close at the same time except for a remaining skeleton crew. These deadlines both created and perpetuated problems. First, to repatriate and disperse them quickly, UNHCR continued to send unaccompanied minors to virtually any relative who was willing to take them. Given the money inducements that were offered, some relatives accepted repatriated unaccompanied minors even if they had little capability or interest in taking care of them. This problem was especially acute in the central Vietnamese province of Thua Thien Hue, which was undergoing its third straight year of drought and famine. Officials of the province sought assistance to avert disaster. They worried about the condition of children, including repatriated unaccompanied minors, who were already being neglected. Despite these serious problems and the failure of NARV to contact one-third of the repatriated children, UNHCR continued to return more children to this area. Second, the NARV staff workers were disturbed and distracted by the prospect that their jobs would soon end. They told us that this affected their performance. Third, many NARV staff feared that difficult cases would remain unresolved. The staff could not address the serious long-lasting traumas suffered by children during their escape or their life in the camps. Fourth, as the closing date approached, unused funds were distributed with less concern for their effect and more to simply get rid of the money. Fifth, cases were closed with the claim that they were "happy endings," even though they did not reflect actual success. Finally, as previously mentioned, six months after a case was closed the files were cleared and sent off, effectively preventing any follow-up or further assistance for those still in need.

The deadline for returning the children was not met. The Vietnamese government delayed accepting the children back home. By the end of 1994, most of NARV's assistance activities had ended, and by March 1995 their children's program ceased altogether. However, several thousand unaccompanied minors still remained in the camps.

In Whose Best Interest?

In August 1995 UNHCR published an upbeat report on repatriated boat people, claiming that they were being well cared for and were benefiting from the new Vietnamese economic reforms, "Returnees can hope to start a fresh life, with a substantial repatriation grant and the help of our offices and those of other institutions. . . . Thanks to a new climate in the countries of origin [Vietnam and Laos], these economies are now booming beyond the recognition of the desperate migrants of 1989 and 1990."[13] (UNHCR 1995a: 10–11).

UNHCR's glowing accounts failed to mention that repatriated unaccompanied minors were neglected, hungry, and mistreated. They had no future in the new Vietnamese economy. NARV itself finally recognized this. Their final report stated that many repatriated unaccompanied minors faced severe problems and regretted returning to Vietnam. The children we interviewed said they would have preferred to stay in the detention camps, where at least they had friends and two or three meals a day (NARV Final Report 1995).

What happened to two brothers and a sister illustrates how children at risk were hustled back to Vietnam, dumped, and forgotten. They were born in Binh Thuan Province, central Vietnam in 1981, 1984, and 1985 (respectively). On 21 March 1988, they escaped from Vietnam with their parents and a nineteen-year-old cousin. The children were then seven, four, and three years old. They traveled through Cambodia, hoping to reach Thailand. Their guide deserted them, and they became lost. A Cambodian found them and led them to a village, where they remained for a year. In their second attempt to cross the border, they were stopped by bandits who killed the parents and abducted a couple of other children who had traveled with their group. When the survivors reached Thailand, on 5 May 1989, the three children and their cousin were placed in Banthad, one of the camps on the border between Thailand and Cambodia. They were moved from one camp to another for three years, finally ending up in Sikhiu camp. They were interviewed and advised to return to Vietnam. They remained in Thai camps for five years.

Because as unaccompanied minors they were considered vulnerable, the three orphans were evaluated by the Thai Special Committee consisting of immigration officials, an expert on child development, and an advisor from UNHCR to determine whether it was in the best interests of these children to be resettled in a third country or repatriated to Vietnam. The children asked to remain with their cousin who had cared for them for more than five years in the camp. But the Durable Solutions Counselor of the Special Committee ruled that the children should be separated from their cousin and repatriated to their grandmother and uncle, disregarding the fact that their grandmother was eighty-three, blind, frail, and dying, and that their uncle was an unmarried, disabled, unemployed alcoholic whom the children did not know. In her letter of request of 29 November 1993, the counselor wrote that their cousin in the camp did not take good care of them and did not want them in his care.[14]

On the contrary, the cousin wrote to us that he and the children were close and they wanted to remain together (Cousin, letter, 26 Aug. 1993). Nguyen, concerned that the welfare of the children was being disregarded, wrote two letters to the UNHCR Director of the Regional Bureau for Asia and Oceania. Nguyen, an expert on Vietnamese children and child welfare, pointed out that in Vietnam there was "no adult relative who could take care of them," that the children did not want to leave their cousin who had reared them for the past five years, and that, based on our observations and interviews in Vietnam, we were convinced that "children returned to relatives other than parents are highly likely to be neglected and are likely to end up on the street. Sending back these three orphans is not in their best interests." Nguyen reminded this official that UNHCR had several choices within their mandate: first, resettle the orphans in a third country; second, let them remain with their cousin in the camp; and, third, have them sponsored in a third country, also allowed within the mandate of UNHCR. A Vietnamese American woman, hearing about these children, offered to do this or adopt them if permitted. Nguyen, calling attention to the United Nations Declaration of the Rights of the Child and UNHCR's own guidelines on Refugee Children, Protection and Care, requested this official to "exercise the UNHCR mandate power to intervene on their behalf and find some humane way to resettle them" (Nguyen Dinh Huu, Letters, 7 Oct. and 4 Dec. 1993). The official refused, for UNHCR and NARV had made pre-return home visits in Vietnam and concluded that, despite the grandmother's declining health and the uncle's questionable character, they were a preferred choice over the others because they presented a good home environment.

The UNHCR and NARV reports that determined the fate of these children show how bureaucratic commitment to a general rule that did not have to be followed prevailed over expertise on child development as well as common sense. Dumping children with relatives who are incapable of caring for them is not an example of best interests but rather of child endangerment. A UNHCR repatriation officer, herself of Vietnamese descent, made the pre-return home visit to the children's grandmother and uncle. She wrote that the grandmother wanted the children to return before she died so that they would know of their ancestors. The repatriation officer observed that the grandmother was blind, frail, and unlikely to live much longer but that she loved her grandchildren.

The repatriation officer wrote that the uncle seemed eager to take care of the children so that he could get hold of their food allowance (U.S. $360, or Đ3.6 million in 1993–1994, for each child). She then discounted this because the uncle said he would put the money in a bank for the children. The uncle expressed concerns that bad people might part the children from their money.

In fact, the uncle wanted more than their food allowance. He asked for additional assistance of 3 million Vietnamese Dong (U.S. $300) to renovate his workshop. He said he would use the increased income to take care of the children. The uncle was given a lump sum of $1,740 dollars, more than six and a half times the annual income of an average family (UNCHR Repatriation Officer's Report, 15 Oct. 1993).

Overseeing the reintegration of the children once they were repatriated was a former social worker from Sweden who, as the NARV consultant, directed the NARV office in Ho Chi Minh City. She conducted another home visit prior to the repatriation of these children. She thought that the uncle would use some of his money to renovate the house in preparation for the return of the three children. She concluded that this was a good home environment into which to send the children. The children were repatriated against their will on 28 April 1994.

In his visit to these children after their repatriation, a NARV Vietnamese social worker wrote that the children got along well with their uncle and neighbors and that the uncle seemed to be taking good care of them. His report made it sound as if everything was going well (NARV Social Worker Monitoring Report, 24 May 1994). However, he told us, "The uncle told me that he used to be an alcoholic, but he has improved since the children came back." We asked, "Why didn't you put this in the report?" He replied, "No one wants to hear it; they only want to hear about successes. These children are neglected; they should never have been returned to Vietnam."

We wanted to see for ourselves that this case was as successful as these reports indicated. In the provincial town of Phan Thiet, we met with DELISA officials and explained why we wanted to meet the children. The officials agreed, and they and the Swedish NARV consultant accompanied us. As we rode, the NARV consultant rationalized the repatriation of the children, "The most important thing is to return the children to their own culture. That is the best solution. Culture is very important. You must understand Vietnamese culture and the extended family. Then you would know that returning these children to their uncle and grandmother in Vietnam was the right and best decision."

The house was filthy and dusty; no improvements had been made to accommodate the children. The blind grandmother was lying on a wooden bed. She was too ill to sit up, so a neighbor lifted her. The only food was an inch of cold soup. Cooking was done on dirt and brick behind the house.

The house contained only two small wooden beds. The youngest child, who wore a soiled and torn shirt, said, "Grandmother and Uncle sleep on the beds; we sleep on the floor." The middle child, the sister, hid in fear near one bed. The eldest brother was severely malnourished and ill. He said, "We are hungry. We do not have enough food to eat." Nguyen asked the uncle, "Where's the food?" He replied, "I'll start cooking soon." Nguyen asked, "Have you been drinking?" The uncle replied, "I've just had something to drink."

Through an interpreter, the NARV consultant asked the children how they were doing. "Fine, happy," said the oldest brother. He did not elaborate. The NARV consultant asked the uncle, "Have you used the money we gave you to develop the fishing business? Are you working on the boat? How about repairs on the house?" The uncle replied, "I haven't done those yet."

Freeman asked the NARV consultant, "What do you think about this?" She replied, "This isn't working. I can see that without even asking anything. Something's got to be done. The uncle hasn't done what we had hoped he would do when we gave him all that money. I remember the grandmother. She was cheerful and energetic, not like now. She has changed. She cannot care for the children any more. But we must do something that fits within the culture. We've got to find another relative or people in the village who will take care of the children. But we should keep the children here; that's the best solution."

A Preventable Tragedy

In Hanoi, we met with the NARV Programme Director for unaccompanied minors. She saw no problems, "I know of no example of money given to an unaccompanied minor that was misused by a family." We disagree. In fact, NARV officials themselves were aware of such abuses, as our examples indicate. Some of these abuses had been made public.[15]

The plight of the three children of Binh Thuan Province was entirely predictable; it is similar to others in which unaccompanied minors were repatriated to relatives other than their parents. These three orphans should never have been repatriated; they had no responsible caregiver in Vietnam. The principle of returning children to their own culture or extended family is a reasonable one, but adhering to it without exception is both inhuman and wrong-headed. It presupposes an idealized and static view of culture. It also assumes that a person's culture is inherently beneficial. But not all cultures are beneficial; some are clearly harmful, especially to children. Southeast Asian refugee and detention camps are one example. The family culture into which these three children were placed, which constitutes a clear example of child endangerment, is another. The assumption that the Vietnamese extended family will automatically take care of a child fails to take into account the actual desperate economic circumstances that face many families. The temporary windfall of NARV moneys does not alter this, as relatives have taken these funds to benefit themselves, not the children who were returned to them.

Not only their relatives but the children themselves have changed during the years the children were confined in refugee camps, and these changes make the readjustment of children difficult. The Vietnamese extended family, not in its idealized nurturing aspects but in its actual functioning, may be exploitative, neglectful, and ultimately harmful to the child. A frequent conflict in the Vietnamese family involves stepparents or adoptive parents and stepchildren. Especially during times of economic crisis, some stepparents simply neglect, if not harass and push out, children other than their own. The girl we rescued from the floor of the coffee shop in Cholon, Ho Chi Minh City, is an example, and her case is by no means exceptional.

Situations of neglect or abuse are very hard to monitor when, as with the three children of Binh Thuan Province, they are in hinterland areas far removed from NARV offices. Similarly, it is unlikely that these two brothers and a sister would or could ask for help. Their desperate situation would have gone unnoticed and unreported had we not visited them.

On 20 December 1993, the UNHCR Regional Director, to whom Nguyen had written two letters, responded, reconfirming the decision of the Special Committee in Thailand and the NARV and UNHCR pre-return home assessments. They agreed that it was clearly in the best interests of these children to be repatriated. To emphasize the rightness of the decision, this officer observed that the NARV Ho Chi Minh City representative also came to the same conclusions.

On 16 February 1994, responding to an inquiry about the three children of Binh Thuan Province, the UNHCR Chief of Operations of the Joint Voluntary Agency in Bangkok, Thailand, which interviews people accepted for refugee status wrote that she could do nothing for these children because they had been screened out. This made them ineligible for resettlement to another country. Furthermore, UNHCR had reported to her on 12 December 1993 that the three children had voluntarily chosen to repatriate.

There was nothing voluntary about their return. A reliable observer in Sikhiu Camp, who was unrelated to the children but knew them well, informed us that the children cried bitterly; they did not want to be separated from the cousin and repatriated. No doubt they were told they had no other choice. But in fact another alternative existed, and officials had been informed of it repeatedly. They could have used the UNHCR mandate power to intervene and to choose adoption and resettlement in the United States. They deliberately chose not to do so.

Instead, on 20 April 1994, the UNHCR Head of Desk, Regional Bureau for Asia and Oceania, wrote us to reaffirm the UNHCR's commitment to repatriate unaccompanied minors without parents to their country of origin and to deny that there was a problem. Nguyen Dinh Huu had written that the process was "patently unfair due to massive outright mistakes." The official dismissed Nguyen's statement as an opinion without supportable evidence.

Several months later, we received a letter dated 19 January 1995 from a Vietnamese NARV field-worker who had been assigned to check on the children. He made no mention of the Swedish NARV consultant's vow on 31 August of the previous year to move the three children out of their destructive environment as soon as possible. Instead he noted that the uncle had received $1,000 to set up a fishing business and assist the children. This was the money that had disappeared and could not be accounted for at the time of our visit. NARV had not even visited the three children again until 21 December 1994, nearly four months after we had discovered their actual condition. The grandmother had died in September, less than two weeks after we had seen her. The Vietnamese NARV field-worker, however, saw no reason to worry because the three children seemed to be happy with their uncle, who seemed to take good care of them. The NARV field-worker wrote that these children needed no further help from his agency. Case closed. Anyway, NARV would cease to assist children at the end of April 1994. His office ceased operation on 15 March 1995.

Contradicting his optimistic claim was NARV's own Monthly Programme Report for December 1994. "Many of these minors when interviewed said that they would have preferred to stay longer in the camps and are now unsatisfied with their present life in Vietnam." Now that the NARV children's program was ending, it no longer had to put a positive spin on its activities.

The field-worker's report, like previous ones, was inaccurate. In December 1995 Nguyen visited the children for a second time. With him was a DELISA official from Binh Thuan Province. The uncle had gained weight but the children were stunted, listless, and emaciated. The house stood unrepaired and food consisted of one small bag of rice. As before, all the money had disappeared.

Because of our previous visit, the DELISA official knew about these children and had expressed concern about the quality of their care. Since Binh Thuan Province, an impoverished and undeveloped area in the southern part of central Vietnam, has no orphanages, he had tried to place them elsewhere. Other provinces refused, since they had too many orphans of their own. DELISA officials of Binh Thuan Province are now seeking foreign aid to help fund the establishment of a shelter for the orphans of their province.

Political Uses of Humanitarian Concepts

Our investigations show that, despite the difficulties of doing so, on-site investigations by trained observers, not subject to the directives of the agencies conducting the surveys, are absolutely necessary to uncover the true conditions under which children are living. The discrepancies between official reports and actual conditions cannot be discovered otherwise.

The neglect of repatriated Vietnamese unaccompanied minors is less the result of the failings of individuals as it is a systemic problem. Countries of first asylum were reluctant to accept Vietnamese asylum seekers. UNHCR responded with policies or guidelines that went beyond its mandate. By attempting to protect and assist screened-out asylum seekers while repatriating them, UNHCR created "widespread confusion about their rights" and compromised its credibility (Marshall 1995:11). At UNHCR's request, NARV tried to recruit people for repatriation and ended up taking responsibility and blame for a UNHCR policy.

A persistent problem was that unaccompanied minors, the most vulnerable of the vulnerable, who were supposed to receive the highest priority to be moved out of the camps, were kept there for years. Since Vietnam was willing to take back children who had not been persecuted, and the special committees were predisposed to repatriate them, the long delays in returning them if they had biological parents waiting were not justified. The situation of stepchildren and minors repatriated to relatives other than biological parents was more troublesome, given the difficulties children typically faced with these adults. Resettlement may have been a better choice for these children than repatriation, and this was within the mandate of the Special Committees, though they rarely chose to exercise it.

Most of the U N H C R officials we met seemed to have internalized the humanitarian concepts they were taught, such as "best interests" and "voluntary repatriation." They accepted the distinction between "refugee" and "economic migrant," despite some controversial refugee status determination decisions that were overturned on appeal. This often occurred after an international outcry about clearly inhumane and erroneous decisions. For example, Nguyen Ngoc Toan, an unaccompanied minor, won an appeal when a Hong Kong judge overruled a U N H C R Special Committee recommendation to repatriate him. The Special Committee had omitted a social worker's favorable summary, forwarded a recommendation of denial, and disregarded clear and pervasive persecution of Toan's family in Vietnam, calling it only "discrimination." The youth was finally resettled with a relative in the United States. The U N H C R response to such situations was that, since most or all flagrantly unjust decisions were caught on appeal, "the procedures performed, in general, remarkably well." But for critics, this did not absolve U N H C R of responsibility in cases such as Toan's.[16]

UNHCR officials are extremely reluctant to admit error, though they do so on occasion. However, U N H C R has not acknowledged error in the cases we have presented. Most officials with whom we spoke were truly convinced of the rightness and the rationality of their views, and their official publications supported them. They see themselves as humane, protecting asylum seekers, properly determining the "best interests" of children, both morally and within their mandate, and justifying their evaluations on the basis of reports, which they believe to be reliable. Understandably, high-level officials, far removed from the children whose lives they were affecting, depended on these reports when they wrote to us. We now know the reports were unreliable.

Officials of U N H C R are frequently transferred from one post to another. Officials rarely stay with or are knowledgeable about long-term problems. Those who are responsible for decisions do not remain to witness the consequences. If they have made errors, these must be dealt with by their successors, a situation which cannot but affect the quality of subsequent decisions.

Critics allege that to question U N H C R decisions or policies, or those of a host country, is to jeopardize one's career and risk being transferred. UNHCR denies this.[17] But U N H C R has no authority to tell a country what to do. The UNHCR may advocate that refugees be protected and admitted, but a country may refuse, limit the activities of UNHCR, deny it entry, or ask it to leave. This must affect how UNHCR officials conduct themselves.

The ideals of UNHCR to protect asylum seekers and of NARV to provide assistance were violated by the pressure to produce successes despite the harm done to unaccompanied minors. To return children to situations of abuse, endangerment, or neglect was to violate the United Nations Convention on the Rights of the Child, the UNHCR Comprehensive Plan of Action, and Vietnam's 1991 Law on the Protection, Care, and Education of Children.

UNHCR and NARV officials used concepts that appeared to express humanitarian concern while actually justifying the mistreatment of children. "Durable solution" was used for solutions that created long-term harm. "Best interests" masked actual abuse and neglect. "Family reunion" was the justification for dumping children on relatives who had no interest in them, and whom the children often scarcely knew. "Voluntary repatriation" was used when what actually occurred was high-pressure coercion or, as in the case of three children of Binh Thuan Province, complete disregard of their wishes and repatriation against their will. "Orderly repatriation" actually referred to forced repatriation.

"Culture" was simplified into an idealized and static list of characteristics, disregarding the fact that cultures, families, and individuals change. This concept of "essential" culture meant that returning children to their culture and country of origin gave the appearance of a policy and practice that was rational and humane. In reality, this not only harmed children but also obscured what actually went on from outside scrutiny. Changes in Hanoi's economic policy were used as an excuse to proclaim that the economic and cultural climate had changed to the benefit of returnees while disregarding the fact that unaccompanied minors were almost completely excluded from any of these benefits. Of course, millions of poor children who had never left Vietnam were also excluded.

The notion of "returning to one's culture," as if it were unchanged at the same time that economic and political changes had occurred, highlights the contradictory rationalizations used to repatriate the children no matter what. Vietnam had changed, but, after spending several years in detention camps, so had the repatriated unaccompanied minors. The world they knew best was not Vietnam but rather the camps.

Anthropologists have come to critique essentialist definitions of culture as overemphasizing uniformity, structure, and stability. Ironically, as anthropologists have moved away from essentialist definitions, non-anthropologists have taken them on, as did the Swedish NARV consultant. Following the lead of UNHCR, she claimed the existence of a cohesive identity for "Vietnamese culture" or "the Vietnamese family," when in fact there is much variation, fluidity of boundaries, and change. Essentialist definitions can be used as a rationalization for actions that have political implications, as was done in the case of the three children of Binh Thuan Province, as well as others.[18]

The concept of culture is neutral, but its misuses further devastated the lives of children, the most vulnerable victims of politics. Especially invidious was applying a principle in general, repatriation to one's own culture, while disregarding its effects on particular individuals. "Happy ending" and "success" were used for cases that were anything but happy, and which were quickly closed and the files sent off so that no one could ever follow up on them. The children disappeared without a trace.

On 16 March 1995, UNHCR announced that it would help to send back all remaining screened-out Vietnamese adults. The forced repatriation of minors had occurred in 1993 with little comment because the "best interests" of minors could legally be determined by adults. However, the repatriation of adults received worldwide attention as breaking with the long-standing tradition of opposing forced repatriation. With the international community firmly behind her, Sadako Ogata, the United Nations High Commissioner for Refugees, proclaimed that those who had been denied refugee status should not expect to be granted asylum. "To those who still linger in the camps in the false hope of being resettled," she said, "I wish to say to them again: Do not lose any more time; seize your opportunity now and return home as quickly as possible to take advantage of international assistance while it still lasts."[19] For unaccompanied minors, her admonition was irrelevant and misleading, since NARV's international assistance for them had already ceased.[20] A joint declaration by thirty countries, including the United States, supported the UNHCR about-face. "There is no option for these people other than repatriation." The U.S. State Department, which had long opposed forced repatriation, now said that rejected asylum seekers "have no option but to return to their country of origin."

The UNHCR Regional Director, who had previously refused to intervene on behalf of the three children of Binh Thuan Province, summed up the attitude of the UNHCR and the international community concerning the Vietnamese asylum seekers, "We feel sure that it is now time for these people to go home. It's time to wrap this up."[21] The UNHCR's Chief of Mission in Hong Kong in 1995 explained why, "These are illegal immigrants, not refugees. We've already gone beyond our traditional mandate. We've operated under a special license to exceptionally exercise our good offices in dealing with the voluntary repatriation of people who are not refugees." He then added, "We have nothing to apologize for in this part of the world. We've provided the solutions" (Marshall 1995:10, 11). Obviously, the sixty thousand asylum seekers who remained in the camps at that time did not share this view.

With these remarks UNHCR officials dismissed themselves from the wreckage of Vietnamese children's lives that was in part allowed to occur by their own failure to implement the high-sounding principles of human rights and children's rights which they proclaimed. By mid-1997, almost all camps had been closed and almost all detainees had been forcibly repatriated. By the year 2000, the remaining Vietnamese boat people had declined to about 3,000. About 1,400 people were unable to leave Hong Kong. About 800 of them were refugees, who for various reasons were not accepted by any country. The last refugee camp, Pillar Point, was closed in May 2000. The Hong Kong government authorized the remaining people, who had been waiting for up to ten years, to be resettled in Hong Kong. These people were ethnic Chinese who were found not to be refugees. Vietnam would not take them back since they could not prove a previous record of residence in Vietnam, and they were considered "stateless." Most of the nearly 1,600 Vietnamese boat people who remained in the Philippines, who had been denied refugee status but were permitted to stay by the Philippine government, lived in a thriving community in Puerta Princesa City on Palawan Island. Another 47 remained stuck in Thailand, though 15 of them had been accepted for return by Vietnam.

What Really Happened to the Returnees?

Our early interviews were conducted in 1991, 1993, and 1994, when the initial problems of reintegration were acute. We were concerned that the repatriation allowances would be taken from the children, that they would not receive the assistance they had been promised, and that their families might not accept them back easily. In 1997 Australian psychologist Maryanne Loughry and Vietnamese sociologist Nguyen Xuan Nghia conducted a follow-up study of the NARV project in central Vietnam. Their research was supported by Norwegian and Danish Councils associated with NARV. They conclude that the repatriated children encountered few problems. They were well integrated in Vietnam, showed few mental problems as a result of the years in the camps, little family conflict, and in most ways showed little difference from local children who had never left. While the returnees had received repatriation allowances to help them reintegrate, the greatest assistance they received was from their own families. According to Loughry and Nguyen, "this assistance has been successful. The children have successfully repatriated and reintegrated" (Loughry and Nguyen 1997:29). They recommend that future programs that integrate children with families use repatriation programs such as NARV.

Loughry and Nguyen distinguish between those who live with both parents, father, mother, relative, spouse, others, or alone, but they make no mention of relationships with stepparents or how they compare with biological parents. The population they tried to reach was less than half of the total number of returnees reported by NARV for that area. In Loughry and Nguyen's group, nearly half had moved and could not be traced. Thus, nearly three quarters of the returnees were nowhere to be found.

We fail to share the optimism of Loughry and Nguyen. Between 1995 and 2000 Nguyen and Dinh Huu made six additional visits to Vietnam, and Freeman returned in 2000. Our observations as well as those of other Aid to Children without Parents volunteers in Vietnam confirm our original findings and contradict their conclusions. When in the camps, the children had been given extravagant promises by NARV and the European Community of assistance for schooling and job training. NARV also promised to help them reintegrate with their family or to find alternatives if their families no longer accepted them. Also promised was assistance in dealing with local Vietnamese authorities. The brochure proclaims, "We will visit you at home, talk with you and your family, and help you if you run into any difficulties."[23] No doubt some children benefited from these promises, but many did not. An ARCWP volunteer who had worked in Palawan camp visited a teenage girl named Dung after she was repatriated to Vietnam. Her family had told her not to return. In his report, he describes what happened. "The family was bitterly disappointed. . . . Dung's siblings no longer knew who she was since she left Vietnam when they were still little. . . . The European Community have stopped their aid and so she no longer had tuition money [for job training]. Her family had to worry about each meal for the day and couldn't take on the costs of Dung's tuition" (Vietnam Thanh Ha 1994:9).

There was little conflict in this family but not because Dung was successfully integrated. Dung had been sent out of Vietnam so that she could be resettled and then help her family economically. She had failed to do this. She had returned because of the promises of NARV but then found the promises to be empty. She felt enormous guilt over her failure. Because of this, she did not talk back or dispute her parents. They in turn were discouraged at Dung's return. They had sent her out because they could not feed her, and they had told her not to return. When she did, they became discouraged at her failure. She had been away for five years; now she had returned as an added economic burden, but she no longer fit easily under their authority; they simply gave up and let her do as she pleased. The lack of conflict signified an uneasy distancing between Dung and her parents.

Even more disturbing were our own findings based on Nguyen Dinh Huu's April 1999 interviews and our joint interviews in September 2000 with repatriated unaccompanied minors. From the moment of their arrival in Vietnam, local low-level government employees systematically squeezed the repatriation allowances out of these youngsters until they had nothing left. The government employees did this indirectly, making it virtually impossible to trace. When children traveled to local offices asking to be reinstated on the household registration card, nothing happened. Without such registration, they were not allowed to enroll in school or job training programs, move to another location, take officially recognized employment, or participate in many other aspects of daily life. The children would return two or three times, each journey often involving an all-day trip. The government employees, who knew the children had repatriation allowances, never asked for anything, but their delayed responses and the way they talked indicated that they were waiting for the children to give them money. The children had a choice: travel back and forth until they had no more money and the registration cards were given or pay the authorities and get the permits quickly. Many children spent all of their repatriation allowances regularizing their household registration cards. Assistance from the European Community fared no better, since the funds to assist the children went through local DELISA employees. The children were unable to enroll until they gave a portion of their money to the government employees. None of the children we interviewed found employment related to the job training they received. Many returnees found themselves shunned in Vietnamese society because they had become contaminated by outside influences. One repatriated youth summed up his experience: "Up to now, nothing in my life is happy."

Humane Alternatives

It is easy to criticize the efforts of others involved in the care and protection of asylum seekers, especially children at risk. It is more difficult to demonstrate realistic alternatives to current approaches, but they do exist. Two examples follow.

On 17 July 1996, agencies of the Philippine government and the Catholic Church signed a memorandum of understanding that allowed Vietnamese asylum seekers in the Philippines to remain there indefinitely. They could return to Vietnam any time they wished, but they would not be forced back. Those who stayed would be given the opportunity to become self-sufficient residents of the Philippines. With donations from around the world, a "Viet Village" in the Philippines was built.[24] (San Jose Mercury News 1996b; 1996c). By 1999, these asylum seekers were economically self-sufficient, and legislation had been introduced to give them permanent resident status; by the end of 2000, they were still waiting for that decision.[25] By mid-2001, we had heard nothing further.

In the late 1970s and early 1980s some countries of first asylum resettled Vietnamese refugees. For example, Malaysia took in about 10,000 people, mainly Muslims; China accepted 230,000 persons of Chinese descent and another 30,000 of Vietnamese descent. But, after the Comprehensive Plan of Action was established, only the Philippines, the poorest of the countries of first asylum, refused to cave in to the international pressure to repatriate by force those Vietnamese who had been denied refugee status. A few people whose status was controversial remained in Hong Kong. All other countries sent them back. Behind them, urging forced repatriation, were the United States, other countries of resettlement, and the UNHCR. The Philippines, persuaded by Philippine Catholics, based its decision on humanitarian not political grounds. Admittedly, the number of people whom they allowed to resettle were small. The decision to resettle them was not easily achieved and probably would not have been made had there been larger numbers. However, the Philippines has shown that in certain circumstances an alternative to repatriation was possible.

We also felt we had a realistic alternative way to protect and assist repatriated unaccompanied minors. As mentioned earlier, we had been assisting them in the refugee camps since 1988 through a voluntary organization called Aid to Refugee Children without Parents (ARCWP), later called Aid to Children without Parents (ACWP), and we felt we could apply our experience to Vietnam. Our approach is to provide humanitarian assistance but remain politically neutral and nonconfrontational. We sensed that the problem for repatriated unaccompanied minors was less that of persecution and more that Vietnam, while willing, was unable to accommodate large numbers of repatriates and unaccompanied minors.

In 1993 we met with officials in Hanoi. We had heard tales of the difficulties that foreign voluntary organizations and businesses had had in gaining permission to operate in Vietnam. We encountered none of this. The officials were humane, focused, and pragmatic. They approved our plan. We selected Hue, in central Vietnam, to start our project because it is a poor area with many repatriated unaccompanied minors and almost no assistance from foreign organizations. Local officials also strongly endorsed our project, and we began our activities in 1995.

NARV was a large-scale, centralized, time-limited, expensive project that covered all of Vietnam. Ours is small-scale and inexpensive, located in one province of Vietnam, and has a more flexible time frame. While we have been initially successful and have avoided many pitfalls that NARV faced, it remains to be seen if others might apply our model successfully in other areas of Vietnam.

We are small-scale by design and sensitive to the potential disruption that our presence and activities might create. We go out of our way to minimize this potential and to monitor our impacts. We do not bring in or display large amounts of money; we are careful to introduce projects in ways that are endorsed by local residents.

All our staff members in the United States are volunteers. Our paid staff is comprised exclusively of local Vietnamese citizens, individuals who are both highly trained and respected in their community. This is significant in light of recent criticisms by an official of the Foreign Aid Receiving and Managing Committee that foreign aid is "abused and misused." In certain projects, up to 70 percent of the aid has gone to the salaries of foreign advisors, who have received large sums in U.S. dollars.[26] Before setting up our project, we met with officials and local organizations to determine what needs were most pressing and neglected. Our projects address those needs and are updated to meet new ones. We have expanded our project to include not only unaccompanied minors but also orphans and street children.

Our projects are realistic; we do not make claims to deliver that which we cannot. Local officials have become skeptical of outside assistance since some voluntary organizations have promised to bring in large amounts of money and new projects and then failed to do so. In contrast, we have implemented several sustainable projects: a children's shelter, a free children's health care clinic, corrective surgery for birth defects such as cleft palate and clubfoot, a preschool and a teenage literacy program, child welfare and emergency relief services, an orphan's calf-raising project, and a program of computer training and English instruction. The computers are supplied by and set up by our unpaid volunteers from the United States. The project prepares students for employment in Vietnam's new economic enterprises.

Because of the history of colonialism and foreign interventions in Vietnam, some officials are uneasy about foreigners who might attempt to exploit them. We have shown that our activities are humanitarian with no hidden agendas. Because of our cordial relationship with local authorities, we are the only overseas Vietnam organization allowed to operate our own office in Thua Thien Hue independently, without working through local organizations.

Virtually everything we have introduced is already known and specifically desired in Vietnam. The introduction of computers and English came as the result of specific requests. The value of self-sufficiency through raising calves is an extension of already existing values. The counseling of children coincides with the activities of Vietnamese social workers. In summary, we are building on already existing values and structures in Hue and among those whom we assist.

Our projects are designed to be compatible with the current social and political environment, to foster self-sufficiency, and to be modified as circumstances dictate. As unaccompanied minors have become adults, ACWP has focused its assistance activities on orphans and street children. We monitor closely the activities and the funds that go into these projects. The relationship between the aid-giver and the receiving youth is not one of equals, but it is one in which the dependency and inequality found at the start of the project shift toward greater independence and equality as the project advances. Youths are given the chance to make it on their own, knowing from the start that the assistance is temporary and intended to enable them to develop economic self-sufficiency as adults.

We ran Aid to Children Without Parents until mid-1999, when we felt we had completed our mission for repatriated unaccompanied minors. In that year, central Vietnam was hit by the worst floods in five hundred years. We founded another nonprofit organization, Friends of Hue Foundation, to provide long-term assistance to the victims of this natural disaster and other impoverished families. Younger volunteers have taken over the administration of ACWP and have moved their assistance activities to southern Vietnam.

Reconfigured Social Fields

The Comprehensive Plan of Action has accomplished its purposes. The detention camps are now closed and clandestine departures from Vietnam have largely ceased, since countries of first asylum no longer admit or allow Vietnamese asylum seekers to resettle in their lands. Those few who continue to arrive are denied refugee status and quickly repatriated. Countries of resettlement no longer face unlimited numbers of Vietnamese seeking asylum. The UNHCR has "wrapped up" the saga of the Vietnamese boat people and turned to other refugee crises in the world. Regarding the delays and problems in setting up the special procedures for unaccompanied minors, UNHCR's Mougne says, "Many of those involved including UNHCR and others made mistakes. I think we have learned some very hard lessons as a result" (Nichols and White 1993:59). Those who have paid most for these lessons are, of course, the unaccompanied minors.

In late 1986 Vietnam approved the "Renovation" (Doi Moi) policy, a thoroughgoing reform of their centrally planned system. Since that time, Vietnam's economic climate has improved, as has its international political relations.[27] Overt political repression has lessened and repatriated Vietnamese are not persecuted, though some have been squeezed for the money they brought back.[28] Vietnam, the second country in the world to ratify the United Nations Declaration on the Rights of the Child, is paying increasing attention to improving the condition of children in the country.[29]

However, after spending years in detention centers, repatriated children have also changed. They have learned to resist authority. In the anticommunist political atmosphere of the camps, they envisioned Vietnam as a place of persecution; many are angry and resentful at being returned. In the camps unaccompanied minors often lived in social units that differed from family units in Vietnam. They learned survival techniques appropriate for the camps but not for Vietnam or the families to which they have been returned. Many are afraid of returning to school because they have missed years of schooling; they are embarrassed to be in classes with younger children. And some, like the shy and withdrawn girl in the Mekong Delta, have undergone terrible traumas while escaping Vietnam or living in the camps.

Officials are concerned about the problems these children bring with them, and the potential threat that some of them pose for the social order. Relatives are finding that some repatriated minors do not have the attitude, discipline, or sense of obligation that they expect to see from children. As Vietnam is reconfiguring itself, so are Vietnam's repatriated unaccompanied minors, who are learning once again how to cope with the imagined families into which they have been placed.

Notes

This essay is drawn from our book, *Storms in Our Lives: Children Seeking Asylum*, (University of Washington Press, 2002, used with permission). Many of the full citations for this chapter appear in the following notes. These mainly include newspaper articles and primary government documents with unattributed authorship. Otherwise, full cites appear in the Works Cited at the end of this book.

1. Hong Kong Government 1994, Monthly fact sheet: Vietnamese migrants in Hong Kong.

2. Freeman 1995:29–41; Gallagher 1994:429–50; Keely and Russell 1994:399–417; Ogata 1994:419–28.

3. See UNHCR, Convention on the Rights of the Child 1989; UNHCR, Comprehensive plan of action: Guidelines for implementation of the special procedures, 20 Aug. 1991; UNHCR, Note on the technical meeting of the steering committee of the International Conference on Indochinese Refugees, 12–13 September 1991, Jakarta;

UNHCR, Refugee children: Protection and care, Draft for field comments, Geneva, 1993; see also Ressler, Boothby, and Steinbock 1988.

4. Muntarbhorn 1992:52–54; Diller 1988; Davis 1991:17–47; Gow 1991; Nichols and White 1993; Robinson 1998:203–209; UNHCR, The comprehensive plan of action, information bulletin, Aug. 1995; UNHCR, Report on alleged corruption in the refugee status determination in the Philippines, Washington, D.C., Oct. 1995.

5. Goodwin-Gill 1983:11; Diller 1988:58; Wain 1981:230–35; Freeman 1989:339–40.

6. UNHCR, Report on alleged corruption in the refugee status determination in the Philippines, Washington, D.C., Oct. 1995, 9, 16; emphasis in original.

7. Boothby 1992; McCallin 1992; Loughry and Esquillo 1994; Nguyen and Freeman 1992; Children Without Parents, Inc. 1991. Refugee concern Hong Kong. Defenseless in detention: Vietnamese children living amidst increasing violence in Hong Kong; Michael Bociurkiw, *South China Sunday Morning Post*, Terrorized in the camp of shame, 6 June 1993; van der Veer 1992.

8. Various articles from the *South China Morning Post* on 8 April 1994 on the Attack on Whitehead Detention Center: Scott McKenzie and Kathy Griffin, Prison ultimatum for 1500; and Growing unrest sparks raid; Darren Goodsir, Blitz against agitators set two months ago; Hedley Thomas, Boots, blasts shatter stillness; and Villagers suffer agony of tear gas; Scott McKenzie, Camp backlash feared; Editorial, The opening battle; also see Report of refugee concern into the events surrounding the transfer of Vietnamese asylum seekers from the Whitehead Detention Center on 7 April 1994; *San Jose Mercury News*, Boat people riot in Malaysia as deportation nears 19 Jan. 1996:16A.

9. Nguyen Dinh Huu and James Freeman 1994; *South China Morning Post*, Beryl Cook, Homeless Viet children spark refugee inquiry, 30 Aug. 1993.

10. Operation Family Reunion. n.d. One-page statement distributed in Hong Kong to voluntary organizations and government agencies, including the U.S. Consulate.

11. James Freeman and Nguyen Dinh Huu 1996:28; articles on Ngo Van Ha from the *South China Morning Post* in 1994: Steve Ball, Viet boy tries to kill himself, 7 Jan.:1–2; Scott McKenzie, Hearing over Orphan Viet's right to review, 19 Jan.:3; Ruth Mathewson, U.S. politician joins protest at return of boy refugee, 23 Jan.:3; Scott McKenzie, U.S. dream comes true for Viet orphan, 8 Feb.:3; Lindy Course and Scott McKenzie, Orphan Ha wins temporary reprieve, 24 Feb.:1, 8; and Editorial, Rule book not always right, 24 Feb.:18.

12. UNHCR, Fifth meeting of the steering committee of the International Conference on Indochinese Refugees, 14 Feb. 1994.

13. UNHCR, The comprehensive plan of action, Information bulletin, Aug. 1995:10–11.

14. Durable Solutions Counselor, Thailand. Letter of Request, Case no. 13, 29 Nov. 1993.

15. *South China Morning Post*, Beryl Cook, Homeless Viet children spark refugee inquiry, 30 Aug 1993.

16. UNHCR, The comprehensive plan of action, Information bulletin, Aug. 1995:6; Gow 1991:30–32; Hong Kong Supreme Court, In the Supreme Court of Hong Kong High Court Miscellaneous Proceedings, In the matter of an application by Nguyen Ngoc Toan, a minor, by his best friend Nguyen Duyen Huu. M.P. No. 3759 of 1990, Coram J. Bokhary in Court; Date of Hearing: 28–31 Jan. 1991, Date of delivery of Judgment: 31 Jan. 1991: 4–5, 6, 12, 14; and articles from the *South China Morning Post* from 1990 and 1991: Viet boy to fight status in 'refugee' test case, 11 Dec. 1990; Refugee status denied to boy despite report, 29 Jan. 1991:1, 4; Ruling in the 'best interests' of boy, 30 Jan. 1991:6; Screening out boy 'breach of natural justice,' 1 Feb. 1991:1–2.

17. UNHCR, Report on alleged corruption in the refugee status determination in the Philippines, Washington, D.C., Oct. 1995.

18. Stephens 1995:3–48; Keesing 1994; Vayda 1994.

19. *San Jose Mercury News*, Article on the UNHCR Sixth meeting of the steering committee of the International Conference on Indochinese Refugees of March 16, 17 Mar. 1995.

20. UNHCR, Sixth meeting of the steering committee of the International Conference on Indo-Chinese Refugees, Geneva, 16 Mar. 1995.

21. *San Jose Mercury News*, Article on the UNHCR Sixth meeting of the steering committee of the International Conference on Indochinese Refugees of March 16, 17 Mar. 1995.

22. Laczo 2000:7; Center for Assistance to Displaced Persons, Yearly Activity Report on the remaining boat people in the Philippines, particularly the Viet Village, Puerto Princesa City, Palawan, Manila: 1 Dec. 1997; Center for Assistance to Displaced Persons, Summary report on the remaining Vietnamese nationals, Manila: 26 Nov. 1999; *Thoi Bao*, Hong Kong dong cua trai ty nan cuoi cung (Hong Long closes the last refugee camp), number 2725, 23 Feb. 2000.

23. NARV Brochure in Vietnamese, Tro ve khong co nghia la tat ca het ma do moi chi la bat dau (Returning home is not the end of everything but the beginning), no date.

24. *San Jose Mercury News*, Philippines decides Vietnamese refugees can stay, 14 July 1996:16A; Carolyn Jung, *San Jose Mercury News*, Viet community unites to aid refugees, 15 Aug. 1996:1B, 4B.

25. Center for Assistance to Displaced Persons, Summary report on the remaining Vietnamese nationals, Manila, 26 Nov. 1999; Sister Pascale Le Thi Triu, Open letter (in Vietnamese), 15 Oct. 2000.

26. *Vietnam Economic Times*, reported in *Thoi Bao*. Tien Vien Tro Cho Viet Nam Bi Lam Dung Va Chi Tieu Sai Lech (Foreign aid for Vietnam has been abused and misused), 13 Aug. 1997.

27. Mya than and Tan 1993; Nugent 1996; World Bank in Vietnam, Vietnam: attacking poverty, 14 Dec. 1996; World Bank in Vietnam, Vietnam: Preparing for take-off?, 14–15 Dec. 1996.

28. *Interaction*, 1995, NGO mission to Vietnam and first asylum countries in Southeast Asia; Marshall 1995; Kristin Huckshorn, *San Jose Mercury News*, Detainees report beatings, 16 Feb. 1996: 1A, 10A.

29. Socialist Republic of Vietnam 1992, *National Report on Two Years' Implementation of the United Nations Convention on the Rights of the Child*, Hanoi: Committee for the Protection and Care of Children.

Part Three

Resistance and Remembrance

Eve Darian-Smith

Beating the Bounds: Law, Identity,

and Territory in the New Europe

In Kent in southern England, you can still imagine walking the Pilgrims'
Way from London to Canterbury across rolling green hills and a village-
dominated landscape. This would involve avoiding, at strategic moments, the superhighways and the drone of speeding lorries. Here, in
this region of historical remnants merging with high-tech modernity, a
peculiar local ritual associated with property rights and community
responsibilities still goes on. This ritual involves the local community,
particularly children, walking the limits and marking the boundaries of
the local parish neighborhood. It is called "beating the bounds."[1]

In this essay, I briefly discuss what beating the bounds involves
and, drawing upon its historical continuities, suggest what its practice
means today. I describe the current revival of this local ritual, associated
with private property and local community rights, to reflect upon the
depth of nostalgia many English people feel, both inside and outside
major cities, for the conservation of the land and the preservation of a
country landscape. I argue, as have others, that the rural landscape is a
significant feature in the collective imagination of what constitutes English cultural identity and a national sense of place.[2] I am particularly
interested in how an aesthetics associated with the country landscape
reinforces, symbolically and metaphorically, a particular consciousness
of law, order, and justice.[3]

In Kent County, for more than a decade, local residents have experienced the building of the Channel Tunnel linking Kent to Nord-Pas de
Calais and, in the wider context, Britain to France. As a result of increasing communications across the channel waters and the breaking up
of national jurisdictional borders, broad changes are occurring both
through the institutional frames of the European Union (EU) and informally through personal networks and community. The consequences of
these changes have been both positive and negative. In contrast to the
initial feeling of despair expressed by many Kent residents at the signing
of the Channel Tunnel Treaty in 1986 about the "invasion" of Europe
and the significant damage to Kent's countryside landscape, there is a
new sense of optimism for the opportunities being opened up by the

EU. Transnational exchange between people living in Kent and the European mainland now permeates local businesses and educational and cultural programs in towns such as Canterbury. For many Kent residents, the presence of the EU is becoming more accepted and acceptable over time.

However, at the same time as increasing connections between people and places across national borders and the channel's watery divide, new boundaries are emerging and old divisions are being redefined. The county of Kent is reclaiming its own identity and asserting its own independence as a region within England and a borderland with France. Elsewhere I have analyzed the apparent retreat to the ideal of a localized community through the reaffirmation of Kent's historical claim as the Garden of England (Darian-Smith 1995a, 1999). Here, I return to the theme of a reintensification of local identity as a feature of postmodernity (see Harvey 1989). The local ritual of beating the bounds illustrates how historical narratives are being revitalized and revamped to meet new political and economic conditions, resulting in a dynamic mix of local, regional, national, and transnational exchange and re-partition.

By interviewing individuals living in Kent, many of whom are members of local environmental groups that have sprung up in the past decade, as well as talking to local Kent lawyers and politicians, I ascertained a widespread popular enthusiasm about protecting the local countryside as well as defying externally imposed change, whether directed from London or Brussels. Evidence of this enthusiasm lies in a variety of forms and places, one of these being the revival of the ritual of beating the bounds. In the past five years, some fifty villages in the southeast and southwest regions of England have revived the local custom. I interpret beating the bounds as an instance and metaphor to highlight the various local activities in Kent responding to anxieties brought about by the increasing presence and power of the EU. This interpretation turns on the extent to which the revival reflects a more generalized surge of interest in re-establishing the significance of locality and village community, even if only as a rather vague idealization.

It has been argued that a moving away from city life and a nostalgia for country living is part of a general swing toward environmentalism, new social movements, and the perceived benefits of postmaterial values (Inglehart 1990). This may well be the case for many Kent residents and weekend commuters from London. What is important in the context of this chapter is whether these beliefs, which support a desire to revitalize local communities, may in fact be generating new strategies of legal politics and legal identity within the EU. To what extent, then, does the reconstitution of locality introduce alternative points of reference in the reproduction of legal meaning that implicitly contest the idea of England as a national center?

Exploring new legal strategies and possibilities of legal redress in the New Europe introduces the underlying aim of this essay. This is a reexamination of legal anthropology that takes law as a field of social action.[4] Law as a field operates through various scales of legal jurisdiction, conventionally framing legal ethnographies between local-level legal interaction relating to cultural identity, on the one hand, through to the level of formal state law, on the other. However, in the New Europe, as elsewhere, the spatial dimensions of law are dramatically changing. By this I mean that no longer can the manner in which a legal jurisdiction marks off and defines the controlled limits of a particular territory (whether national or subnational) be presumed stable (if it ever could). Under a European legal regime, both the "local" and "national" are clearly inadequate as two extremities along a gradation of applicable legislation and governance. For unlike the regime of international law, which is based on the interaction between nation-states,[5] the EU brings into focus new hierarchies of legal order, new territories of legal meaning, and new avenues of legal redress that challenge the notion of nation-state sovereignty.[6] European law introduces additional points of reference by which to organize ethnographic analyses of the possible relations between law and people. At the same time it dramatically alters those already existing.[7] In short, the growing impact of a European law suggests the need to rethink the boundaries of what may be relevant legal and social fields in new transnational state entities (see Darian-Smith 1995c).

What Is Beating the Bounds?

As mentioned above, beating the bounds involved a community gathering to walk around the outer boundaries of the local neighborhood or parish in a public procession. It was a highly symbolic event that marked the territorial limits of the village, defining "insider" and "outsider" and the complex bundle of social relations that informed a feudal community.

Throughout premodern England and into the eighteenth century, beating the bounds exemplified a set of mutual social relations and a powerful legal ideology that went beyond the realm of property rights in legitimating peasant and emerging working-class activities. This in turn informed popular notions of justice in social contexts that transcended parish limits, such as the right to take up arms against exploitation and the right to certain forms of social welfare (Bushaway 1992:114; see Thompson 1991, plate ix). Beating the bounds was one of numerous rituals that solidified people's places in society as laborers or manor lords, as well as their mutual responsibilities within the local community.[8] It helped smooth over internal class conflicts and intercommunity rivalries and hostilities by reasserting the significance of the parish system vis-à-vis the bleak future represented by the outside world. This consolidation of community was important given that England's medieval system of feudal tenure was based on a hierarchy of reciprocity and exchange. Beating the bounds affirmed a lord's duties to his poor tenants, as well as the peasant's right to bring their lord to trial through an established system of manorial courts. The terms of this reciprocal relationship and the balance of hierarchical power began to shift significantly throughout the seventeenth and eighteenth centuries with the emergence of the industrial revolution and a middle class (Holmes 1962; Williamson and Bellamy 1987). But there are enough cases on record to suggest that the threat of legal redress by a parish poor against their superiors held some force (Daniels 1988:45; Drescher 1964:91). Thus, continuities of custom allowed poorer people the potential to stand their ground, to assert their inherited rights, and to take "combative, socially-critical and threatening roles" (Bushaway 1992:130; see King 1989).

Critical to the endurance of any village community was the capacity to define its local constituency. In fortifying the parish's spatial limits, beating the bounds also identified those who lived beyond the village as "savage" while the insiders were "civilized." Beating the bounds established a discourse of exclusion and inclusion, demarcating who had rights (or not) to charity, access to common lands, and historically to a lord's knights for military protection. "Those within the boundary were a part of a particular moral world and those without were outsiders" (Bushaway 1992:126). This moral dimension of insider/outsider is disclosed in written records of beating the bounds as a slippage of word use between "processioning" and "possessioning" is often found. Such slippage suggests that, in a particular way, the local community belonged to, or was in the possession of, the parish. In many ways the performative ritual stressed that a relational sense of locality was inextricably bound up with a moral and legal code of rights identifying community members. It is important to note how land was featured as the basis of moral and legal values, since the homeless, another type of poor, were excluded from participating and were deemed "naturally" immoral.

According to the historian John Brand in his *Observations on the Popular Antiquities of Great Britain* (1795), beating the bounds has its origins in the Roman festival of the god Terminus, who was considered the guardian of fields and landmarks and the keeper of peace among men (see also Reed 1984). It occurred on the third day before Accession when the minister, churchwardens, choir boys, and local community would processionally walk around the limits of the parish, and stop to beat sticks of willow and chant songs beside white boundary stones.[9] The procession blessed nature's bounty. More importantly, it represented a liminal moment in which intercommunity tensions were subordinated to a reinforced sense of justice that stressed the property owner's responsibilities to the parish poor. According to John Brand:

> These religious processions mark out the limits of certain portions of land, under which the whole kingdom is contained; and in all these the principle of God's fee is recognized by the law and the people. The . . . church-rate is admitted as due throughout the bounds, and the tithes, also as a charge on the parish; but, together with these admissions, there is formed in the mind a mental boundary, and a sacred restraint is placed upon the consciences of men, that co-mingles religious awe with the institution of the landed right and landed inheritance, and family succession to it. . . . The walking of the parish bounds on the *gang-days*, in religious procession, very materially contributed to form and keep fresh in the mind of each passing generation the terms on which property was held, and some of the duties belonging to the holding (1795:197–98).

In reinforcing local knowledge about land and clarifying community responsibilities, beating the bounds helped sustain a "mental boundary" around the parish and determine its spatial borders. In times when parish boundaries were rarely created by statute or evidenced in writing, "unless the bounds were occasionally patrolled, this knowledge might be lost." This explains the encouragement given children to participate in the procession as the new generation charged with remembering parish history and, also, the peculiar custom of bouncing or bumping the choirboy—holding him by the ankles and gently touching his head to the ground—to reinforce his memory.[10]

In the course of my fieldwork other dimensions of the custom were revealed. My interview with Mr. Humphreys raised the issue of local borders as barriers not only against people deemed undesirables but also against devastating disease. Mr. Humphreys, a retired lawyer living in Barham, Kent, was somewhat of a local expert, having written an article on beating the bounds in the *Kent News* (a pamphlet published by the Kent branch of the Council for the Protection of Rural England [CPRE]). He explained that the article was written because the custom was "of topical interest" to a Kent audience since "there were quite a lot of parishes doing it last year" (interview, 25 Feb. 1994). With respect to the ritual's history, Mr. Humphreys stressed that establishing the parish or manor limits was critical in order to exclude incorrigible rogues, vagabonds, and itinerants as well as migrants fleeing religious prosecution from countries such as France and Belgium. The local elite was anxious not to have to feed and clothe another parish's poor. Moreover, Mr. Humphreys thought this need to exclude outsiders stemmed from European outbreaks of black death in 1348 that periodically spread into England.[11] People traveling from distant lands generally disembarked on the shores of East Kent, the closest coast to France. These foreigners were more likely to be carriers of disease and, not surprisingly—especially in the light of contemporary panics about outbreaks of the plague in India—"were not looked upon kindly."[12]

The Region of Kent as Place and Symbol

The geographical proximity of Kent to mainland Europe, particularly France, points to the larger contexts in which local activities in southern England, both then and now, should be situated. The history of Kent is long and complicated, but central to the narrative is the region being the front line of defense against European invasion. During the Second World War and the infamous Battle of Britain, defending the nation characterized the heroics of Kent residents and their fortitude against German attack (Rootes 1980). Thus, geographical proximity has meant that Kent's historical as well as its continuing physical importance and symbolic role in the well-being of the nation is greater than that experienced by most other counties in England.[13] Of course, the significance of Kent's place in the national imagination is not static, and its shifting role will be discussed more fully in the latter part of this essay. At this point, what I want to stress are the historical themes and continuities that form the basis for the current national interest in Kent County as a continuing emblem of England and Englishness.

Historically, Kent has been relatively autonomous as a regional entity in England. Up until the centralization of English law in the eighteenth century, this autonomy was in part due to Kent having its own distinct legal system.[14] Jurisdiction helped solidify the county's boundaries, within which all men were supposedly born free (Everitt 1986:12; Sandys 1851:89). More concretely, the legal custom of *gavelkind*, a law of inheritance peculiar to the common law of Kent, reinforced its territorial boundaries. Gavelkind dictated that nonecclesiastical property had to be equally divided between all surviving sons, and, by ensuring the subdivision of land, reflected the church's desire to maintain its landholding superiority against powerful families. While gavelkind prevented the formation of large secular estates, it did grant Kent residents the freedom to buy and sell land without a lord's permission (Williamson and Bellamy 1987:74). On this point gavelkind differed substantively from the common law of England. Yet, despite this difference, up until the nineteenth century legal theorists argued that Kent law was the English system's juridical precedent and embodied "the pure sources of the English constitution."[15]

Indeed, an important element to this study is the extent to which Kent mythically represents England's ancient roots and legal antecedents. English law embodies an imagery of old England grounded in a rustic countryside and natural landscape (Goodrich and Hachamovitch 1991:159–82; Darian-Smith 1999:17–40). This sentiment reflects a legacy of folklore built up both by Kentish residents in premodern England and, since the seventeenth century, by an emerging modern English nation.[16] The county's autonomy, represented by Kent's Saxon motto "Invicta," meaning unconquered or untamed, set a particular interpretative frame of reference toward Kent. Kent's ancient Saxon derivation and its singular symbolism lent it a specific mythologized identity within English nationalist discourse.[17]

The official mythologized narrative about Kent in England increasingly came into conflict with the parish-based narratives Kent residents held about themselves. Prior to the consolidation of England, Wales, and Scotland to form the modern British nation under the Act of Union in 1707, the hundreds of villages in southeast England were most immediately linked economically and legally to Kent (Jessup 1974:128; Holmes 1962:61). But the industrial revolution and the rise of specific regions of production that attracted labor migrations shattered the parish system, and village life slowly disintegrated in the eighteenth century (Horn 1984:211–42; Mingay 1990:168–98). While Kent never became highly industrialized, neither did it retain its singular autonomy. London swelled, spread, and dissolved the county's northern borders. This helped generate a self-consciousness of identity in which people took pride—and today a number still do—in declaring whether they were maids and men of Kent, or Kentish men.[18] The breakdown also meant that for local residents identification with Kent county existed increasingly in competition with nationalist loyalties toward the idea of the modern British state.

Conflict between national, regional, and local identities was clearly expressed in the opposition toward the move to centralize English law. Legal centralization by the nation necessarily involved the diminishment of local legal custom and, hence, the declining need to beat the bounds of the parish. Thus, the rise of a national English system from the early eighteenth century stripped village life of its basic legal relations governing social responsibilities and membership rights within the local community. In Kent, with its own peculiar legal code and lingering rural economy, the codification of English law had a dramatic impact. It shattered the nexus between law, land, and community that informed the Kentish locality and replaced it with a restructuring of law more appropriate to the imperial nation's political, economic, and territorial contexts and conquests.

The Codification of English Law and the Decline of Legal Custom

The codification of modern law in the eighteenth century exemplified the emergence of England as a nation-state. This legal process was both cause and consequence of a range of social and political changes that accompanied the decline of church and aristocratic powers, the rise of capitalist ideology, and an emerging industrial economy whereby wages slowly replaced former tenant-farmer arrangements.[19] Moreover, change was often met with local forms of resistance.[20] Yet, despite local pockets of opposition to change in Kent, by the mid-nineteenth century village life was dramatically different from what it had been at the turn of the century (Jessup 1974:134–42). Industrial regions, such as those characterized by Welsh coal fields or Manchester cotton factories, were firmly established in the west and north. These regions superseded the older counties as the primary unit of politics.[21]

Law played a central role in these rapid social, political, and economic changes in Kent. Industrialization, though not having such an overt impact in Kent as other areas, nonetheless drastically altered the infrastructure of its parish and county community relations. This was primarily due to the grounding of capitalism in a laissez-faire ideology of contractual liability dependent upon a uniform, predictable, and enforceable legal system (see MacDonagh 1980). The peculiarities of Kent law such as the intestate rule of gavelkind could no longer be tolerated under the rubric of English common law. Such local legal inconsistencies were eliminated through the enclosure acts and streamlining of property devolution. These legal changes made landlord-tenant relations a matter of "free contract" by eradicating the validity of customary responsibilities and village obligations.[22] Thus, enclosure "did not merely involve the consolidation of scattered property and the fencing and hedging of fields, but also represented the triumph of individual ownership over the rights of the rest of the community. Walls and hedges serve a practical agricultural purpose, but they also have a wider, symbolic significance as the boundaries of a private landscape" (Williamson and Bellamy 1987:94, 192–208; see also Bryant 1967:293–304). As E. P. Thompson notes, land privatization shattered landlord responsibilities to the poor and thus undermined "an alternative notion of possession" located in the "petty and particular rights and usages which were transmitted in custom as the *properties* of the poor" (1991:184).[23] Furthermore: "Common right, which was in lax terms coterminous with settlement, was *local* right, and hence also a power to exclude strangers. Enclosure, in taking the commons away from the poor, made them strangers in their own land."

Industrial growth, then, was necessarily accompanied by a reassessment of the function of law with respect to land rights and state control, which made local people "strangers" and altered the reproduction of community identity within the rural landscape. An intended, but often unremarked upon, consequence of legal centralization was the puncturing of any remaining social and cultural ties local villages had with their long-standing lords. For a codified law better served an emerging culture of entrepreneurs and fostered a diminishing imperative to designate the particularities of a locality—legally and socially.[24] By the mid-nineteenth century, the moral and ideological codes that sustained premodern rural customs based on a reciprocity of needs and acknowledged rights between the have and have-nots were severely shattered.[25] Normative legality, existing in informal and unidentified local communities without legal standing, and thus outside the logic of English state governance and a philosophy of corporate individualism, was denigrated and eventually abandoned (see Rose 1993:124–25).

In Kent, as elsewhere, local outbreaks of resistance did not halt the advance of modern capitalism and the accompanying transition in notions of individualism, both with respect to other individuals and with respect to the state.[26] One consequence was that beating the bounds all but died out by the end of the nineteenth century, highlighting the instability of the village entity in the rural landscape. Explicit in this dismantling of the village parish system was the declining significance of legal customs and norms in the reproduction of locality.[27] Individualism, utilitarianism, and rationalism, and the English legal system that embraced these concepts, reigned supreme throughout the eighteenth, nineteenth, and twentieth centuries. However, the transition to the ideal of an autonomous individual operating independently from surrounding community values and historical contexts was never fully achieved. And, particularly since the late 1960s, with the rise of new social movements and other philosophies that seek to reinstate the significance of the collective community, the values embodied within English law are now being openly challenged.

Beating the Bounds in 1994

According to the Open Spaces Society,[28] there has been an unprecedented resurgence of interest in beating the bounds since 1989. Over fifty villages performed beating the bounds in 1993, and even more villages participated in 1994. The society has been the main stimulus to current interest in beating the bounds. From the society's perspective, the ritual's importance lies in its public declaration of interest in local commons, helping to reinstate an informal property regime that puts value in "public" land—and so runs contrary to a utilitarian-based law and economics position endorsed by Thatcherism. According to one of its pamphlets, on Rogation Sunday:

There are all too many interests keen to encroach on the margins of our commons and greens. If no one objects in time, it can mean common land is permanently lost. So beating the bounds is just as important *today*. It reminds your local community that they *have* a common or green with a boundary to be guarded, and in the process also shows them how much enjoyment and interest the area has to offer. It's a practical and enjoyable way to protect a valuable part of our heritage. (Open Spaces Society n.d.: 2)

Most of the villages identified with performing beating the bounds are in southeast and southwest England (Open Spaces Society 1993, 1994). One of these is Fordwich, a small and well preserved village about four miles outside Canterbury where issues of local heritage are taken very seriously.[29] Here, beating the bounds is performed every year and is very much a local rather than a tourist event. Dressed up in muddy Wellington boots, anoraks, woolen sweaters, and limp cloth caps, people arrive in the main square around 10 A.M. on the Sunday before Ascension Day, armed with their dogs and the anticipation of a hearty pub lunch. It is a family event, friendly and congratulatory, as people slowly walk the outskirts of the village pointing and tapping with walking sticks the few remaining boundary stones designating the parish limits. In some cases, a child "bumps" these boundary stones (in imitation of the old custom of bouncing the choirboy) to remind the child of parish limits.

Of course, the village of Fordwich is not representative of the general Kentish landscape. Many villages, even the smaller ones, are now populated by people who do not know each other, such as the touristy village of Chilham which is occupied by a disproportionate number of London's weekend commuters prepared to pay handsomely for their "rustic" retreats. Tranquil rural life is, for the most part, an illusory ideal. Nonetheless, it is important to reflect upon this nostalgia for a disappearing countryside. In the context of this brief discussion, the aesthetic deterioration of the countryside is of secondary importance to the forms through which this loss is being perceived, vitalized, and politicized.

In Kent, the revival of beating the bounds is one of many expressions of a popular anxiety about the need to preserve the landscape and, specifically, a communal right to public property. Beneath this anxiety, however, runs the related but deeper concern in the English sensibility of identification with the land. This is linked historically to the loss of empire and more currently to the diminishing of Britain as a political and economic world leader. In recent years this fear has become even more intense, as illustrated by the commodification and commercialization of heritage, which has become a huge English industry (Walsh 1992; Ashworth 1994).

Against the heritage background, the resurgence of interest in beating the bounds becomes both more complicated and more interesting. This is particularly so when its main advocates tend not to be native Kent residents but more recent arrivals from London and other urban areas who escape the city in search of a sense of morality, community, and locality in which to play out their rural fantasies. This indicates that the beating the bounds ritual is now much more polyvalent in its symbolic referencing than its historical parish derivation initially suggests. In Barham, according to Mr. Humphreys:

> A lot of the people living here are ex-urban people really, and, funnily enough, the chairman of the Parish Council who organized the previous beating of the bounds was a Londoner, who became a farmer. . . . He came here and took an enormous interest. It's rather like a convert, I suppose, whereas local people took it all rather for granted. It's often like that, when an outsider picks things up. . . . It came I think with broader education, which happened with the war and which took longer to get down to East Kent, mind you. I'm not sure that ought to have gone on record. . . . Another thing is that all that happened through the women's institutes in those days [i.e., interest in local history], and you hear more about it now because it's the projection business; there's a Barham Society, a Petham Society, an Ash Society, and all of these are independent of the Parish Council, and they all started thinking about it. I think partly its because other people come from other areas and want to find out where they've come to, search around, and get to know the people who live here (interview, 25 Feb. 1994).

The resurgence of interest in village customs and local practices cannot be dismissed as simply sentimental yearnings for a past golden age. In consciously linking the past with the future, the force of custom rests on its symbolic capacity to historically ground and, in a sense, legitimate shifting cultural aspirations. Custom today, as throughout history, exemplifies particular social ideologies and community relations. Of course, it is important not to overly interpret. There is an attractive element of security in the continuities of ritual, and most people would agree with Mr. Humphreys that they participate in beating the bounds "for fun, really." Yet, I argue that the current impetus, especially by "city" people,[30] to revive a practice so central to the production of locality in premodern life is more telling of deep social and political undercurrents than is immediately apparent. At the forefront are people's anxieties about England (and Kent's) future place in a united Europe. Thus, revitalizing an old land ritual is about more than merely the asserting of historical continuities. Customary ritual is also a way of remaking the world, of changing the present, of redirecting a sense of history.

Other Local Community Activities

Beating the bounds is only one of many local events in Kent that seek to reinstate a sense of local community imagined through a rural landscape. The Open Spaces Society, Common Ground, and other charities fear that the privatization schemes promoted by recent conservative governments threaten the remaining common lands accessible to the general public. In questioning the central government's ruling capitalist ideology and the so-called "enterprise culture" fostered under Thatcherism (Heelas and Morris 1992), the Open Spaces Society and Common Ground intrinsically come into conflict with the dominant mode of Tory politics. For instance, in 1993 the Open Spaces Society launched an "Open Spaces—Special Places" campaign and established a charter. This charter sets out proposals for legislation to guarantee the protection of open land for collective recreational purposes. Importantly, the Open Spaces Society advocates that local authorities be vested with the control of common land. This contests central government efforts over the past decade to divest local bodies of power, which results in the declining significance of local government structures and the removal of local geographical variations—what Richard Johnston has called the replacement of "place by placelessness" (1991:245). Thus, in seeking to reinstate legally the value of localism through generating interest in common lands and village greens, the Open Spaces Society promotes an alternative sense of justice that ultimately rejects exclusive property rights and selfish individualism.[31]

The Open Spaces Society's aims resonate somewhat ironically with other local practices in Kent, even those more explicitly insurgent in nature. At one extreme are the few but conspicuous itinerants that claim rights to squat on common land.[32] More significant in terms of their political strength are the many supporters of the environment who are involved in a variety of projects concerned with noise, pollution, road construction, bicycle paths, and rail lines, as well as the stabilizing of microenvironments exclusive for the survival of rare species of birds and wildlife. In Kent, the Council for the Protection of Rural England (CPRE) has heightened anxiety about losing the island-nation and, specifically, the "Garden of England" as a national landscape. To counteract this sense of loss, CPRE promotes European law as a potential strategy for achieving "better decision-making and greater public participation in the decision making process," which it claims "can result in tangible, practical improvements in procedures and legislation" (Sheate 1992:90). On the ground, CPRE's "Campaigner's Guide to Using EC Environmental Law" outlines step-by-step how local lobby groups can petition Brussels and bring attention to the British government's numerous environmental transgressions. This strategy was put into action when CPRE joined up with four Kent groups, including the Kent Association of Parish Councils, as the local watchdog body on the implementation of the Channel Tunnel Rail Link (Kent Action Group 1993). What this sort of activity suggests is that there is an emerging tendency to use EU leverage to strengthen local control, both against private enterprise and the national government.

Now that the Channel Tunnel is finally operating, the forms and strategies of local Kent politics have shifted. The focus of contention has moved away from the tunnel itself toward the implementation of the fast rail link between London and the coast. Energies have been dispersed. What remains, however, is an invigorated sense that Kent's environment is of value and must be protected. This has resulted in independent umbrella bodies such as the Canterbury District Environmental Network that seeks to link up small volunteer groups, bicycle clubs, and local green interests. In early 1995, the network involved fifty-one organizations, ranging from regional branches of Friends of the Earth, Greenpeace, and The Body Shop, to Kent Bat Group, Kent Farming and Wildlife Advisory Group, and Action on Canterbury Traffic group. As an indication of the extent of their activities, during the unusually cold and miserable winter of 1995, these groups nonetheless organized fifty-three events, workshops, conservation tasks, and evening information nights. One member from the Chartham Conservation and Recycling Enterprise, which, like many of these groups, began in the past five years, informed me:

> We were not directly influenced by the Channel Tunnel, but like many of our parishioners, we are concerned about the effect on Kent countryside that the works have caused. Our conservation activities are mainly concerned with the parish of Chartham, e.g. maintenance of Public Rights of Way, tree preservation and preservation of ancient features such as Parish boundary banks and stones. (private correspondence, 23 Nov. 1993)

This sentiment was reinforced by the leader of Canterbury Conservation Volunteers, another local environmental group:

> In the past few years, there has certainly been an explosion of public interest in conservation issues, and I'm sure the Channel Tunnel has played its part in convincing local people that they have to do something before the Kent countryside gets swallowed up. . . . The development generated by the Tunnel will certainly be a major catalyst to this trend. (private correspondence, 19 Jan. 1994)

This sense of locality is further supported by emerging groups such as the Canterbury group of LETS (Local Exchange Trading System), which replaces money with a supposedly medieval system of bartering through the exchange of goods and services. This group was set up in early 1994, and as yet it is too early to comment upon its success. What is crucial about this system, which is also in operation in Manchester, South Devon, and elsewhere, is both its objections to governmental authority and its use of an alternative unit of currency, which means that it can only operate within a limited local territory (Worpole 1994:171). In Canterbury, the unit of currency has been called "Tales" (as in *The Canterbury Tales*) in order to immediately identify the local vicinity in which the system operates. According to Andry Ryrie, a former businessman and now coordinator of Canterbury LETS, "By using an interest free unit of currency, which only has value locally, people are given the chance to regenerate community facilities and spirit rather than see the fruits of their labour taken for investment in more lucrative markets elsewhere" (*Kent Adscene*, 14 Jan. 1994; *Guardian*, 25 April 1995:13).

This brings the discussion back to the wider symbolism embodied in beating the bounds. Just as beating the bounds rearticulates the village space, these other activities, be it a hedgerow restoration project or the setting up of a recycling scheme, are also committed to building up a locality and carving out a sense of place.[33] For the first time, people from various political perspectives are becoming involved in local politics and have helped push green issues to the forefront. The underlying question asked, and one that was used for a regional meeting organized to discuss health, transportation, and the environment, is "What Kind of Kent?" (26 Feb. 1994 Maidstone).

The sense of anxiety over what constitutes Kent County is certainly increased by an encroaching London suburbia. But, from the perspective of Kent, this is a long-standing problem. In recent years, what has propelled the anxiety to new heights is the proposed fast rail link that would physically join London to mainland Europe. As travelers race at 210 km/h (130 MPH) through the Kentish landscape—further diminishing perceptions of space within England *and* expanding spatial relations within Europe (see Schivelbusch 1986:33–43)—residents fear that a sense of local identity, formerly determined by Kent's isolation from London, will be destroyed. Hence, there are real concerns that tourism, vital in the reproduction and survival of the symbolic garden landscape, will be diverted elsewhere.[34] (Images hover of the seedy and depressed Isle of Thanet on the Kent coast as a constant reminder of the vital importance of the tourist dollar.) For locals, the most dreaded consequence of the fast rail link is that the perceived distinction between city and country will be confused and blurred.[35] With these fears in mind, I argue that many of the local and regional activities mentioned above seek to metaphorically establish new boundary stones in the "possessioning" of Kent. They implicitly evoke a spatial relation that seeks to differentiate and impose distance between what is going on at the ground with what is thought to be happening in London. In short, local practices seek to reinstate "mental boundaries" and re-mark territorial borders that identify the limits of membership.

I am not suggesting that Kent residents are any less patriotic or nationalistic than other English citizens in support of their homeland. I am arguing, however, that precisely because of its projected garden image and "old-world" charm, the impact of Europe's physical intervention in Kent is that much the greater. So, unlike the north of England, where the concept and implications of a European Union are rather remote, in Kent there is no getting around it. In local newspapers, at school, on supermarket shelves, and in the streets, there are consistent images, sounds, and choices reminding Kent residents of their increasing perception of spatial proximity to mainland Europe. This is reinforced through Kent County Council whose administration is now orchestrated both through the British government and through the *Euroregion*, which is a transborder legal institution created by the EU to link Kent to Nord-Pas de Calais and the three Belgian regions of Flanders, Wallonia, and Brussels Capital. Over the past five years the Euroregion has attracted £35 million of EU regional funds and is establishing multiple transborder networks.

Kent in England

All of this transborder activity suggests that Kent is confused about its future role as England moves toward an integrated Europe. And it is this ambivalence that lays the foundations and potential for a greater reception to European law. When feeling unjustly ignored by London and forced to make their own way, Kent residents are possibly more inclined to explore what mainland Europe has to offer.[36] Historical narratives about the familiarity of London and the strangeness of Europe are disturbed. At the very least, Kent residents are directly confronted with a range of possibilities existing outside England. For instance, issues of subsidiary and regional autonomy will have increasing import in Kent. These EU schemes seek to reinstate power in local authorities and so contradict the British government's policy of national centralization. A second area of conflict is the Social Charter, spelled out in the *Maastricht Treaty* (1992), and finally signed by Britain in 1997 in Amsterdam. The British government was the only member-state to refuse initially to accept the Social Charter. But now that job opportunities for English people in mainland Europe are opening up, particularly with the fast rail link, Britain's "opt-out" on implementing EU directives regarding workers' rights to representation, child labor, and maternity pay is increasingly less tolerated by other EU countries. A third area of significance is property law. Existing controls in France, Denmark, and other member-states control a person's absolute right to own certain land. The French legislation, for example, requires that all farmland must be monitored by locally-based statutory authorities who determine the fitness of a potential landowner. This directly conflicts with modern English law and the principle of absolute ownership, unfettered by any responsibilities to conservation or a notion of collective rights to the environment. But since a great deal of people in Kent are concerned with green issues, it is through European environmental law that many people are being introduced to the potential of Brussels as an alternative site of justice and superior juridical power.

Analogous to the reforms that centralized English law in the nineteenth century, what is now being experienced is a new phase of legal concentration with Brussels as its center. But whereas locality (and custom) had only a limited role in Margaret Thatcher's Liberal economy, the EU is making efforts to accommodate local territories. Brussels is implementing legislation and legal institutions, such as the Committee of Regions, in an effort to promote grassroots local participation. Thus, for Kent residents, the legal conditions through which it may forge and maintain its future regional identity are changing. Certainly it is too early to predict the long-term effects, which in the end may not be extensive; however, what is important is that EU law is fragmenting national legal narratives and the "flat, contiguous and homogenous space of nationness" (Appadurai 1996:189). To put it differently, EU law is disrupting the mythology of modern western law (Fitzpatrick 1992) or what Katherine Verdery has called conventional "state-subject relations" (Verdery 1992:10). And it is such disruption that is granting local custom the space to make a comeback, on new terms and conditions. In this light, I characterize the ritual of beating the bounds as both a funeral march and celebratory promenade.

Ironically, while this destabilizing confusion about what constitutes Kent's identity is going on within Kent, at a national level, Kent County is perceived as the landscape most symbolically English. This affirms that the relationship between law and property as embodied through a particular landscape is no less intense in constituting the national identity as it is in constituting that of Kent. The difference lies in the English sensibility being rooted in the island-space of Britain, the "fortress built by nature for herself against infection and the hand of war." (Shakespeare, *Richard II*). This island sensibility upholds the inextricability of land with national identity and is significantly defined and defended through English law that sustains the nation-state's autonomy. In short, the very idea of England relies upon its physical and symbolic territorial independence.

In being forced—so to speak—to beat its own bounds, England has concentrated its attention once again on Kent as emblematic of English heritage and custom. Kent symbolizes a cozy garden, but, curiously, this garden that has survived the advance of industrialization also represents ethnic homogeneity and resistance to foreign invasion. These images are now being manipulated and distorted, particularly by the media. Thus, allied to the blurring of lines between country and city, between rural landscapes and the suburban sprawl, Kent's bounded limits have become fluid and reflexive, denoting a resurgence of interest in a rural identity that cannot be divorced from its national symbolism of idyllic permanence. What better than the garden of England, framed by the white cliffs of Dover, to provide England with the biggest and most symbolic of all boundary cornerstones?

So it is perhaps not just a coincidence that in 1992, in the midst of talk over the devaluation of British currency and its replacement by the new European Currency Unit (ECU), the English ten-pound note was redesigned with a "quintessentially English" image. This was an illustration adapted from Dickens's *Pickwick Papers*, and it depicts a cricket match played on a village green in the heart of Kent, framed by a marquee and Parish Church tower (Andrews 1992). Similarly, it is fitting that in 1990 the infamous *Sun* newspaper urged its twelve million readers to travel the twenty-three miles to Dover, stand on Shakespeare's cliff (beneath which the Channel Tunnel runs), hold up their fists in a rude gesture towards France, and shout in unison "UP YOURS DELORS" to the President of the European Commission, Jacques Delors (*Sun*, 1 Nov. 1990).[37] But perhaps the most telling example of the importance of coastal borders in the makeup of the English identity is the publication entitled *Coastlines*, published by the British Council to mark the United Kingdom presidency of the European Council of Ministers in 1992. Here explicit mention is made of the Channel Tunnel drawing Britain closer to mainland Europe. In light of increasing European "partnership"—rather than unity—*Coastlines* commemorates the enduring need for Britain to maintain its coasts, which, it points out, the nation has more of than any other member-state and which are symbolic "not so much as a barrier, but as a natural frontier" (*Coastlines* 1992:1).

The complicated and tense relations between the EU and Britain can only be hinted at here (see George 1990). Suffice to say that since 1992, when the Maastricht Treaty strengthened the role of the European Parliament and diminished the powers of member-state's representatives, English relations have become worse, not better. Britain appears determined, almost as a matter of principle, to take an isolated and contrary stand to every other state member. Because of this reluctance, there is periodic talk of a two-track Europe with Britain being relegated a second-level player. For instance, Britain has decided not to participate initially in the European Monetary Union that commenced in 1999 despite the pro-European stand adopted by Tony Blair's Labour Party, which was overwhelmingly voted into government in May 1997.

In this wider European context, Kent County has renewed significance in the national political landscape as evidenced by the booming heritage industry. As the bounded garden of England, its very character depends upon it being an anomaly within what is otherwise projected as a highly industrialized, but now floundering, nation. Thus integral to Kent's garden imagery is both its capacity to affirm England's past glories and greatness and, at the same time, defuse the import of the Channel Tunnel and its symbolism of an encroaching Europe. In other words, Kent's garden imagery provides a comforting reassurance that London remains the disciplinary center (the landowner and gardener) of a significant political and economic power. The important corollary to this is that the English remain culturally unique. The irony, however, is that at the same time the image of Kent is being used to support the idea of nation, its local practices are increasingly being orchestrated through Europe and specifically by European law. Hence this increasing mediation of Kentish identity through Europe undermines Kent's symbolism in the English imaginary at the same time that it is affirmed.

Conclusion

By way of conclusion I wish to stress that in contexts increasingly transnational, we can no longer assume a state-territorial structure. Nor can we presume a directly derivative relationship of locality to the state. In exploring law as a field of social action in the European Union, it becomes increasingly clear that new scales and new spatial spheres of legal interaction, interpretation, and consequence are emerging.

This essay has articulated one instance where the varied responses of national, regional, and local spheres of action to law come into conflict and shape the way law as a field of social action constitutes and defines its sphere of application. In other words, I have tried to show that it is as important to study how different contexts and places react to law as it is to analyze to whom, how, and why different laws apply. In England, Kent residents, and particularly the Kent County Council, have reacted with guarded enthusiasm to the idea of Europe and the potential of

Brussels as an alternative system of justice. At the same time, the British government, answering to an increasingly powerful EU, has taken a stand on sovereignty that encourages it to act with a determined inflexibility. England has backed itself into a corner. And the EU exacerbates the whole situation by recognizing that its future legitimation depends on grassroots support. It anxiously acknowledges and attempts to give aid to local and regional communities, and a potent example of this is the EU's sanctioning of the transborder *Euroregion* that institutionalizes Kent's links to Nord-Pas de Calais, Flanders, Wallonia, and Brussels Capital.

What I wish to demonstrate is that in exploring law as a field of social action in increasingly transnational contexts, the first question that must be asked is what law and what jurisdiction are operating? An answer is required before there can even be an attempt to articulate a field, be it semiautonomous or otherwise. No longer can there be presumed a directly derivative relationship between locality as defined against and through the state. Similarly, there cannot be assumed one primary legal order, one territorial jurisdiction, and one pivotal authority around which pluralist perspectives and interpretations of law can oscillate, resist, and reshape. In Europe, new legal hierarchies, new territories of legal meaning, and new avenues of legal redress are emerging and bring into question each country's legal sovereignty. Additional points of reference and conflict are emerging below and beyond the level of the nation-state, and, at the same time, affect what that level means and how it continues to be defined. Of course, none of this is entirely new or revelatory. Nation-states have never been stable legal units. It just so happens that current events in the New Europe explicitly highlight and seek to institutionalize these political and social processes, suggesting the need to re-examine and give weight to local customs as innocuous as beating the bounds.

Notes

Thanks to Carol Greenhouse, Kay Warren, and Elizabeth Mertz, as well as the editorial reviewers for their very helpful comments. A special thanks to Peter Fitzpatrick. The essay draws on material gathered during field research in England from 1993 to 1994 and appears in more expansive form in *Bridging Divides: The Channel Tunnel and English Legal Identity in the New Europe*, which was published by the University of California Press in 1999. A shorter version of this essay appears in *Political and Legal*

Anthropology Review (1995):63–74. Research was supported by grants from the National Science Foundation and the Wenner-Gren Foundation for Anthropological Research.

1. Recently, tourism has greatly promoted a widespread appeal and commercial value in the quintessential English countryside (see Urry 1990). Also important has been the emerging concern in English environmental issues, peaking in political terms in 1989 with the rise (and demise) of the Green Party. These and other factors such as the imposition of EU environmental standards have been of critical significance in altering England's city/country relationship (Darian-Smith 1999).

2. See Williams 1973; Viswanathan 1993; Waller 1983; Lowenthal 1994; Walsh 1992; Wright 1985; Shoard 1987; and, generally, Mingay 1989b.

3. Today, the force sustaining England's legal imagination relies upon the image of absolute property ownership in a naturalized "old England," where tradition, common sense, and legal precedent play a significant role. Evoking a past when the nation's economic and political stability flourished, the country garden landscape associated with Kent County today provides an organic metaphor for a particular temporal and spatial landscape that mythically represents the imperial glory of England, the identity of Englishness, and the superior authority of English law (see Darian-Smith 1995a).

4. See Sally Falk Moore's profoundly influential essay on law as a semiautonomous social field (Moore 1978:54–81). For an analysis of Moore's essay in terms of rethinking what is understood by the expression "legal pluralism," see Griffiths 1986.

5. "In the international society . . . each state caters to its own needs and must have a power potential for doing so. Power is excessively possessed and exercised by states, an arrangement which the law sanctions through sovereignty. There is no authority above the states either for limiting their power potential, or regulating the manner of its use. Such limitation and regulation are matters of agreement among the states and enforceable only by each individually" (Levi 1980:545). This analysis of state cooperation applies to institutions such as the United Nations and NATO, which are conglomerates of state powers and exert authority on the basis of consensus among state representatives. When acting under these international umbrellas, a group of states can force a country to comply with, for instance, standardized environmental standards. But this does not undercut state sovereignty per se, rather it forces a state to comply through fear of economic sanctions and international media condemnation.

6. I have in mind here Marilyn Strathern's notion of "focus," that is, the bringing into view particular scales or levels of action that are today commonly thought of as "local" and "global." As Strathern notes, "If one focuses on the local it vanishes in the realization that one person's local forms are another's global ones, and vice versa. This is a cultural practice we might wish to make explicit" (Strathern 1995b:30). In this sense, the EU does not create a new global level, but it does provide the conditions through which so-called transnational relations may be constructed, produced, articulated, and substantiated.

7. As John Ruggie has argued, not only may "the institutional, juridical, and spatial complexes associated with the [European C]ommunity . . . constitute nothing less than the emergence of the first truly postmodern international political form," but that understanding this new entity "requires an epistemological posture that is quite different from the imperious claims of most current bodies of international relations theory" (Ruggie 1993:140, 169).

8. Parishes, by definition, contained a small church and were the basic units of ecclesiastical jurisdiction. On average, they contained 300 to 400 people. Thus town parishes were cramped compared to those in agricultural communities. Whether in towns or villages, the importance of beating the bounds was that it ensured property owners provided for the parish poor and, as a corollary to this, that small communities retained a measure of local authority and autonomy (see Holmes 1962:42, 59–67).

9. There are numerous variations on this theme. For instance, the opening scene in Thomas Hardy's *Tess of the d'Urbervilles* depicts a women's club that had walked for hundreds of years in an annual "processional march of two and two round the parish. . . . In addition to the distinction of a white frock, every woman and girl carried in her right hand a peeled willow wand, and in her left a bunch of white flowers" (Hardy 1891:6–7).

10. Bouncing or bumping the choirboy was intended to impress the place of the boundary marker upon the child. In 1830 a trial was reported in the *Observer* newspaper that a man fishing within Walthamstow parish limits was bumped by the parishioners to remind him of his boundary transgression. In the mid-1970s when beating the bounds was performed in Barham parish, Kent, the churchwarden's grandson was apparently bounced on the only remaining boundary stone (interview 25 Feb. 1994).

11. See Brand 1795:201; for impact of the plague in Kent, Jessup 1974:63; Mingay 1990:59–63.

12. I have explored links between imagining disease and imagining foreignness elsewhere in the context of England's current obsession with the infiltration of the rabies virus (Darian-Smith 1995b). Of significance to this relationship, both now and in the past, is Kent's physical proximity to mainland Europe and the vast networks of interaction across the channel that heighten the desire and intensify the need to exclude "polluted" outsiders.

13. In 55 B.C. Julius Caesar declared Kent the most civilized part of England and placed it on par with occupied Gaul. Even then it appears that the area of Kent was remarkably removed from the rest of the country. By the end of the fifth century, after the Roman legions abandoned England and returned to the defense of Rome, the Saxon kingdom had been firmly established. King Ethelbert (560–616) governed and made Kent one of the most advanced of all Saxon kingdoms. Its prestige caught the attention of Pope Gregory who in 597 sent Augustine and his forty missionaries to preach Christianity to the English "heathens." On their way to London, these religious messengers stopped and settled in Canterbury and later in Rochester, building at each site grand cathedrals. As a result of Augustine, the Pope established the position of Archbishop of Canterbury and declared Canterbury the ecclesiastical See of England. Kent was again invaded by the Normans in 1066, who were eventually defeated by the English, and shortly thereafter London was declared the new capital. Yet, despite this transfer of power, Kent continued to grow in political and economic stature by further developing its military fortifications, ports, dockyards, trading fleets, church administration, and legal system (for recent commentaries of Kent history, see Jessup 1974; Bignell 1983; Brandon and Short 1990).

14. Kent was not alone in having its own system of tenure and inheritance, which differed between places largely according to the social structures that accompanied woodland or village landscapes (for a fascinating discussion of the intricacies of the English landscape based on medieval agricultural practices, see Williamson and Bellamy 1987:45). As MacFarlane has noted, "The situation is made more difficult since at no date between 1250–1750 could a single book have summarized the customs of the manor in England" (MacFarlane 1978:106).

15. See Sandys 1851:307, 7–15, fn. 1 at 17, and (for differences between the two systems) 92; also Elton 1867.

16. For instance, Michael Drayton's poem of 1622, "Poly-Olbion," stressed the autonomy of Kent's legal customs, which were of critical importance to the county's defense of the greater English freedom from foreign law:

> O NOBLE KENT, quoth he, this praise doth thee belong,
> The hardest to be controld, impatientest of wrong.
> Who with the *Norman* first with pride and horror sway'd,
> Threwst off the servile yoke upon the English layd,
> And with a high resolve, most brauely didst restore
> That libertie so long enjoy'd by thee before.
> Not suffring forraine lawes should thy free customes bind,
> Then onely show'dst thy self of th' ancient *Saxon* kind
> (cited in Sandys 1851:90)

17. For an interesting connection between the myth surrounding the English nation's Saxon descent and its implications of racial purity, liberal law, and democratic institutions that accompanied a growing English nationalism in the mid-seventeenth century, see Francis Whyte's *For the Sacred Law of the Land* (1652) and Richard Hawkins's *A Discourse of the National Excellencies of England* (1658), which are discussed in MacDougall 1982:62–70.

18. Time and again, especially when talking to the elderly, I was asked whether I knew about this distinction—rather, I suspect, to test me. The popular explanation is that men of Kent lived east of Canterbury, Kentish men west. While some people today may not recognize this historical distinction, there appears to remain evidence of a strong sense of Kentish identity, particularly among the older generations. The Association of Men of Kent and Kentish Men has four thousand active members and twenty-three branches ("Guarding Kent Traditions," *Kent Life*, August 1993, 40). It is interesting that a recent dictionary of Kent dialect, drawing on an earlier 1888 version, explains that historical records dating back to 1066 suggest that the phrases Kentish Men and Men of Kent merely involve "a distinction without a difference" (Major 1981:126).

19. In the nineteenth century, the railway was crucial in opening up labor markets and communications. Cities such as Manchester and Liverpool grew at spectacular rates. By 1848 one could travel by train from Edinburgh to London. The reduction of travel times between towns and places led to an "enormous shrinkage in the national space" and instrumentally united the British nation and reorganized its political economy (Thrift 1990:463; see also Kellett 1969; Faith 1990:58–70; Schivelbusch 1986:33–43).

20. For instance, the economic depression that followed the Napoleonic War harshly affected rural Kent, giving impetus to popular movements such as the Swing Riots of 1830–1831 and the Courtney Rising of 1838 when the poor demanded higher wages and lower food prices (see Mingay 1989a, 1990:154–64). Across the nation, events such as the Peterloo Massacre of 1819 and the Chartists campaigns in 1839, 1842, and again in 1848 helped raise a popular consciousness about the poor and electorally underrepresented.

21. There is an interesting correlation between the first official census taken in England in 1801 and the rise of the regional scale of differentiation (and the fall of public concern in smaller localities) at roughly the same time. As has been noted, this was partly because many types of government-administered data collections and surveys such as the *General Household Survey* and *New Earnings Survey* adopted the regional scale and so officially enshrined its spatial value (see Savage 1989:247).

22. The history of English property law leading up to the general enclosure acts of 1836, 1840, and 1845 is very complicated (see Turner 1984; Burt and Archer 1994; for subsequent history, see Douglas 1976; Cox 1984). Parliamentary enclosure involved the reorganization of over 21 percent of England's land but did not affect all places equally (Turner 1984:133). What is important for this discussion is the ideological assumptions that enclosure embodied and promulgated.

23. Furthermore, it brought about much hardship by denying small farmers their rights to pastoral commons (sometimes called "wastes") and eliminating a valuable safeguard against economic hardship. As William Cobbett declared against large farms in his *Political Register*, "I learnt to hate a system that could lead English gentlemen to disregard matters like these! That could induce them to tear up 'wastes.' . . . 'Wastes' indeed!" (Cobbett 1821:520–21). Cobbett goes on, "I am convinced that Paper-money, Large farms, Fine houses, Pauperism, Hangings, Transportings, Leprosy, Scrofula and Insanity, have all gone on increasing regularly to-

gether" (Cobbett 1821:508). This list reflects the degeneration of public health resulting from the decline in village life, where formerly the poor and mentally ill would
have been accommodated and supported.

24. After the 1834 introduction of the poor laws, the parish was not held morally
responsibility for rural poverty. Nor was defense and protection against crime any
longer within the parish domain. Moreover, the remapping of new county court
districts in 1846 denied local justices of the peace—the traditional enforcers of village
law and order—their social, economic, and legal standing (MacDonagh 1980:118).

25. It would take the franchise-widening Reform Bills of 1867 and 1884, driven by
the enthusiasm of the conservative leader "dizzy" Disraeli, to lay the conditions for
the emergence of the British welfare state.

26. Dahlman argues that the open-field system never existed in Kent, particularly
East Kent, and that therefore, enclosure and property subdivisions were probably not
experienced as a change to the same degree there as in other parts of England
(1980:111, 153). This helps explain why the Kentish landscape still retains many
features of a preindustrial age, allowing it to maintain the image of a "back garden"
to the rest of the nation. Kent became peripheral to industry while at the same time
remaining critical to the processes of modern nation-building as a marker of the
past's golden history and the future's technological progress. Yet despite this idealized stagnation, village life and its legal and social customs were fundamentally
disrupted by the acceleration of legislative reform.

27. On the decline of the countryside, see Horn 1984:211–42; Mingay 1990:168–98.

28. The Open Spaces Society located in Henley-on-Thames, Oxon, was established in
1865 by public-spirited reformers (including John Stuart Mill) in response to the
enclosure acts and the widespread appropriation by the state of common lands
(Walsh 1992:71). The citations for the Open Spaces Society publications in this
chapter are as follows: Beating the Bounds List of Events on Rogation Sunday 16 May
1993 and also 8 May 1994 and ". . . And What Will You Be Doing on Rogation
Sunday?" no date of publication.

29. Here, the community is keen to preserve its local traditions and heritage as a
reminder of the days when Fordwich was a thriving inland port in the twelfth and
thirteenth centuries. Indeed in 1994 under the direction of a local historian, the
community of some fifty households created a film about the village's history that
stressed its rise and decline, its still functioning "ducking stool," which once low-
ered witches into the Great Stour River (now only a few feet deep), and the village's
parochial legal jurisdiction administered in what is England's smallest town hall
(McIntosh 1975).

30. Other anthropologists have pointed to the irony of incomers to small villages and
towns who often take over local committees and groups in an effort to "keep alive"
local customs that the native populations are not particularly concerned about (see
Forsythe 1982:94–95; Rapport 1993).

31. On the paradoxical convergence of Green and Conservative perspectives in England, see Gray 1993.

32. Gypsies, as well as the homeless in general, also provide a reason to enforce local laws and community membership as a strategy of exclusion. Thus, they play an ambiguous role in a moral discourse of exclusion—at times the subject of the law and at other times denied legal standing and so ignored by the law altogether.

33. The Kentish Stour Countryside Project puts out a pamphlet calling on landowners, farmers, community groups, Parish councils, and schools to become involved in the conservation and preservation of hedgerows. The pamphlet states that "[w]ith the disappearance of hedges, Rights of Way can be threatened as many follow original hedge boundaries. Footpaths may be ploughed up, making public access more difficult. Traditional field systems are lost, and the sense of place altered" (Kentish Stour Countryside Project, Wye, Kent).

34. In economic terms, it has already been projected that a transport corridor bypassing Kent will be detrimental to the region. (Vickerman 1991).

35. "New technologies may not only lead to new arrangements of people and things. They may, in addition, generate and 'naturalize' new forms and orders of causality and, indeed, new forms of knowledge about the world" (Akrich 1992:207).

36. Mr. David Crowhurst, a Conservative councilor representing the Cheriton area, said: "We won't forgive Mrs. Thatcher for the contempt she has shown for local democracy. She has rushed ahead with indecent haste in a cynical, unacceptable and undemocratic manner." He said Mrs. Thatcher and the Conservatives could have created a "political graveyard" for themselves in East Kent (*Daily Telegraph* [London], 21 Jan. 1986). At this time, local resistance to the government was labeled "a pioneering exercise in grassroots democracy" (*Times* [London], 18 Sept. 1986).

37. George Orwell writing on English patriotism comes to mind: "There can be moments when the whole nation suddenly swings together and does the same thing, like a herd of cattle facing a wolf" (cited in Mander 1963:200).

Nancy Ries

"Honest Bandits" and "Warped People":

Russian Narratives about Money, Corruption, and Moral Decay

In the 1980s, we started with pluralism, and ended with banditism.
—Vitalii Tsepliaev, "Onward, to the Triumph of Capitalism?"

Perestroika (1986–1991) was an era of fervent unveiling: the manifold problems of Soviet society were exposed in all the media; official ideology was delegitimized as the depths of Communist Party corruption and hypocrisy were exposed; shocking histories of revolutionary and Stalinist terror were told and retold. These were the years of glasnost—the policy of transparency decreed by Gorbachev in early 1987 as part of his remedy for bureaucratic, technological, and social stultification. Glasnost quickly overtook the narrow boundaries Gorbachev had set for it, however. For a few years, there was a euphoric sense that all the dark corners of society would be exposed to public scrutiny, and that this exposure might serve as the basis for creating a democratic and just social order.

One of the bitter paradoxes of post-Soviet Russia is how quickly all sense or pretense of transparency evaporated (and with it much of the popular faith in democratization). The veiled complexities of communist prevarication have given way to manipulations of public information that are more open but all the more mystifying for their visibility, and all the more troubling for their ubiquity. Many of the conversations I had with people in Moscow and Yaroslavl during ethnographic fieldwork touched upon the idea of the profound cynicism (tsinism), which many claim characterizes post-Soviet Russia from top to bottom. People talk about cynicism to describe a general context of moral corruption and dishonesty, where it seems that everyone is engaged, to some degree, in cheating, lying, swindling, and stealing—whatever it takes to capture one's share of the available economic resources. Those higher up on the socioeconomic or political ladder are cast as the most cynical, because, while pretending to care about the general welfare, they take advantage of myriad opportunities to enrich themselves at public expense.

As an interlocutor, I take these discourses about cynicism at face value—as embittered expressions of lost faith and political grounding. At the same time, I regard them as a dynamic and powerful field of socio-cultural production. Through talk about cynicism (and through cynical talk), people actively deconstruct whatever legitimizing discourses or practices are presented on behalf of the reformulated political-economic order, and thus regularly inoculate themselves against any naive belief in state or market ideology; at the same time, the notion of ubiquitous cynicism explains and justifies their own less-than-honest actions— actions such as misrepresenting their income on tax declarations or as criminal as hijacking trucks or perpetrating scams. Finally, but perhaps most importantly, cynicism in its many guises is metaphoric short-hand—a way of encapsulating, depicting, and circulating a view of the present world.

The phenomenon of all-delegitimizing cynicism is not, of course, only a post-Soviet one. Under different guises (kitchen table humor, absurdist art forms and talk, participation in the black market) it was quite common in Soviet times.[1] However, in the late years of communist rule in Russia, many still heralded the innocence of the people (narod) in contrast to the corruption of those with power. This claim of popular innocence is one of the things that began to disappear in the early 1990s with the demise of Soviet rule. Thus, the particular cultural contours of post-Soviet cynicism, the metaphors employed to explain the spread of cynicism in Russia, and popular ideas about possible paths of re-demption from the traps of cynicism are the central issues explored in this essay.

Cynicism emerged for me as an ethnographic issue in Yaroslavl,[2] Russia, during the summer of 1995, not in the form of abstract discus-sion, but through vivid narratives centered on two dominant and inter-connected themes: money and the mafia. Not surprisingly, in this new market economy people spoke constantly about money: getting it, keep-ing it, spending it, hiding it; losing it to thieves, swindlers, relatives, or tax authorities; making do without it. As my close friend Olga declared: "This is all anybody talks about anymore: money, money, money. All you hear, even as you pass people on the street, is limony [literally "lem-ons"—then slang for "millions"] as people discuss their crazy ideas, their schemes, their dreams.[3] This is so even among children." I heard a great deal of speculation about other people's money: who had it and by what mysterious means they got it, how they spent it or lost it. Although much of this talk centered on the pragmatics of money, there was a significant moral dimension to these narratives, as well.

People also spoke constantly and colorfully about the mafia, describing personal encounters and engagements with so-called "bandits" [bandity], the thievery, extortion, bombings, shootings, and poisonings attributed to the mafia. As with conversations about money, these stories seemed to invoke simultaneously "the real mafia" and what Katherine Verdery (1996:219) calls "the conceptual mafia" or "the-mafia-as-symbol."[4] One of the ironies of the new capitalism in Russia is the multivalent conceptions of the mafia as both the *destroyer* of any hopes for justice and social order and also the most likely potential *source* of justice and order. To this point I will return later in the essay.

In narratives about money and the mafia, people used a semimythical vernacular to express in a simple, linear fashion the enormously complicated, multidimensional realities of their changing society. To some extent, these condensed narratives seemed keyed to my presence as an interested outsider. I was interviewing people to try to understand something of their reality, but that reality had so many new complications, and there were so many new secrets, that it was hard to convey it except by way of these parables.[5] Through their symbolically charged metacommentaries, people conveyed a general image of the political, economic, social, cultural, and moral complexities, contradictions, and conflicts of their world. These were complexities and conflicts that they faced and were aware of every day, not as abstract issues, but as real dimensions of every social transaction and encounter.[6]

An "Honest Bandit"

I was initiated into the worlds of mafia and money (both real and conceptual) on my first day of fieldwork in Yaroslavl; for this initiation I remain grateful to Pasha, an acquaintance who played a clever ruse on me, probably as an act of sly pedagogy designed to upturn my scholarly pretensions. Although not his main intention, his ploy immersed me all at once in local orientations and practices which would otherwise have become clear only slowly.

Pasha was virtually the only businessperson I knew when I arrived in Yaroslavl to study changing conceptions of work. I called him on my first day in town and asked him if he would set up interviews for me with other people in business in the city. Perhaps irritated because I didn't first invite him for tea (or something stronger), Pasha said he was too busy to help me, although he would think about my request. Within an hour, however, the phone rang, and Alesha, a friend of Pasha's, offered his services as informant.

At noon the next day, Alesha picked me up in a battered, black Mercedes, and we drove to a cafe. The hostess greeted Alesha warmly and seated us in a curtained alcove. After Alesha ordered our meal, he said, "Okay, so what do you want to know?" I politely inquired as to the nature of his business. After a long pause and a piercing but amused look, he said "I . . . am a bandit."

I raised an eyebrow and smirked, trying not to show that I was taken aback. Here I was, on my first full day in Yaroslavl, sitting across the table from a gangster. And the gangster was grinning at me, tracing my reaction, pleased at his ability to disarm a foreign ethnographer.

"Aaah," I said, somewhat at a loss for words. "I had assumed from what Pasha said that you were a businessman."

"Well, yes, I am a businessman. I am in the business of building roofs." Fortunately, I had learned in a conversation with a young student the night before that "roofs" (kryshi) was bandit slang for the various forms of protection the mafia offered. During the rest of my summer in Yaroslavl, and later in Petersburg, Moscow, and Tver, I heard this term invoked constantly—in a short span of time it had become a key cultural referent throughout Russia. I asked Alesha to explain what it meant to provide roofs for people.

> Well, the traders and speculators are always cheating each other. They borrow money and disappear with it. They take goods on consignment and don't pay for them. They are always out to cheat each other, to make money however they can. Goods get stolen out of warehouses and stores. We protect the businessmen from each other. We ensure the collection of debts and recover stolen goods. Our clients' partners know who is protecting them, whether our clients have good kryshi or not. A good krysha means good business.

"Does every business have a krysha? Even the babushki selling potatoes and mushrooms from their rucksacks on the sidewalk? Do schools and hospitals have kryshi?" I asked. He smiled patiently, and it was clear he recognized in my questions the international image of Russian mafia bandits as scoundrels who terrorize the urban population with their "racket":

> We don't make a point of "covering" the *babushki*. But they are constantly hassled by street criminals and alcoholics. So they ask our guys to protect them. So every month they pay maybe twenty, thirty bucks [Alesha spoke of money only in dollars], and we watch over them. The hoodlums know they better not mess with the old ladies because our guys are watching out for them. And schools don't have *kryshi* because there's no money involved. It's only when there is some kind of money that people need protection. Understand, Nancy, we don't go out and seek our clients: *they come to us*, our clients approach *us* to provide them a service which they need.

"You seem like a nice guy," I said, "Do you mind being a bandit? How do you feel about what you do?"

> Bandits are known for their honesty, we protect our clients from being cheated, we enforce their contracts, collect their debts for them, ensure some kind of normal business relations. They know they can count on us. Eventually, this will become, I would like to have it become a legitimate business, a regular kind of collection agency like you have in America.[7]

I asked him how he got into this "business," how it was structured, and how it operated. He explained that he had been an engineer, with an advanced degree, and had worked as a unit director in a local factory. But he was also an athlete, a weight lifter and a boxer with many trophies.

> When all this began, the master under whom I apprenticed proposed starting a gang. Within four years, we built up our gang to the point where we now have an echelon of "middle managers" [*brigadiry*] and thirty "soldiers" [*boitsi*] working under us.

"This is a delicate question, and you don't have to answer if you don't want, but . . . do you ever have to . . . kill anyone?" I inquired. Alesha paused before answering.

> No, there are few killings, it isn't necessary. Although sometimes there are fights among the different gangs [*brigady*] in town. We try to get our men to keep out of trouble, for instance, only to go to

"our" restaurants and bars [I thus realized we were in one of Alesha's protected cafes]. When different gangs mingle, there can be trouble. We try to enforce a policy of discipline. Our boitsi shouldn't drink too much, or smoke even. They should be family men, decent, orderly people.

"And what about the police?" I inquired.

The police know us. They know all the bandiugi [an affectionate diminutive of bandity] in town, who works for whom, whom we protect. They know everything. And they rely on us to provide order which they themselves can't; they don't have the resources. There would just be chaos if not for us, because the businessmen are incapable of running their affairs in an orderly way. Most of them are uncivilized! You know, the Russian people. It's not the decent businessmen who are driving around in Mercedes cars. They live in a more modest way, they have family values and don't need the show-off of fancy homes and cars; it's only those from the working-class backgrounds who need to show off their new wealth.

He went on to explain that he had been arrested in the spring of 1995 and spent an entire month in prison, without charges being filed.

I was lucky to get out after a month, it could have been a lot longer. But I wasn't telling them anything they wanted to know. I just smiled and held my tongue. In general I was well taken care of there. The other prisoners took care of me, because they knew who I was, they brought me so much food I gained five kilos while there. I would sit in my bunk, and the others would bring me food, I didn't even have to leave my cell. Though I had to spend the days without any clothes on, to keep the bedbugs away! It was okay there, however; the cops even gave me mattresses and blankets, you often have just a metal plank to sleep on. I was well treated. And then they just let me go, because they didn't have any charges against me, and I didn't talk. In general the police just have a quota to fulfill, they have to arrest a certain number of us every month, to show they are doing their job.

"What about your wife? Wasn't she upset that you were in jail? Didn't she cry?" I asked.

My wife didn't cry, she was very strong, she understands. My wife is a "good kid" [molodets]. My mother cried.

Honest Bandits and Warped People   **281**

The rest of that day and the next, I spent driving around Yaroslavl with Alesha as he made his rounds. First we met some men in a parking lot outside of a notary public; Alesha sold his old Mercedes, took temporary possession of a decrepit Soviet-era Lada (he explained that he was getting ready to buy a jeep, the only kind of vehicle appropriate for driving the terrible local roads), and then drove to a furniture store (belonging to one of his clients) where he checked the forty hundred-dollar bills he had received for his Mercedes on their counterfeit-currency detection machine. Then we visited other clients together. What was remarkable to me was the ease with which he (and I with him) moved through the ranks of the city: we dropped in on the director of a newly founded private university, walking right in on (and asked to join) some kind of power-lunch; we visited bankers and store-owners, walking freely and unannounced into their offices. Nearly everyone was polite and many were even friendly with Alesha, and he was always polite and soft-spoken, although I sat in a vestibule while a verbal altercation, which I could just barely hear behind closed doors, took place between him and a bank director. At the end of our first day together, we dropped in on his partner, who didn't seem particularly glad to meet me, in part, perhaps, because he was busy taking care of his dying mother, who rested on the couch while Alesha and his partner talked "business."

Everywhere we went, Alesha greeted people he knew on the streets; some, he explained, were also bandits from his or other gangs; others were businesspeople whom he "protected." He was clearly an energetic participant in the flow of activity in the city. At one point we drove up to a set of kiosks to buy some snacks. A policeman jumped out of a jeep parked nearby and greeted Alesha warmly. There ensued a discussion about the policeman buying some ammunition for his "hunting rifle" through Alesha. We stopped in at Alesha's apartment (an average Soviet apartment but with brand new Scandinavian furniture) to pick up some documents he needed; there Alesha unlocked a gigantic safe and proudly displayed to me his collection of firearms and a block of hundred-dollar bills about the size of a breadbox.

During the two days we spent making rounds, Alesha seemed eager to let me observe his business, and he patiently, though elusively and without many details, answered my questions about the structures and practices of the local mafia and its role in the current social and economic system. To this day, I don't know why he agreed to meet with me, or why he was as open with me as he was; when I asked him at one point, he just said, "Why not?" and laughed. My best guess is that it was a form of entertainment for him. He seemed to enjoy performing his identity as a bandit for an awed and interested foreign woman.[8] It is also possible that to some extent he was parading my presence as a sign of his legitimacy and importance, although in general I felt I had very little social capital compared to the obvious wealth and status of him and his clients. In any case, through Alesha, I made contacts with a wide range of people with whom it would have been difficult to meet otherwise, and several of these contacts proved valuable in the development of my networks in the city. To travel the streets with a bandit was to observe the patterns of interconnection and power that structure a postcommunist Russian town; it was also to experience a mysterious, charmed kind of passage across hierarchical boundaries and between a variety of social realms.

Later, in conversations and experiences with other informants, I had many opportunities to gauge the veracity of Alesha's representations of self, city, and society, and to understand the hidden factors in the various transactions I observed with him.[9] While it was difficult for me to discern the degree to which he believed his own claims to legitimacy and service of the common good, I decided that this was not really the main issue: what was important was the enthusiasm with which he employed these legitimizing discourses, which were his personal refractions of a much wider sphere of talk about trust and deception, alliance and conflict, civility and chaos, work and scheming, morality and socio-spiritual corruption.

In his narrative about the role of mafia gangs, Alesha depicts the landscape in postsocialist (or newly capitalist) Russia as a place of weak governance, where the state has insufficient resources and incentives to protect people's interests or those of business. The mafia, on the contrary, has the wherewithal and the will to provide order at ground level where it is needed—and it is needed wherever money is at stake. Alesha depicts the mafia as honest, decent, and disciplined in contrast to low-level businesspeople, whom he casts as unscrupulous, ostentatious, and immoderate; in this he is invoking the popular image of "New Russians" (*Novye Russkie*)—the Russian nouveaux riches who are represented in jokes, media stories, and everyday talk as uncultured, uneducated, and thoroughly corrupted by the thirst for money. During the rest of my fieldwork in Yaroslavl, what was striking to me was the degree to which Alesha's basic construction of the social terrain of contemporary

Russia and the mafia's function in this landscape was echoed in conversations I had with many other people. How was I to explain the fact that elderly, impoverished pensioners described their world in more-or-less the same terms as those used by a successful member of the contemporary Russian mafia? Was Alesha cynically echoing the popular construction because it conveniently legitimized (some of) his business activity? Or were these discourses, dialogically reinforcing and building upon each other, capturing—in the symbolic codes of narrative—some crucial dimensions of the restructuring social world?

Privatization: Views from Within

Although the success of enterprise privatization in Russia has been acclaimed by some outside observers (see, for instance, Aslund 1995 and Blasi, Kroumova, and Kruse 1997), the perspective of Russian citizens who have not been leading participants in the process is not nearly as sanguine. Until the fiscal crises of the late 1990s, the voices of neoliberal politicians, businesspeople, writers, and scholars could be heard around the globe, hailing the birth of capitalism in Russia, conceiving it as the cradle of eventual democracy and prosperity for all. In conversations with international harbingers of optimism during fieldwork in Russia, I was often struck by the passion with which they espouse their worldview, not noticing that their triumphalist declamations do not always echo on the ground.[10] There, local discourses about privatization and marketization are contextualized within a cluster of intertwining phenomena: overnight fortunes and unpaid workers, pyramid schemes and vouchers, "swindles" [obman] and violence. These form basic points of local conceptions of society, economy, and polity.

The spectacle of (seemingly) overnight fortunes has been quite vivid throughout Russia; I say seemingly since in fact many of these fortunes were far from instant; instead they represented, on the one hand, the lifelong maneuvering of Soviet-era elites whose positions allowed them to turn power or status into capital during the late Soviet and early post-Soviet years, and, on the other hand, they represented the proceeds from Soviet-era black market activities, which served as excellent start-up capital in the late 1980s and early 1990s.

Gorbachev's 1988 decree permitting the formation of cooperatives provided a significant opportunity for those poised to privatize. Only a small percentage of the actual economic strategizing that took place during those years was publicly evident, in the form of small retail shops and services that began to appear. Less visible but more meaningful were the enrichment strategies of communist bosses, factory and shop directors, upper- and mid-level KGB functionaries, ministry bureaucrats, and other socialist-era elites, who created cooperatives as devices through which to siphon capital, equipment, labor, and other resources into privately held enterprises. When privatization went into full effect in late 1991, this process escalated dramatically in scope.[11]

Overall, the financial machinations of the elites entailed little investment in productive industry; on the contrary, since they often involved industrial directors, managers, and party bureaucrats conspiring to dismantle and sell off equipment and raw materials which lie within their domains, many productive enterprises devolved into trading organizations or holding companies, and the managerial elites transferred the capital thus acquired into offshore bank accounts or into their privately held cooperatives. Thousands of new banks were registered, and while some were legitimate, many others were merely covers for quasi-legal investment or money-laundering.

Having far more capital than most people, Soviet-era, black-market traders similarly found themselves in a prime position to start cooperatives that would allow them to invest, launder, and build on their existing wealth by entering the sphere of trade on a serious scale. One wealthy Moscow woman explained that her husband made his first fortune in the 1980s by illegally duplicating music and video cassettes for sale on the black market. When he became free to use that capital openly, he started buying and selling real estate in central Moscow. When I interviewed this woman in 1994, the couple was building their first house—a fifteen-room mansion, complete with gazebo, statuary, and fountains, on a lavishly landscaped, four-acre parcel near Moscow.

Nearly everyone I have interviewed has a tale to tell of a friend, relative, colleague, or acquaintance who amassed a considerable fortune after 1991. Such stories were often tinged with awe and aversion, since so many fortunes had their base in the semicriminal shadow economy. In 1994 in Obninsk, a town several hours south of Moscow, a nursery-school teacher told me of a locally infamous, former *fartsovshchik* [Soviet-era slang for foreign currency speculator, a word that connotes a general sleaziness]. Her description vividly summarized the popular image of New Russians who are seen as uncultured, uneducated, and unscrupulous persons who have accrued unthinkable wealth through criminal or quasi-criminal means, and who live in vulgar splendor, tinged with an aura of violence:

> Ten years ago he was kicked out of his apartment and fired from his job for "speculating." He just barely avoided going to prison for his activities. Everybody knew him from childhood, he was always getting in and out of trouble. Now he is the town's richest businessman, with a dacha, a house, several cars, and his own bodyguards. He drives around town in an entourage, his own armored Mercedes surrounded by the cars of his bodyguards with their submachine guns.

While seeing such New Russians aggressively and visibly cruising the streets of the cities, towns, and villages, and while watching their directors building new dachas, purchasing foreign vehicles, and refurnishing their private offices in grand style, most workers are themselves earning salaries below the official subsistence level, are being laid off, or are working for months on end without being paid. Families use a variety of strategies for coping with this. Many of these strategies are similar to those employed in the Soviet period. People depend on relatives, friends, and colleagues for mutual assistance; they employ the science of frugality developed over a lifetime; they rely on the domestic production of foodstuffs (especially via dacha gardening); they do part-time, nighttime, or weekend work, and they engage in many forms of trade to make extra money. Hoarding food, utilizing public benefits and discounts, and pilfering from the workplace remain as common as they were in Soviet times, although the specific contours of these practices have changed somewhat, with new opportunities and constraints.[12]

There were a few moments in the mid-1990s when some people believed that they, too, might partake of the bounties of privatization and make their own overnight fortunes. As part of the official privatization program, in 1992 the Yeltsin administration announced that a voucher worth 10,000 rubles (around $24 at the time) would be distributed to each Russian citizen for investment in the newly privatized enterprise of their choice. Many people believed that their vouchers gave them an opportunity to participate in the future of Russian economic development, although many others realized right off that this was an absurdly insignificant amount of investment capital and regarded the entire campaign as a reflection of the cynical stance of administration reformers toward the population.[13]

In the same years that vouchers were being distributed (roughly 1992 to 1994) a range of investment schemes arose. Billboards, subway cars, and newspapers were plastered with advertisements promising enormous returns on investments; it was common to see ads offering several hundred percent yields on deposits (measured in dollars instead of constantly inflating rubles). The MMM company was the most active promoter of such investment opportunities, and their witty television ads were a topic of widespread public attention and amusement. These depicted Russian folkloric characters, the affable urban simpletons Lenia Golubkov and his family, who used their MMM profits to buy, first, new kitchen appliances, and then fur coats, purebred dogs, a vacation abroad, and a fancy new dacha. These humorous ads worked their magic, and people lined up at investment points all over Russia to hand over their vouchers—and often their entire savings. Being, in fact, nothing more than a countrywide pyramid scheme, MMM collapsed in 1994 when investors began to complain about not receiving their interest and not being able to withdraw their capital. Its director, Sergei Mavrodi, was charged with tax evasion and other financial crimes, but he later ran for and won a seat in the Russian parliament by promising depositors to return their capital if he was elected.[14]

MMM was only the most visible (and most brazen) of hundreds of similar financial pyramids, in which tens of millions of hopeful Russian citizens invested what little capital they possessed.[15] The media in 1995 were full of accounts of angry investors lined up outside the locked doors of these bankrupt firms in hopes of gaining some of their money back. While most of these schemes were ultimately simple, others were more complex marketing pyramids, less prone to sudden collapse but equally unrewarding for most investor-entrepreneurs.

For many the experience of investing in these schemes provided an introduction, in one form or another, to the new world of *obman* (deception and swindling) and to the weird cosmologies of capitalism as well. People by the millions fell for the promise that their investments would "deliver almost preternatural profits . . . yield wealth *sans* perceptible production, value *sans* visible effort" (Comaroff and Comaroff 1999: 281). As one of my Moscow friends put it, "This is our necessary education in economic reality. We invested our money, believing the promises of advertisement, and now we know better, but it is a painful lesson." (She had invested and lost two hundred dollars, the equivalent for her family of two month's salary, and, more importantly, a large chunk of their savings). Quite a few of my informants described their own or their friends'

experiences losing money through such schemes, international, national, or local. They spoke with bitter irony about their own naïveté in
the seductive new marketplace of trickery and con. There were many
ways to be swindled on a large or small scale. Regular day-to-day shopping often entailed hidden risks, and although these might seem relatively insignificant, they created an atmosphere of mistrust and furthered
the sense that everyone had become cynical and corrupt. Although the
development of markets and the ubiquity of kiosks selling everything
from beer to footwear has made shopping much easier than it was in
Soviet times, people regularly remark on the problem of discerning fake
or counterfeit products from genuine name brands: traders sell cheap
imitations of designer clothes, and imported liquor bottles are filled with
illegally-brewed grain alcohol that is tinted with food color.[16] Savvy
consumers have developed numerous ways of discerning the real from
the fake,[17] and the sharing of shopping experiences and advice is a
regular topic of conversation. Writing about consumption habits in
contemporary Russia, Caroline Humphrey comments that people buy
from kiosks with the "certain knowledge that they are being 'cheated' "
and, she argues, with a full understanding of the various mechanisms
through which that cheating is perpetrated (1993:51). "Public markets,"
she writes, "have become huge fairs of disingenuousness" (63).

Property transfers also present a significant risk of swindle. With
privatization, buying and selling property became legal, and property
transfers occur at a furious pace. The market, however, is full of shady
real estate agents and crooked developers, who have worked out myriad
ways of cheating people out of their money or their property. They sell
properties that don't belong to them, abscond with deposits and down
payments, snare customers in high-interest loans that they can't repay,
or get people to sign away their property by taking advantage of the
complex bureaucracy involved. This last method has been especially
effective in swindling elderly people who don't understand the intricacies of contracts. Explaining why she dare not sell or trade her apartment, whose mortgage payments she could no longer afford, one small-
scale businesswoman declared that "if they want to swindle you, they
will find a way. The agents know the ins and outs of the paperwork. No
matter how savvy and careful we are, they are many steps ahead of us
with their little tricks." My friend Olga, a schoolteacher, and her husband Yuri, a bookkeeper (one of the "prestigious" new professions, in
which a person could earn a decent salary, at least until the banks

collapsed in 1998), told me their story of a property swindle which took place in 1995:

> We tried to buy another apartment. We found some agents, and they showed us a place, and we put a deposit down on it. Then they refused to give us the apartment or our money back, the whole thing was just a huge swindle. We tried to get some guys to help us get the money back, we had our own *krysha*, but the agents' krysha was stronger, and our krysha couldn't break through theirs.

People engaged in business or trade face the challenge of avoiding swindles and dealing with unreliable partners, clients, and suppliers on a daily basis; the risks involved correspond, of course, to the scale of the business being transacted. Hence the ubiquity of *kryshi* in business. It is no exaggeration to say that everyone doing business has some kind of "roof"—whether supplied by bandits, the police, or some other form of official connections (or all of the above).[18] "Where money flows," as one businessman said, "there is always a risk of swindle, because money attracts swindlers like flies; swindlers have a nose for money or property changing hands." The bandit Alesha summed up only a small part of the situation when he said "the traders and speculators . . . borrow money and disappear with it. They take goods on consignment and don't pay for them . . . goods get stolen out of warehouses and stores."

These are only the most direct forms of swindle in business. The general atmosphere is one of fierce competition for capital, resources, properties, supplies, control of specific markets, industries, or geographical regions, official support and favors, and so on. To engage in business in Russia is to engage in an elaborate, multileveled, and constant struggle to maintain even a slight advantage in these various arenas. While this description (and these bellicose metaphors) apply to capitalism everywhere, Russia entirely lacks a framework of state regulation and oversight within which business "battles" may take place; there are no final arbiters for the conflicts that constantly arise, and there are few developed moral or ideological constraints on bad behavior. Such conditions make the field of enterprise a frightfully slippery one in which rights, rules, alliances, and obligations constantly change. One of the key colloquialisms in contemporary Russian is "*krutit'sia*," meaning simultaneously "to turn, spin, revolve, whirl, squirm, circulate, twist, contort."[19] It is a common piece of local knowledge that

Honest Bandits and Warped People **289**

only by knowing how to *krutit'sia* can one keep one's head above water in any kind of enterprise. The Russian mafia are, in a sense, the masters of this dance. Their occupation entails a kind of "meta-spinning" among different realms of enterprise, within and between different social fields and different levels of hierarchy.

In the absence of reliable, coherent, and accessible state arbitration in business matters, the mafia are also, of course, the primary suppliers of mediation, compensation, and conflict resolution services. For many businesspeople, they provide the only controlling or coercive apparatus readily available. Their range of services includes the common *razborka*—meetings between two opposed parties that are mediated by the bandits representing each side. The outcomes of *razborki* may depend on communicative shrewdness or on some logic of justice, authority, alliance, or brute force (or a combination of these). If razborki fail to resolve a conflict, the mafia may be engaged to utilize more drastic means—everything from "unpleasant encounters" to assassination.

For those who haven't spent much time in Russia, the specter of the mafia may appear terrifying, astonishing, and exotic. From a local perspective, however, kryshi, razborki, murders, bombings, and assassinations have become surprisingly normal features of the daily landscape, of conversation, of humor, and of popular culture. It is not uncommon to see groups of five or six "flatheads"[20] aggressively marching, almost in formation, through a metro station or along a street; "there they go, off to a razborka!" my Russian companions say with droll humor. Several businesspeople have described their experience with razborki in interviews. Half-joking references to kryshi and protection money are a standard feature of much conversation.

The media regularly report the murders of businesspeople, politicians, and journalists; people joke about the ignominy of low-price, thousand-dollar hits, and there are plenty of anecdotes about hired killings gone wrong.[21] This realm of murders and assassinations is not far removed from the experience of most people; on the contrary, many have stories to tell of their close encounters with bandits, of murders or bombings they have witnessed, and so on. One acquaintance, a woman engaged in very small-scale egg distribution in Moscow, described how she was dragged into a car and driven to a forest, where some bandits to whom she owed money threatened to strip her naked and drive away if she could not explain how she planned to pay up. A music teacher reported that her cousin, a security guard, had noticed a grenade taped to his neighbor's door as he was leaving for work; he called the police who removed the grenade, but they could not figure out why the neighbor, a businesswoman, had been targeted. In Moscow during the summer of 1994, I was twice in the vicinity of bombings, close enough to hear the explosion and witness the ensuing commotion. The interesting aspect of these experiences for me was to observe, in myself as well as in those who tell me their own stories, a sense that these events were entirely explicable, as horrifying but as common a part of contemporary life as automobile accidents. Thus does an aura of violence become an almost banal part of existence.[22]

The Metaphysic of Money

Thus far, I have presented only a general outline of some of the contours of socioeconomic life in the developing markets of Russia; there is, obviously, much more to it. But the phenomena described above form the basis for widespread declarations about the "cynicism" that seems to have infiltrated the social fabric. However, most people—even the mafia bandit Alesha—are not so cynical that they do not seek to explain and justify the social changes they have experienced. As people watch others and, indeed, find *themselves* energetically participating in the scramble for resources—learning to *krutit'sia* on whatever level—ideas about the power of money serve as symbols of the compelling force behind all this activity and its resultant changes in social relations.

Contemporary Russian narratives often describe an expanding sphere of uncontrollable corruption, greed, duplicity, and savagery, a dystopic realm where the values of charity, compassion, love, art, and labor have all dissolved under the inescapable hypnosis of what many refer to as "the cult of money." There are multiple positions from which this social image is cast and a wide range of inflections that vary according to age, education, ethnicity, social status, degree of involvement in the marketplace, and economic experience. Nonetheless, certain central images are remarkably consistent, part of the general, "commonsense" view of the changed social world.

The symbolic construction of money as an almost animate, destructive agent serves in Russia, as elsewhere,[23] to summarize the immensely complicated dynamics of systemic transformation. As Jonathan Parry and Maurice Bloch (1989) have theorized in *Money and the Morality of Exchange*, at issue in these fetishistic discourses about money is the question of how two overlapping, interdependent, but separate spheres of social life—the long-term sphere of collective values and the short-term sphere of private striving—are to be reconciled or articulated. In any society, they argue, both of these spheres are necessary to social and biological reproduction, yet each must be insulated from the other in reliable, stable, and socially legitimized ways. The fetishizing of money may occur when the natures of the exchanges between these two spheres is under contest, and this is surely the case in Russia as it has been throughout the postsocialist world. Conversations about money mark a general effort to define profound structural changes in moral terms; money is, in a sense, a symbol of the force which has dissolved the socialist institutions, practices, ideologies, and commitments that seemed (for better and for worse) so sturdy and unmalleable.

Katherine Verdery writes that "as a once-socialist economy increases the play of market forces, it opens up spaces for radically new conceptions of the economy and the place of money in people's lives" (1996:181). In socialist economies, of course, most people had few ways to amass capital or multiply their money without direct investment of labor. In moving away from the logics of socialism, people must come to grips with the seemingly magical quality of money in a market system, where money begets money, goods accrue value through trade, familiar work practices have given way to mysterious forms of economic activity, and income discrepancies create utterly disparate, incommensurate worlds.

Where traditional boundaries of moral and group identification have been effaced, the flow of money can be cast as the primary agent of that effacement. Where it seems that personal integrity, moral limits, concern for the welfare of the larger community, and a desire to perform "honest work" have disappeared, the thirst for money can be invoked to make sense of that disappearance. One irony here is that money has been reinvested with the fetishistic power it had in communist propaganda as an agent of spiritual and social corruption.

A retired schoolteacher, Viktoria, whose family was managing quite well through a variety of means (including renting their apartment to me for the summer), lamented that:

> We are morally damaged. Look at how men these days are glued to their televisions, and what are they watching? All the American films so long denied them but especially the martial arts films. Our old

Soviet films all had some moral base, which wasn't bad. In fact the philosophy of communism corresponded to Christian philosophy. The only problem then was at the top with the officials. They gave us those moral messages but we didn't mean anything to them, we "little people," and they lived their comfortable lives behind a curtain, that was the *real* iron curtain, hiding their happy lives from us. Now it is all out in the open, and nobody is ashamed. Now we all know what it is about, and everybody wants to get rich and live like our leaders always lived, even the children are already totally damaged, totally warped.

Viktoria's commentary sheds light on many aspects of the discussion at hand. In a few verbal strokes, she constructs a history of class relations, posits certain alignments of cosmology and ideology, and conveys the emotional effects of moral confusion and decay. In particular, Viktoria suggests that there was always a social realm wherein money circulated and corrupted—the sphere of the communist elites—but that the "little people" were excluded from, in a sense *protected* from, that corrupting force by the fixed barriers of power and privilege. When she says "even the children are already damaged," she implies that there no longer seems to be any reliable separation between the spheres of innocence and corruption (childhood and adulthood, people and elites).

In this vein, another teacher described her disdain for the changes she witnessed in her ten-year-old nephew: "He's really charming, but he smokes and trades already. Kids today only think about money. When I asked him what he thought of a pretty girl in his class as a possible future wife, he said, 'No, she's too poor.'"

The thirst for money is said to motivate extreme breaches of social relations—even those of kinship. Kolia deplored the collapse of family values, saying: "It is sickening what is happening nowadays to children. People just toss their kids out on the streets, to fend for themselves, so they can save money. It was never like this before. Now there are thousands of abandoned kids."

The media has reported a few cases of people who murdered their own parents or grandparents so as to inherit and sell their apartments, and such stories are picked up and spread to vivify the claim that money drives people to the most abominable behaviors. Tales of friends, relatives, and associates cheating or abandoning each other for the sake of money are not uncommon.

Despite claims that now everybody is corrupt, there is a logic of degree: most people concurred that the moral waters are murkier the higher one looks. The more money a person has (or the more money that circulates around a person), the more corrupt he or she must be. Government officials and the new business class are seen as being the most corrupt of all, as being utterly disinterested in what happens to "the people" as long as their pockets are full and their dachas protected by high walls. Discourse is somewhat slippery and contradictory on this point, however. The thirst for money creates moral corruption, while, at the same time, existing moral corruption may allow the thirst for money to take hold. (This must be so if the speaker perceives himself or herself as being relatively immune to money's power).

Many people invoke the notion that the willingness to work for money has disappeared. Presumably, nowadays many people want to get it magically, instantly, and without labor; this idea seems to reflect most vividly the lack of fit between socialist ideologies about the honor of work and the evil of speculation. Talk constructs a standard opposition between real work, which does not bring a person money, and those dishonest or unproductive activities that do make money. In contrast to the transparency of "real labor," moneymaking activities are murky and mysterious. My friend Olga talked about an acquaintance who works as a cleaning woman in a fancy shop where they sell nothing but some kind of German skin balm—so expensive that few can afford it. "The cleaning woman says all she does in the mornings is gather up vodka and wine bottles, and she wonders what her employers actually do during the day." Olga also passed on the story of an engineer who works in a joint venture. "He signs a few pieces of paper every month and gets a huge salary. I have no idea where the money comes from to pay people like that for nothing."

Trading, the predominant (and most visible) economic activity of the day, feeds into the image of moneymaking as an activity by which money is made without work. Russian streets are now crammed with private shops, kiosks, and small stands, and it is imagined that the owners of these enterprises make "piles of money" without working. This, of course, reflects Soviet-era and even pre-Soviet Russian constructions of trade as immoral speculation. As Mikhail, a retired scientist, put it, "nowadays anybody will kill anybody else for any little thing." His son heartily disagreed, however, saying: "If that's true, then why would all these people sit all day in kiosks, selling vodka, when they could just as easily kill someone?" His father retorted, "What kind of work is that, sitting in a kiosk? That isn't work. Those people just can't figure out whom to kill."

Sometimes deserving people do make money, but there is often some kind of "miracle" by which this occurs. A young seamstress, Anna, who dreams of being a fashion designer, cast things in an eminently folkloric vein in the following story:

> Russians don't really want to work, you know. It is too hard. One of my friends went to Florida and stayed with a Russian émigré there. He said it was beautiful and everybody was rich, but he couldn't stand it. Life there was too crazy, the phone was always ringing, there were always dozens of messages on the answering machine, business calls to answer, too much bustle, exhausting. Russians don't need that kind of insanity. Though we are living in poverty now, we wait for miracles, like always. All poor Russians wait for miracles, like Ivan the Fool from Russian fairy tales, who always did everything wrong but married the princess in the end anyway. But miracles do happen nowadays. One artist I know brought some paintings to Moscow to sell in a park. An Italian wandered by, fell in love with his work, brought him to Italy, toured him around, lavished millions on him. He came back loaded with money and bought himself an apartment in Moscow!

Such winsome accounts are overshadowed in conversation by those which highlight a logic alien to fairy tales, however. In older Russian tales, the honest (though perhaps lazy or foolhardy) hero usually prevails, and the villain gets his or her punishment; however, contemporary stories more often emphasize the inversion of this moral logic. Kolia put it starkly: "Look at who gets rich nowadays. Not people doing honest work or anything productive. Just those people who know how to steal, are willing to steal and kill and swindle to get what they want. People kill their own parents to get their apartments to sell. We are warped."

The image of two intimately connected but utterly unequal social groups, the "honest" people who have played by the rules and only gotten poorer and the former communists, businesspeople, traders, and bandits who have stolen everything they possibly could, was constantly voiced by other working people and pensioners with whom I spoke. At a birthday dinner for Pasha's father—a meal featuring homegrown potatoes and mushrooms gathered at the dacha—Pasha's mother lamented bitterly about the impossibility of living on their pensions and the fatal insult that was being delivered to the people who had worked so hard their entire lives. Having sat desultorily silent during most of the meal, the father finally said:

> There's no future for Russia, it's twenty or thirty years away. The government does not serve the people, it just wrings them dry and steals from them. Our mayor, our governor, what do they do? They just travel to exotic lands supposedly to make "deals"—they go to Portugal, Japan, Europe, on money from our taxes and stay in fine hotels, eat fancy meals, buy presents for their mistresses. They live like tsars already, but they want more. Our own factory director, having piles of money of his own already, demanded that a shipment of wood for the factory be put aside, so he could use it in his own dacha. They have everything, but they want more. And we, who have worked all our lives, have nothing.

Striking incongruities were sometimes encountered in relation to such discourses, however. I spent quite a lot of time talking with Viktoria, my landlady for the summer. Many of our conversations hinged around her depictions of the poverty in which her family and her friends now live, and the "moral insult" that this represents to pensioners.

> I don't understand. People work for forty-three years and find themselves paupers. Is that fair? No, it is dishonest. The government has treated us very very badly, insults all of us who endured everything. And look at all the stuff in the bazaar, what an insult. None of it is Russian, traders just go to Poland or Turkey, buy stuff, bring it back here to sell. While our local factories sit empty. There used to be no shoes to buy, now the bazaar is full of piles of shoes to enjoy but they are all imported, and our shoe factory sits empty. Now, we honest people are still as poor as ever. It is no wonder that nobody wants to live honestly anymore. If you live honestly, you starve. Regular workers are just starving nowadays. The minimal sum required for living is now officially one and a half million rubles per month per person, and we get 150,000 each as pensioners, so we live *one hundred times worse* [sic] than the minimum standard. While the big guys and the criminals get rich, resting on our backs.

I made no comment on the flaw in her mathematical calculation, which was repeated a number of times during our acquaintance. I took it to indicate her affective response to the degree of separation she sensed between herself and the newly rich. There were other puzzling moments in her discourses and practices, however. Viktoria and her husband had gone to live for the summer at their dacha, in order to rent their apartment to me for the sum of two hundred dollars per month. This money, she explained, they would use to pay part of their grandson's thousand-dollar tuition to the new private university. It was unclear to me, at first, how they raised the rest of his tuition; as the summer progressed, however, I realized that they must have had several ways of earning money on the side. One day someone called offering an apartment on the Volga River for sale. I passed this message along to Viktoria. Later I overheard her asking her husband "did you advertise that you wanted to buy an apartment on the Volga?" He said he had and took the caller's number. Clearly the family had some capital to invest. During the entire summer, she brought home vast quantities of berries, mushrooms, tomatoes, and other produce for preserving, saying, "this, and the potatoes we are growing at our dacha, is the only way we old people can survive anymore." And yet, on another day she described the forty-dollar electric teakettle she planned to buy. "Imagine, it boils water in two minutes and shuts itself off so that it won't boil dry!" The inconsistencies in our conversations—her descriptions of their extreme poverty and the evidence I saw to the contrary—may have been her attempts to assuage the moral repugnance she felt toward shadow income. As someone who had spent her entire working life in the Soviet system, where these realms were clearly marked and income on the side might be disguised, she could not easily see her family's extra income as legitimate. The director of the private university, who I met during my travels with Alesha, explained this, saying:

> Since, in Soviet times, people had no way to earn money legally aside from their official jobs, since so much economic activity was in the shadows, it is natural that now they hide and do not even in many cases appraise their own incomes. So while they complain of having no money, they are getting money on the side, which they do not even really count consciously as income.

My friend Tania offered an alternative explanation, however:

> She is ashamed at how she is cheating you, Nancy! Taking two hundred dollars for such a place, from an unsuspecting foreigner. She

has to make you think she is really poor, so you will feel good about giving her an insane amount of money for the apartment, an apartment that you can't even really work in, because she is always there herself![24]

I did not agree, however, that Viktoria was consciously manipulating my feelings. Rather, it seemed to me that she was working on her own self-construction, trying to perceive herself as a "good person," living the life of relative poverty which was for so long ideologically constructed as connoting honesty and morality among nonpowerful Soviet people. Current realities gave her family economic opportunities not directly related to their own labor, and it was necessary for her to frame these in terms of the predominant ideologies of the past.[25]

People in their forties and fifties, who came of age during the Khrushchev "thaw" (a period of relative liberalization in the early 1960s) more openly express their cynicism—the conflict they negotiate between moral values and pragmatic necessities. My friend Larissa joked bitterly that "there is no mafia, we are all mafia now," referring to her sense that there is no way to survive economically if one behaves ethically. Olga and her husband, Vasia, honest and hardworking people, were approaching the point of impoverishment when they found themselves considering a way of getting a kickback from suppliers at Vasia's workplace; it was clear that this was the way his colleagues were making money. I was taken aback as I heard myself encourage them to do this; "What am I saying?" I asked aloud, and Larissa replied, sardonically, "You see, it's inescapable, even you are getting as corrupted as we are!"

More striking than these generational divergences in discourse are the distinct ways that social status shapes people's representations of money and morality. While conversations with "working people" constantly revealed an ideological struggle to coordinate moral and pragmatic interest (or, to put this in Parry and Bloch's terms, to navigate the shifting, blurry lines between long-term collective interests and short-term personal needs), conversations with successful and powerful people reflected these concerns in abstract and detached language. It might be argued, and I think most of my Russian friends would agree, that the greater a person's corruption, the less he or she would be bothered by the problem of social cynicism. A couple of examples illustrate this point well.

When I visited Yaroslavl's new private university with the bandit

Alesha, the director showed me around the poshly renovated building and was especially proud to show me the computer center whose appointments and technology rival those of many well-endowed universities in the West. He explained that the university had received grant money from the German government for the retraining of Soviet military officers, that they had established a sophisticated computer laboratory and were training the officers (and some of their wives) in systems design, programming, and other high-tech applications.

A few days later, I returned to the university by myself for a formal interview with the director. I asked what the main problems in business in Russia today are, and he said:

> There is no culture of agreement here; that is the main problem. There is no mode, for example, of dividing property. So, two guys, longtime friends and colleagues, working together, start to disagree about the direction of their business, and they come to the point of splitting up. But it is impossible for them to figure out a way to divide their capital rationally, to appraise its value correctly. So they fight, and then they call in their respective "bandits" who assist them in working things out. Banditry [banditizm] is thus a normal phenomenon in times like these. It is necessary to get people to pay their debts in the absence of a developed legal system and a developed business culture. The Chechen mafia has been fulfilling this function for a long time in Poland. I cannot predict how long that will be the case, but it is slow to evolve. Also, there is always a margin of people who do not really have the talent or means—the capital—to start their own businesses, but who want to get ahead. Banditry is for them a way.

This explanation frames current reality in starkly functional, pragmatic terms with no hint of moral questioning and no expression of anxiety or uncertainty about the future. During our tour of Yaroslavl, I had asked Alesha who the director was and how he had founded this university. Alesha explained that the director had been a top city official, a highly-placed Communist Party member. During the transitional years, he was able to get the German grant and some other capital—Alesha's explanation here was vague—and acquired buildings for the university to renovate. It was clear that, like many former party leaders and managers, the director had been able to transform his power and connections into a new platform for the greater accrual of power, wealth, and prestige—his chauffeur drives him around in a new Volvo, and he just returned from a grand tour of American universities where he was on a quest for partnership arrangements. I asked Alesha whether, in his view, it was mainly those with top party connections who were doing really well today. He said:

> Well, those people, who were even then very active and businesslike [*delovye*], and who were shrewd and had good connections, of course things have been much easier for them, and they are doing quite well today. But if a person is *very smart* . . . he can do anything, even without those connections.

Being "smart" means being active, energetic, and ambitious [*delovoi*]; it also means being shrewd, always on the lookout for opportunities to make money or gain power; and, especially in the current context, it seems to mean negotiating the margins of danger and taking risks, but only those for which you have adequate "cover."[26] Cover—the protection of "roofs"—is partly structural, dependent on the net of connections and the security of status, and partly charismatic, a function of one's ability to intimidate and charm. Alesha, too, seemed confident about the possibilities for making money, maintaining power, and living well; this sanguine optimism was the key feature of the speech and mode of self-presentation among the mafia, elite businesspeople, and government officials alike. In conversations and interviews with such people (including a group of mafia gangleaders with whom I sat through a dinner party charged with the drama of threats and brutality), I never heard a single expression of concern about the corrupting power of money.

Another encounter shows this nonchalance in stark relief. While visiting a bank with Alesha, I had a short conversation with its public relations director, a sophisticated man in his early thirties. Without any irony or hesitation, he told me the following:

> We try to "control the press" so the public does not get scared about their investments; they are very nervous right now after MMM and everything. This is easy, since there is no free press here, no fourth estate. We just pay journalists to write what we want them to, and the people believe anything in print. Although it is hard when you have investments from regular people. They have the strange habit of coming to collect their interest and then turning around and cursing the bankers, calling us "scoundrels" because they are sure we are

getting very rich off their money. They are earning 300 percent a year from us and calling the bankers scoundrels.

This man seemed to have no sense of how cynically his words rang. This suggests how powerful the discourses of particular status groups can be in shaping social perceptions. The general surround of "businesslike" [*delovoi*] talk is like a powerful filter through which very few of the concerns of other social groups penetrate. This man clearly had no idea why bank customers cast bankers as "scoundrels," although his own brief rendition of how he uses money to control the press is a flagrant articulation of the general spirit of cynicism and public swindling which so many people decry.

The Dangerous "Cult of Money": Retribution and Redemption

Contemporary stories and laments about a population warped by the cynicism and moral debasement that circulate with money do not stand alone. Rather, they are almost always in implicit or explicit dialogue with transcendent images of a near or distant future in which some form of social redemption will occur. Espousing a logic of retribution—human, magical, or divine—many of the stories depict the dangers of the "money cult," and the circulation of these stories may act as a subtle form of interpersonal warning, a pedagogy of moral order couched in almost folkloric forms. At the same time, this circulation represents a collective discursive effort to imagine "ways out" of the morass of moral confusion, to resolve the urgent question of establishing boundaries of right and wrong, private and public: in short, to revise the contours of social order in relation to changed patterns of economic and political practice. In the absence of any common ritual forms for navigating these unfamiliar waters, public and private discourse is arguably the key sphere in which a moral order can be renegotiated and moral anxiety is expressed.

Narratives describe three main forms that retribution may take against those engaging in the cult of money: wealthy people experience psychospiritual, financial, and physical dangers. Those who fall prey to the temptations of money must cope with their constant vulnerability to the general ennui that may result when money is one's highest value; they are also liable to being swindled, robbed, kidnapped, or killed. A Moscow feminist described a complicated chain of psychological despair in the lives of New Russians:

You know who's suffering the most now? The wives of the rich businessmen. They have everything, but life is totally boring. They are not involved in their husbands' intense business activities. The men think their wives should be happy, with their fancy kitchens and clothes, but these women have nothing to do or be involved in. All the patients in a new neurosis clinic are the rich husbands who are going nuts because their wives are so unhappy.

Anxiety is another primary psychological penalty paid by the wealthy. I heard a number of tales of how people turned in others to the police or the bandits in exchange for money, or tales of people who were killed when they made a wrong move or tried to cheat someone.[27] Families are also under threat. Several unrelated people in Yaroslavl told me the same story of a woman working in oil refining (still a partly state-controlled industry) who managed to divert huge sums into her own pocket by working hand-in-hand with the mafia. Presumably, she tried to hide some of her income from the mafia to avoid paying them their full share of the profits. As a result, the bandits kidnapped her two children and held them for a huge ransom (one person said $200,000, another twice that). In the end, she paid them and got her children back. "Why would anyone want to live like that, having to worry all the time that your children would be kidnapped?" asked a woman, hearing this story at a dinner party.

In Yaroslavl in early August 1995, the media reported the brutal slaying of a married couple who had made a fortune in the beverage distribution business. Discussing a newspaper report about the killing, the artist, Kolia, explained:

You see, there is no point in making big money. People are greedy. As soon as they see large sums flowing, they demand their percent. This couple probably got greedy, maybe they tried to hide some of their income, or maybe their competitors got annoyed with them for grabbing too much of the market here. It's all swindling and fraud; it isn't worth it to try to do anything; you work hard, figure something out, make some money and you think you've done it, and then somebody takes it all away from you. There's no point in trying to make money. People are greedy. As soon as they see it flowing, they want it. Or you get killed if you cross someone. This is normal business in Russia today: it's the cult of money . . . very simple. And money attracts trouble like a magnet. Because of this, there will never be a normal business climate in Russia. Everyone just wants big bucks as fast as possible, and will do anything to get it. It is a very murky water.

As in many Russian cities, the edges of Yaroslavl have sprouted with beautiful and preposterously large private homes, always surrounded by tall brick walls that are topped with barbed wire and security cameras. These are the fortresses of the New Russians. Expressing both awe and disdain at their vulgar grandeur, my friends would show me around their dacha villages, pointing out these new structures and passing on rumors about who the owners were supposed to be and the shady ways they were said to have made their money. These houses stood as symbols of the miraculous new wealth in their midst, but they also conjured tales which reinforced the idea that the cult of money brings on the demise of its most fervent devotees.

A number of times I rode the bus past a particular red-brick palace, and each time my companions would point and explain that it was the house of a particularly ruthless politician, recently murdered in his own home despite his barbed wire, bodyguards, and electronic security system. I spent many evenings listening as people told strings of tales about such murders, all hinging on the inevitable connection between moneymaking and death. On one level, these were just stories people told with eagerness and thrill, like kids telling slasher stories around a campfire. But these were pregnant with a kind of occult significance as well: they signaled a belief in the inevitability of some manner of social redemption, some ultimate reconciliation of the contradictions of morality and money. As Pasha, my trader friend explained:

> It is not at all worthwhile to make a lot of money, you just attract attention and get yourself killed. It is much better to stay very small, stay in your own small corner. Of course everybody has to pay for *kryshi*—there is no getting around that. But if you stay little, take care of your debts, pay your percent for protection, you have a chance to be okay, make a little money and survive. But you have to be very careful, not to step on anybody's toes, not to go over the limit.

In Moscow in 1994, I visited my old friend Andrei, a poet and artistic impresario. He had moved from his old communal flat, which he had proudly inhabited for decades, into a nice large apartment that a businessman, who valued everything Andrei had done in Soviet times to help underground artists, had bought for him. After hearing him describe this generous gift, I asked Andrei to tell me what he thought about all the social changes around him, and he took off on a descriptive flight:

Suddenly, into this life in which the Russian people have been conditioned to perceive poverty an accomplishment, a sign of cleanliness and morality, suddenly into this life flies a sixteen-year-old boy behind the wheel of a Lincoln, and the question arises: when did he succeed in earning enough for a Lincoln? Any fool understands what it means: He killed somebody, he robbed somebody, the racket, kidnapping, and so on. Everyone understands. Where did he manage to earn it? This sixteen-year-old kid with hardly anything on his face to shave? The people see this and go into wild shock. All understand: hard work, honest labor now means nothing. There's a guy, he's survived the war, and here he is earning a minimal salary, nowadays twenty thousand rubles—what is twenty thousand now? It means one breakfast. Per month. That is the minimum wage, what people earn who are washing floors, working their hands raw, and these people see the kid with the Mercedes. . . . Philosophers, scientists, make sixty thousand a month. That's three breakfasts. To express this in Russian language is impossible. Even artists can't describe this contrast of two Russias. Even our humor is dying. What can you say about this new world of ours? Nothing. But I'll tell you: When the big companies let out at night, the new rich pour into the street, and they are all drunk. They have been drinking all day. I have seen it with my own eyes, on the main streets, in front of the fancy new buildings. Our new wealthy class files out of their gleaming skyscrapers, wearing their Armani suits, and they are all falling down drunk, falling into puddles with their Armani suits. All they can do at work is drink. They know there's no future, for them or for us. They live in mortal fear, in mortal shame, and to forget about it they drink until they fall down. This is the world we live in now.

In Andrei's fantastic realism, Russia is a new Babylon, one in which the cult of money leads to "mortal shame and fear," the first signs of an impending, inevitable world-collapse. Money earned "magically"—that is, dishonestly, through the sorcery of corrupt practices—also destroys "magically" and the New Russians, as the avant-garde of corruption, are the first to sense this inevitable destruction. Stories of this sort form a broad discursive tapestry; they weave the seemingly senseless social phenomena of a radically changed world into a clear theodicy, whereby—

at least in narrative—everything makes sense: there may be no just future on earth for the poor workers or professor, but neither will the "wealthy class" enjoy the illegitimate fruits of their corruption.[28]

Redemption through the Mafia

To see corruption as something which is morally bad needlessly burdens the task of analysis. It suggests that there are evildoers who can be punished. We must expect, however, that people who act in particularistic and corrupt ways in not making a clear distinction between public and private affairs have few other options. They are part of societies in which the distribution of power is far more uneven than in certain nation-State societies where people can, quite apart from personal merits, afford to be "honest."—Anton Blok, *The Mafia of a Sicilian Village, 1860–1960*

If money is the fetishized agent of social decay, the agent of redemption that appears in many stories is, strangely enough, the mafia. This is implicit in Andrei's tale, for everyone knows that the "mortal fear" the New Russians feel is fear of being killed, and the mafia are, of course, the professional agents of murder. But a representation of the mafia as a redemptive agent is much more broadly cast in Russian talk. That Alesha depicted himself as an "honest" bandit may not be surprising; what is striking, however, is how widespread and explicit are notions that the mafia may be the most reliable provider of social and moral order.

Until I encountered actual bandits and heard all kinds of bandit stories, it would have been hard for me to imagine the degree to which the mafia and its members have been constructed and experienced as a normal, necessary, and even comforting presence in day-to-day life. Conversations I had in 1990 and 1992 showed that the mafia was, for most people, the supreme symbol of evil and terror. Four or five years later, however, the shadow of evil was projected onto other social groups, and the terror the mafia provided was sometimes represented as the means by which avarice and corruption might be reined in. A few selections from local discourse suggest the contours of this conception.

A student in the private university who described himself as struggling to stay honest in a corrupted world, nineteen-year-old Lenia offered his image of possible futures:

I see two forms of government for Russia in the future. The first will be the type proposed by Zhirinovsky [an eccentric nationalist politician], with a crackdown on crime; although what Zhirinovsky promises is impossible: a wealthy, comfortable life for all. He promises vodka for all the men, but sober husbands for all the women! This is of course a fairy tale. The other type of government will be made up by the mafia, and this is a more rational way to go. The bandits understood economic reality, they will set things up in a rational way. And you know, the majority of business people are not driving in Mercedes-Benzes, they live modestly, value family life. It's only the real working-class people who get suddenly rich and need everything fancy, to show off. By the way, the Russian mafia now has more methods of torture than there were during the Spanish Inquisition. They are really advanced.

In this construction, the mafia—because it is both rational and "advanced"—will ensure some kind of social normalization. Lenia's depiction echoes that of the director of his university, who said that the bandits fulfill a crucial function in the absence of a developed legal and business culture that is "slow to evolve." Kolia, the artist, told a story that reflected these themes:

> I made fourteen thousand bucks selling my old apartment. I gave my ex-wife half. The next thing I knew, some of her gangster friends came and stole the rest from me. That was all the money I ever had, and it was actually all mine, because that was my apartment before I even met my wife. I had just wanted to help her out, but she wanted everything. After that the gangsters stole the money from her! In the end, Alesha helped me, and he managed to get me three thousand back. That was all he could do. He's a decent guy, he gave me the whole three thousand, didn't take a cut. He said, "Kolia, I respect you, you're a good fellow, I just wanted to help you out and I don't need to make money off of you." He's a good guy.

Although I wondered whether Alesha really gave Kolia all the money he recovered, I decided that was not the most important point of this story. Here we have a traditional tale of good bandits and bad, fighting it out, with the good bandit achieving at least a partial victory.

Other stories about mafia gangsters emphasized their less pragmatic functions. One woman told me about having met one of Yaroslavl's top mafia leaders at a spa, and she enthusiastically described how he generously treated her and her companions to fancy meals and drinks and entertained them with his stories of life in the racket; she expressed regret that this man had recently been poisoned while he lay in a hospital bed getting treatment for alcoholism. Marina, an ethnographer who had recently moved to Yaroslavl from Yekaterinburg, the proclaimed mafia capital of Russia, told me that:

> the funerals of bandits have become the most important public ritual, much more interesting than other holidays. People turn out in droves to watch the long parades of fancy black cars going in entourage to the funerals. They watch the newspapers to know when the funerals will be. It is a regular event in town, people are thrilled by it, fascinated to see these parades of the rich and powerful.

What are these stories about the mafia saying, and why are they so prevalent? Katherine Verdery suggests that mafia talk circulates so actively in postsocialist societies "because it symbolically expresses many of people's difficulties in the transition." Among the general meanings that mafia-talk may encapsulate, Verdery suggests that since they flexibly mediate a variety of social fields, the mafia may stand for the "invisible horizontal linkages" integral to market economies, and as such they may symbolize people's suspicions that those linkages are morally questionable. Mafia, she proposes, "is a symbol for what happens when the visible hand of the state is being replaced by the invisible hand of the market. . . . [i] in this sense, the image of mafia perhaps gives voice to an anxiety about statelessness, alongside other forms of insecurity" (1996:219).

While Verdery is quite right about what the mafia can symbolize, I think she has conveyed only half of the picture. The "conceptual mafia" that she describes does not fit the one depicted in the Russian stories above; these stories do describe "real bandits" but gloss them with a symbolic varnish of generosity, helpfulness, and judiciousness, and relay a sense of the awe (not altogether disapproving) with which the populace regards mafia rituals.

Ethnographic encounters suggest that there are a number of "conceptual mafias" circulating at once in postsocialist contexts—just as there are any number of real and competing mafia gangs. Local talk, in fact, makes this quite clear. Interviewing five young workers at a Yaroslavl bread factory in 1995, I asked them whether they would vote in the upcoming elections. They all said no. One man said: "Why should we vote when it is all rigged and political offices are just bought and traded?

It is nothing but a giant mafia up there. We must simply try to live on our own down here and get by without politics."

As so many others do in casual conversation and media discussions, this man applied the metaphor of mafia not to the "real" mafia but to the "government" mafia—to those who are seen as invisibly, conspiratorially, and effectively mastering social resources and power to the detriment of the people "down here." My trader friend Pasha made these categories of mafia even clearer for me. One day, after hearing one of his long complaints about how hard it is to do business and still stay honest in Russia, I asked him whether he ever fantasizes about living and working elsewhere:

No! I totally love my country, my motherland. I don't want to live anywhere else. This place nourishes my soul, with all its craziness, mysteriousness, and unpredictability. I would die anywhere else, couldn't live. But I can't stand the corruption. Everyone who has power or money is corrupt. The politicians—that is our true mafia, each and every one of them: the *real* mafia. The street bandits, who you have met, they are basically honest, hardworking guys. The real corruption is at the top, and it is the politicians, from top to bottom, who are the real criminals. I think they should all be taken out and shot. That is the only way for Russia to become a clean and civilized place: like Stalin did, we should just round our leaders up and destroy them. We pay our taxes to them and it just goes in their pockets. I am not against supporting the poor, the elderly, but I think the best way is for us to do this independently: give me three *babushki* to support and I will happily, joyously support them! Directly! Without the intervention of the fucking mafia government which takes the largest percent just for themselves. This is the way our country should be arranged. I am an honest businessman, and I pay my taxes diligently, but I resent it, because I see the poor old women on the street and I know I could do a better job of taking care of them, just assign me three *babushki* and I will take care of them until they die. Another thing that is really pathetic: the way the old people believe in and give their last kopecks to the church. They are totally happy to give their last kopecks for the reconstruction of the local churches. But then you see the priests driving around in Mercedes, really! And living it up on the money the poor, believing *babushki* give them. The priests today are also the real mafia. Getting rich from two directions, from the contributions of the people who want to believe in something again and from the huge investments of the government, which is trying to prove its spirituality by rebuilding the church. Wherever you have such money pouring in, there is corruption and evil. I'm not, but if I were a terrorist, I would be a revolutionary. I think it is necessary, on a regular basis, to take certain groups of people out and shoot them, to restore the purity of our society.

However frightening Pasha's passionate diatribe may seem, I think it vividly presents the sociocultural paradoxes of postsocialism and capitalism in Russia and the tangles of hypocrisy and cynicism in which people feel themselves caught. State power disintegrates and reintegrates, but though it pretends to move toward democracy and justice, it in fact seems as inaccessible, inconsistent, and involuted as before. It seems unwilling to distribute resources as needed—whether to feed the old *babushki* or guarantee a general rule of law in which market mechanisms might function. In such a context, it is no wonder that the bandits are sometimes cast as social redeemers. As depicted in public mythology, the "real mafia" seems to offer what the weak (or unwilling and self-interested) state cannot. Street bandits are accessible and flexible. They are sympathetic and fair—if the price is right. They are "protective." They offer arbitration services, and they mete out legalistic decisions in somewhat predictable ways. They are controlled by fixed internal regulations (the well-known mafia hierarchy and code of conduct) and thus *seem* to operate within a frame of social morality. They are relatively transparent; their mode of operation seems straightforwardly visible and thus negotiable. They fulfill functions of discipline and punishment—often, significantly, *capital* punishment. In short, they seem to embody the very qualities that characterize strong states. And, as a final touch, they render a range of ritualistic spectacles (such as momentous funeral processions) through which legitimate states normally glorify collective agency and undying commitment.[29]

In a sense then, however paradoxical it may seem, *one* of the conceptual mafias in contemporary Russia functions as a discursive projection of people's yearnings for a rational, distinct, and strong state apparatus. We, western ethnographers and others privileged by life experience in more stable societies, might be inclined to judge this as a highly mystified projection. After all, it is the mafia that has facilitated the liquefaction of legal parameters and the less-than-legitimate privatization of public resources by former Communist Party bosses and powerful others; it is the mafia that has made grotesque murder a predictable outcome of competition in business and politics. Yes, the spiritual integrity that some discourse attaches to the Russian street mafia is of questionable veracity. Nonetheless, despite all of the mystification I may detect in their talk, I often find myself thinking that because of the stark forms their economic "re-education" has taken, my Russian interlocutors perceive the structural realities of class, power, and transaction in the capitalist marketplace more clearly than I ever will.

Notes

For thoughtful and critical assessments of this essay and its ideas in various incarnations, I am grateful to Bruce Grant, Svetlana Golybina, Carol Greenhouse, Julie Hemment, Natalia Kulakova, Michael Peletz, and Kay Warren. Generous funding for fieldwork in 1994, 1995, and 1997 was provided by the Joint Committee on the Soviet Union and its Successor States of the Social Science Research Council and the American Council of Learned Societies with funds provided by the State Department under the Russian, Eurasian, and East European Training Program (Title 8). Research in 1997 was funded in part by a Fellowship Grant from the National Council for Soviet and East European Research, under authority of a Title 8 Grant from the U.S. Department of State; neither the council nor the U.S. Government is responsible for my findings or this essay. I am also grateful to Colgate University for research leave and for support in 1997 from the Colgate Research Council. Selected portions of this essay are reprinted from Nancy Ries, *Russian Talk: Culture and Conversation during Perestroika.* Copyright © 1997 Cornell University. Used by permission of the publisher, Cornell University Press.

1. For phenomenological discussions of Soviet cynicism, see Yurchak 1997, Kon 1996, and Humphrey 1993.

2. Yaroslavl is an ancient Russian city about two hundred kilometers to the northeast of Moscow. In the Soviet period it was transformed into a center of heavy industry, primarily dedicated to the manufacture of automobile engines and parts. With the collapse of heavy industry in the postsocialist economy, many of Yaroslavl's plants sit inactive, and vast numbers of workers inhabit the limbo of semiemployment, with all of the complex and shadowy survival strategies that this necessitates.

3. In 1995, a million rubles equaled about two hundred dollars and a million was a standard monetary referent, both concrete and symbolic. In some circles, however, people used *limony* to refer to millions of dollars, not rubles. *Arbuz* (watermelon) was a slang way of indicating a billion (dollars or rubles), a metonym, I assume, from the smaller fruit but also an allusion to the heaps of watermelons sold on city streets every summer by traders, who are presumed to earn "piles of money" this way.

4. Verdery notes the prevalence of talk about the mafia (or various mafias) in all postsocialist societies and suggests that exploration of the ways the conceptual mafia is used in postsocialist discourse can reveal much about local perceptions of social and political upheaval.

5. In my work on Russian discourses during the time of perestroika, I have argued that the key narratives (particularly laments) I was hearing in 1989 and 1990 were widespread, not tied to my presence as an outsider (Ries 1997:83–84). In contrast, many narratives I heard in Yaroslavl in 1995 seemed keyed to my foreignness. While in the last years of the Soviet regime people were collectively and ritualistically mourning the past and bemoaning the uncertain future, by 1995 that future had arrived, and local conversations were focused on the close-at-hand specifics of survival. These specifics were probably viewed as being both beyond my comprehension and inappropriate to discuss with a relative stranger. Only a handful of close friends openly described their economic strategies, and indeed it was only among old friends that I had enough background knowledge to make sense of the complex trajectories of survival activity.

6. This is another crucial way that post-Soviet narratives were different from those of perestroika. With the evaporation of the ideological construct of Soviet Communism and the hegemony of the Soviet state, abstract and totalizing discourses and local practices that had been keyed to state power were now decentered. This entailed a personalization and fragmentation on both ideological-discursive and practical levels.

7. Alesha seemed to speak without irony here; clearly he was unaware of the popular image of collection agencies in the United States. Discursively striving toward legitimacy, he unwittingly underscored its opposite.

8. A month later, due to a connection I made through Alesha, I happened quite accidentally to be at a dacha outside Yaroslavl that, to my surprise, turned out to be the safe house that his gang used for meetings. Without warning a group of eight mafia leaders, including one who Alesha told me was the head of a big Belorussian gang, showed up for a *razborka*—bandit slang for a meeting to sort out differences. All afternoon these eight men energetically "performed" their bandit identity for me, even threatening to stick my feet in concrete and throw me in the nearby river if I turned out to be a CIA spy and not the innocent anthropologist I claimed. It was clearly amusing to them to enact an identity borrowed directly from American gangster films. Sensing this—and recognizing my own sense of the Hollywood thrill of it all—I was not as unnerved by the situation as I might have been.

9. For example, through discussions of mafia activity and culture with several informants, I learned that boxing clubs were a cradle of criminal enterprise even in Soviet times and that Alesha had probably been involved in underground activity even long ago; I realized that the vehicles being traded were quite probably stolen; and I was given hints that suggested that Alesha's gang had recently carried out at least one hired killing. I also began to understand that the street-level protection racket provided only a relatively small source of mafia income, but that this local base was crucial to the large-scale, intergang, and even transnational criminal activities in which gangs like Alesha's were engaged.

10. I have had many occasions to converse with western businesspeople and scholars during fieldwork and travel in the 1980s and 1990s; most vivid for me were the three days I spent working as a translator for top company executives during the gala grand opening of Moscow's first McDonald's. I regret that I have not had time to undertake an ethnographic study of the discourses of westerners engaged in business in Russia; if one wants to encounter the ideology of capitalist colonizers in a most naked form, Russia offers a prime research site. While some western agents of business and democracy have been made quite cynical by their experiences, many espouse the idea of the "natural" social progress that the "free market" will deliver. Discourses about "the survival of the fittest" resound abundantly.

11. "*Privatizatsia*" (privatization) is often bitterly referred to by the rhyming neologism "*prikhvatizatsia*" which plays on the verb "*prikhvativat*" (to grasp, grip, or clutch) and on the colloquial "*khvatkii*" (tenacious, shrewd, crafty). This pun reflects popular awareness that privatization has been a process whereby people in power grabbed resources in a shrewd and greedy manner. Quick privatization was energetically promoted by the IMF, the World Bank, and armies of neoliberal foreign advisers representing the interests of global markets. Instructive are Janine Wedel's (1999) study of the entanglement of international interests in Russia and Michael Burawoy's (1997) trenchant remarks on privatization theory and practice. For realistic assessments of the privatization process, see, for example, McFaul and Perlmutter (1995) and Nelson and Kuzes (1995).

12. Although focused on very different kinds of communities in Russia—collective farms in rural Buryatiya—Caroline Humphrey's (1998:444–505) discussion of survival strategies and the ideological and practical dilemmas they entail is very instructive here.

13. The Russian anthropologist, Alexei Istomin, has commented (in a personal communication) that each voucher invested represented a person's symbolic acquiescence to privatization policies; in this way, he argues, the administration cleverly "purchased" people's naive consent to "shock-therapy" programs that did not represent their best interests. Joseph Blasi, Maya Kroumova, and Douglas Kruse (1997:77–79) make high claims about the success of the voucher program in creating a "people's capitalism," but I have not encountered a single person who has earned anything, whether cash or influence in factory management, from the program. Blasi, Kroumova, and Kruse cite figures for voucher investment, but they fail to report that a significant portion of these investments vanished into pyramid schemes or fly-by-night banks.

14. Under a law of their own creation, elected members of the Russian Parliament cannot be prosecuted for crimes while in office; Sergei Mavrodi, MMM's founder, thus escaped criminal prosecution by gaining a seat in the parliament. People voted for him chiefly out of desperation, imagining his election to provide a chance for them to get their investments back. For a fascinating discussion of the narrative effectiveness of MMM advertising, see Borenstein 1999.

15. See Katharine Verdery's detailed discussion of similar pyramid schemes in Romania, where, as certainly was the case in Russia, many of the savvy first investors—those who made huge windfalls before the pyramid collapsed—were members of the political-economic managerial class. Verdery hypothesizes that among other results in the former socialist societies, such schemes "nourished segments of the rising bourgeoiscracy that feeds off the primitive accumulation realized under socialism in both public and private domains" and that they "helped to produce two opposing social groups; one whose new wealth enables them to make money and dominate politics, and one, increasingly impoverished and disenfranchised, who will see riches as immoral and risk as unrewarded" (1996:202–203). Because government regulation of investment firms is so weak, such pyramids have been widespread throughout Eastern Europe; Albania's experience, where angry investors took up arms and rioted throughout the country in 1997, has perhaps been the most vivid example of the vast scale and serious consequences of these scams. Comaroff and Comaroff describe a complex of such schemes in post-Apartheid South Africa, which, like Russia, experiences "a promiscuous mix of scarcity and deregulation" (1999:281).

16. One wholesale-market worker described a box of shirts she was given to sell in a kiosk; the neck labels read "Made in France," while inseam labels read "Made in Korea," and labels on the plastic wrap read "Made in Italy." Her boss instructed her to remove the inseam label and the plastic wrap so that buyers would think the shirts were made in France. In a similar case, a friend explained one of his friend's frozen-food business: he imports expired product from Europe and has his employees restamp the boxes with new expiration dates; this man pays off the state inspection agents at the border so he can import his inventory without problems.

17. Some of these strategies are almost mystical in nature. There is, for example, a folkloric inventory of ways to discern real vodka from cheap grain alcohol. This can be a deadly serious situation; there have been numerous instances of people being poisoned by drinking "vodka" that turned out to be derived from industrial alcohol.

18. On various forms of krysha, see particularly Shlapentokh (1996).

19. The anthropologist Dale Pesmen (2000) has written a brilliant semantic analysis of this key term and its many correlated forms. It must be noted that the ability to krutit'sia has always been adaptive in Russia. Practices implied by the traditional proverb, "khochesh'zhit'? Umei vertet'sia" (You want to live? Know how to spin/prevaricate) carried on through the Soviet years in the various forms of blat, the complex system of favors and "pull." Ledeneva (1998) provides a comprehensive ethnographic treatment of blat, and includes a discussion of its transformations in post-Soviet years; see also Pesmen (1996) on the metaphysics of blat transformations in recent years.

20. This is the expatriate community's slang for bandit-types, whose uniform style is crew cuts and black leather jackets.

21. Several such jokes concerned the murder of Versace, who was the designer of choice for bandits: "A New Russian makes a phone call somewhere in America after the murder of Versace. He says 'I ordered Versace . . . but the guys took me literally!' " The verb zakazat' means to order goods, but can also mean to order a killing.

22. It is crucial, however, to note that I did not experience any sense of personal danger related to this kind of violence in Russia. In the ocean of money flowing freely (especially in Moscow) today, an American academic is a very small fish indeed.

23. See Taussig (1980) for an extended case study of the metaphysics of money in a transforming system; see also Comaroff and Comaroff (1993).

24. While living in Yaroslavl, I learned that I could have rented a better apartment for much less, and many people commented that it was a swindle to charge me so much rent for that space, especially given the fact that my landlords, their grandson, and two dogs were frequently home, though they had promised to come only once a week to do laundry. Late in the summer, having heard my complaints about having no privacy, Grisha, one of my acquaintances, wanting, I think, to demonstrate to me his connections and his toughness, phoned Viktoria and made a veiled threat to gather his bandit buddies and come "take the two hundred dollars back from them." It was a mystery to me why my hosts suddenly disappeared to their dacha, leaving a note saying they would return only in two weeks, until my acquaintance proudly told me about his phone call. I was horrified, I felt that there was "evil on my soul" (thus do local constructs become part of an ethnographer's own worldview), but in spite of this I did manage to enjoy my privacy; thus did I benefit directly from the threat of banditizm.

25. Elsewhere I have described popular discourses of "mystical poverty" (Ries 1997:126–60). See also Dale Pesmen's (1996; 2000) discussions of the ways in which monetary exchanges could be purged of immoral connotations through complex avoidance practices.

26. As Max Weber noted in "The Social Psychology of the World Religions" (1946: 276), "strata in possession of honor and power fashion their status-legend so as to claim a special and intrinsic quality of their own, usually a quality of blood." Delovoi—"businesslike"—seems to me just such a symbolic quality, perhaps not a quality of "blood" but certainly an essentializing mode of explaining why some people had status and others did not.

27. The fact that these are usually tales about "distant acquaintances" or "acquaintances of acquaintances" suggests the mythic quality of such stories; while they may be real occurrences, they are probably more rare than the constant talk makes them seem.

28. I am grateful to John Borneman for the observation that these kinds of narratives are a contemporary theodicy. See Weber's (1946) "Social Psychology of the World Religions."

29. This image of socially redeeming mafiosi is vividly reflected in popular literature. In the books of Alexandra Marinina, by far the most popular detective novelist in Russia today (as well as a professor of jurisprudence and state criminal investigator), one recurring character is Eduard Petrovich Denisov, the aging mafia boss of a small Russian city. In Marinina's 1997 *Playing on Foreign Turf*, Denisov is depicted as a highly principled man, who runs his city with an iron hand, guaranteeing freedom from crime, high employment rates, well-provisioned schools and hospitals, orderly, "swindle-free" commerce, and a satisfying urban ritual life. Though he is a bandit, on principle Denisov refuses to trade in weapons, drugs, or historical treasures. Marinina is, of course, invoking an international popular culture archetype here, but it is one with poignant resonance in Russia today.

Judy Rosenthal

Trance against the State

In the context of recent government discourse and events of national importance in Togo, cross-ethnic and cross-regional possession trance, with its ethics of radical reciprocity, takes on a certain political irony. While a government-controlled press accuses "southerners" of tribal hatred against the north, these very southerners honor northern cultures by hosting and worshiping northern spirits during Vodu rituals. Both Gorovodu and Mama Tchamba, the spirit possession orders central to this essay, have contested government accusations of tribalism and separatism, undercutting the "necessity" of excessive social control claimed by the state.[1] There is no doubt that these *Atikevodu* (medicine Vodu) orders are vehicles of cultural resistance to the abuses of state power. Resistance in this case is endemic to Vodu ritual, which is a time and place for reshuffling power relationships internal to southern Adja-Ewe and Guin-Mina communities in their historical ties to African peoples of "the north," as well as those coming from their predicament with and against states.

In this essay, I examine Vodu ritual as political resistance. My principal implication is that African countries moving toward their own forms of democracy must take into consideration the sorts of law, power, and identity that Vodu and similar African religions create, so that the state governments, in turn, may receive legitimation from the people.[2]

This essay is thus, first of all, an examination of the ways in which Mama Tchamba and Gorovodu in southern Ghana and Togo have often employed religious forms of political resistance to colonial and authoritarian states. On occasion this resistance is explicit; otherwise it is perhaps unintentional, implied in the very nature of Vodu, and of Atikevodu in particular. My reading of ritual joins much recent writing that has established that ritual is political and has explored the complexities of implicit and explicit resistance.[3] In this essay the data and interpretations go further, suggesting how this is accomplished. By means of ritual, identities and hierarchies are made fluid; in the context of oppression, this fact in and of itself makes ritual politically active. The essay details historical and contemporary contexts in which Vodu worshipers have addressed oppression with and through the fetish. Though conventionally categorized as religious practice by anthropologists and others (for example, colonial administrators), Vodu orders are as political as they are religious by virtue of their deconstructions and reconstructions of identity and hierarchy through periodic redistributions of agency, responsibility, personality, and power. Vodu people have taught me that in Gorovodu and Mama Tchamba, social identity is fluid at every level, always turning on itself, refusing to remain fixed. They have also taught me that much of what is Vodu transcends or leaks past issues of states and resistance. It just "is," like life itself, in its ravishing incommensurability, and that is what makes it so very resistant. This is the essay's major ethnographic theme.

Second, taking issues of Vodu identities and political resistance to some of their logical conclusions, this essay indicates that social fields such as Gorovodu network are not unified, nor are they separable from the history they create or the histories they resist, including those produced and chronicled by colonial and authoritarian states. Third, I provide some details about the political context in which I gathered data and interpretation of Gorovodu and Mama Tchamba, that is, what pushed me to investigate the resisting capacities of these religious orders and their thoroughly political nature.

Vodu Practices and Interpretations

The *Voduwo* are slave spirits. Hundreds of years ago peoples of the north—Haussa, Mossi, Tchamba, and Kabye—passed through Eweland. Some of them suffered hardships and had to sell their children to our ancestors. These children did everything for us. They worked their whole lives and made their masters rich. When they grew old and died, the objects we had taken from them upon their arrival— cloths, bracelets, fetishes, sandals—these things became Vodu, and the slave spirits came and settled in them and became our gods. If we do not serve them, generation after generation, we become ill and die. It is beautiful when the Vodu comes to possess you. It is good. (Gorovodu and Mama Tchamba priestess in Togo, quoted in Rosenthal 1997:183)

Gorovodu and Mama Tchamba are specific orders of the Vodu (or Tro) culture widespread in southern Ghana, Togo, and Benin, among Adja-Ewe, Guin-Mina, Fon, and related groups.[4] Gorovodu and Mama

Tchamba communities (networks of informally affiliated "congregations") worship the spirits of their ancestors' slaves (*amefeflewo*; literally, bought people) from the north. During spirit possession rituals, when the *brekete* rhythm is drummed, spirit hosts (*trosiwo*) go into trance and become, through mimesis, these northern spirits who heal, protect, and provide law (*ese*) for their southern worshipers.

Gorovodu and Mama Tchamba are descendants of Atikevodu orders formed during the colonial period and called "fetish worship" by colonial British administrators. Vodu worshipers today call the material vodu or god-object "the fetish" (*le fetiche* in Togo and Benin), and a spirit possessing an adept may also be called "the fetish." This indigenous cooptation of the colonial word is interesting, given that the term *fetisso* (first used by the Portuguese) was usually something of an insult, a classification created by Christians who found such libidinally charged "idol-worship" titillatingly disgusting. However, "made things" with sacred intent is exactly what material vodus are; thus, although the colonial connotations were racist, the moniker was ethnographically correct.

As the quotation that introduces this section indicates, Atikevodu people have typically romanticized the north, appropriating northern objects for their rituals and worshiping erstwhile immigrants from the north. Spirits of bought people from savanna regions are said to be "wild" (*ada*), just as northern peoples (*dzogbedzitowo*) are seen as wild compared to southerners; such wildness is perceived as both dangerous and beautiful, and therefore is recreated in dramatic fashion during possession ceremonies (Rosenthal 1995, 1997). The spirits of these northern slaves, now vodus (gods), come back to possess the descendants of their previous owners.[5] Spirit hosts speak a glossolalia full of northern sounds, including Kabye, Losso, and Tchamba words. Worship of slave spirits is itself repayment of ancient debt, for the bought people are said to have created wealth for their owners, or, more correctly, their adoptive families and in-laws, as bought people inevitably married into the lineage of their "buyers."[6] Upon being recreated and worshiped, atikevodus still "work" for their new owners/worshipers, providing them with protection, healing, sacred law, and the rapture of trance. Worshipers also work for the slave spirits, building them shrines, speaking to them daily, satisfying their desires for special foods and drinks, drumming rhythms, celebrations, and opportunities to dance through the bodies and minds of spirit hosts.

Major Gorovodu and Mama Tchamba ceremonies in coastal villages may attract five or six hundred adepts and visitors, for all inhabitants of the host village and other Vodu villages are welcome, and even tourists may attend Gorovodu rituals. They often last three days and nights—Friday, Saturday, and Sunday. Seated on one side of a large ceremonial ground, drummers begin the performance; they play breketé until the audience swells and spirit hosts arrive. Periodically, many in attendance will dance across the ritual space; talented breketé dancers, elders, and children are honored by women who dance behind and fan them with their hip cloths. The crowd sings songs honoring spirits of northerners and thereby calls the Gorovodus so that they will come and dance breketé in ecstasy. After a while, spirit hosts who had begun by performing (dancing), suddenly appear to be "performed." That is, they go into trance—at first with a certain struggle and what appears to be suffering—and then they dance fiercely and beautifully in a state of grace, crying out rapturously or bawdily, shouting or cooing, and imperiously demanding certain songs and variations of the breketé rhythm and other rhythms from the north. Special assistants (*senteruawo*) guide them into the Vodu house (*voduhome* or *trohome*), dress them in costumes from the north, and cool them with water poured from northern kettles. At times the possessed rush to particular individuals, including children who are ill, and carry them into the Vodu house to wash them with sacred water in which they have put healing plants (*amasi*). Or, with the help of priests (*sofowo*), they administer *atike*, medicine made of burnt ingredients.[7] Gorovodus may also warn against behavior that is not respectful of Gorovodu law (ese). Law here includes all the usual commandments against murder, theft, adultery, and amoral or malevolent magic (*adze*, *dzoka*, or *bovodu*); it covers dietary prohibitions (*ekonuwo*), instructions for performing a host of different rituals, and principles of "speaking pain" and "speaking desire" (*enudzidzi fonufo*) to the deities and to one's family of sibling worshipers (guarding against keeping bitter conflict, rivalry or hatred bottled up). Ese also includes the divine demand for possession trance during ceremonies, the excessive enjoyment of which is paradoxically a gift both for and from the northern spirits.

Political Context of the Ethnographic Project

I visited Togolese Vodu neighborhoods and villages for the first time in 1985, when I began living with a Togolese friend near Lomé.[8] Several women who were spirit hosts from a village we frequented told me that I must write about Gorovodu. Their urging sent me to graduate school in anthropology and then back to Togo for research. I knew the ethnographic work might involve certain risks: In 1985 and 1986 bombs were discovered in Lomé. The military regime in power since 1967 had increased its control of citizens through frequent police and military arrests of those suspected of opposition to the government, in particular many Adja-Ewe and Guin-Mina southerners. The government press accused southerners of tribalism directed against the northern regime.[9]

The friend I was living with had been arrested several times for his political associations, and many of his friends were in prison or in hiding. We both became afraid for his freedom, so I suggested we get married "under the law" to get him off the hit list. Apparently our marriage did protect him; friends informed us that he was no longer under surveillance, for a person becoming a U.S. citizen could not actively resist the Togolese regime.

After spending three years in the United States, we returned to Togo so that I could carry out dissertation research. During our stay from 1990 to 1992, opposition to the regime increased. An attempted coup in 1989, supposedly organized from Ghana, had been put down with considerable loss of life. Many Togolese were clamoring for a "conférence nationale" so that the many different ethnolinguistic groups and associations in the tiny country could come together to form a basis for democratic elections and constitutional reform.

In the narrow sense, I found most Gorovodu and Mama Tchamba people to be passive opponents of the regime as far as political activity was concerned; some publicly spoke out for democracy and against state abuse. Even so, they were pointedly not anti-north. Like most people I spoke with in the south, whether of southern, northern, or mid-country origins,[10] Vodu worshipers were not concerned about the ethnic identity of a future, democratic president. They were not tribalists. Like most people, they wanted an end to egregious state nepotism and violence against civilians; they wanted proportionate government participation for all ethnic groups.

My research on Vodu was eventually cut short by a burst of political violence that cost many Togolese lives. One night in 1991 a curfew was suddenly declared, and thirty people were murdered in the Lomé neighborhood of Bé, a quarter famous for its Vodu practices. The victims had been surprised while walking in the streets, going about their business, quite unaware that a curfew existed. They paid a high price for their ignorance of the latest government news: they were shot, bayoneted, or bludgeoned to death and dumped in a lagoon. Some of the women were found with children still on their backs. This slaughter was a warning to the people of Bé: they should not be involved in any political change except on the side of the present regime. However, the people of Bé responded by writing their own riot act—laying out their dead neighbors and family members in front of the U.S. Embassy in the broadest possible—international—daylight. As it happened, the outside world had other priorities.

Friends from Bé explained that they had chosen the U.S. Embassy because they believed the United States to be the most powerful foreign power.[11] They wanted the world to know that nothing would make them bow to the regime. They wanted the deaths to mean something, to be a sign of future change.[12] Bé, with perhaps a thousand lineage and neighborhood Vodu shrines and sizable Gorovodu, Mama Tchamba, and Yewe[13] communities, is known as a seat of resistance to the regime; all of the Vodu orders are considered to have politically active components at one level or another. In Bé, Vodu agency is proclaimed or suspected during nearly all events and activities. Nyekonakpoe, where my husband grew up, is another Vodu-charged neighborhood with a similar reputation. Although people from Bé and Nyekonakpoe have often been arrested, threatened, and jailed, they have not been easily intimidated.

After the uproar of outrage over the Bé slaughter, including street demonstrations by market women, the president agreed to suffer a national meeting. Togolese from north and south and in between created a conférence nationale that gave them jubilant hope.[14] But the regime put an end to the democratic experiment on 2 December 1991 with the use of tanks and guns against the provisional democratic government. That day my family and I, along with hundreds of people from the settlement where we lived, walked to the highway where we could hear the artillery firing on the presidential *Primature*, fifteen miles away in Lomé.

The situation grew worse in 1992. Some well-known opponents of the regime were killed, as well as ordinary citizens just walking in the street, including children buying bread. My family and I were warned by a trosi in trance that we were in danger of death. Still I clung to my fieldwork. But in July my husband and children and I were obliged to hurry secretly across borders to escape the "political police" after a passport was confiscated and wild accusations, punctuated with death threats, were hurled at us in a kangaroo court. We may never know for sure whether our close association with Ewe and Mina Vodu communities contributed to a police perception of us as undesirable.

Our close call, the obvious significance of the Bé events and the responses to them, and the labeling of the Bé and Nyekonakpoe quarters as "enemies of the state"—all this filled me with urgent curiosity about the political implications of Vodu. For a long time I had been formulating questions about the nature of Atikevodu during colonial times. I wondered whether there was something inherently "resisting" about medicine Vodu orders. Did the present situation demonstrate a continuity of certain Vodu practices and concepts, including relationships to state power, that had developed during the colonial period?[15]

In 1994 I spent the summer alternating between the Ghana National Archives in Accra and a Gorovodu community in a Tema shanty town. According to anthropologists of the colonial period, medicine vodus were created and worshipped in the south for their healing "work" (edowowo) and their "witch-finding" capacities (azelele) (Field 1948; Fiawoo 1971). Reading between the lines of colonial records, I realized that Atikevodu a century ago had also provided law or ordered power (ese)[16] and the gift of sublime enjoyment through possession trance (vodufofo). Most significantly, with the help of the Tema Gorovodu community, I became convinced that during the late nineteenth and early twentieth centuries fetishes from Northern Territories brought to Akan regions also offered an aesthetics and ethics of north/south relationships in southern Ghana and Togo, including ways to interpret the history between northerners and southerners that broached the trauma of slavery (File 11/1/1243),[17] (Field 1948). Such practices predictably included a framework for continuing all the usual sacred services that were provided by many Vodu deities. But it also produced references to history in the "modern" sense, including the long years of the Atlantic trade and the resulting slave economies in West Africa, followed by colonial regimes. Documents pointed to issues of countervailing powers and supported my belief that the strength of Vodu during that period, as now, lay in the mimesis of possession trance, the intense desires it provoked and satisfied, and its social and spiritual relevance as a force that held its own against the abuses of state power.

Although it is not my present aim to discuss exactly what the state is and how it dominates, I do wish to signal my agreement with certain writers who problematize notions of the state and of resistance. For example, in the introduction to this volume, Carol Greenhouse writes:

> [P]eople may not necessarily act deliberately against the state, yet their acts nonetheless transgress the self-representations of state agencies. . . . [T]he state is not an agent in its own right performing this or that function. Rather, the ethnographic focus is on people who claim to act in the name of the state, drawing their salaries and wages from the public payroll, dressing for work—perhaps in uniform, perhaps not—and setting off for their offices or outposts. (Greenhouse, this volume, 8, 11)

This demystification of the highness and coherence of the state is appropriate to the pages that follow. It does not suppose the state any less violent than if it were monolithic and fully coherent; as Vodu people know only too well, many little people who act in the name of the state also carry large guns. Clearly, the Atikevodu social field was alienated from the colonial state, whether the state erupted in the persons of Native Authorities, colonial police, or British Chief Commissioners of one region or another. And Atikevodu itself was in a constant state of flux, as further discussion will demonstrate.

Vodu Law and Power

In my efforts to interpret relationships between sacred mimesis and state control, I have come to think that it is precisely through possession trance that Gorovodu and Mama Tchamba orders build and maintain their resistance to state power and centralization, as well as to outside definition.[18] Such ritual (re)creates key relationships and empowers Vodu collectivities over and above other interpretive frameworks, political bodies, and designs of social control. While this moral resistance may often be implicit,[19] it is sometimes conscious and explicit. During the recent political upheaval in Togo, many Vodu legends in circulation indicated a clear (if not militant) partisanship—for example, the trance message urgently warned my husband and me that the long arms of the authoritarian state were about to eject us.

In one narrative a young Vodu priest, who was compelled to earn his living as a soldier because jobs were rare, went AWOL during the events of December 1991 when the Togolese army put an end to the experiment in democracy and terrorized civilians. In order to return to the barracks after the carnage was over and also avoid severe punishment, the priest tied a talisman of the Gorovodu Banguele around his arm. According to legend, his superiors did not see him or even notice that he had not taken part in the killing of his own people. Earlier, during the summer of 1991, numerous villagers had gathered around battery-operated radios listening to the "conférence nationale," pulling for the "démocrates," yelling words of long-distance encouragement to speakers they recognized (see other examples in Rosenthal 1993).

Gorovodu law-power (*ese*) does not, however, stand in some necessary or full opposition to the existing legal systems inspired by French law in Togo and English law in Ghana, that some Vodu adepts call "everybody's law" ("*la loi de tout le monde*"). This expression indicates at least a partial recognition of law created by the state, of its possible usefulness and eventual legitimacy as a cross-ethnic institution, a clearinghouse for local or ethnic justice systems confronting each other. Vodu law directly opposes official law only when official law turns on Vodu orders; that is, when it is at its most oppressive as a tool of the state.

According to many informants, Ewe Vodu people have never taken to high degrees of centralization, not even those foisted on them by their own leaders (see also Greene 1996) and much less those brought by colonial administrations and contemporary dictatorships. The informants make it clear that Gorovodu ese possesses its own logic, political form, ethics, and aesthetics, above and beyond state legal systems and enforcement. Possession by the gods makes the host the walking, talking law itself, as well as a figure of absolute ecstasy. No law or ravishment imposed from the outside could be as stunningly convincing and desirable. Certainly torture and death at the hand of the state are convincing, too, but only as utter evil; whereas Vodu ese protects and gives life to all its "Vodu-eating children" (*troduviwo*), who also (ideally) give and protect life and never take it.

Vodu law clearly covers more than the mere rules of law or the power of social control. Coupled with sacred trance, ese is reproductive of Ewe and Mina life itself, of culture and meaning, "identity" (a plural affair) and happiness (*dzidzokpokpo*), as well as local justice. So, there is no question among Vodu people of abandoning such law that is flesh of their flesh and, even further, their "destiny" or "divinity" (translations of ese or Se, with a different tone). Notwithstanding all the above, Vodu law is now in agreement with the broad outline of "everybody's law," if not with that of the law enforcers, who tend not to be "everybody." Instead of judging today's states, national governments, and legal systems to be bad in themselves, Vodu people seem to take for granted the necessary existence of a plurality of powers and justice systems that cover much of the same ground, yet are all necessary, given the multiplicity of life itself and the many different levels and scales of social (dis)organization. For example, official Togolese law and Gorovodu ese both punish murderers, but it is the gods not humans that punish in Gorovodu, and any Gorovodu practitioner or other villager known to have murdered with literal weapons would be delivered up to the state court system. It is said that if everybody's law does not act, unrepentant murderers will die without a single mark on their bodies, by the "knife of the spirits." There are, to be sure, forms of killing other than through outright murder, for example, through adze or unthinking bovodu (forms of malevolent magic), and in such cases state law may or may not be interested. Gorovodu ese specifically forbids building up rivalries and wishing harm upon one's enemies. It provides special rituals to purge passionate envy, bitterness, and death wish (n'bia), which Vodu people say everyone has from time to time. As moral law, it goes further than state law in preventing murder by making the desire for someone to die a conscious matter for confession and dismantling.

At another level, Afa divination (Afakaka), working hand in hand with Gorovodu, provides a form of "personal law" (Afase) that creates radical individuality, a form of selfhood that overlaps with human groups, deities, and the forces of nature.[20] All these components remain connected to permutations of ese as the law and power of social control, as deity and as destiny, both personal and collective. Only thirty-five years ago, there was a Vodu imperative to resist colonial law and forces of order, which, judging by letters in the national archives, were almost always experienced as unjust. And now there is an evasion of everybody's law when it is accompanied by the army and police force; that is, when it works against the Vodu people, as has often been the case in recent periods. Vodu people do not, therefore, delude themselves with ideas of temporal or secular equality in such a diversity of law stuff; they know perfectly well they are subaltern in the face of state artillery and terrorism, and they struggle to protect themselves by lording their spiritual power over the state.

This is not to say that Vodu worshipers feel intrinsically subaltern. Rather, their interpretive framework includes their knowledge of the state, its interpretation of them as subaltern, and its subsequent willingness to kill them. However, Vodu ritual has also helped worshipers to survive the very real terrors of the state, including torture and death, and to protect themselves from collective and individual psychic trauma and despair.

In summary, Vodu law at various levels is inextricable from Vodu culture and society itself, and it functions as an alternative to state legal systems. This fact has, on occasion, made colonial administrators and contemporary dictators very nervous, as the next section will show.

Atikevodu in the Colonial Records

Almost as grating on state nerves as Vodu law (and quite connected to it) have been Vodu practices of crossing borders—literal national borders as well as more metaphorical sorts of borders, limits, and boundaries during ritual and spirit possession.[21] In coastal Ghana and Togo this border activity was seen as trouble by colonial regimes. Particularly troubling were the "medicine fetish" orders, including those now consolidated as Gorovodu. The northernness in such religious practices, including a significant number of ritual objects brought from the Northern Territories, was a sign to administrators that uncontrolled exchange was happening between the coastal peoples and the northern territories. (As I have already pointed out, northern style was a source of pride to the Atikevodu adepts, who represented it in sumptuous detail.)[22] Claims by colonial administrators and by Vodu people themselves that a certain politicocultural orientation was constitutive of Atikevodu were reinforced by such trappings of resistance that came from the north of the Gold Coast or from a mythic north as distant as Mali. Atikevodu orders thus looked blatantly political to some colonial governments, whether or not they were intended to be: "These fetish people are openly antagonistic towards missionaries and such like, and secretly towards the White Administration" (File 11/1/952). Their most direct resistance to the state probably began during the 1880s and increased around the turn of the century.

Another notable peculiarity of Atikevodu before independence was its tendency to change names and details of practice. In fact, Vodu and Tro orders of all kinds (all "fetish worship" in the records), changed during the period of the Atlantic slave trade.[23] They also changed over and over again during the colonial period for the very purpose of remaining as much the same, or as much themselves, as possible in the face of British, German, French, and Christian attempts to control them or to wipe them out. This chameleon capacity to protect their own cultural and spiritual being by being all things to all aggressors is particularly notable in the medicine cults that were forerunners of Gorovodu. They would be in flux in any case, given that Atikevodu, with its worship of northern spirits, is about flux, traveling, change, transformation, and relations with the foreign. And the fact that their practice was marked in particular ways by troubles with states and border crossings was linked to this metaphorical and spiritual flux. Also significant was the fact that on numerous occasions Atikevodu orders were accused of working at cross-purposes with colonial or state authorities by supplanting official law and political authority with their own powers.

Numerous documents from the colonial period in the Gold Coast are entitled "fetish removal" or "fetish ban." I examined at length about twenty such files. These documents contain a fragmented but detailed narrative, case after case, of the ways in which the colonial government, with the help of village Christians (sometimes newly converted ones), undertook the destruction of indigenous forms of worship. The British suspected with good reason that the vodus did not approve of colonial rule, so many colonial administrators approved the tearing down of shrines and the imprisonment of priests. Even so, committed officially (no doubt sincerely, in some cases) to a certain freedom of religion, they did not ban all Vodu worship. But local and specific Vodu and Tro orders found to be "unhealthy for the population" were made illegal in village after village all over the "Muster Kolonie" (Togo) and the Gold Coast: "[The Dente fetish] is undoubtedly a bad fetish . . . [it has] far-reaching influence, not only personal, but also political" (File 39/1/221).

As soon as one medicine fetish was removed, another sprang up in its place with an entirely different name and which the worshipers swore was wholly different from the recently deposed deities. But both native Christians and British administrators began to understand that the "same" fetishes (or were they exactly the "same"?) were resurrected under different names all over the coast and inland for two hundred miles—among Ewe, Fanti, Asante, Adangbe, Ga, and Akwamu.

Local Christian and colonial administrative accusations against the "medicine fetishes" were, however, almost always the same: they had come from elsewhere; they were foreign, moneymaking, and exploitative. (Ironically, these were the same complaints that the people had about the colonial government.) Often the banned fetishes were said to be versions of the vodus that now compose the Gorovodu pantheon, especially Ablewa (also Abrewa, Abirewa, etc.), the first order to be banned and which was found all over the coast among a variety of ethnic groups. Today Gorovodu includes not only Ablewa and Kunde, but also Sunia Compo, Sacra Bode, and Banguele Ketetse, all of which were banned at one time or another in one region or another, under one alias or another, during the colonial period.

Accusations that local fetishes were really Ablewa in disguise are common in the cases documented between the turn of the century and the 1950s.[24] For example, the Secretary for Native Affairs, Victoriaborg, Accra, wrote on 30 September 1916: "Sir, I have the honour to transmit, herewith, a copy of a letter from the Omanhene of Akim Abuakwa reporting the revival of a fetish called 'KUNE' originating from Nkoranza in Ashanti; and similar in its practices to 'ABEREWA,' and to suggest that the matter be brought to the notice of the Chief Commissioner of Ashanti" (File 872/250/10). Kune (Kunde) is indeed similar to Ablewa today as they are "man and wife," father and mother gods, in Gorovodu.

A letter from the archives file titled "Nkora Fetish" (Case #24, 1926), holds that the new fetish is a form of Ablewa: "It is a mischievous, money-making foreign importation. It came from the French territory and found its way to Ashanti Akim and having been ousted from there has established itself in Akim Abuakwa. . . . the ceremonies, dancing costumes, and make-up are similar to those of Abrewa. . . . There were charges that the Nkora priest had tortured a girl to death, but in fact she died from tuberculosis. There was rivalry between the people of the Salvation Army and the devotees of the Nkora fetish" (File 11/1/952). Also in this case file is a letter from the Omanhene Akyim Abuakwa. He writes, "It is needless to say that the decision of the government to suppress the fetish has caused much anxiety and restlessness among the people."

The Ghana National Archives contain a number of letters from local Christians, including policemen and native authorities, as well as from British administrators, which warn that the fetishes were in competition with British justice and British interests, and that Vodu fetishes competed with local Christian groups. A similar number of letters from chiefs and priests warn that the fetishes are of and for the people and must not be destroyed or banned. These writers seem to hope that a transcendent justice might prevail and that the colonial rulers might understand their common religious humanity. (I am tempted to say their "equal rights," given the egalitarian tone in Ewe villages.) One might imagine an almost systematic religio-political struggle between locally approved headmen and -women and the British-appointed native authorities, usually Christians, who were backed by colonial administrators and who identified with and attempted to serve colonial interests.

Intrinsic to this struggle was the very definition of the Atikevodu people, their name, and the "artificiality" or "authenticity" of their practices. The question of who is capable of judging "authenticity" in the religious sphere ranges beneath the surface of these records, but is never articulated as such. Sometimes colonial anthropologists were asked whether a given fetish was a "real" one or an "imported" one. Rattray answered to one such question, for example, that the Dente fetish was what made Kratchi the important place it had once been and that its revival should be permitted (File 11/1/751).

Early on, these fetish worshippers understood the strategic necessity of changing names and even the details of practice and discourse to camouflage their order. In any case, they had never been sticklers for remaining the same, and theatrical performance, including costumes brought from the north or modeled after northern ones, was part of their practice of the sacred. They were exceedingly convincing actors, if I can judge by the talents of the Gorovodu worshipers I came to know years later.[25] Reading the archives, one gets the impression that if the stakes had not been so life-threatening the Atikevodu people might have thoroughly enjoyed the game of hide and seek they seemed to be playing with the colonial officers, the police, and certain local Christians. Certain administrators no doubt realized this. For example, J. C. Fuller, Chief Commissioner of Ashanti in a letter dated 30 October 1916 said: "My experience is that there is no phase of native life that lends itself to such unreasoning criticism as these spasmodic fetishes—facts become so distorted, rumors so exaggerated that Political Officers may well be excused for taking an unduly serious view of a new fetish. . . . To watch a known movement is much easier than to discover secret and mysterious rites, which invariably follow premature coercive action [on the part of the colonial administration]" (File 872/250/10).

Other letters in the archives include "permission requests" asking that Atikevodu shrines might be erected in villages without undue police intervention. Such is the correspondence between the Secretary for Native Affairs in Accra and the Provincial Commissioner's Office in Winnebah, dated 13 June 1922, which includes a letter from the Omanhene of Agona to support Chief Bobikuma's application for permission to set up the Hwemisu Fetish: "I beg to forward herewith for your approval and return an application from the Chief of Agona Bobikumah respecting a certain medicine called 'Donkor' which has been brought into his town for the welfare of all the inhabitants therein. . . . I have carefully examined the medicine and found it to be a good one both for Adults and Children" (File 11/1/1243).

Although the title of the correspondence is "Hwemisu Fetish," the Omanhene of Agona calls it "Donkor medicine," a clue that connects Hwemisu with Gorovodu, as *donkor* is the Twi word for a slave from the northern grasslands region. A Gorovodu priest from Togo says that Hwemisu was precisely an early name for Banguele, the warrior Iron God and "hot-death" spirit protector beloved by Gorovodu worshipers. This same letter confessed that "no concrete case of the Fetish having been injurious to the person has been reported" (File 11/1/1243). Another report on Hwemisu (from the Provincial Commissioner's Office in Koforidua, 11 September 1922) predictably included the Ablewa accusation: "in the main the Dances, Shrines, Medicine, etc., are identical [to Abrewa], and both Commissioners are of the opinion that it is the prohibited 'Abrewa' under another name and strongly recommend that it should be prohibited" (File 11/1/1243).

Anthropologists also have a difficult time trying to discover whether such-and-such a vodu in the past is the same as one existing now, or whether in fact it was a totally different one, or whether the Fante version is a faithful translation of the Ewe Tro or rather the original (or rather unfaithful). These turn out to be the wrong questions. A more interesting approach is to follow the multicultural narrative trail left in the colonial records and in the songs and dances of worshipers, and further, in the details by which vodus are somewhat the same and somewhat different from each other, as distanced in time and in space and through camouflage for resistance to the colonial order.

Colonial and Christian Reactions to Atikevodu

The letters against medicine fetishes betray an almost palpable anxiety among Christians and British administrators about the "foreignness" and the "spreading" of Vodu worship—both of which were grounds for pride among the "medicine children"—as though fetishes were like rabbits multiplying in the most frenetic fashion, ever contaminating one ethnic group after another with no respect for centralization, or for linguistic, ethnic, and, less so, administrative boundaries.

One senses that there was another sort of panic related to this concern about rapid reproduction: a fear of well-worn categories coming unglued, a decentering of the usual judging faculties, a malaise related to the ontological status of "the fetish," that god-object absolutely Other to Christian and Western notions of deity, power, and being. Suzanne Preston Blier comments on the subject of related Beninese Fon sacred objects: "*Bocio* arts . . . express not only an aesthetic of negativity, but also what Kristeva calls *frappe* or shock" (1995:28). It is as though the fetish were a *passage a l'acte* that outsiders were loath to gaze upon, the knowledge of which produced either shame or prurient excitement in many Western observers. Blier further notes that "commoner" bocio objects often involve tying and binding, even chains that are reminiscent of the state of slavery in Dahomey throughout the period of the Atlantic Slave Trade—during which, in the Fon area, domestic slavery was marked by some of the same forms of cruelty known to slaves who crossed the Atlantic.

But the "negativity" that certain Vodu objects inspire in Europeans may not be only about aesthetic statements of class and caste embodied in sculptures (28), nor about evil in the strict sense. It could well be about what is repressed, what the subject of the colonial unconscious wishes to remain unconscious and without words. This may indeed include the unspeakable horrors of Asante, Fon, and Atlantic (and Ewe?) slavery, but it also evokes the incommensurability of cultures. Jacques-Alain Miller reminds us that what Europeans cannot "take" (in all the senses of the word) from colonized others is "the particular way the Other enjoys" (in Žižek 1993:203). Included in the "peculiar way [the Other] organizes his enjoyment," Žižek says, is "the surplus, the 'excess' that pertains to this way: the smell of 'their' food, 'their' noisy songs and dances, 'their' strange manners, 'their' attitude to work" (203).

But most peculiar and disturbing of all to colonial masters was the way the Vodu Others created and enjoyed their gods with such unthinkably carnal spirituality.[26] Unlike God is for peoples of the Book (Christians, Jews, or Muslims), a fetish is a created god, a divinity fashioned through and for desire, and its worshipers say as much; this alone is scandalous to many Western minds. To be sure, the fetish is not created out of nothing; it is a bringing together of matter, the forces of nature, the power of slave spirits, and human longing. The fetish is a strengthening of desire for enjoyment and for life itself that flames before life, during life, and after death. It is the product of a "doing" or a "making" (fetisso) that meddles with the borders between the human and the divine. Its disturbing incommensurability leaves it "similar, not similar to something, but just similar," yet consciously unrecognizable (Taussig 1993:33, quoting Roger Callois). The Vodu fetish created—and still often does—a relationship of the uncanny with the foreign, Christian, or Islamic observer, a disquieting strangeness that often attracted or repelled with great intensity.

If god-objects provoked strong reactions, the spirit possession was even more destructive of comfortable, familiar references and knowledge of the world. Colonial administrators and Christians sometimes wrote of the repugnance they felt toward fetishes and possession trance (see accounts in Verger 1957, 1968). Vodu thus possessed a shock value that left many Western hearts deeply troubled, with a wound on the border between their conscious selves and an Other World which they had seemingly conquered. These same attitudes may be seen today, not only among Europeans and Americans, but also among numerous West African Christians.[27] As a Gorovodu priest once told me, "The fetish is frightening and monstrous—that is why it is so beautiful." This aesthetics of negativity was thought to protect, to guard from attack, to nurture without creating envy, to do battle without shedding blood, to keep evil away from the village, to keep an edge of freedom in an area controlled by the colonial Other.

Predictably, the problem of legal authority was articulated during colonial times: "[Fetishes] divert litigation which should properly come to the Colonial Tribunal" (File 11/1/886). Vodu and Tro people had their own law that they put above the colonial justice system: "The Asogli State Council, headed by the Howusu as Native Authority, decided that the Atando Fetish was undesirable. This Fetish has virtually been fulfilling the function of a tribunal, and, recently, as a result of a complaint made to the Police, a charge was laid before the District Magistrate, and the Fetish Priest was convicted [of not 'rescinding' the Fetish]" (File 39/1/515). How fascinating that priests were told to "rescind," that is, annul or cancel out, their gods. Colonial authorities indeed understood that they were engaged with a different sort of sacred practice.

Often there were admissions that evidence of the wickedness of fetishes was lacking; there was simply a conviction that they should be banned "for the good of the people": "[A]lthough I have very few facts to produce, I am inclined to the opinion that the Fetish is a bad one and dangerous. . . . There are indications that this fetish is against public morality and if allowed to continue will attract to itself members of the various Christian Missionary Bodies" (File 11/1/1243). The state thus took it upon itself to protect Christians from the seduction of Vodu power.

In some cases justice was summary, even when guilt was not proven:

> In 1912/13 the Germans executed the late Head Fetish Priest and his accomplice the Chief of Tariasu by hanging them publicly. The King of Kratchi, who is a fetish priest as well, escaped to British Territory. . . . There are serious charges made against them, such as open rebellion against the German government and plots against traders (German Subjects) and officials; blocking the Caravan Routes to Lomé, and many cases of murder committed on strangers and Natives. (File 39/1/221)

In numerous instances Vodu men and women were fined or imprisoned, and sometimes they were killed. And in virtually all cases, the god-objects were destroyed and shrines were pulled down, and sometimes even the huts or houses in which priests lived were leveled. Occasionally individuals sued authorities for destruction of property. At least one priestess actually won her case (File 9/12/22).

Colonial rulers apparently felt a repugnance toward each other that was at times almost as great as that toward Vodu, and they competed with each other in their concern over fetish-spreading and importation. Each colonial administration blamed the other for the spread of fetish worship, for the permeability of the borders; or, in some cases, self-righteously, they blamed each other for unjust persecution of fetish worshipers. By 1912 at the latest, the Atikevodu tendency to celebrate and ritualize cultural flows between north and south was perceived as a threat to colonial regimes. Also seen as a threat was the Vodu passage across literal east-west borders; ignoring state boundaries, Vodu followers traveled to each other's ceremonies all along the coast. All of these crossings remained highly problematic almost until national independence.

Medicine cults were often accused of being from the wrong side of the border, even during the 1940s and 1950s (Maupoil 1961:55). When the fetish came from the "other" colony, a British administrator wrote in the Gold Coast: "I have never known a fetish brought from French territory which does not possess objectionable features. . . . From such a small fetish from French Country sprung all the 'Abirewa' palaver" (File 11/1/952).[28]

In 1936 several Togolese Catholic and Protestant clergymen published tracts against "Goro," or "Kunde," charging that it was imported from Ghana, that its priests took advantage of people, especially women, and that it drew backsliding Christians into its ranks, to the detriment of Christianity. Monseigneur Auguste Hermann, apostolic vicar of the Lower Volta, wrote: "Since 1926 a newly-invented fetish has been introduced all over the territory of the Lower Volta. Everywhere, adroit pagans and apostate Christians employ this new cult as a means of acquiring authority over the people" (Cessou 1936:33).

Bishop J. Cessou, apostolic vicar of Togo, believed Gorovodu dated from 1912 or 1913 in Togo; he said that it was not successful at the time, given that the German government was vigilant against "all that came from the Gold Coast" (1936:7). Bernard Maupoil, author of the otherwise generous ethnography, La géomancie a l'ancienne Côte des Esclaves, quoted the above sources to show that Gorovodu was "imported from Gold Coast" and that it was a menace to public order, as it was a secret society, "half confessional and half political" (1961:55).

Here we have not only protests over the border crossing and foreignness of Gorovodu and crisscrossing accusations about its "other European" origins, but also about its half-pagan/half-apostate-Christian nature, and, lastly, about its half-and-halfness in the realms of religion and politics. Adding all these complaints to those in the colonial archives, where witness is borne to the Vodu tendencies to change names, to turn into a different fetish at the slightest hint of a ban, to challenge all sorts of boundaries and identities, we find quite an aggressive body of anti-Vodu confusion. The colonial administrators were apparently not aware of yet another marvelous half-and-halfness; that is, Vodu practices of gender plurality, including the wifeliness of spirit hosts, whether men or women, and the notion that men and women can be both male and female at different times and in different contexts (Rosenthal 1997).

What is so interesting about Vodu worship is that this crossing and half-and-halfness are the signifying crux of the worshiping (and worshiped) matter. The very word *tro*—the Ewe preference for reference to the deified spirits (more often called *vodu* by Mina and Fon)—in its verb form, means a "turning" or "turning into" something or someone else, a "transforming" or "changing," a "turning back on itself." The gerund is appropriate in English; in Ewe *tro* is also a noun made of a verb. Turning or transformation is the very nature (culture) of fetishes: god-objects who or which are half-spirit/half-matter, created gods who re-create their worshipers and give them the ecstatic privilege of becoming half-divine in the possession trance.

Given the naturalness of their "turning," the urgency of their own law, and the necessity to go on worshiping their gods in order to continue creating the world as they knew it, in their own image rather than in the colonial image, how could the Vodu people interpret colonial states and their laws as anything other than perplexingly unjust? They certainly never gave their own stamp of legitimation to British rule in the Gold Coast or to German (and later French) rule in Togoland. And it was no wonder the colonial administrators and missionaries could not fathom the meanings and laws of Vodu orders; to British, French, and German eyes they appeared to be "disorder" in the extreme. To be sure, the agendas of the Vodu worshipers and those of the colonial administrators and native authorities were interpreted on the two sides in mutually incomprehensible manners.

Of course, not all of the Vodu people could have been saints. Some of them probably were charlatans, as Christians and native authorities said (with apparently thin evidence). But even the cheats and the greedy priests would know that power could not be accumulated and centralized under the Gorovodus. That was the very political principle that made such cults utterly at odds with colonial governing principles (and later with "independent" authoritarian states). The banning, fining, and imprisonment and, on occasion, death penalties that colonial regimes employed to stamp out Atikevodu worship were unthinkable to the worshipers. They came to understand that representatives of colonial power were not quite of the same order of human beings as Vodu people.

Mimesis and Resistance

Thus the savanna spirits were not the only conduits for northern cultural flows to the coastal south of Ghana, Togo, and Benin. Colonial sorts of northern infusion began to inspire rituals and spirit possession orders, both similar and radically dissimilar to Gorovodu and Mama Tchamba. The white men and women whose images gave rise to mimesis certainly were strangers, northern, and "wild" in the eyes of the south. They were all this in the eyes of more northern and Sahelian peoples, too: for example, the Zabrama men from Niger who brought the Hauka possession cult to Ghana during the 1920s. The stunning film *Les Maîtres Fous* by Jean Rouch shows Hauka adepts possessed by no less than the British colonial governor-general, Commandant Mugu (the "wicked major"), "Madame Lokotoro the doctor's wife," and other white "notables" whose images were worthy of reproduction in these Africans' very bodies and souls. Here we have reproduction of the colonial world in the medium of African bodies and psyches; or, was it rather a truly Zabrama world in the medium of colonial images? Either way, the mimetic Real erases the distinction between the medium and the message. And, in both cases, the practice of sacred mimesis provided means through which such resistors might co-opt some of that incomprehensible foreign power for their own strength. Wild, white characters with extravagant pomp and ceremony (French in Niger and then British in Gold Coast) had so amazed the Zabrama with their exotic otherness that there was nothing left to do but "become" them for a ritual time, so as not to become undone by them on another, more final, level. And, whoever would let herself be possessed in trance possessed symbolic wealth of considerable value.

Such mimesis carried certain risks. As Michael Taussig tells it, "The Hauka were jailed in 1935 for mimicking [in possession trance] the white man who possessed their very bodies, and Rouch's film was banned in the 1950s for mimicking that mimicking" (1993:243).[29]

Thus, mimesis of colonial characters was not entirely unlike Gorovodu mimesis, but it was certainly of a different political complexion, given the obvious fact that British administrators were never slaves of the Hauka worshipers, nor did they ritually "marry" or practice other forms of reciprocal symbolic exchange with the Zabrama. They were never the ones in the subaltern position, except perhaps when they were being transformed into Hauka images. Hardly interpretable as a form of sacred debt payment (as in the case of Gorovodu and Mama Tchamba), Hauka possession appears to have wrested from dominators part of the power those colonial strangers otherwise would not share with the native governed. This could be read as a seizing of reparations.

Some might argue that the situation in Togo today does rather resemble this scenario to the extent that a number of government northerners have power over southerners. But most Ewe do not see it that way; they do not believe that northerners as such dominate southerners, but realistically understand the regime to have both northern and southern, as well as French support over and against the people of Togo in general, all regions included. Thus, to the extent that colonial hegemony was different in important respects from today's predicament, we can say that Hauka and Atikevodu possession come at power from opposite directions. But in both cases mimesis levels out power relationships, at least for the time of trance, and even such a parenthetical "time-out" brings strength to the rest of life.[30]

If not a systematic form of resistance to colonial power through recuperation of its images, Hauka was at least a powerful signifying on images of whiteness and foreign domination, an invitation to be vampirized by wild colonial otherness in order to trap it, control it, and wield it, to crack its borders and thereby enjoy it for oneself and one's own people. It was a trance by the colonial state—and yet against it— which vaccinated the hosts against the violence of state takeover; it was a homeopathic neutralization of colonial hegemony accomplished by taking in the state and swallowing parts whole. If the colonial governor was taken in—and thus took over—by the Hauka spirit host, who was taking whom for a ride? Who was agent, or where was agency acting? Was hegemony turned inside out, at least for the period of trance (and perhaps beyond)? Was resistance carried out by not resisting? In any case, lives were altered, and the reenactment of the *passiones* was a constant text to that effect.[31]

The Hauka becoming of the colonial, foreign Other obviously did not include quite the same Romance of the North that accompanied (and still accompanies) the becoming of the slave spirits through trance in Atikevodu ceremonies. (The Hauka worshipers were themselves the people of the north whose culture the Vodu orders imitate.) Mimesis of colonial power and personality was a different genre, a theatre of surreal signifying, accompanied by incredulous admiration for colonial technology and a fear for one's life as well as for the collective identity that was always a shifting affair. I have not seen signs of Hauka in Ghana; perhaps it has disappeared since that country gained independence and was outlined with more "domesticated" borders. It is still alive in Niger where it originated as resistance to French rule and has now joined other sorts of possession groups, still satisfying the "need . . . to make sense of the ongoing European force" (Stoller 1992:156). Vodu worship of northern slave spirits, for its part, has intensified.

As for Gorovodu agency through mimesis, its spirit hosts maintain that they are not doing anything, not controlling or commanding or making anything happen. Their priestly cohorts (often former spirit hosts), on the other hand, make what appear to be exaggerated claims of creative making and doing. They "make," "form," or "prepare" gods, by placing natural and cultural ingredients in relationship with each other in order to call forth and attract spirits that then inhabit the materials or fuse with them, enliven them, and bring the breath of life and strong, individualized personality to the abstract creations of the priests. Vodu priests co-create deities, for spirits of the dead submit to their powers and are thus turned into gods more powerful than their creators. Vodu spirit hosts co-sacrifice themselves; they submit to the blazing power of spirits in order to erase the limits, to fuse with the north and have their personhood blown away and yet expanded to fill all time and space. In Vodu practice, agency and structure, intentionality and unconscious desire, individual and collective drive go round and round, north and south, hot and cold, all metaphors mixed.

Conclusion

Today, Vodu orders are not faring badly in Ghana and Benin. Even so, there are now more than a million Christians on the coast who some-times despise the Vodu people and may tell them, as did the first Euro-pean visitors, to throw their fetishes into the sea and (these days) to accept Jesus as their personal savior. (My family and I were repeatedly admonished to do so while in Ghana in 1994.) But, the phenomenon of evangelizing Christians aside, some of the Atikevodu people in Togo are not getting along much better with the postindependence state than they were with the German and French colonial states, even though they are no longer banned. Their answer to borders, curfews, martial law, and the declared "fixity" of ethnic identity continues to be Vodu ese (law/power) and trance. Spirit possession and the law it gives rise to constitute the very backbone of Vodu worship in its active and latent resistance to authoritarian states—and, sometimes, to the accompany-ing capitalist political economy.

Structural and discursive resistance in this case can simply mean an insistence on adhering to Vodu practices of community (the "big Vodu-eating family") and conceptualizations of foreign others, especially northerners. It lies in the fact that Vodu people continue to interpret reality through Vodu law and Vodu meanings of life and categories of relationship, including parameters of regional exchange and of ethnic, regional, or linguistic specificity, even when other interpretations and laws dominate the political and military scene. That is to say, politics of ethnic identity, practices of strict hierarchy and centralization, and privileging of a capitalist political economy that characterize the state have been straightforwardly refused by Vodu people at certain times and circumstances; otherwise, they have been reinterpreted, reworked, transformed, or ignored when possible. An implicit refusal to be defined and controlled by the state is quite visible in the colonial records and continues in current practices, although today there is no explicit Vodu resistance to national government as such. An Atikevodu aesthetics of ethnic difference and regional exchange that challenges modern state practices and ideologies continues to be represented sumptuously during possession ceremonies.

This penchant for overcoming dualisms and divisions does not mean that Vodu people do not believe in distinctions or in "two sides of things." They virtually worship the culturally invented, two-sidedness of things, whether the things in question be regionalized, gendered, classed as hot or cold, or classed or cast in some other way. At the same time, they imagine that borders and other distinctions are constructed for purposes of crossing, and that sides are divided up precisely so that they may fuse from time to time.[32] In a word, Vodu cultural logic is more a "both/and" business than an "either/or" affair, although its "both/and" does include "either/or," notably in the effect to interpret and integrate the colonial "either/or" logic.

Gorovodu people at the turn of the century took this artful turn even with the distinctions between Vodu, Islam, and Christianity. Today priests still say that the Gorovodu rules are like the Ten Commandments; and many of the ritual props for possession ceremonies are from the specifically Muslim north, with even a goddess called "Allah" in some Gorovodu shrines. However, I would never suggest that Atikevodu in its various forms should be imagined as a primarily "syncretic" form of Vodu as distinguished from other, more "indigenous" or "pure" forms. If Atikevodu was syncretic during the colonial period and again recently, Vodu cultures have always been syncretic, as have been their predecessors as well as the religions from which they have generously accepted numerous fragments.

In the case of Gorovodu and Mama Tchamba, these fragments or components include concepts, names of gods, material trappings, and segments of rituals for all-new combinations. We might argue that the Adja-Ewe and Guin-Mina cultures are also syncretic and combinative in the extreme, as are very many cultures in West Africa and elsewhere in the world. It is unthinkable that a West African coastal religion could somehow be purely authentic, frozen to some point of origin. Such rigidity would keep it untainted, unmoved, and perhaps unnoticed by all the actors and theaters of history, its own and those visiting it, intersecting it, in and through which it has in fact reinvented and renewed itself when possible. Purity or fixity of identity is unknown to the Gorovodu and Mama Tchamba interpretive frameworks; it is just as unthinkable to Adja-Ewe and Guin-Mina cultures. Nor is there an Adja, Ewe, Guin, or Mina people or culture in the sense of an ordered, integrated ethnic entity. It would seem that Vodu orders (seen ethnographically as social and ethereal fields) take as a point of honor the refusal of unitary identity (centralization is not an Ewe value). Yet there is a certain coherence about them since in Ewe worlds, fixity or centripetal orientation arguably lacks sacred, performative dynamism at every level of exchange.

Gorovodu worshipers and deities have never stood still. They have, however, stood noddingly by as accomplices to Christian, Islamic, and other "foreign" elements that, at their (Adja-Ewe and Guin-Mina) bidding, slipped into the already "foreign" Vodu order just as uncannily as spirit hosts slip into the "being" of foreign spirits. It has been this disorder of things that keeps Gorovodu turning, changing, and traveling, so as also to keep on being the same, that is, transforming where it matters more urgently on all the crisscrossing borders.

In this way numerous West African spirit possession orders both accommodated and resisted colonial states through practices of crossing real and metaphorical lines and through mimesis and camouflage. They also resisted through a multiplication of difference; that is, by changing names and details of practice, a sort of opposite to mimesis. The Vodu people involved were agents—victims and victors—in these histories, acting in them and reshaping them by altering their very identities at individual and collective levels, which were simultaneously personal and political. Gorovodu and Mama Tchamba worshipers today also play the chameleon, "changing colors" for the state and for themselves, continuing to admire and become the stranger peoples of the northern savannas.

It is important to acknowledge that the very libidinal and mimetic nature of Vodu and Tro spirit possession powerfully attracts human agency away from the designs of national governments and capitalist political economies. The uncanniness of spirit possession and god-creation that repels Europeans attracts Vodu people. Trance is the motor (vu, also "spirit") of modes of local and regional exchanges of power and wealth that demand reciprocity. The desire that creates fetishes, health, individuality, and enjoyment among Vodu people is the same that creates material wealth. But material wealth cannot be a final end in itself. The strongest desire among Vodu worshipers, on the part of spirit hosts, spirits, and the entire attendance, is no doubt the craving for possession trance itself; that is, for a return to the founding of law, power, and exchange in rapture, a visit to the unrepresentable Real, beyond or prior to the symbolic order, and yet also its birthplace.[33]

With the above in mind, we must realize that if the Atikevodu avatars were and are the response to certain colonial and authoritarian states, and to the suffering and damage such states have brought to Vodu people,[34] then in principle forms of Vodu will continue to exist even when these political and historical contexts change and new, as yet unimagined, contexts arrive.[35] As to whether new Vodu orders will be the same as Gorovodu and Mama Tchamba, the answer must be yes and no. As we have seen, Vodu orders do not stake much importance on remaining identical to themselves.

Flagrant indeterminacy and a talent for change no doubt have contributed to the fact that Vodu forms—always as political as they are religious—persist today on three continents and countless islands. And such being-for-itself is precisely what has made the existence of possession trance over hundreds of years inseparable from the varied and fluid political climates of the Gold Coast/Ghana and the Slave Coast/Togo. The "itself" Vodu is "being-for" includes constant parsing of power, relentless explosion and redistribution of identity, and continual re-creation of relationship. "It" always (re)members and then transforms historical and contemporary hierarchies. Gorovodu and Mama Tchamba can thereby afford to include the state in their agenda and cosmology—preferably a legitimized and democratic state. Thanks to this ability, they are very different from colonial and postcolonial states whose military, police, and bureaucratic agencies refuse to share power with Vodu. Vodu orders allow for other powers, not imagining their own to be strictly "their own," never supposing Vodu to be the sole agency at work, maintaining a perspectivist position on good and evil. In this way Vodu is both oppositional and inclusive, turn by turn; it categorizes relationships in binary oppositions that it proceeds to overcome. While it works to incorporate and refigure bits and pieces of others' agencies, including representations of northern cultures as well as fragments of colonial and neocolonial states, it does not imagine itself to have exhausted the multiverse of power; it does not create a vision of totalizing control. It offers itself as a universal possibility but does not hold an agenda of universal or even local takeover. Vodu orders play transgressively and very seriously with identity, power, and hierarchy, so as to allow worshipers to live both life and death to the farthest reaches of material and imaginative complexity.

Gorovodu and Mama Tchamba insist on crossing over, riding borders, and altering states. They offer the worshiper as altar, the pure expenditure of the person (Bataille 1985) who is suddenly annihilated only to spring back as human, divine, and animal at the same time, dead and alive in a heartbeat, master and slave locked in an embrace, north and south in a sacred marriage. Concepts of reciprocity and re-creation in Atikevodu never stop turning, giving way to redistribution of powers, pleasures, identities, and raptures at every border and every level of logic and being. Today, Gorovodu and Mama Tchamba, however friendly they remain toward European and American cultures, however kindly they include fragments of Islam and Christianity in their aesthetic repertoire, amount to a resolutely pagan provocation to the West.

Notes

I wish to thank the individuals, institutions, and agencies responsible for the following fellowships and grants that enabled me to engage in fieldwork and archival research for this article: Fulbright-Hays Dissertation Research Fellowship, Charlotte W. Newcombe Dissertation Writing Fellowship, Sage Scholarship from Cornell University, Faculty Research Initiative Grant and Faculty Research Fellowship Award from the University of Michigan-Flint. I also wish to thank Gorovodu sofowo Awudza, Dzodzi, Fo Tete, Ganugbe, Koliko, and Seydou; tronsiwo Adjo, Afi, Comfort, Cudjo, Koffi, Kponsi, and Pearl; kpedzigawo Kafui, Kuma, and Seydou; Edith Wood, archivist at the National Archives of Ghana; Samuel Kumodzie; Etienne Ahiako, anthropologist at the ORSTROM, Lomé; Tom Kumekpor, University of Legon; Sandra Greene, Cornell University; and especially Carol Greenhouse, coeditor of this collection, who also organized the American Anthropological Association panel, "Altered States; Altered Lives" (1994), where I presented an earlier version of this paper. Finally, I wish to thank my husband for help of all kinds, professional and personal.

1. Although this essay is about Vodu resistance to colonial and authoritarian states, it is important to remember that the constructions of ethnic and national identities put in question by Gorovodu and Mama Tchamba may not be entirely different from those employed by or occurring in modern liberal states as well. The identity politics of minorities in bourgeois democracies and the national identity that can accompany or even supplant identity politics for a majority of citizens are both problematic for Vodu practitioners, who practice other, perhaps otherwise complex, sorts of personhood and community.

2. See, for example, Owusu (1995); Skinner (1995); and Sklar (1995) on the possibilities of such recognition and practice in West Africa today.

3. In particular, I am referring to the ethnographic work of Amadiume (1987); Apter (1993); Boddy (1989, 1994); Comaroff and Comaroff (1991, 1993); Masquelier (1993); Matory (1993, 1994); Stoller (1989, 1992); and Taussig (1993).

4. Although they are not called Vodu or Tro among other coastal groups, similar practices and god-objects also exist among Akan peoples in Ghana. "Fetishes" I saw among Fante priests along the highway to Cape Coast in 1994 were exactly the same as the Gorovodu god-objects. Ablewa or Abirewa (discussed later in this essay) is well-known among Asante and still exists near Kumasi (as I found out in 1996).

5. I have found few reports that Gorovodu actually existed as such in the northern regions of Ghana, Togo, or Benin, or in Burkina Faso, although I have asked colleagues who work in these "norths" about such a possibility. In the cases I did find, it was said that the cult had been introduced by northerners (Kabye, in one case) who had "taken" it from Asante across the border in Ghana. The origins of these "northern" deities seem to me to be in border crossings themselves—ethnic, regional, sacred, national, linguistic, political, and imaginary. But I have not ruled out future fieldwork in any of the possible "norths" that can be singled out. Indeed, the work of M. J. Field (1948) indicates that both Sunia Compo and Nana Wango, of the Gorovodu pantheon, probably did come from the Wa district in northern Ghana. The "north" can mean many different things to people living in the south—north of the coast, north of Kumasi, the "real" Ghanaian, Togolese, and Beninese norths bordering Burkina Faso, Burkina Faso itself, and so forth. It often means "Hausa" (Awusa), which itself may refer broadly to Muslims as well as to actual Hausa people, of which there are many along the coast. The Hauka cult was brought to Ghana (colonial Gold Coast) from Niger by Zabrama immigrants (Stoller 1989, 1992).

6. At present, north-south alliances between free people are not rare. I have met several Gorovodu priests who are married to women from the north and who have become spirit hosts, thus doubling their northernness in trance. Some of our Ewe friends in Lomé have married northern husbands. For example, our lawyer (from a prominent family), one of my husband's cousins (from a poor family), and a popular recording artist whose northern husband is a well-known journalist and opponent of the regime have all done so.

7. Atikevodu is very successful in treating crises of paranoia and hysteria and in bringing sufferers of psychotic breaks to the lucidity necessary to mourn their losses and continue on with life. I assisted a Gorovodu sofo as he treated two such cases over a period of several months.

8. Unlike colonial governments, the Togolese government has never officially prohibited Vodu orders. It is not difficult for a person living in southern Ghana, Togo, or Benin to establish connections with a Vodu village or community.

9. While the president and about 80 percent of the army and police force are from the north, such Losso and Kabye northerners account for only some 30 percent of the total population of Togo. Adja-Ewe and Guin-Mina southerners compose another 30 or 40 percent. Groups found in the middle are often not mentioned and are thus erased in this dichotomizing political discourse, although they also are divided into "southerners" and "northerners" by the town of Blitta, which is said to be the middle of the country.

10. My husband and I had many friends and acquaintances from the north, including neighbors from all walks of life and colleagues at the University of Benin. From 1990 to 1992 we were present during countless political discussions in which northerners argued detailed positions with regard to issues of governance. They were all on the side of democracy and constitutional reform with the exception of several very young and uneducated men who touted "killing anyone who is against the president." Such young tyrants were quickly reproved by their elders of the same ethnic group. Mid-country people—Akposso, Danyi, Bassar, and so on—also freely spoke their grievances against the regime and their desire for a more just form of government.

11. They would not have chosen the French Embassy, as they were convinced that the French government was soft on the dictatorship. Numerous newspaper articles appeared in both the Togolese nongovernment press and the French press from 1990 to 1993 blaming the French government for encouraging the national conference and then betraying the Togolese people by supporting the regime when push came to shove.

12. In Gorovodu a violent or "hot" death (dzogbeku) need not be a waste; survivors must wring strength from it. Thus the "hot" vodus of the Banguele group in Gorovodu are said to be spirits of slaves who died violent deaths, and that is why they are so powerful for protecting their worshipers from such a fate. But worshipers sometimes wish to die a violent death so as to join their beloved Banguele after death. (After death only one specific element of the person [luvo] can join the conglomerate Vodu; another, the reincarnation personality [dzoto] may be reborn in the lineage; other components join the cosmic soup of the universe.) But a person cannot really choose her death or cause her own or anyone else's, for that is strictly against the law. Anyone who "sees death coming" while in his village dies a "cool" or "house" death, which is good.

13. The Yewe cult was also at one time called "foreign" in Eweland. It is related to the

Shango and Yemoja, spirit possession cults once integral to the Yoruba Oyo state (Matory 1993, 1994). Yewe Vodu wielded considerable power in the Ewe Anlo state in the nineteenth century (Greene 1996). Although Gorovodu and Mama Tchamba share many cultural traits with Shango, Yemoja, and Yewe, including conventions of possession trance (and some Ewe women belong to Yewe, Gorovodu, and Mama Tchamba), they are also easily distinguished from these older cults. They carry a charge of "mixture" and border-crossing which has a more international flavor than do the older orders. They do, however, "send out the sign" (Matory 1994:80, 132) in similar ways; in the Togolese case this includes implicit (and sometimes explicit) disputing of government interpretations of ethnic identity, north-south relationships, and recent political violence.

14. I am told it is still possible to view the sessions of the month-long conference on videotapes that are available from the U.S. Embassy.

15. Gorovodu and Mama Tchamba orders have never rallied explicitly against the government; nor are they structured in such a way as to actively resist the regime in any organized fashion. From 1985 to 1993 most Vodu adherents were Ewe and Mina, thus southerners, and this colored them politically in the most obvious manner. Even so, it has often been said by Togolese northerners and southerners alike that the latent strength of the south for rising up against the regime, or for doing anything else of importance, lies in Vodu. Even Christians and Muslims are apt to say such things. Vodu has its reputation.

During 1985 to 1993 Vodu orders were not prohibited, and Vodu worship as such was not in peril. But numerous Vodu communities located in areas known to be strongholds of resistance to the present regime, such as Bé and Nyekonakpoe, were particularly vulnerable to attack by soldiers and police practicing state terrorism.

During the past decade the political turmoil in Togo has often been called tribal conflict not only by the government press but also by African and European outsiders who think Ewe and Mina southerners and Kabye and Losso northerners are divided into hostile tribal and regional factions. In fact, until the coup of 2 December 1991, there was very little evidence of actual ethnic hostility in Togo except for the activities of the feared, near mono-ethnic army and police force.

After the coup, some parties opposing the regime did in fact reject their northern members and thus played the government's divisive game. In 1993 when numerous army officers who belonged to the secret "Military Movement for Democracy" were fatally purged, it was known that members of both southern and northern ethnic groups were included (Le Monde, 6 April 1993). Thus, while there was a "northern-ethnic" majority at every level in government and the military, some of those opportunistically faithful to the regime were actually southerners, and some of those who struggled against it were northerners.

But Gorovodu and Mama Tchamba practices in and of themselves fly in the face of the "tribalism" assessment as well as in the face of authoritarian state power. They practice reciprocity across time and regions and perform rituals as compensation or debt payment to the north for the southern enslavement of numerous northerners during the last century (both for the Atlantic voyage and for domestic slavery). However, this does not mean that there is never any Ewe ambivalence about northerners or former slaves, as I have discussed elsewhere (Rosenthal 1995).

As a great number of northerners were also implicated in the slave trade, there is no concept of an "innocent north" and a "guilty south." Vodu people expect northerners also to carry out ritual concerning their "debts" to enslaved people. In the Mama Tchamba order all deities are spirits of slaves that married into Ewe and Mina patrilines.

16. All kinds of law or "power" in Ewe culture may be referred to as *ese*. The adjective *se* means "hard," "strong," "forceful," or "powerful." "Ese si domeda," or "the law which brought me here" into this life is individual, personal law or fate, said to exist very specifically for each human being even before conception. This fate is indeed a "hard thing" (*nuse*), for life is often full of difficulty, if not tragedy, but it is a law which can be handled or acted upon through Afa divination. Wise people find out their Se, or Afa destiny (personal law) and then attempt to live a scrupulously conscious life in order to avoid the pitfalls written into their personhood from the beginning of time, as well as to enjoy the happiness that is uniquely theirs.

17. This "File" citation and those that follow are found in the Ghana National Archives in Accra.

18. I include here anthropological outsiders. I myself have found no unifying or encompassing theoretical discourse that can stand up to the complexities of Gorovodu and Mama Tchamba, so I must content myself with fragmented attempts, half-postmodern-literary/half-structuralist, to interpret them, and must employ "emic" Vodu concepts themselves as theoretical tools.

19. Jean and John Comaroff discuss what they call "nonagentive power," but what in Atikevodu is considered to be propelled by both human and spirit agency, such as that manifested during spirit possession and in countless details of ritual and everyday Vodu life: "[N]onagentive power proliferates outside the realm of institutional politics, saturating such things as aesthetics and ethics, built form and bodily representation, medical knowledge and mundane usage. . . . Yet the silent power of the sign, the unspoken authority of habit, may be as effective as the most violent coercion in shaping, directing, even dominating social thought and action" (1991:22).

Or, as they say it even more recently and inclusively, commenting on ethnographic and anthropological tendencies of the past few years (and here we can certainly include possession rituals in their consideration of "rites"):

> "Rites" are increasingly being treated, alongside everyday "routines," as just one form of symbolic practice, part and parcel of the more embracing "discourses" and "technologies" that establish or contest regimes of rule. . . . Rather than being reduced to a species of ceremonial action that insulates enchanted, self-

reproducing systems from the "real" world, then, ritual may be seen for what it often is: a vital element in the processes that make and remake social facts and collective identities. Everywhere. (1993:xvi)

In her extensive review of the anthropological literature bearing on this subject, Janice Boddy has the final word on the present acceptance of spirit possession and its concerns as "always already resisting":

Researchers currently locate possession in wider spheres of human endeavor, as speaking to quotidian issues of selfhood and identity, challenging global political and economic domination, and articulating an aesthetic of human relationship to the world. And whether central or peripheral, possession has been shown to be about morality, kinship, ethnicity, history, and social memory—the touchstones of social existence. Here morality and resistance are one. (1994:427)

20. The highly individuated Ewe person cannot, however, be an individualist in the Western sense without bringing shame upon himself. An Ewe individual is not a "whole person," either, but rather a crossroads of relationships including a reincarnation personality (dzoto), death soul (luvo), shadow (vovoli), spirit-double that may survive death (gbogbo), and all the components of one of the 256 Afa divination life signs (kpoli), including specific plants, animals, mountains, and rivers, and weather phenomena. This is a multitotemic construction of the self wedded to other, nontotemic, elements, for a person also overlaps with the being and personality of any Vodu that might have "accompanied her into this world" as well as with any Vodu that possesses her.

21. The "crossings" or overcomings of binary oppositions I write about in this essay are not spoken of as "border crossings" by Ewe speakers themselves. Many of them are just "crossings" or "travelings." For example, when a person first goes into trance an onlooker might say, "Eyi emogodo," which means, "She went to the other side of the street." I have also heard "Eyi Dagati" or "Eyi Yendi," indicating that the spirit host has suddenly been transported to northern towns. Indeed, borders such as that between Ghana and Togo did not exist until the colonial period. (The Ewe word for literal borders is edin and is used primarily in reference to state-defined national borders.)

Binary oppositions in Vodu culture, such as hot/cold, wild/tame, foreign/domestic, and male/female, are "crossed over" symbolically during Vodu ceremonies in the sense that the either/or identity of opposites is overcome, giving way to a both/and relationship embodied (and inspired or "inspirited") by the spirit host in trance. The word etrototo means "turning" (turning into, turning around, transforming, etc.), and my etic border metaphors in this essay are a subcategory of etrototo, that is, of crossing from one level of classification to a higher, more inclusive (or more plural) one, or from one symbolic state to another.

22. An especially telling example of northern garb may be found in the "warrior/

hunter shirts" (adewuwo) worn by Gorovodu and Mama Tchamba priests during ceremonies today. These shirts are copies of those worn during colonial times to protect wearers from German and English bullets during a period when some Vodu groups were explicitly anticolonial (according to several Togolese Gorovodu priests). The adewu was already, in colonial times, a copy of Sahelian or northern warrior garb, similar to that worn by Mandé hunters during ceremonies. (Maria Grosz-Ngate informed me of the Mandé ritual shirts; Lisa Aronson [1995:81] writes about these hunters' garments and includes a photograph of a fine Malian "adewu.")

23. Vodu orders were always changing, and new ones came into being even during the time of the Ewe Anlo state (from the seventeenth to nineteenth centuries), which had very limited powers. Sandra Greene, in her history of Tro worship, social change, and gender among Anlo Ewe, has argued that the Yewe Tro order, which took over much of the authority previously possessed by the Nyigbla order, gave women back some of the power they had lost when land became scarce and fathers married their daughters to whomever would add land to the family—or at least not take it away. (Ewe are patrilineal.) On becoming a Yewe priestess, a woman could not be forced to marry someone against her will. She had her own powers and a community that existed apart from lineage organization, even if mothers and daughters often belonged to the order. Greene believes that some Yewe priests may have been involved in the Atlantic slave trade, employing their powers for the material and political interests of their shrine (1996:123–33).

24. I noted about ten cases of Ablewa accusation in the small number of files that I examined, not including the reportedly swollen file entitled "Abirewa," which was mysteriously missing from the archives when I was there.

25. This is not to say they are "acting" when trance occurs; there is no doubt in the mind of anyone watching Gorovodu rituals that possession is a secondary state.

26. It is obvious that even today the subject of Vodu objects and practices produces a particular excitation in many Europeans and Americans, even those living in Ghana, Togo, and Benin. More than one expatriate that I met in Togo told me that I would eventually find the Gorovodu people committing murder, sacrificing babies, or engaging in sexual orgies. Not all of these individuals were missionaries; some were working in embassies. One missionary priest who is an excellent ethnographer of Adja-Ewe cultures, and who was very helpful to me, is reputed to have burned down the church he himself had built when he discovered that his parishioners were still engaging in Vodu worship. It is said the Vodu people then made him leave the village for his action was totally incomprehensible and, to their eyes, criminal. (In my husband's natal village, parishioners attend church and then go to Vodu rituals—the priest knows this and is resigned to it.)

In the university classes I teach in the United States, students from very different backgrounds clearly have internalized the Hollywood representations of Vodu, and it requires considerable work for me to undo such images (and I don't always succeed). Indeed, Hollywood racism with regard to African religion is even more devastating than the comments of early traders and colonial writers, some of whom left descriptions that were fairly neutral (e.g., in Verger 1957).

27. African contempt for African culture is common among devout second or third generation Christians who have never practiced Vodu. Such attitudes are not easily predictable—I know numerous Togolese and Ghanaian Christians who are respectful of Vodu. But a certain number warn of the "Satanism" in Vodu and are just as intolerant as many Europeans and Americans, perhaps even more so. On the other hand, hundreds of times (especially when I was teaching English at the U.S. Cultural Center in Lomé) I heard West Africans sneer and laugh at the mention of Vodu, claiming that Vodu practices were stupid and superstitious; and months later I would find out that these individuals in fact practiced Vodu. They apparently had learned their attitude of contempt from Europeans and Americans and used such expressions to protect themselves from the questions of curious outsiders. Even so, some West Africans may be truly of a mixed mind about their religious practices.

I do know many Togolese who practice both Christianity and Vodu (but some would argue they in fact are assimilating Christianity to Vodu) and are utterly unapologetic about the mix. Perhaps they do not ask themselves questions about apparent contradictions between monotheism and polytheism or between the worship of god-objects on the one hand and the Christian taboo on idols on the other. They are not concerned about doctrine or issues of logic; they are participating in two different cultures, and that is a good thing as far as they are concerned. (Many West Africans can live with contradictions while engaging in sacred rituals, just as a good number of anthropologists can.)

28. In fact, there is evidence from the archives, as well as in the rich use of Twi language in Gorovodu songs, that Abirewa began among Asante, in "British Country."

29. Paul Stoller has written about this film, the people who "starred" in it, and Rouch, the more-than-ethnographic film artist to whom we are all indebted for such a magnificent "mimesis of mimesis" (1992:145–60).

30. Fritz Kramer suggests that the motors for mimesis of colonial figures and of African northern peoples are images of "*passiones*," modes of intense experiences which have transformed those possessed by them (1993:58–63): "The passiones become psychic states, transient moods or a lasting mark and imprint which form under the 'impression' left by particular encounters" (61). Michael Taussig, in his important study of mimesis and alterity, captures well the compelling nature of mimesis:

> Note the magical, the soulful power that derives from replication . . . the magical power of replication, the image affecting what it is an image of, wherein the representation shares in or takes power from the represented—testimony to the power of the mimetic faculty through whose awakening we might not so much understand that shadow of science known as magic . . . but see anew the spell of the natural where the reproduction of life merges with the recapture of the soul. (1993:2)

Trance against the State **349**

31. Although my interpretation of Hauka is not exactly in the same words as Stoller, and he may not altogether agree with me, my ideas draw on his conclusions as well as on Taussig's work.

32. A story about an event that occurred several years ago helps to demonstrate the multileveled relevance of the border theme:

> Mawusi in Aflao was a smuggler. He had a good "honest" life as a smuggler and never hurt anyone. But he attended a fetatotro [a Gorovodu "turning-of-the-year" festival] and left it early to go across the border so as to bring back some goods that would have made him a great deal of money. He couldn't pass it up even though Afa [divination] clearly informed him he was not, under any circumstances, to cross the border during the fetatotro. When the border guards called him to stop, he didn't hear them and kept on going, so they fired and killed him. All because of money. What a waste. And he was otherwise a very good sofo. (Rosenthal 1998)

Smuggling, turning (back), and crossing are carried out literally and symbolically in this narration and its context. (Are not the slave spirits "smuggled" into the south each time there is a possession ritual?—do they not smuggle themselves into their hosts' bodies?) Even so, aware of the secular danger in crossing literal borders, the Afa diviner warned the priest not to cross the line that night. Mawusi's inability to turn down monetary wealth in order to cash in on symbolic goods at the turning-of-the-year festival caused his death; his preference for crossing state borders rather than spiritual ones hastened his "crossing of the river."

33. Jacques Lacan's translator, Alan Sheridan, says with regard to the "real":

> [The "real"] stands for what is neither symbolic nor imaginary, and remains foreclosed from the analytic experience, which is an experience of speech. What is prior to the assumption of the symbolic, the real in its "raw" state. . . . This Lacanian concept of the "real" is not to be confused with reality, which is perfectly knowable: the subject of desire knows no more than that, since for it reality is entirely phantasmatic. . . . (Lacan 1977:ix, x)

One might say that the Lacanian Real is what escapes language, at bottom, enjoyment and suffering (*jouissance* and *angoisse*), which are never representable; nor can they be remembered in their "real" fullness (Rosenthal 1998). I interpret spirit possession to be precisely a visit to the Real.

34. Gorovodu and Mama Tchamba may be said to include the "historical consciousness" that Boddy (1989:347, 48) refers to in connection with Zar cults in Sudan, although their history is surely different from the Western varieties. I would also say that they are commentaries on "modernity" as is *orpeko* possession among Masaai women (Hodgson 1997), although the modernity they both embody and contest is not conceived of in terms similar to the occidental modern. Vodu possession, however, is desired and held out, unagressively (as it was during the colonial period), as an old/new alternative to Christianity or as an activity that might be engaged in alongside a person's Christian practices, whereas the women possessed by *orpeko* must be exorcised.

35. However, lest anyone think that possession trance, as practiced by Ewe Vodu worshipers, began with state formation or as a form of political resistance to colonialism, let the records speak (e.g., in Verger 1957); Vodu and mimesis of spirits were already alive and well when the first Europeans arrived in West Africa. Vodu no doubt took new forms during the colonial period along with similar spirit possession orders among neighboring peoples. Gorovodu in particular, in its present Ewe and Mina form, did begin with various Atikevodu cults during colonial rule, as previously discussed. And it may have been strengthened during the past ten years by the political problems in postindependence Togo as, by all accounts, it has been growing rapidly.

But any Ewe Vodu worshiper will say that practices of possession trance have always had their own *raison d'etre*—trance in Gorovodu erupts as "being" or "just life itself," that is, transformation, the rapture of living in the midst of difference, differentiation, otherness of all kinds, and then of overcoming these differences for a sacred period. So, as far as emic explanations go, any adaptive characteristics or functions that Atikevodu might provide, any political uses it might be put to, are predicated upon its being-for-itself. In other words, within a general Vodu logic, given that Gorovodu and Mama Tchamba are historically marked and motivated, it also must be understood that whatever political system "comes along," there will always be an appropriate Vodu agency at work with or against it, and most likely both.

Part Four

Conclusion

Elizabeth Mertz

The Perfidy of Gaze and the Pain of Uncertainty:
Anthropological Theory and the Search for Closure

Why should we care about the promises that can be made or broken through gaze, when one person looks into another's eyes? We begin to answer this question by stepping back into the setting of Carroll Lewin's essay in this volume—a Polish ghetto during the Holocaust:

> In April, Tory confronts Miller about the slaughter of five thousand Jews from Vilna who were supposed to have been transported to Kovno but instead were taken to Ponary and killed. Tory wants "an open, human conversation"; he knows that when Miller "is not angry, and is alone with me in the room, he is capable of speaking as one human being to another." Miller is elusive, but, when pressed by Tory, he shifts the responsibility for the slaughter of the Vilna group to the Gestapo. Tory reads this as an "unspoken admission" and concludes that "under his Nazi uniform there is some spark of humanity." Miller continues "with eyes cast downward" and reassures Tory that nothing will happen to Kovno ghetto: "I give you my promise." Fifteen months later, Kovno ghetto is liquidated. (Lewin, this volume, 54)

This haunting vignette captures a profound and painful dilemma, one with which anthropologists and others are still struggling—a fundamental conundrum that defies the tools of rationalist theory and traditional social science method. On what can we rely in drawing conclusions about other human beings? If we cannot impute some core regularities or structures, some fundamental humanity, some measure of certainty to the external indicia we are given, then how is any kind of social connection or understanding possible?

In this exchange between Jewish leader and Nazi, it is not only the social order that has been turned upside down but the very fabric of human connections—the minute-to-minute communicative signals and gestures upon which sociality itself depends. Desperate for some certainty in an increasingly violent and insane situation, Tory searches Miller's face and voice for indications of humanity, for the signals that permit any shared understandings to emerge in human communication. In retrospect it may be tempting to respond with scorn to such naïveté: given the situation, surely it was folly to expect any of the usual conventions or signals to hold. Tory's search for certainty, for structure—for his people's survival—did indeed hang upon very slender threads: on a downcast gaze, on a tone of voice, on the words "I promise." Yet it is upon just such slender threads, woven together in a multitude of daily interactions, that the fabric of human interaction and sociability is built. It is through regularities of experience with just such minute cues that children build the growing understandings and expectations that permit them to become members of families and social groups.[1] What, then, do we make of an adult's attempt to make order out of life-threatening chaos by clinging mistakenly to such small, important signals—and what do we take from the failure of this attempt and many others like it?

In 1973 two bank robbers in Stockholm held four people hostage in a bank for almost a week (Strentz 1982:149–50). During that time the robbers threatened the lives of their hostages many times but also showed them occasional kindnesses. For example, when one of the women attempted to call her children and was unable to reach them, she began to cry; her captor "touched her cheek" in a consoling manner and urged her, "Try again, don't give up" (Graham, Rawlings, and Rigsby 1994:2). By the end of the siege, the hostages had developed tender feelings for the robbers and antagonistic feelings toward the police who were attempting to save them. In the wake of this event, scholars studying trauma have noted similar reactions in other victims and have tracked what came to be known as the "Stockholm Syndrome" among survivors of a number of terrifying situations, including concentration camp victims, battered women, and abused children (31). Interestingly, among the factors researchers have identified as contributing to the development of this syndrome are the degree to which the hostage and captor make eye contact, the amount of general contact and communication between them, and the extent to which the hostage is dependent on the captor for survival over extended periods of time (25). It has been suggested that this bonding arises out of a hostage's need to survive and that it provides a person who is living under the high stress of a life-threatening situation with a way to keep functioning (Strentz 1982:150–52; Herman 1992).[2] In the process, the perpetrator of violence is viewed as a savior; bonds of trust with those who might actually save the victim are undermined, as the victim's sense of reality turns upside down in the service of hope. This is a phenomenon frequently noted among children from abusive homes, who must somehow reconcile the harsh reality of family abuse with the necessity of trusting and relying upon some primary caretaker for survival (see Courtois 1988; Freyd 1996). Warren presents an intriguing parallel in her discussion of the tactics used by terrorist states: the "creation of divided realities, the exploitation of radically different rationalities, and the blurring of victimizer and victim" that are used to discourage organized resistance by undermining "the bond of trust between citizens, community members, and close family relatives" (Warren, this volume, 385).

At a very fundamental level, then, these cases demonstrate how people struggle to impose meaningful structures and pictures of reality on the situation when ordinary and predictable ways of interacting disappear—how far they will strain to avoid the pain of acknowledging the potential perfidy of the ordinary cues and signals upon which they have always relied.[3] A warped vision that provides reassurance and continuity, it would seem, is sometimes preferable to a more accurate assessment that acknowledges the dangers, chaos, and untamed uncertainties of volatile situations—and perhaps, to a lesser extent, of human existence generally. Or, to view it through a different lens, these victims are rejecting an accurate vision of themselves as lacking much real agency, refusing to accept that they are in imminent danger of annihilation and powerless to do much about it. To accomplish this rejection, they must imagine themselves inhabiting a world in which there is some hope, in which there is some possibility of reaching, reasoning, or connecting with the people who hold the power of life and death. As Greenhouse has eloquently explained in this volume, ethnographies of political instability force us along with our subjects to rethink many key ideas, including our conceptions of agency. What sort of agency is this, then, that refuses to acknowledge its own powerlessness—that insists on finding a "normal order" where none exists, a "human" response where inhumanity is prevailing, safety where there is danger? It might be tempting here to romanticize such denials, pointing to the spirit it takes to assert even such residual agentive force (that is, exercising the power to refuse to acknowledge a lack of agency). Or one could note, in a social constructionist vein, that perhaps such denials can make themselves true in some cases—that by refusing to accept powerlessness, people give themselves the hope that is needed if they are to go on struggling to live. Indeed, this observation is in part accurate. And yet we also encounter in these cases a limit to such a social constructionist vision: no matter what "reality" these victims constructed to evade their lack of power, many of them would die and suffer terribly at the hands of those who controlled their fates. If, for some, denial of the danger was a life-saving psychological move, for others it may have been a trick that took away any last opportunities for resistance or struggle.[4] As Warren (this volume, 386) notes, the conflicting rationalities within which Jewish leaders struggled "at once made life livable and left intact structures of control that would take it away."

It is precisely these kinds of conundrums and paradoxes that animate this collection of essays on life in unstable and changing states. If, instead of turning away from these difficult dilemmas, we rise to the challenges they pose, we find our own categories and models shifting and at times exploding. This is a turn toward complexity and away from easy answers. Victims can at times "construct" their ways into survival but at other times, to their own detriment, conceal from themselves the truth about the dangers they face. The same act of denial can be an assertion of agency (indeed, a means to survival) and a delivery of ultimate power into the hands of aggressors. As Greenhouse's introduction to this volume explains, it is precisely when society is being remade, when states are dissolving and transforming, when at-times violent change is underway, that we see most clearly the dynamic, improvisatory, and performative aspects of the cultures, societies, and lives that anthropologists have always studied. And, at the same time, the limits and underlying commitments of social science concepts and methods are revealed and brought into question—as, for example, when we find notions of social construction both crucial and inadequate to mapping what is happening. De Nike's analysis of postunification attacks on East German judges, prosecutors, and law professors "finds individual and collective phenomena seeming at once to confirm and undermine the analytical utility of Habermas's behavioral and dialogic model of 'intersubjectively shared traditions' of 'cultural values' " (this volume, 105). Or, taking another example, Greenhouse has argued powerfully for a new "uncoupling" of structure and agency in order to take better account of the way the "illusion of . . . concreteness" of society is always being remade in interaction. As in the work of Jean and John Comaroff, these articles attempt to capture both "a constantly unfolding, mutating, unruly process and an infinitely intricate order of evanescent, often enigmatic, relations" (Comaroff and Comaroff 1997: 19).

Reacting to the difficult ambiguities that emerge from this kind of research, these authors have also turned to reflexivity—not as a flourish, but as a brass-tacks methodological necessity. In a sense, here we see anthropology pressed to its core, as the women and men who perform the ethnography find themselves asking not only about the role of their own concepts and cultures in their research, but side-by-side with their subjects, digging down to examine the very constitution of selves, agency, and society as it occurs from minute to minute in action and interaction. In Zabusky's words, "[a]s I rode the gyres with [my informants] . . . I realized that I was trapped as well, trapped in an iron cage of my own making, but from which, nonetheless, there could be no escape" (this volume, 139–40). Drawing on her own field research in Guatemala as well as the articles in this volume, Warren incisively delineates the reflexive challenge posed for anthropologists when they are "not exempt from the cultures of terror [they] seek to describe," and yet must "position themselves so that they can narrate the interplay of . . . conflicting rationalities" involved (this volume, 386).

The Pain of Uncertainty and the Search for Closure

If the essays in this volume uncover conceptual and methodological challenges that arise from studying social transformation, they also centrally confront the ethical and emotional aspects of things falling apart or changing beyond recognition.[5] We have seen that victims of violence at times turn away from confronting their lack of control over their fate. Faced with potentially paralyzing uncertainty as to whether they will live or die, and with no means to influence the outcome, they force certainty, create knowable parameters, imagine closure and order where none exist. But, as a number of the authors in this volume indicate, this response is not limited to the subjects of anthropological studies: social scientists, too, have sometimes balked at uncertainty, reaching for relatively fixed concepts of rationality and structure to capture lived realities that may be far more fluid and unpredictable.[6] Greenhouse discusses the challenges to the anthropological imagination posed by "modern uncertainties." Warren warns that "the question for engaged ethnographers is how to resist becoming complicit in the misrepresentation of normative (nationalistic) politics as stable systems" (this volume, 381). And Lewin notes that social scientists have often avoided facing the "unambiguous trauma and terror of the Holocaust" (this volume, 37) in part because it might defy the closure that is an accustomed part of taming events through explaining them in social science categories. Drawing on the work of Zygmunt Bauman, Lewin goes on to discuss the related problem that such events fit poorly with models of progressive rationalization or order in society: "if we, as anthropologists seek to reject muteness on evil such as that epitomized in the Nazi genocide . . . [w]e need to jettison the idea that this genocide was an aberration or failure, rather than a product of modernity" (this volume, 37). In a strikingly parallel vein, feminists have argued that in order to confront adequately "the reality and extent of sexual violence," it will be necessary for social scientists to move beyond a frequent characterization of such violence as aberrant or unusual—a kind of denial that, these feminist authors argue, reflects an "unwillingness to believe that 'normal' healthy human beings can be, without their own complicity, so frequently and so severely victimized by men who appear 'normal'" (Fitzgerald, Lonsway, and Payne n.d.:3; Meier 1993:1311).[7] This is a theme taken up by the activists with whom Elizabeth Faier worked, who complain that it is difficult to upset the settled picture held by many people of rape as unusual. Here resistance to domination takes the form of resisting a false security—a security based upon the comforting image of society as a fundamentally safe and orderly space for women. Like the social scientists criticized by feminist scholars, many laypeople seem to prefer the certainty promised by such settled and orderly models of human existence. And acceptance of these orderly visions undercuts urgent calls for change, denying the need for social reforms.

We can hear then, in some of this scholarship, grounds for an indictment of social science for its inability to confront pain, uncertainty, lack of closure, and, perhaps in a more controversial vein, for its unwillingness to face what Lewin calls "evil." Psychologists studying violence have echoed this indictment:

> The study of psychological trauma has a curious history—one of episodic amnesia. . . . This intermittent amnesia is not the result of . . . lack of interest. . . . To study psychological trauma is to come face to face both with human vulnerability in the natural world and with the capacity for evil in human nature. . . . [W]hen the traumatic events are of human design, those who bear witness are caught in the conflict between victim and perpetrator. It is morally impossi-

ble to remain neutral in this conflict. The bystander is forced to choose sides.

It is very tempting to take the side of the perpetrator. All the perpetrator asks is that the bystander do nothing. He appeals to the universal desire to see, hear, and speak no evil. The victim, on the contrary, asks the bystander to share the burden of pain. (Herman 1992:7).

And perhaps it is not only the lay bystander who struggles over accepting this burden, but social scientists as well. Another psychologist points to the difficulty for many in facing humankind's fundamental vulnerability to betrayal by others, and she coins the phrase "betrayal trauma" to describe the problem:

Betrayal is the violation of implicit or explicit trust. The closer and more necessary the relationship, the greater the degree of betrayal. Extensive betrayal is traumatic. . . . Betrayal trauma theory posits that under certain conditions, betrayals necessitate a certain "betrayal blindness." . . . (Freyd 1996:9)

Again, as with the "Stockholm Syndrome" or the Jewish leader, Tory, we see the difficult and painful character of acknowledging the real frailty of the social connections, structures, and signals that permit trust and sociality to develop; and we see the reasons why it might be tempting to turn away from instabilities and unpredictabilities that, while strikingly visible in more dramatic moments of human experience, actually render everyone vulnerable in frightening ways. How much more comforting it is to theorize a world in which structure and predictability reign—in which injustice, violence, and betrayals of key social norms are exceptional.[8] Perpetrators of violence, whether they are states, organizations, or individuals, can exploit this desire for comforting beliefs and stability.

Anthropologists working on issues of violence have also pointed to the inadequacy of standard social science conventions of representing the disorder and emotion involved; by the time we have told the story in the removed voice of social science narrative, our very account has tamed—and thus obliterated—much of the immediacy and lack of structure that characterized the events.[9] Indeed, the control and closure that result from telling the story of what happened as a narrative with a known ending—about an event of a certain type—move the readers away from an essential aspect of the lived experience.[10] Although this is a difficulty that may never be completely surmounted, it can be amelio-rated by use of discursive strategies such as Faier's first-person "eyewit-ness account" to describe a tenuous, potentially eruptive moment. As Faier takes us face-to-face with villagers who threaten to get their guns, the fact that she has placed herself in the narrative brings an immediacy to our reading; we realize that in that moment our narrator herself could not be sure of the outcome. We can for a time stand in the ethnogra-pher's shoes (and thus closer to her subjects' positions) at an unstable instant in which, quite literally, life and death might hang in the bal-ance. And in moving imaginatively that much closer to moments where the narrative's ending is uncertain—where the unthinkable conclusion hovers closer than is comfortable, we may also be able to reach closer to Ichlas at the moment before she was killed by her brother in the name of "honor," reliving if only fleetingly a point in time at which she looked into familiar eyes and imagined another ending—a moment before the violent explosion of cultural and personal boundary-crossings made death the certain ending of the tale.

If scholars studying some of the bleakest moments of human history and interaction are urging us away from the complacency of closure in social science analysis, so, too, are researchers operating in less trau-matic realms. Thus, psychologists attempting to develop adequate theo-ries of the self or the person have moved increasingly away from static, bounded conceptualizations toward more contextual, processual, and fluid approaches. Psychologist Kenneth Gergen writes of "the break-down of the knowable self" in contemporary understandings, noting that "as the sense of self as a singular, knowable set of essences is questioned, so doubt is cast upon the existence of other bounded en-tities" (1991:17). Gergen urges us, in a move reminiscent of Wittgen-stein and others, to view "the locus of understanding [as] removed from the heads of individual persons and placed within a relational space" (1990:602). Vincent Crapanzano describes "the constitution of the self and other" as "the result of momentary arrests in a continuous dialecti-cal movement," a movement that is in crucial ways shaped by contextual features of linguistic exchanges (1990:419). The field of "cultural psy-chology" and its many relatives in anthropology, linguistics, and other fields are all centrally concerned with the exploration of this decentered, processual approach to the psyche (see Shweder 1990; Wertsch 1985).

In parallel fashion, a number of authors in this volume—building on similar theoretical approaches developed by anthropologists and so-

X

ciolegal scholars in recent years[11]—point out the inadequacies of static, bounded conceptions of person, nation, locality, and place and urge us toward more turbulent, shifting perspectives. Here is ground less amenable to the safe, comforting security of easily-drawn boundaries and clear centers; here are spaces constantly in flux and remade by the people who inhabit them.[12] Just as we are pushed to confront the instability and potential perfidy of everyday human signals and connections, we are urged by this scholarship to confront the pain of ambiguity, uncertainty, and paradox in human cultures, geographies, and societies—to turn away from the comfort of closure toward ethnographic accounts that do better justice to the lived realities of human existence. (Of course, we should avoid idealizing ordered systems, remembering that pain can lie in certainty and order as well.)

The Palestinian women in Faier's account occupy this in-between territory, struggling with their own blurred personal boundaries as they fight against accounts of an honor killing that render the murder an accepted and acceptable ending to some stock narrative. If Ichlas was a prostitute, one narrative would go, then her behavior creates social disorder and brings shame on her family; her death at the hands of a family member is fitting because it will return social order and family honor. In another version, the disorder was caused by Ichlas's violation of the boundary between Jewish and Palestinian societies and states, while yet another narrative described her as literally embodying a violent clash between two other incompatible worlds and identities—modern cosmopolitan versus traditional village. In this latter case, the embodied collision of two incommensurate worlds is visible in the war between the immediate surroundings and her dress and manner, in the way her body crosses and violates boundaries. And, once again, her death offers a resolution of this conflict by actually removing the offending body and restoring order. In all of these narratives, the honor killing offers closure—a restoration of order. The Palestinian feminists seek to unsettle these comforting narratives by offering a more upsetting story in which the killing creates disorder and injustice. This story opens the door on a world in which women's safety is far from certain, in which rape is possible, in which no woman can with certainty guarantee herself immunity from an honor killing. At the same time, the feminists who work to unsettle settled narratives are simultaneously living with blurred boundaries of identity and disbelief, and Faier does not attempt to resolve this ambiguity for us. Some are vividly caught in-between and are vocal about their confusion—or even hospitalized for their mental anguish—while others bear the collision of transforming worlds and states more quietly.

Anthropological Accounts of Unstable and Transforming States: In-between Concepts, Disciplines, and Epistemologies

Because they occupy and tell us of the "in-between," the essays that comprise this volume capture well the sense of vertigo familiar to those of us who find ourselves frequently bridging distinct worlds, disciplines, or epistemologies—a position that Maria Lugones refers to as "world-travelling":

> I think that most of us who are outside the mainstream U.S. construction or organization of life are "world-travellers" as a matter of necessity and survival. . . . In describing a "world" I mean to be offering a description of experience, something that is true to experience even if it is ontologically problematic. Though I would think that any account of identity that could not be true to this experience of outsiders to the mainstream would be faulty even if ontologically unproblematic. Its ease would constrain, erase, or deem aberrant experience that has within it significant insights into non-imperialist understanding between people. . . . (1990:390–402)

Lugones explains that we can learn a great deal about interstitial moments—moments of fluidity and translation—from those inhabiting the margins of power, who experience such world traveling as an urgent and constant necessity. If everyone must at times travel across boundaries, if "selves" are always somewhat fluid, if all social experience at times slides from clear structures into provisional, constructed, and contested spaces, then it may be not the most elite and privileged— those abiding closest to seemingly stable centers—who can teach us the most about these ubiquitous aspects of human life and society.[13] And, of course, as Zabusky's essay vividly demonstrates, sometimes the lessons can come from increasingly unstable centers, as the boundary between center and margin blurs.

In the study of our subjects' blurring boundaries—and our own—we are often called to work in-between and question the boundaries of disciplines, theories, and concepts. The idea that work from the margins (and transforming centers) can advance the central understandings of social science is underscored by the authors in this volume. Indeed, as Judy Rosenthal pointedly implies, it may be that those we study were there ahead of us, understanding more fully the paradoxical and fluid character of social relations long before Western social scientists began to grasp the traps and promise of such a vision:

> This penchant for overcoming dualisms and divisions does not mean that Vodu people do not believe in distinctions or in "two sides of things." They virtually worship the culturally invented, two-sidedness of things. . . . At the same time, they imagine that borders and others distinctions are constructed for purposes of crossing, and that sides are divided up precisely so that they may fuse from time to time. (this volume, 339)

Rosenthal's at-times deeply ironic commentary counterposes the alarmed response of those who prefer neatly divided, static categories to Vodu people's incessant boundary-crossing and their easier acceptance of complexity and motion in the social ordering and disordering of life.

Ries, in describing the inversion of expected social ordering she found in postcommunist Russia, speaks of the odd discourse that locates order and even safety in the Mafia, commenting wryly: "Despite all of the mystification I may detect in their talk, I often find myself thinking that because of the stark forms their economic 're-education' has taken, my Russian interlocutors perceive the structural realities of class, power, and transaction in the capitalist marketplace more clearly than I ever will" (this volume, 310). Their continually unsettling discourse poses street bandits as occasional sources of social redemption from "the tangles of hypocrisy and cynicism in which people feel themselves caught" (this volume, 309), as they navigate a disappointingly chaotic transitional time. The cynical talk of ordinary folk in Russia, with its constant critique of capital accumulation and state power, "actively deconstruct[s] whatever legitimizing discourses or practices are presented on behalf of the reformulated political-economic order" (this volume, 277)—refusing the proferred depiction of an orderly movement "toward democracy and justice," insisting on a vision of state power as equally as "inaccessible, inconsistent, and involuted as before" (this volume, 309).

Echoing these themes in the work of Rosenthal and Ries, Parnell contrasts more orderly models of a central, centered state and its concomitant discrete (clearly defined and owned) parcels of land with the more disordered geography that emerges from ethnographic study: "Conflicts that grow out of the disorganization of multiple ownership of land . . . reveal a composite rather than a Western state" (this volume, 148). Similarly, Eve Darian-Smith's article tells of an intriguing response to European unification in the border area of Kent: a peculiar combination of increasingly porous boundaries—between England and Europe, between Kent's claim to local autonomy and EU law—and a renewed defense of clear, strong borders for Kent as an old boundary-maintaining ritual is revived. And, just as psychology-from-the-margins may yield a truer, more adequate vision of the processual-self experienced even by those at the center, Darian-Smith and Parnell show us how ethnography-from-the-margins can advance the central project of developing "a theoretical language that allows us to talk about community and state at the same time" (Parnell, this volume, 177, paraphrasing Chatterjee 1993:11). In both cases, work in margins and destabilized centers allows us to see through the inaccuracy of unrealistically ordered social science models and advances our understanding where more centrally located, normal-science projects have remained mired— that is, aware of their inability even in less obviously fragmented situations to capture process but unable to extricate themselves from this bind. Sounding a theme close to the hearts of many of the authors in this volume, Clifford Geertz has recently written of his "sense that one is continually putting together ordered pictures and having them come apart just at the moment one gets them more or less put together; that the tension between an urban tradition a long way from dead . . . and an urban life outrunning that tradition's categories is pervasive, chronic, and not obviously resolvable," thus accepting the in-between scholarship (and social world) of which these essays speak.[14]

For James Freeman and Nguyen Dinh Huu, the view from the margins yields a grim assessment of Western-based bureaucracy and theories as they have impacted the lives of refugee children. This narrative tells of cumulative traumatization of these children, first as they fled Vietnam, then as they struggled to survive in refugee camps, and finally when the United Nations High Commissioner for Refugees (UNHCR) forced them to repatriate from the camps—at times to certain abuse and neglect. We learn that the "culture" concept played a role in the ideology that spawned this forced repatriation. As Freeman and Nguyen relate these children's stories, they move from the more anthropological genre of ethnography into an account that is unabashedly engaged and judg-

366 Elizabeth Mertz

mental. Albeit through the pages of volunteers' letters and case workers' reports, we hear the voices of abandoned children living in brutal and inhumane circumstances: one child prays to die in his sleep in order to avoid the temptation of suicide, which he regards as a sin. We hear the sharp contrast of official reports ("[T]he uncle seemed to be taking good care of them" [this volume, 228]) and of ethnographic observation ("The middle child, the sister, hid in fear near one bed. The eldest brother was severely malnourished and ill. . . . The uncle had gained weight but the children were stunted, listless, and emaciated" [this volume, 228, 231–32]). And then the authors move to a more engaged stance, condemning the UNHCR's actions, describing their own efforts to intervene, and taking a normative position. Here then is a blurring of the boundary between ethnography and social action—between social science and moral judgment. This convergence is more usually the domain of law or policy studies.

Because I am trained both in anthropology and law, much of my work has attempted to bridge these two distinct and at-times warring epistemologies. There is a strong tug-of-war between the mandatory normative engagement of legal studies, at times perhaps without sufficient critical thought, and the more contemplative and careful stance of the anthropologist, at times perhaps shirking moral engagement. My legal colleagues repeat tales of the heartless anthropologists who evade ethical responsibilities by hiding behind the "culture" concept or various brands of relativism. My anthropologist colleagues express their dismay at the "bottom-line" mentality of legal scholars, so obsessed with instrumentalist analysis of situations that they run roughshod over the complexities, nuances, and moral ambiguities. The articles in this volume suggest some new bridges—but also, of course, some added complications—to be found in this core tension.

In a sense postmodern long before the term became popular, some would chastise anthropology (along with postmodernism generally) for undermining or exploding fixed meanings and conceptual categories to a point where moral judgment becomes impossible—indeed, where no standpoint can even be carved out from which to assert the "reality" of events or perceptions.[15] Facing daily confrontations with urgent issues of violence and responsibility, many activists and lawyers respond with an irritated sense that such epistemological skepticism is a luxury only academics removed from the demands of engagement can afford. Once we have stepped through the postmodern looking glass, how do we avoid a nihilist vortex where any account is as valid as another? The murderer's denial of responsibility, after all, is just another perspective (see Frohmann and Mertz 1994:846–48). If there is no fixed "truth" or even "reality" to assert in the face of such denials, from what vantage can those who abuse power be called to account for their actions?

How, then, is anthropology to respond to such critiques, which have come from within as well as from without? There is certainly some validity to concerns about the moral and epistemological implications of anthropology's use of the culture concept or its reliance on relativism (see Freeman and Nguyen in this volume; Mertz 1987). And yet, the answer is surely not to assert singular, fixed standpoints; indeed, full recognition of the dangers of such a monologic approach has always been one of anthropology's most important contributions. This kind of singular point-of-view is of course particularly problematic when it implies a lack of careful attention to the complicated "on the ground" experiences and understandings of the people in question. Indeed, this is one of the best and most powerful arguments, made in many of these essays, for the value of ethnography.[16] The ethnographies in this volume take us through the fixing and unfixing of social realities as states are reformulated and cultures transformed.

Perhaps, then, the more interesting question becomes not whether there is any fixed reality, but rather what the significance is of asserting a singular, nonnegotiable truth at particular points in the history of a social shift. When does such an assertion of reality help in contesting abuses of power, and when does it aid a hegemonic impulse that obliterates dissent and difference, asserting a unity of perception when in fact there are a variety of important viewpoints to be considered?[17] There are numerous examples of times when the insistence on particular, fixed, verifiable "facts" has obscured a larger reality and, conversely, of broad-scale descriptions that, in glossing over complicated nuances and divergent viewpoints, have failed to capture important truths. If we shift the question to asking about the effects of taking one position or another in a given situation, we move our focus to asking which perspective does the least damage—or, less pessimistically, which captures social reality more accurately in particular contexts. As Jean and John Comaroff remind us, if all attempts to analyze social life must at times resort to "working essentialisms," we are left primarily with "the crucial question [of] how this is done, to what degree and effect; also, whose interests are served, whose subverted" (Comaroff and Comaroff 1997:406). Again, there is no easy answer. Rather, this is a pain-in-the-neck shove into an ongoing calculus: assessing our own situations relative to those of our informants as well as to the professional discourses with which we engage, while also judging our informants' situations relative to a plethora of possible contexts. This entails a further push out of any fixity of perspective—one akin to the plunge that Albert Einstein urged on sister disciplines some time ago.[18] It poses an analytic issue and a reflexive or ethical one, both of which will have to be considered not only as we interpret what we observe but also as we compose our own texts.

Ethnography in unstable situations and transforming states is a par- ticularly well-suited site for confronting these issues. For the ethnographer, it would seem, the task is in part how to sustain an "appropriate modesty"[19] without flinching from "famine, violence, suffering, and other forms of terror"—without, in Lewin's words in this volume, remaining "mute about evil" or becoming an unwitting collaborator in the production of human misery, as Freeman and Nguyen warn us is possible. In abandoning any lingering yearnings for purity—a search which anthropological work should long have brought into question in any case—scholars will have to accept partial solutions, concepts that are useful but flawed; they will have to themselves self-consciously occupy margins. This is reminiscent of a similar injunction by some of the critical race theorists in the legal academy, who have taken issue with the relativizing and deconstruction of fixed "rights" urged by critical legal studies. Instead, they urge that we inhabit the gray area between complete acceptance of the "rule of law" as a panacea, and complete rejection of formal law as a possible solution to some problems. As Patricia Williams reminds us, reliance on informal norms is a luxury only "insiders" to social systems can afford; while most assuredly imperfect, the language of "rights" has at least provided a toehold to which outsiders could cling in attempts to climb and enter the strongholds of the privileged (1991:146–55). We hear, then, a repeated theme—a call to accept the partial, the less-than-perfect, a call to inhabit the uncomfortable interstices of stable categories and unstable critique, a call to humility about the constructs with which we must work but also a call to engaged scholarship. The articles in this volume thus sound a theme found in the work of a number of other anthropologists currently urging a revival of "public interest" scholarship, following in the footsteps of earlier similar anthropological efforts (Nader 1999; see also Hymes 1969).

X If anthropology, along with a number of other disciplines, is now caught even more "in-between" than is its usual wont—struggling between a postmodern shattering of fixed standpoints, on the one hand, and, on the other, its often-accurate perception of "systematicities"— then perhaps it is from work on transformation at the shattered centers or vibrant margins of societies that a new post-postmodern approach

X will emerge. The work in this volume suggests that this next step of the anthropological journey—which, in many ways is at the cutting edge of a journey that much of Western social science seems poised to undertake[20]—will push us still further beyond the comfort of stable concepts and fixed social structures. At the same time, while embracing uncertainty and accepting the lack of closure that is found in much of what we study, these authors also insist that we notice, respect, and take account of the systematicities and anchors to which our subjects (and we) cling (see Rosaldo 1993). Here is a space that is truly "in-between"—between fixed reality and completely relativist deconstruction and between concepts, disciplines, and epistemologies. It is arguably a space anthropology has occupied, if only in partial and uneasy ways, for some time.[21]

Fragmented Realities, Structured Truths: The Ethnography of Transforming States

X And so we turn to the ethnographies in this collection for the guidance they provide in navigating this perplexing space between structure and chaos, improvisation and constraint, social construction and raw power—a space in which choosing one of two comfortable "either/ or" poles is no longer a satisfactory response.[22] Within these articles the nested contradictions appear as mutually entangled and sometimes even mutually constitutive—as paradoxes resistant to easy or clear resolution.[23]

Thus Zabusky's essay describes the increasingly fragmented sensibility of ssd scientists' professional lives. However, this fragmentation conceals a more coherent undercurrent that is in some sense deceptive; it pulls people into cooperation with a system whose movement may be fighting against the tide of pure science that these scientists believed they were riding:

370 Elizabeth Mertz

The shifting centers that accompany the transnational processes of big science and European integration produce not only improvisation and cynicism but dreams and domination as well. . . . [E]veryone feels out of control, pushed and dominated by forces that they cannot see and over which they have no control. . . . For [SSD scientists], the forces of big science and European integration seemed, on the one hand, to make their work possible and, on the other, to lock them in prisons. (this volume, 138)

Trapped in the "iron cage" created in part by their own desires, in part by the larger movement of capital, organizations, bureaucracies, and funding, these scientists spoke of "a clean and pure science . . . unfettered and free," while experiencing a daily, distracting fragmentation of their enterprise. Similarly, the fragmented lives of the child refugees in Freeman and Nguyen's account permit bureaucrats concerned with career progress and an appearance of success to perpetuate distortions that conceal the way their own system is deeply complicit in the very disruption it is supposed to prevent. And, again, in Lewin's account, we witness the Judenrate, pulled in by the false lure of potential safety, participating in a Nazi system that uses the fragmentation it creates to conceal the fact that those who participate risk contributing to their own—and their peoples'—ultimate destruction. Rosenthal describes the ways in which myths of ethnic fragmentation in Togo have been used to cover up state violence, with the government attributing arrests "by police and military" to the necessities of coping with virtually nonexistent "tribalism" (this volume, 320). And Gordon's account tracks the rising panic over rumors of "Native risings" and "Native unrest" in Namibia that fed support for ever-tightening laws to limit indigenous people's movements, culminating in "the routinization of terror in day-to-day interaction" in the service of colonial capitalism (this volume, 77).

Thus, on the one hand, these ethnographies tell of surface fragmentation on top of hidden systematicities. On the other hand, however, we also see the lure of a mythical, fixed, safe reality throughout many of these ethnographic accounts—a drive for stability or justice, a will to make a coherent story even where none exists. And, as we have noted, this is a lure to which social scientists are not always immune. So, a favored colonial trope that renders indigenous practices as "customary law" and searches for "authentic," singular voices to speak for complicated, polyvocal societies in effect freezes into static form the fluid, shifting, and threatening practices such as those of the Vodu orders. And, we have increasingly come to recognize anthropology's complicity in such mistranslations. In Gordon's account of Namibian vagrancy law, the colonizers move still further, in effect trying to freeze the people themselves into static form, clamping down on dangerous freedom of movement so as to produce a docile workforce. And Parnell demonstrates the inadequacies of ordered models of the state to capturing the fluidity of an increasingly decentered state, enacted in splintering communities and sprawling land disputes. Darian-Smith shows us the concerted reassertion of fixed boundaries occurring in Kent just at a point where the line between England and Europe as territories, along with the boundary between British and EU law, is blurring. Searching for belated closure, De Nike implies, a West German legal system that never fully confronted its own Nazi past now excorciates East German judges whose erased history contains a far more decisive rejection of Nazi jurists and legal outcomes. As Faier's ethnography of Palestinian feminists reminds us, even the rebels who seek to destabilize dominant narratives can feel the vertigo that results when these accepted stories and patterns give way to a less reassuring and more disordered picture that takes account of violence and powerlessness. Or again, we saw in Lewin's account of Tory's conversation with Miller the way in which social actors may cling stubbornly to appearances of normal life and interaction in highly abnormal circumstances—in denial of the potential perfidy of "normal" conversation, of the daily signs we use to signal continuity of meaning and to build trust in human connection and society.

This web of talk is one of the key means by which bureaucratic myths of normality and stabilized situations are perpetuated. Thus, lulled by webs of talk and writing that insulate them from the harsh realities of displaced Vietnamese children's lives, bureaucrats at a far remove can hide from a fractured, painful truth and still live with themselves—indeed, can even feel good about what they're doing. When Judenrate listened to such webs of talk from Nazi officers, they misrecognized the degree to which this pacifying discourse concealed ongoing genocide—a fracturing of life and society beyond comprehension. For the activists in Faier's article, resistance to gendered social domination and injustice required an ongoing battle to unsettle views of the social order as fundamentally safe and nonviolent—of violence and perfidy as routine rather than unusual. Quoting Dean MacCannell, Gordon also reminds us that "[t]he spread of fascism depended on a set of everyday social practices. . . . The capacity for self-delusion enabled settlers [in Namibia] to suppress or gloss over the obvious in order to normalize a terrible event, 'coolly re-inscribing the event into the realm of the ordinary' " (this volume, 79–80). Vagrancy laws in Namibia, Gordon argues, provided just such a reinscription of the colonizers' disruption of indigenous society and culture, rendering it as a commonplace legality regulating everyday conduct.[24]

These authors also remind us of the ways in which our own discourse can become part of such a misleadingly tranquilizing "web of talk": like the UN bureaucrats, social scientists are at times at risk of participating in discourses that project distorted images of closure and safety while people's lived experiences are to the contrary.[25] Rosenthal and Ries in particular urge humility in this regard, counterposing their informants' more processual, irreverent, and destabilized understandings to arguably more limited social science models. Thus more sedate models of the social order that look to the state and the market as central organizing forces, Ries argues, would fundamentally misunderstand the daily paradoxes confronting Russians today. The myth and status of the "honest bandit" that emerges in such a crazy, mysterious, and unpredictable social context is not easily analyzed using carefully ordered models of markets, states, or capitalism. Interestingly, however, it is precisely a more turbulent process of capitalist development that animates much of the transformation Ries describes.

Thus, behind the fragmentation of lives on the ground, there is often yet another level that is not random or fractured at all, but is rather a movement of systematic interests well-concealed from view, a movement of state, capital, colonialism, and patriarchy that cares little for the splintered lives it leaves in its wake, yet generates a benign appearance that is part of its mode of progress. Here, then, is a complex, double edge[26]—an unreal stability masking fragmentation, yet a fragmentation that results from a very real systematicity. The essays in this volume, in presenting ethnographic and historical accounts of capitalist processes, bring us insistently face-to-face with dilemmas that are at once ethical and intellectual. If we avoid analysis of the systematicity, we participate in an untruth that perpetuates the fracturing of human lives. If we turn away from the fragmentation and unpredictability as it is made real in our subjects' lives, we distort their truths.

And from what standpoint can we see or assert any of this? The contributors to this volume are exemplary in demonstrating how, in remaining close to the ground, ethnography can stay true both to the lived reality of destabilized and improvised lives, some of which know no happy endings, and to an unmasking of the forces at work behind the fractured surface. At times this work calls for a move into multiple, shifting perspectives and voices, while at others it calls for assertion of fixed truths and realities. For those with anthropological training, to engage in the kind of judgment Freeman and Nguyen unapologetically put forward ("not all cultures are beneficial; some are clearly harmful") may seem heretical and even dangerous. Certainly the past several decades of anthropology have revealed the dangers and erroneous conclusions that follow the unthinking imposition of scholars' versions of Western morality—or even simply (!) their conceptual schemes—not only in non-Western settings but also in the West as well. But, in another sense, in taking this kind of stance—accepting the inevitably partially compromised or impure position of some engagement in the worlds we study and relinquishing our remaining shreds of hubris about the ability of our own discourse to stay above or beyond social construction—we are simply returning to the kind of unabashed socially engaged impulse that has been an important part of the anthropological tradition at least from the days when Franz Boas's forthright stance against racism set the standard for our fledgling discipline.[27]

Notes

I would like to thank first our coeditor and the source of the core "agentive force" behind this volume, Carol Greenhouse. The elegance and intelligence of her scholarship, as many of us know, are matched only by her generosity of spirit. Our field and many of its junior (as well as senior) members are much the richer for her willingness to give her time, energy, and ideas in so free and ungrudging a fashion. Working with Carol and with Kay Warren on this project has been a truly rewarding intellectual and collegial experience. In addition, I would like to thank a number of colleagues for discussions and ideas that contributed to the conceptualization developed in this article: Clint Francis for sharing his exciting thoughts about the importance of paradox to theorizing societies and selves; Ross Cheit, Jennifer Freyd, Judith Herman, Ken Pope, and Anna Salter for scholarship from beyond the bounds of anthropology that has also courageously confronted the pain of perfidy and uncertain safety in human society; Cynthia Bowman and Kim Lonsway for discussions of closely related issues that informed my thinking; John Comaroff and two anonymous referees for their very helpful comments on an earlier version of the essay; Judith Shapiro for an exciting introduction during my earlier training to many of the issues discussed here. I thank Marcia Lehr for helping me with research and for tracking the "Copenhagen" syndrome to its correct venue. And, of course, I thank the contributors to this volume not only for their "paradigm-shaking" ethnographic work but also for the risks they took by sharing their questions and uncertainties.

1. As Elinor Ochs notes:

> Caregivers are concerned with children's affective competence and . . . children quite early in their lives attend to, recognize, and act on displays of emotion by others in their social environment. [Some researchers] report that by nine months of age infants can monitor the facial expression of affect of mothers and will act differently toward some third object according to the affect displayed. Through this type of monitoring, termed social referencing, . . . infants are socialized. . . . These frames lay the groundwork for attitudes, opinions, values, and beliefs that evolve over a lifetime. (1988:169)

Schieffelin (1990) provides sociolinguistic analysis of the ways in which Kaluli children develop fundamental orientations toward others, themselves, the social world, authority, gender, autonomy, and interdependence—indeed, sociality itself—in and through often minute or subtle linguistic and interactional cues. Ochs (1988:227) similarly notes the centrality of indexical (or contextual) linguistic cues in shaping the ways in which Samoan children learn to "engag[e] with the world" (see also Schieffelin and Ochs 1986).

2. Indeed, some studying this phenomenon have urged those working with hostage-taking situations to encourage formation of bonds of this kind between victim and captor as a way of increasing the likelihood of survival for the victims (Strentz 1982:160–61).

3. Of course, anthropologists and others who self-consciously travel into new situations where they expect these cues to differ may not be surprised to experience "misfires" at key moments.

4. And we can note this, as Lewin, in this volume, urges us to, without post hoc judgment, keeping in mind "that singular normative standards cannot relate to behavior under conditions of unrelenting stress and terror." (citing Zygmunt Bauman, this volume, 56).

5. I owe this felicitous formulation to one of the anonymous reviewers of the volume.

6. To be sure, this is not always the case; social scientists have also embraced ambiguity or even refused to see systematicity that arguably undergirded what they deemed to be unique or locally specific circumstances. And anthropologists in particular have at times preferred the humility of acknowledging uncertainties and indeterminacies in complex social events to determinist models delineating which of a myriad of happenings and patterns decisively caused a particular outcome to occur. (I am indebted to John Comaroff for this observation.) Indeed, Freeman and Nguyen are unhappy with the degree to which relativist models borrowed from anthropology have resulted in too little decisiveness in analyzing the systematic brutalization of children. It is not my intent to unduly celebrate or excoriate scholarship at either end of this continuum; it is precisely my point that each approach can be appropriate or misleading, depending upon the situation to which it is applied. I take a major contribution of the authors in this volume to be their insistent troubling of set polarities and distinctions—their rich exploration of the paradoxes that lie in the tension between uncertainty and systematicity.

7. See also Mertz and Lonsway 1998 on the issue of how broadscale social and cultural refusal to "see" the realities of abuse and violence aids a process of denial.

8. Scholars studying incest have particularly noted the discomfort that many seem to feel in acknowledging the possibility of betrayal at the level required for parents to actually molest or injure their children. And this discomfort extends to the children themselves, who have been found to participate in forms of denial—no doubt in part because of the pain involved in accepting the possibility of such a level of perfidy from the people upon whom they most depend for love and survival. See, for example, Courtois 1988; Freyd 1996; Herman 1992. Of course, if they are oppressive, structure and predictability can also carry a terror from which people wish to flee.

9. There have been some notable attempts by anthropologists to struggle against the narrative conventions that render ethnographies less effective in conveying some aspects of social realities (see, for example, Crapanzano 1990 and Feldman 1991 for attempts to confront the problem).

10. For discussions of the way that metapragmatic typifications in naturally occurring speech and in linguistic analysis of necessity reify the contingent and fluid nature of language, while at the same time forming a vital "backbone" for the ongoing structuring of speech, see Silverstein 1993; Mertz 1998; Mertz, Njogu, and Gooding 1998.

11. Greenhouse's introduction gives a useful map of this work; for another overview, see Mertz 1994a, 1994b.

12. For a similar "exploding" of a fixed, safe conceptualization of ethnographic time, see Greenhouse 1996.

13. Susan Gooding (1994) has, for example, powerfully exposed the conflict that arose when members of the Colville Tribes' more sophisticated understanding of the fluidity of social identity collided with the more static views of the U.S. legal system.

14. Geertz notes that it is "necessary, then, to be satisfied with swirls, confluxes, and inconstant connections; clouds collecting, clouds dispersing" and also suggest that it "may just be . . . that all understanding . . . trails life in just this way . . . [f]loundering through mere happenings and then concocting accounts of how they hang together" (1995:2–3). Michael Silverstein (1993) has outlined a model of language and understanding that details a similar kind of process in which the ongoing flow of talk is continually monitored and regimented at the metalevel, after the fact (if only by seconds).

15. During the question-and-answer period following a panel in which I recently participated at the Law and Society Association's annual meeting, a younger colleague stood up and diffidently—even apologetically—commented that she was puzzled. Having diligently deconstructed and reflexively situated knowledge in her work, what was to be done next? And where did this leave us? A number of colleagues have commented quietly, with some embarrassment—making an observation that seemed almost heretical to voice in these postmodern times—that it appeared that there were some things that were, well, "objectively" ascertainable. These things were not decomposable depending on position or viewpoint—things we would all generally agree existed or happened in the world, even if we might interpret their significance quite differently.

16. See discussion of Larson in note 19 below; see also work by Nahum Chandler on DuBois and the concept of double-voicing (1991).

17. Geertz has suggested a somewhat similar approach, asserting that "[t]he issue is: What do you get in saying that [taking a particular point of view about societies]? Where does it get you? There are other figurations. . . . What recommends mine? (1995:19).

18. I do not mean to imply that anthropologists have indulged unduly in the "comfortable fixity" of perspective, as the discipline has always specialized in unsettling settled perspectives. However, on the issue of "relative relativism," the anthropological debate has at times taken the form of asking the field to choose "either/or" rather than "when" it makes sense to choose a fixed standpoint or assert relativity of perspectives. Mark Goodale (1998) has argued for a shift of this kind in legal studies that would borrow from developments in scientific fields such as physics and mathematics.

19. I borrow the term from legal feminist Jane Larson, who suggests that one solution to this dilemma is a necessary maturation for social scientists who still cling to the notion that they can maintain a form of purity—of remaining above and outside of the imperfect morality that accompanies engagement for all other human beings (including those studied by social scientists). She terms this the development of an "appropriate modesty," the acceptance of the partial and human character of academicians' awareness and judgments (Larson, personal communication). This entails accepting the possibility that one's stance might turn out later to have been flawed in some way and also accepting the reality that one's work might impact events.

20. As Clifford Geertz notes, the "unsettledness is hardly limited to anthropology, of course, but, in one form or another, is perfectly general in the human sciences. (Even economics has begun to squirm; even art history.)" (1995:133).

21. Some might argue that there is nothing new in all of this, but, as Geertz (1995:129–30) and many other anthropologists have noted, including the contributors to this volume, that there has clearly been a shift in the degree of sensitivity that anthropologists now feel around issues of representing the life experiences and cultures of others—one that seems clearly linked to reflexive, postmodern, and sub-altern movements.

22. This does not imply that there is nothing that any one can do about problems; I argue here for wrestling with the difficult issues and dilemmas that emerge in unsettled states, even in the absence of any clear resolution or solution. And, indeed, the writing of ethnographies that engage in this kind of struggle is arguably one form—albeit "humble and humbling"—of "doing something." (I quote here from an anonymous reviewer, to whom I am grateful for making this point.)

23. Comaroff and Comaroff discuss the ubiquity and power of simplified models of change, legal and otherwise—not only among colonizers and colonized, but also among scholars (see 1997:366–67, 406–7). On "customary law," see Moore 1986.

24. See Lazarus-Black (1994) on the social construction of legalities and illegalities.

25. On issues of sexual abuse, a number of scholars have pointed to ways in which social scientists have at times been collusive in a misleadingly tranquilizing dis-course about the social problems involved (see Cheit 1998; Freyd 1996).

26. I draw here upon Moishe Postone's (1993) work on Marx, in which he analyzes a "double character" to capital, labor, and time under capitalist systems—and, indeed, to the very categories used in attempts to understand capitalism itself. In his view, labor in these systems has a double character as at once abstract and concrete, creating a new kind of social mediation that is "impersonal, abstract, and objective" (158–60). As a result, new forms of domination and alienation appear in these societies, forms that are less clearly based in "direct compulsion" than were feudal forms (160). This arguably suggests a normative "double edge" to the "double character" of capitalism as explained by Postone, so that the abstract character of labor in capitalist societies at once fuels new powerful forms of alienation and domination but also yields at least the potential for new liberatory directions. At a much broader level, my description of a complicated, double-edged process echoes that of John and Jean Comaroff, who insist that colonialism be conceptualized as "simultaneously, both a monothetic and polythetic business, everywhere the same yet different, obviously singular yet palpably plural" (1997:19). The essays in this volume similarly yield a picture of apparent paradoxes—fragmentation that belies structure, coterminous with orderly surfaces that deny fragmentation.

27. See, for example, the speech in which Boas asks his audience to consider "a problem that has for a long time been agitating our country and which, on account of its social and economic implications, has given rise to strong emotional reactions and has led to varied types of legislation"—the issue of antimiscegenation laws (1940:3). He concludes the talk with a plea for a reasoned antiracist approach to the problem (1940:13–14; see also Boas 1986).

Kay B. Warren

Toward an Anthropology of Fragments,

Instabilities, and Incomplete Transitions

The post–cold war era has been a watershed for anthropology as it has been for many of the societies and communities that anthropologists study. This volume's essays on Vietnamese refugees, the fallout of German reunification for East German jurists, and the rise of the powerful informal economy in post-Soviet Russia illustrate the diverse and changing legacies of the period. The transitions from socialist and capitalist authoritarianisms to varieties of market-driven democracy are neither linear nor unilateral processes, although the commentators and politicians who make their livings by characterizing such developments have for the most part been slow to recognize this (Weisberg 1999). Those commentators who praise global neoliberal economic integration, which would dismantle highly centralized socialist state economies and the protectionist markets of the West, do not always acknowledge that this moment is only one of several historical waves of capital expansion with its Janus-faced array of new possibilities and harsh dislocations.

The modernist impulse to see rational progress or "the end of history" in these political and economic transformations is thwarted at every turn by far more complex and less controllable realities (Fukuyama 1993; Scott 1998). Once one considers the complex interplay of politics and economics in a world of striking cultural diversity, it becomes evident that change does not generate shifts from one coherent formation to another. Howard De Nike's essay for this volume captures an important dimension of the post-socialist political and economic transition in Germany through a case study of the troubled unification of the democratic and socialist legal systems under the mandate of the West German judiciary. His analysis illustrates the central role of history and memory in the consolidation of West German dominance—the strategic conflation of the Nazi and communist periods used to strip the senior generation of East Berlin judges and prosecutors of their legitimacy and jobs while the West German establishment embraced their own past as one of unproblematic anti-fascism. This analysis illustrates the doubleness of bureaucratic memory through which the past is reconstructed in terms of a highly partisan present to justify the marginalization and disintegration of a high-status social field. That there were more collegial alternatives to the scapegoating of the post-WWII generation of jurists in other parts of Germany underscores the political choices that were involved in this "democratic" and apparently authoritarian transition.

If De Nike's essay captures the fulcrum point of a classic post–cold war nationalist transition, then Stacia Zabusky's essay on big science and European integration documents the emergence of new post-nationalist formations of elite work. These ephemeral virtual networks demand great individual creativity and the tolerance of fragmentation and uncertainty in the face of ongoing work-group and institutional instability. This pattern echoes what Aihwa Ong (1999) describes as "flexible citizenship" in the post-nationalist world of global capital flows.

Communities, whatever their scale, continue in heterogeneous ways to reconstitute themselves as they make the world their own, inevitably in the face of tremendous economic and political constraints on their actions. As a result, anthropology has increasingly become the study of instability and fragmentation, of systems caught in contradictory currents of change. It is important to recognize that Carol Greenhouse's and Beth Mertz's framings of this problematic in terms of ethnographic feasibility and a humanistic quest for ethical understanding and this essay's concern with political economies are all parts of the same project.

The analyses in this volume respond to these sea changes with a range of issues and framings. The authors seek to characterize current national and transnational engagements and to explore historical processes in terms specific to their ethnographic contexts. The case studies illustrate that, while instability may be a marker of our era, it is hardly a monopoly of the present. Michael Taussig (1992, 1997) has critiqued the unreal—or rather surreal—character of stability and the ways political regimes attempt to mask their destructive fragmentation of social life for international audiences, even as they characteristically pursue policies to heighten insecurity and uncertainty in the lives they seek to control (Sluka 1999). Most often, fragmentation has been attributed to state violence, to dehumanizing colonialism and authoritarianism. At times this construction affirms a hierarchy of nations with unspoken hubris: the West is democratic and above violent internal politics; others are not. Some of the most striking current political anthropology, however, questions this formulation in subtle ways, widening our understanding of fragmentation and violence through findings of violent fragmentation across authoritarian and democratic regimes (Tambiah 1997; Aretxaga 1997, 1999).

The question for engaged ethnographers is how to resist becoming complicit in the misrepresentation of normative (nationalistic) politics as stable systems. And how not to leave unprobed constructions that normalize the danger of Otherness as threats that emanate from outside stable systems or as sedition from within (Warren 1993, 1999). The concept of stability twinned with the ominous threat of instability conjures a world of bounded units—the territorially defined nation-states of political science and the discrete cultures or societies of anthropological accounts—in what plays out to be (as often as not) a defensive support of the status quo of power arrangements.

There are several ways out of this situation. One is to study the political acts of conjuring, idealizing, and protecting stability, of representing populations as bounded nations or cultures, and of pursing modernist rationalism as an end in itself. This is what Scott (1998), Holston (1993), Fox (1990), Ferguson (1994), Schirmer (1999), and others have done so well in powerful social critiques. Another is to focus on instability itself, on communities caught in contradictory transformations to pursue the current tensions and mismatches of neoliberal capitalism and democracy that are played out in the practice of local and national politics. This is what Tambiah (1997), Aretxaga (1999), Comaroff and Comaroff (1999), Nash (2001), the contributors to Sluka (1999), and many of the essays in this volume do.

Such projects involve first moving away from a uniquely state-centric analysis, from national interest as the most important measure of political calculation, to a more finely grained picture of multiple centers of politics and social interests. They are also increasingly a move away from regional studies—originally a product of cold war research funding that channeled transnational studies down the well-trodden path of great-power spheres of influence and toward a more fluid sense of transnationalism and international connections (Kearney 1996; Appadurai 1996). This reframing calls for a recognition of the impact of the heterogeneous global flows of capital and culture through emerging regional economic blocs, border transgressing mass media, major institutions promoting international law and human rights, nongovernmental organizations (NGOs), and the ever more complex diasporas of refugees, immigrants, and migratory workers. Few of these patterns are novel, as the feminist anthropological literature on footloose transnational industrial production made clear twenty years ago (Nash and Fernández-Kelly 1983).

Much is now being made about the impact of neoliberalism and the jarringly rapid transnational flow of capital without concern for state borders. Grassroots protests against the World Trade Organization (WTO), International Monetary Fund (IMF), and World Bank policies that mushroomed after 1999 have brought these issues into the realm of public debate. There is now recognition that state sovereignty has been weakened as countries are subject to powerful and volatile economic forces beyond their immediate control.

Transnational patterns of investment and currency speculation pursue profit maximizing strategies that cast the world in terms of economic markets rather than in terms of the security of families and communities (Trouillot 2001, Nash 2001, Stephen 2001). From the national perspective, the issue is not just what producers are paid for their labor and companies for their exports but also how countries cope with transnational industries and their capacity to cut jobs and relocate at will to pursue lower production costs and less regulation.

Before financing major development projects or rescuing national economies in monetary crisis, international organizations routinely insist on structural reforms consistent with global norms for World Bank and IMF loans. Thus, loans are granted on conditional terms that compel economic restructuring. The resulting pressure to privatize what have conventionally been public services threatens government job patronage, great and small, and the services and subsidies that keep transportation and food prices lower for the poor than markets otherwise demand. A growing gap between the rich (who are able to benefit from these currents of change) and the poor (who face economic stresses and unpredictabilities that endanger their basic subsistence strategies) appears to be the price of doing business in the neoliberal era.

While aggregate statistics show that the growth in income gaps began to level off for some world regions in the 1990s, the reality looks very different when one examines individual communities and displaced populations that suffer the brunt of uneven economic development. The Zapatista rebellion in Mexico, riots and ethnic tensions in Indonesia, and the mass uprising that triggered the 2000 coup in Ecuador demonstrate the intensity of citizen responses to these economic shocks.[1] The 2000 demonstrations against the IMF and World Bank were designed to highlight the interconnected character of the global economy, the overwhelming debt burden carried by some of the poorest countries, and the severe repercussions of neoliberal reforms for the most vulnerable populations.

Increasingly, we see regional blocs emerging: the EU, NAFTA, and other regional trade alliances that reflect the erosion of any one state's ability to respond to local needs. Nevertheless, it remains very difficult for anthropologists who have worked on states with aggressive authoritarian histories to support the argument that states are growing irrelevant in the global economic order. Despite the global economy and the intervention of the international community into selected regional disputes such as the Kosovo war, it is still clear that many states maintain coercive powers over their citizens and that militaries still use the language of national security to repress dissent. History continues to hold many lessons for us on this score.

One thematic that crosscuts the essays in this volume is the coercive nature of states and the ironies of colonial rule. Robert Gordon's essay on the South African administration of Namibia after World War I is particularly astute in rethinking the issue of state violence, power, and subjectivity in a colonial situation. This colonial state was by all measures underadministered. The mission of civilizing the native communities and establishing the rule of (procedural) law was used by those in power to assert the legitimacy of an ethnically stratified polity. Colonial procedures and social rituals, as invented traditions, were tactically used to heighten the distance between the colonizers and the native communities. Lacking the capacity for full-scale surveillance, the government solved the problem of state control through policies that devolved substantial powers to the settlers. The measure of vagrancy legislation was not, Gordon argues, the rate of arrests but rather that this policy, in effect, gave settlers special powers as state surrogates, including the capacity to intervene at whim in the lives of native families.

Yet, following this power arrangement in practice reveals important ironies about colonial rule. While the colonial system normalized and legitimized settler violence, it failed to calm their anxieties about the possibility of native revolts, and this anxiety was exacerbated by the settlers' own demographic and political fragmentation. As Gordon shows, there is only the delusion of an exit from the contradictions of a colonial political formation built on this particular combination of the rule of law, violent control, and settler anxiety. The analysis raises the issue of how much the controller was controlled as state policies designed a highly brittle and ambivalent role for their local surrogates.[2] In response, one wonders how often native communities played on their capacity to precipitate settler panic.

Carroll Lewin analyzes another colonial form in her examination of the process through which German occupiers instituted ghettos to forcibly segregate Jewish populations in the newly conquered territories of Eastern Europe during the Holocaust. Resettlement was used by the Germans to strip Jews of their property, to force them into slave labor for the war effort, and ultimately to subject them to extermination. At the center of German occupation was an imposed system of self-rule through Jewish councils (Judenrate) that were given the duties of dealing with the conflicting demands of German bureaucracies and regulating many aspects of ghetto social life, including the rationing of food, organization of forced-labor squads, provision of basic services, and the fulfillment of deportation quotas to what turned out to be death camps. In a climate of terrible violence and uncertainty, Nazi policy created terrible existential dilemmas for the ghetto populace.

By pursuing these dilemmas, Lewin addresses an issue which Gordon's framing does not, the response of the subaltern to the hegemonic modes of control that envelop them. Through case studies of the council leadership in the Lodz, Warsaw, and Vilna ghettos, she illustrates the varied approaches that leaders brought to their roles—and the varied responses of other Jews to their actions—as they worked under the unstable Nazi deception that by cooperating with German authorities they could help their fellow Jews. Lewin takes a second analytical pass on ghetto politics to show how the system of conflicting German and Jewish rationalities (or cultural logics) fit together in this terrorist state. The horror is that the desire to find even a contingent morality and mutuality was destined to fail in the face of this factionalized—and merciless— power structure. Only the interplay of deception and denial kept alive the illusion that work would slow deportation, that the loss of some would permit the survival of others, and that resistance would only bring collective repression. Lewin would likely agree that German-imposed Jewish self-administration in the ghettos was an extreme variant of a common political form that reappears in the present neocolonial terrorist state and promotes forms of self-rule and self-surveillances in addition to death squads and genocidal policies that undercut resistance.

The creation of divided realities, the exploitation of radically different rationalities, and the blurring of victimizer and victim is typical of the structures of control imposed by violent states (Aretxaga 1996; Sluka 1999; Warren 1999). In order to divide civilians from the organized resistance, states have invested a great deal of energy in undermining the bond of trust between citizens, community members, and close family relatives—the very people upon whom individuals were dependent for survival—by forcing people to spy on each other or encouraging people to settle old scores by secretly reporting their enemies to the state. States use a variety of strategies to accomplish these forms of control, yet one commonality in the patterns is the demonization and dehumanization of the Other so that those captured in this category fall outside the routine discourse of moral claims.

As I have found in my research on Guatemala, the fragmenting of social fields produced by counterinsurgency violence fosters internalized violence directed at the community itself. It also compels local culture makers to seek ways of expressing the resulting crisis of meaning in innovative ways—at times through surrealist imagery that transcends the representational limits of language—and causes people to seek cultural forms through which they can validate communal life, however momentarily. In Guatemala, these countercurrent responses to violence emerged at a moment in the 1980s when community survival was at stake (Warren 1998). As in the German case, there has been great dispute over wider citizen awareness of the genocide.[3]

The problem for the anthropological study of state terrorism—given limited access to the original events and the ambiguous status of memory[4]—is to represent the terms of conflicting rationalities and existential dilemmas in situations where power is dramatically skewed. In such situations, those in power seek to control civilians through practices that heighten insecurity and foster the displacement of political violence onto other social antagonisms. If one looks across violent regimes, there is no universal pattern to be found, so the ethnographic goal remains that of understanding the variety of situations and their outcomes. Lewin would add to this burden the challenge of revealing the ways that, in such overwhelming circumstances, people seek a quotidian normality—the macabre children's games and organized cultural activities of the ghettos—and the mimesis of moral mutuality and humanity that some Judenrate selectively extended while negotiating with their captors, even as genocidal politics made a mockery of it.

It is the interplay of these different rationalities during the German occupation that, as Lewin observes, at once made life livable and left intact structures of control that would take this away. The challenge for ethnographers of coercive states is to position themselves so that they can narrate the interplay of these conflicting rationalities. This is extraordinarily difficult in war zones where anthropologists are not exempt from the cultures of terror we seek to describe. During our field research, many of us experience existential dilemmas that echo the chronic uncertainties lived by those with whom we work. We come to know about and witness events that for a variety of ethical reasons we cannot fully reveal (Warren 1989, 1998, 2001). For contemporary anthropology, the interpretive dilemma becomes finding ways to portray the coexistence of powerful kinds of authoritarianism that have been changed by intensifying transnational economics and the resulting social dilemmas.

A second thematic in these essays is globalization. Ongoing theorizing by Carolyn Nordstrom, Michel-Rolph Trouillot, and Aihwa Ong suggests that anthropologists are repositioning themselves in response to a variety of new circumstances. Nordstrom (2000a, 2000b, n.d.) argues for a new form of economic anthropology. Her goal is the creations of methodologies and ethnographic forms to study wartime trade alliances, or "shadow networks," that crosscut countries, languages, and identity groups in Angola and Mozambique. As she observes, there has been little ethnography that examines internal wars as interstate events that generate transnational patterns of exchange (2000b:14). The recent convergence in Africa of weak states, chronic warfare, and crosscutting markets has spurred the development of transnational social fields that are the conduits for what Nordstrom terms "il/licit trade," which often operates in the same spheres of influence as formal trade (2000a). War in remote corners of the world creates the demand for a jumble of commodities, services, and humans, demeaned as expendable objects. While regional and international markets are hungry for "local products" such as gems, strategic minerals, oils, drugs, timber, mercenaries, and war orphans, wars also generate the demand for weapons, private armies, computers, and luxury goods for wartime elites. There is a particularly anthropological dimension to this project in that these informal economies generate their own alliances, norms for exchange, and authority structures. Nordstrom criticizes the conventional focus on formal institutions and the consequent neglect of informal economies in these situations.

Nancy Ries's essay in this volume on the collapse of state socialism in Russia takes on Nordstrom's agenda, the tracing of the growing impact of vibrant informal economies where states are weak, in a very different context. In Russia, as the state lost the power to politically and economically regulate the economy, settle disputes, or enforce contracts, elements of the shadow economy filled the vacuum. Ries argues that the continuities in this cultural system are striking. For many citizens, participation in the informal economy through strategies of mutual assistance, domestic gardens, food hoarding, and pilfering remain key to survival in the face of meagre and often late paychecks, massive inflation, and dwindling benefits and employment from the state. Aggressive entrepreneurs have the option of working in the ever-expanding shadow economy that has left urban life saturated with illegal activities and violent enforcers.

Life with the Russian market economy has given rise to a great deal of culture work, especially the crafting of narratives by the general populace to express their growing cynicism and to make sense of the uncertainty of authority, reciprocity, and risk in the new world order. What is striking in these narratives of moral economy is the Russian yearning for a strong institutionalized state, one in which, for some, an idealized and locally responsive mafia would supply order and enforcement that the official state cannot (or does) not. This marks a shift across the 1990s from the dread of the mafia as a source of great evil to acceptance of its role in ordering social relations. Although Ries ascribes a particularly Russian imagery to this situation of eroding trust, ironic dreams of a well-ordered world are not uncommon for postauthoritarian states in other parts of the world.

The populations of Latin American countries, such as Guatemala, have struggled after the antiguerrilla wars of the 1980s with the loss of legitimacy of their legal systems, growing criminal delinquents who prey on the common people, and chronic economic uncertainty. Interestingly, local communities there have also been faced with the task of making sense of the ways violence breaks down trust and reciprocity and, in Guatemala, they have used Maya legends of transforming selves to explore the existential dilemmas of the danger of trust (Warren 1998).

Since the return to civilian rule in the late 1980s and the rise of general crime since the disarming of the guerrillas, civil patrols, and the military, one hears an undercurrent of yearning for rescue from social disorder by leaders who express law-and-order politics and populist concerns, even if in the past these same figures were associated with brutal counterinsurgency violence against civilians. In a number of Latin American countries, similar desires have been very cleverly manipulated by parties on the Right.

Michel-Rolph Trouillot (2001) agrees that despite the strident rhetorics of sovereignty and nationalism it is time to rethink our understanding of states in light of globalization. He advocates approaching the state as a multiplicity of social fields, boundaries, and institutions. For him, ethnographic research becomes the study of ongoing events and processes that reflect the dynamics of transnational power relations, the circulation of capital and growing concentration of economic power, and the restructuring of labor markets. In the volume, several essays reveal how complex, heterogeneous, and violent these social fields can be, especially for those at the margins. Phil Parnell focuses his description of poor Filipinos struggling for urban land and housing in the context of the "composite state," the result of fragmented cultures, alliances, and patron-client relations. Elizabeth Faier traces the fragmented lives of Palestinian feminist activists and nationalists in Israel who attempt, at great personal cost, to find ways of bridging the disjunctures between their multifaceted lives as urban activists and as rural daughters. They struggle with the tensions involved in social advocacy on two fronts, with the gendered realities of their daily lives, and with the possibility of honor killings by their own family members for their challenges to traditional patriarchy.

Trouillot offers a conceptual innovation, the study of transnational and state powers through their effects. Among these "state effects" are the production of individualized subjects, collective identities, languages of governance, and jurisdictional boundaries (4). With international development policies stemming from neoliberal economic models, states are yielding major functions to private groups and corporations. Moreover, as international organizations and NGOs assume state functions in areas such as economic development, peacekeeping, and education, they produce state effects in their own right. The ethnographic challenge I would add, is coming to a fuller understanding of the interplay between transnational effects and domestic politics.

James Freeman and Nguyen Dinh Huu's study of Vietnamese refugees in this volume illustrates the interplay of states and the UN system of governance in the lives of unaccompanied minors who fled the country after the U.S. military retreat and the fall of Saigon in 1975.[5] These children were relocated to camps in Hong Kong, Thailand, the Philippines, and elsewhere, and the authors focus on the violent ironies of contemporary transnationalism in which states determine who is an alien at their borders, and international organizations have the power to redesignate refugees as illegal immigrants. Even as these detention centers became permanent homes over the years, their substandard living conditions and limited schooling and job training continued to underscore the refugees' transitory status and were seen as appropriate ways to encourage the asylum seekers to return to their homeland. Though Freeman and Nguyen do not discuss life in the campus in any detail other than the incubation of alternative families and a violent youth culture, one suspects that the resulting political culture included the demonization of communism even as Vietnamese society moved on and readjusted to the end of the cold war. This would have contributed a bizarre time warp to the inmates' many other dilemmas. Beyond fearing persecution, youths did not have the basic social skills and education to return to daily life in 1990s Vietnam, and they realistically worried about the prospect of inadequate support from distant relatives with their own problems.

Freeman and Nguyen make a case for the injustice of Western-centric models of aid delivery promoted by the United Nations High Commissioner on Refugees (UNHCR) and their NGO affiliates which acted as state surrogates in determining the fates—including forced repatriation in 1993—of these children. As NGO activists themselves, Freeman and Nguyen argue that there were a variety of options beyond the breakup of camp families and the forced repatriation of siblings to distant relatives, which were left unexplored yet might have better served these minors as they faced adulthood. Their critique of the UN bureaucracy—its discourse and practice of assistance—echoes Lewin's discussion of the modernist need for closure which, in its quest for order as recognizable progress, denies the complexity of situations that fail to conform to this vision of change. In their view, this powerful transnational bureaucracy—with its own sovereignty and state effects—escapes accountability for its actions in a way that leaves its model of intervention intact no matter what its result. The rationality of the UNHCR's actions rested in the organization's methods for weighing the eligibility of individuals for third country asylum and, absent this possibility, creating conventional understandings of the best interests of children. The UNHCR bureaucracy rotated staff through standardized positions with the result that officials were moved on before they could see the consequences of the decisions they made. On the grassroots level, NGOs did much of the monitoring and were pressured to generate reports that fit within the organization's procedures and time frame. The authors charge that, in the worst situations, officials created a kind of double-speak that hid the actual mistreatment of children in the humanitarian language of "durable solutions," "family reunions," and "orderly repatriation." For the Vietnamese refugees, the problem was that this language assumed a stability of culture, country, family, and individual psychosocial development that cannot exist in a world where change has produced such radical disjunctures. In this context, to see stability where there has been very little is a misstep with severe consequences.

Viewed in a global context, I would add that it becomes apparent that international organizations are constrained by a crisis life cycle in which it is important for cases to be closed out—that is, successfully resolved in order to give meaning to the effort and to encourage international financial support—so the system can move on to the next crisis. The children became victims of a transnational boom-bust cycle in the funding of crisis aid, as Stephen Jackson has so insightfully pointed out, one that often generates its own unanticipated violence and corruption (1999). As a result, the state effects of these international organizations have their own life cycle that influences the organizations' responses toward the people they reclassify in the fateful interplay of domestic and international policies.

Finally, Aihwa Ong's view of globalization (1999, n.d.) emphasizes regionally specific patterns of development that emerge from the differential demands of the global economy. The consequent degrading of state power has produced new political geographies that can be characterized by their "graduated sovereignty." On the one hand, high-tech production in global information cities, industrial corridors, and growth triangles in Southeast Asia concentrates economic power that crosscuts state boundaries. Elite employees at these global centers cultivate identities and political subjectivities that echo transnational rather than national flows of capital. Yet other regions are marginalized by this process, especially when they are stigmatized as sources of cheap labor or as backwaters of economic change.

The question for Ong, however, is not the presence of these new hierarchies but rather the insecurities and responses that these regional patterns engender in those who benefit from them as well as those who suffer from diminishing state services, fragmented citizenship, and growing economic insecurity. She argues for a reorientation of ethnography to study the ways that elite subjectivities are reshaped by languages of religion and community that stand apart from the conventional discourse of politics and social citizenship. Her dual perspective further argues for a special role that N G Os can play in communities that find themselves exploited and marginalized by neoliberal economics. Here she would have ethnographers focus on the ways that transnational norms of social justice have been appropriated in local efforts to build novel forms of social capital and self-reliance in order to cope with changing patterns of uncertainty and risk.

Ong's comprehensive framing of globalization leaves one with the feeling that many of us have part of the story without seeing the whole, and that anthropology, with its new commitment to multisited field research, needs to foster more integrative and collaborative research methodologies. One can see the contributions in this volume by Stacia Zabusky (on high-tech science in the European Union) and by Eve Darian-Smith (on the reinvention of Kent localism by both urban interlopers and locals who appropriate European Union law as a tactical weapon against encroachment and state regulation) as contributing to Ong's call for the study of regionalisms as consequences of new forms of transnational production and politics. For the fuller European case, one would want to add more on the issues of guest workers and the transnational labor pools that European countries draw upon for their economies.

This volume's essays argue that analytical insights about the nature of transnationalism, power, and changing subjectivities can be garnered by studying a variety of historical and current situations. The challenge for anthropologists studying contemporary situations is conceptual and ethnographic. How do we research situations of flux and fragmentation even as we are experientially and structurally part of the story? How do we create ethnographic genres to convey our findings? One way is through narratives of absence and displacement that capture the contradictory currents of change, changing social fields, and the failure of state institutions and older models of citizenship in the face of difficult transformations and transitions. Another way is to trace the social struggles and culture work of people attempting to make sense of and cope with the particular kinds of fragmentation and displacement they experience. Nordstrom, Trouillot, and Ong remind us of the importance of studying the intimate interpenetration of the local and the global and the importance of informal as well as formal power structures. A third approach argues that the anthropology of outrage—that is, the act of taking sides in political disputes and economic crises—is not sufficient in itself. Rather, anthropology's unique capacity is to stand back and understand conflicting rationalities though more encompassing models that reveal the wider array of political economic interconnections and existential dilemmas of living in the global era.

Notes

My thanks to Carol Greenhouse for stimulating exchanges throughout the process and to coeditor Beth Mertz and the volume's contributors for their thought-provoking essays on such a wide range of issues. One of the most invigorating aspects of this project has been its transgression of anthropological norms that generate homogenous research networks on narrowly defined common issues.

1. Scott's classic (1977) comes to mind as an explanation for the powerful moral tone of many of these rebellions.

2. Gordon does note that this system was not as hegemonic as it might seem, especially when viewed from a gendered analysis.

3. Goldhagen (1996) argues for wider awareness in the case of Germany, and I suspect that upon closer inspection this would be more common in other cases. One could certainly argue that denial is a form of awareness.

4. Memory will always pose complex interpretive issues for anthropology. Violence fragments experience as Scarry (1985) and Aretxaga (1997) suggest. As the testimonial literature illustrates, there is a range of genres for representing memory, each with its own narrative constraints (Montejo 1999; Warren 2001). And there is the ever present issue of the doubleness of memory, the ways the past is reconstructed in terms of the contested present, as De Nike's essay in this collection illustrates so well.

5. As Malkki (1995) observed for the refugees of the Burundi genocide, the bureaucratic status of "refugee" and the cultural distinctiveness of "refugee camps" trumped other needs and identities.

Contributors

Eve Darian-Smith is Chair of the Law and Society Program at the University of California, Santa Barbara.

Howard De Nike is an anthropologist, independent scholar, and consultant based in San Francisco.

Elizabeth Faier, an anthropologist, is Assistant Professor in the Jepson School of Leadership Studies, University of Richmond, Virginia.

James M. Freeman is Professor of Anthropology Emeritus at San Jose State University, California.

Robert Gordon is Professor of Anthropology at the University of Vermont.

Carol J. Greenhouse is Professor of Anthropology at Princeton University.

Nguyen Dinh Huu, a social worker, is founder and Executive Director of Aid to Children Without Parents, Inc.

Carroll McC. Lewin is Associate Professor of Anthropology at the University of Vermont.

Elizabeth Mertz is Professor of Law at the University of Wisconsin–Madison and Research Fellow at the American Bar Foundation, Chicago.

Phillip Parnell, an anthropologist, is Professor of Criminal Justice at Indiana University–Bloomington.

Nancy Ries is Associate Professor of Anthropology at Colgate University.

Judy Rosenthal is Associate Professor of Anthropology at University of Michigan–Flint.

Kay B. Warren is Professor of Anthropology at Harvard University.

Stacia E. Zabusky, an anthropologist, frequently teaches at Ithaca College.

Works Cited

Abélès, Marc. 1992. *La vie quotidienne au Parlement européen.* Paris: Hachette.

Abraham Fund, The. 1992. *The Abraham Fund Directory.* New York: The Abraham Fund.

Abu-Lughod, Lila. 1991. Writing against culture. In *Recapturing Anthropology,* edited by Richard Fox. Albuquerque, N.M.: School of American Research Press.

——, ed. 1998. *Remaking Women: Feminism and Modernity in the Middle East.* Princeton: Princeton University Press.

Adam, Heribert. 1971. *Modernizing Racial Domination.* Berkeley: University of California Press.

Adelman, Madelaine. 1997. Gender, law, and nation: The politics of domestic violence in Israel. Ph.D. diss., Department of Anthropology, Duke University.

Adelson, Alan, and Robert Lapides. 1989. *Lodz Ghetto.* New York: Penguin.

Akrich, M. 1992. The de-scription of technical objects. In *Shaping Technology/Building Society: Studies in Sociotechnical Change,* edited by W. Byker and J. Law. Cambridge: MIT Press.

Alonso, Ana Maria. 1994. The politics of space, time, and substance: State formation, nationalism, and ethnicity. *Annual Review of Anthropology* 23:379–405.

Amadiume, Ifi. 1987. *Male Daughters, Female Husbands: Gender and Sex in an African Society.* London: Zed Books.

Anderson, Benedict. 1991. *Imagined Communities: Reflections on the Origin and Spread of Nationalism.* Rev. ed. London: Verso.

Andrews, Michael. 1992. Englishness and English Landscape. Open Lecture, University of Kent, Canterbury.

Antoun, Richard. 1989. *Muslim Preacher in the Modern World: A Jordanian Case Study in Comparative Perspective.* Princeton, N.J.: Princeton University Press.

Appadurai, Arjun. 1991. Global ethnoscapes: Notes and queries for a transnational anthropology. In *Recapturing Anthropology,* edited by Richard Fox. Albuquerque, N.M.: School of American Research Press.

——. 1996. *Modernity at Large: Cultural Dimensions of Globalization.* Minneapolis: University of Minnesota Press.

Apter, Andrew. 1993. Atinga revisited: Yoruba witchcraft and the cocoa economy, 1950–1951. In *Modernity and Its Malcontents: Ritual and Power in Postcolonial Africa,* edited by Jean Comaroff and John Comaroff. Chicago: University of Chicago Press.

Arad, Yitzak. 1982. *Ghetto in Flames.* New York: Holocaust Library.

Arad, Yitzak, Yisrael Gutman, and Abraham Margaliot, eds. 1981. *Documents on the Holocaust.* Jerusalem: Yad Vashem.

Arendt, Hannah. 1963. *Eichmann in Jerusalem.* New York: Penguin.

——. [1967] 1971. *The Origins of Totalitarianism*. London: George Allen and Unwin.

Arensberg, Conrad Maynadier. 1937. *The Irish Countryman: An Anthropological Study*. New York: Macmillan.

Aretxaga, Begoña. 1997. *Shattering Silence: Women, Nationalism, and Political Subjectivity in Northern Ireland*. Princeton, N.J.: Princeton University Press.

——. 1999. "A fictional reality: Paramilitary death squads and the construction of state terror." In *Death Squad: The Anthropology of State Terror*, edited by Jeff Sluka. Philadelphia: University of Pennsylvania Press.

Aronson, Lisa. 1995. Threads of thought: African cloth as language. In *African and African-American Sensibility*, edited by Michael W. Coy Jr. and Leonard Plotnicov. Ethnology Monographs, no. 15. Pittsburgh: Department of Anthropology, University of Pittsburgh.

Ash, Timothy Garton. 1993. *In Europe's Name: Germany and the Divided Continent*. New York: Vintage Books.

Ashworth, G. J. 1994. From history to heritage, from heritage to identity: In search of concepts and models. In *Building a New Heritage: Tourism, Culture and Identity in the New Europe*, edited by G. J. Ashworth and P. J. Larkham. London: Routledge.

Aslund, Anders. 1995. *How Russia Became a Market Economy*. Washington, D.C.: Brookings Institution.

Badran, Margot. 1991. Competing agenda: Feminists, Islam and the state in nineteenth- and twentieth-century Egypt. In *Women, Islam, and the State*, edited by Deniz Kandiyotti. Philadelphia, Pa.: Temple University Press.

Badran, Margot, and Miriam Cooke, eds. 1990. *Opening the Gates: A Century of Arab Feminist Writing*. Bloomington: Indiana University Press.

Bahloul, Joëlle. 1992. *La maison de mémoire*. Paris: Métailié.

Baier, Kurt. 1958. *The Moral Point of View*. Ithaca, N.Y.: Cornell University Press.

Baker, Houston. 1993. *Black Studies, Rap, and the Academy*. Chicago: University of Chicago Press.

Barley, Stephen R., and Julian E. Orr, eds. 1997. *Between Craft and Science: Technical Work in U.S. Settings*. Ithaca, N.Y.: Cornell University Press.

Barnes, Annie S. 1997. Comparative study of policing in America. *Droit et Cultures* 33 (1):97–110.

Barrow, Clyde. 1993. *Critical Theories of the State: Marxist, Neo-Marxist, Post-Marxist*. Madison: University of Wisconsin Press.

Bataille, Georges. 1985. *Visions of Excess: Selected Writings, 1927–1939*, translated by Allan Stoekl, with Carl R. Lovitt and Donald M. Leslie Jr. Minneapolis: University of Minnesota Press.

Battaglia, Debbora. 1995. On practical nostalgia: Self-prospecting among urban Trobrianders. In *Rhetorics of Self-making*, edited by Debbora Battaglia. Berkeley: University of California Press.

Bauer, Yehuda. 1989. Jewish resistance and passivity in the face of the Holocaust. In *Unanswered Questions*, edited by François Furet. New York: Schocken Books.

Bauman, Richard. 1986. *Story, Performance, and Event.* Cambridge: Cambridge University Press.

———. 1992. Performance. In *Folklore, Cultural Performances, and Popular Entertainments: A Communications-Centered Handbook,* edited by Richard Bauman. New York: Oxford University Press.

Bauman, Zygmunt. 1987. *Legislators and Interpreters: On Modernity, Post-modernity and Intellectuals.* Cambridge: Polity Press.

———. 1989. *Modernity and the Holocaust.* Ithaca, N.Y.: Cornell University Press.

Baumann, Gerd. 1996. *Contesting Culture: Discourses of Identity in Multi-Ethnic London.* Cambridge: Cambridge University Press.

Bellier, Irène, and Thomas M. Wilson, eds. 2000. *An Anthropology of the European Union: Building, Imagining and Experiencing the New Europe.* Oxford: Berg.

Belmonte, Thomas. 1979. *The Broken Fountain.* New York: Columbia University Press.

Ben-David, Joseph. 1971. *The Scientist's Role in Society: A Comparative Study.* Chicago: University of Chicago Press.

Benthall, Jonathan. 1997. Speaking of suffering. *Anthropology Today* 13 (3):1–2.

Bentley, Eric. 1971. Afterword to *Thirty Years of Treason: Excerpts from Hearings before the House Committee on Un-American Activities, 1938–1968,* edited by Eric Bentley. New York: Viking Press.

Berger, Peter, and Thomas Luckmann. 1967. *The Social Construction of Reality.* New York: Anchor.

Berliner Zeitung. 1992. Stasi-Akten offenbarten Rechtsbeugung—Ex-Militaerstaatsanwaelte stolperten ueber ihre eigene Gruendlichkeiten. 30 April.

———. 1993a. Sozialgerichte vor Antragsflut. 22 Jan.

———. 1993b. Anwalt Schnur droht Entzug der Zulassung. 20 July.

———. 1994. Ein Anschluss unter dieser Nummer—*Gregor Gysi und "IM Notar" wurden von der Stasi unter derselben Registrierung gefuehrt.* Oct. 29–30.

———. 1995. Ernuet Anklagen wegen Rechtsbeugung: DDR-Richter und Staatsanwaelte sollen vor Gericht. 21 Jan.

Bhabha, Homi K. 1994. *The Location of Culture.* New York: Routledge.

Bignell, Alan. 1983. *Kent Lore: A Heritage of Fact and Fable.* London: Robert Hale.

Blasi, Joseph R., Maya Kroumova, and Douglas Kruse. 1997. *Kremlin Capitalism: Privatizing the Russian Economy.* Ithaca, N.Y.: Cornell University Press.

Blier, Suzanne Preston. 1995. *African Vodun: Art, Psychology, Power.* Berkeley: University of California Press.

Bloch, Maurice, and Jonathan Parry, eds. 1989. *Money and the Morality of Exchange.* Cambridge: Cambridge University Press.

Blok, Anton. 1974. *The Mafia of a Sicilian Village, 1860–1960: A Study of Violent Peasant Entrepreneurs.* Prospect Heights, Ill.: Waveland Press.

Boas, Franz. [1928] 1986. *Anthropology and Modern Life.* New York: Dover Publications.

———. 1940. *Race, Language, and Culture*. New York: Free Press.

Boddy, Janice. 1989. *Wombs and Alien Spirits: Women, Men, and the Zar Cult in Northern Sudan*. Madison: University of Wisconsin Press.

———. 1994. Spirit possession revisited: Beyond instrumentality. *Annual Review of Anthropology*, vol. 23.

Boothby, Neil. 1992. Displaced children: Psychological theory and practice from the field. *Journal of Refugee Studies* 5 (2):106–22.

Borenstein, Eliot. 1999. Public offerings: MMM and the marketing of melodrama. In *Consuming Russia: Popular Culture, Sex, and Society since Gorbachev*, edited by Adele Marie Barker. Durham, N.C.: Duke University Press.

Borneman, John. 1992. *Belonging in the Two Berlins: Kin, State, Nation*. Cambridge: Cambridge University Press.

———. 1997. Europeanization. *Annual Review of Anthropology*, vol. 26:487–514.

Borofsky, Robert, ed. 1994. *Assessing Cultural Anthropology*. New York: McGraw Hill.

Bourdieu, Pierre. [1966] 1974. The sentiment of honour in Kabyle society. In *Honour and Shame: The Values of Mediterranean Society*, edited by J. G. Peristiany. Chicago: University of Chicago Press.

———. 1977. *Outline of a Theory of Practice*, translated by Richard Nice. New York: Cambridge University Press.

———. 1984. *Distinction: A Social Critique of the Judgment of Taste*, translated by Richard Nice. Cambridge: Harvard University Press.

———. 1990. *The Logic of Practice*, translated by Richard Nice. Cambridge: Polity Press.

Braham, Randolph. 1989. The Jewish Councils: An overview. In *Unanswered Questions*, edited by François Furet. New York: Schocken Books.

Brand, John. [1795] 1853. *Observations of the Popular Antiquities of Great Britain*. Rev. ed. by H. Ellis. London: Henry G. Bohn.

Brandon, John, and Brian Short. 1990. *The South East from A.D. 1000*. London: Longman.

Breckenridge, Carol A., and Peter van der Veer. 1993. Orientalism and the postcolonial predicament. In *Orientalism and the Postcolonial Predicament: Perspectives on South Asia*, edited by Carol A. Breckenridge and Peter van der Veer. Philadelphia: University of Pennsylvania Press.

Breitman, Richard. 1991. *The Architect of Genocide: Himmler and the Final Solution*. Hanover, N.H.: University Press of New England.

Brenneis, Donald. 1990. Shared and solitary sentiments: The discourse of friendship, play, and anger in Bhatgaon. In *Language and the Politics of Emotion*, edited by Catherine A. Lutz and Lila Abu-Lughod. Cambridge: Cambridge University Press.

Browning, Christopher. 1986. The Revised Hilberg. In *Simon Wisenthal Annual 3*, edited by H. Friedlander and Sybil Milton. White Plains, N.Y.: Kraus.

———. 1988. Bureaucracy and mass murder: The German administrator's comprehension of the Final Solution. In *Comprehending the Holocaust*, edited by Asher Cohen, J. Gelber, and C. Wordi. New York: Peter Lang.

——. 1992. *The Path to Genocide: Essays on Launching the Final Solution*. Cambridge: Cambridge University Press.

Bryant, John. 1967. *Protestant Island*. London: Collins.

Bull, Martin J. 1993. Widening versus deepening the European Community: The political dynamics of 1992 in historical perspective. In *Cultural Change and the New Europe: Perspectives on the European Community*, edited by Thomas M. Wilson and M. Estellie Smith. Boulder, Colo.: Westview Press.

Burawoy, Michael. 1997. Review essay: The Soviet descent into capitalism. *American Journal of Sociology* 102 (5):1430–44.

Burawoy, Michael, and János Lukács. 1992. *The Radiant Past*. Chicago: University of Chicago Press.

Bureau of Forestry Development. 1981. Position Paper of Region 4, Bureau of Forestry Development on the Legality of the Alleged Title of the Payatas Estate Improvement Company. May 23:7.

Burt, Richard, and John Michael Archer. 1994. *Enclosure Acts: Sexuality, Property, and Culture in Early Modern Europe*. Ithaca, N.Y.: Cornell University Press.

Bushaway, R. W. 1992. Rite, legitimation and community in Southern England, 1700–1850: The ideology of custom. In *Conflict and Community in Southern England*, edited by B. Stapleton. New York: St. Martin's Press.

Butler, Judith. 1993. *Bodies That Matter: On the Discursive Limits of "Sex."* London: Routledge.

Center for Policy Analysis on Palestine. 1992. *Facts and Figures about the Palestinians*. Washington, D.C.: Center for Policy Analysis on Palestine.

Cessou, J. 1936. Une religion nouvelle en Afrique Occidentale: le "Goro" ou "kunde." Etudes Missionnaires, Supplément à la Revue d'Histoire des Missions, Paris, "Les Amis des Missions," t. IV, no. 1, April:1–39 and no. 2, Nov.:230–43.

Chandler, Nahum. 1991. The force of the double: A reading of W. E. B. Du Bois on the question of the African-American subject. Paper presented at the 1991 American Anthropological Association Meeting, Chicago, Ill.

——. 1996. The economy of desedimentation: W. E. B. Du Bois and the discourses of the Negro. *Callaloo.* 19 (1):78–93.

Chatterjee, Partha. 1993. *The Nation and Its Fragments: Colonial and Post-Colonial Histories*. Princeton, N.J.: Princeton University Press.

Chatty, Dawn, and Annika Rabo, eds. 1997. *Organizing Women: Formal and Informal Women's Groups in the Middle East*. Oxford: Berg.

Cheit, Ross. 1998. Junk Skepticism. Paper presented at the 1998 Law and Society Association Annual Meeting, Snowmass, Colo.

Clapham, Christopher. 1982a. *Private Patronage and Public Power: Political Clientism in the Modern State*. New York: St. Martin's Press.

——. 1982b. Clientism and the state. In *Private Patronage and Public Power: Political Client-ism in the Modern State*, edited by Christopher Clapham. New York: St. Martin's Press.

Clark, J. C. D. 1991. Britain as a composite state: Sovereignty and European integra-tion. *Culture and History* 9/10:55–83.

Clifford, James, and George Marcus, eds. 1986. *Writing Culture: The Poetics and Politics of Ethnography*. Berkeley: University of California Press.

Coastlines. 1992. London: The British Council.

Cobbett, William. 1821. *Political Register*, vol. 39. London: John M. Cobbett.

Cohen, Stanley, with Mohammed Haj Yahia. 1989. Crime, justice, and social control in the Israeli Arab population. Publication in the research project, The condition and status of the Arabs in Israel under direction of Henry Rosenfeld. Tel Aviv: International Center for Peace in the Middle East.

Cohn, Bernard. 1988. The anthropology of a colonial state and its forms of knowl-edge. Paper presented at the Wenner-Gren Foundation symposium, "Tensions of Empire," Mijas, Spain.

Cohn, Carol. 1987. Sex and death in the rational world of defense intellectuals. *Signs: Journal of Women in Culture and Society* 12 (4):687–718.

Cole, John. 1977. Anthropology comes part-way home: Community studies in Eu-rope. *Annual Review of Anthropology* 6:349–78.

Comaroff, Jean. 1985. *Body of Power, Spirit of Resistance*. Chicago: University of Chi-cago Press.

Comaroff, Jean, and John L. Comaroff. 1991. *Of Revelation and Revolution: Christianity, Colonialism, and Consciousness in South Africa*. Vol. 1. Chicago: University of Chicago Press.

——, eds. 1993. *Modernity and Its Malcontents: Ritual and Power in Postcolonial Africa*. Chi-cago: University of Chicago Press.

——. 1997. *Of Revelation and Revolution: The Dialectics of Modernity on a South African Fron-tier*. Vol. 2. Chicago: University of Chicago Press.

Comaroff, John, and Jean Comaroff. 1992. *Ethnography and the Historical Imagination*. Boulder, Colo.: Westview Press.

——. 1999. Occult economies and the violence of abstraction: Notes from the South African postcolony. *American Ethnologist* 26 (2):279–303.

Cooper, Frederick. 1994. Colonizing time: Work rhythms and labor conflict in colo-nial Mombasa. In *Colonialism and Culture*, edited by N. Dirks. Ann Arbor: Univer-sity of Michigan Press.

Cooper, Frederick, and Ann Laura Stoler, eds. 1997. *Tensions of Empire*. Berkeley: Uni-versity of California Press.

Coronil, Fernando. 1997. *The Magical State*. Chicago: University of Chicago Press.

Corrigan, Paul, and Derek Sayer. 1985. *The Great Arch*. Oxford: Blackwell.

Council for the Protection of Rural England. 1992. *Campaigner's Guide to Using EC Environmental Law*. London: Warwick House.

Courtois, Christine. 1988. *Healing the Incest Wound: Adult Survivors in Therapy.* New York: Norton.

Courtwright, David. 1996. *Violent Land.* Cambridge: Harvard University Press.

Coutin, Susan. 1997. The political subject in U.S. asylum law and in Salvadorans' narratives of persecution. Paper presented at the 1997 Law and Society Association Annual Meeting, St. Louis, Mo.

Cowan, Jane. 1991. Going out for coffee? Contesting the grounds of gendered pleasures in everyday sociability. In *Contested Identities: Gender and Kinship in Modern Greece,* edited by Peter Loizos and Evthymios Papataxiarchis. Princeton, N.J.: Princeton University Press.

Cox, Andrew W. 1984. *Adversary Politics and Land: The Conflict over Land and Property Policy in Post-War Britain.* Cambridge: Cambridge University Press.

Craig, Gordon A. [1982] 1991. *The Germans.* New York: Meridian.

Crapanzano, Vincent. 1985. *Waiting.* New York: Penguin.

———. 1990. On self characterization. In *Cultural Psychology: Essays on Comparative Human Development,* edited by James Stigler, Richard Shweder, and Gilbert Herdt. Cambridge: Cambridge University Press.

Dahlman, Carl J. 1980. *The Open Field System and Beyond.* Cambridge: Cambridge University Press.

Dajani, Souad. 1993. Palestinian women under Israeli occupation: Implications for development. In *Arab Women: Old Boundaries, New Frontiers,* edited by Judith E. Tucker. Bloomington: Indiana University Press.

Daniel, E. Valentine. 1996. *Charred Lullabies: Chapters in an Anthropography of Violence.* Princeton, N.J.: Princeton University Press.

Daniels, S. 1988. The political iconography of woodland in later Georgian England. In *The Iconography of Landscape,* edited by D. Cosgrove and S. Daniels. Cambridge: Cambridge University Press.

Darian-Smith, Eve. 1995a. Legal imagery in the garden of England. *Indiana Journal of Global Legal Studies* 2 (2):395–411.

———. 1995b. Rabies rides the fast train: Transnational interactions in postcolonial times. *Law and Critique* 6 (1):75–94.

———. 1995c. Law in place: Legal mediations of national identity and state territory in Europe. In *Nationalism, Racism, and the Rule of Law,* edited by Peter Fitzpatrick. Aldershot, England: Dartmouth Publishing Company.

———. 1999. *Bridging Divides: The Channel Tunnel and English Legal Identity in the New Europe.* Berkeley: University of California Press.

Davis, Leonard. 1991. *Hong Kong and the Asylum-Seekers from Vietnam.* New York: St. Martin's Press.

Dawson, Graham. 1994. *Soldier Heroes: British Adventure, Empire, and the Imagining of Masculinities.* New York: Routledge.

De Nike, Howard J. 1994. Criminal prosecution of GDR judges: A cultural perspective. In *New Definitions of Crime in Societies in Transition to Democracy*, edited by Uwe Ewald. Bonn: Forum Verlag Godesberg.

———. 1997. *German Unification and the Jurists of East Germany: An Anthropology of Law, Nation and History.* Moenchengladbach: Forum Verlag Godesberg.

Deleuze, Gilles. 1993. *Critique et clinique.* Paris: Les éditions de minuit.

Desjarlais, Robert, and Arthur Kleinman. 1994. Violence and demoralization in the new world disorder. *Anthropology Today.* 10 (5):9–12.

Diller, Janelle. 1988. *In Search of Asylum: Vietnamese Boat People in Hong Kong.* Washington, D.C.: Indochina Resource Action Center.

Dimock, Wai Chee, and Michael T. Gilmore, eds. 1994. *Rethinking Class.* New York: Columbia University Press.

Diner, Dan. 1992. Historical understanding and counterrationality: The Judenrat as epistemological vantage. In *Probing the Limits of Representation: Nazism and the Final Solution,* edited by Saul Friedlander. Cambridge: Harvard University Press.

Dirks, Nicholas B., ed. 1992. *Colonialism and Culture.* Ann Arbor: University of Michigan Press.

Dirks, Nicholas B., Geoff Eley, and Sherry B. Ortner, eds. 1994. *Culture/Power/History: A Reader in Contemporary Social Theory.* Princeton, N.J.: Princeton University Press.

Dobroszycki, Lucjan. 1980. Jewish elites under German rule. In *The Holocaust: Ideology, Bureaucracy, and Genocide,* edited by H. Friedlander and Sybil Milton. Millwood, N.Y.: Kraus.

Donat, Alexander. 1978. *The Holocaust Kingdom.* New York: Holt, Rinehart, and Winston.

Douglas, Roy. 1976. *Land, People, and Politics: A History of the Land Question in the United Kingdom, 1878–1952.* New York: St. Martin's Press.

Dresch, Paul. 1986. Significance of the course of events in segmentary systems. *American Ethnologist* 13:309–24.

Drescher, Seymour. 1964. *Tocqueville and England.* Cambridge: Harvard University Press.

Duara, Prasenjit. 1995. *Rescuing History from the Nation: Questioning Narratives of Modern China.* Chicago: University of Chicago Press.

Dubisch, Jill. 1991. Gender, kinship, and religion: "Reconstructing" the anthropology of Greece. In *Contested Identities: Gender and Kinship in Modern Greece,* edited by Peter Loizos and Evthymios Papataxiarchis. Princeton, N.J.: Princeton University Press.

Duiker, William J. 1995. *Vietnam: Revolution in Transition.* 2nd ed. Boulder, Colo.: Westview Press.

During, Simon, ed. 1993. *The Cultural Studies Reader.* London: Routledge.

Durkheim, Emile. 1983. *Durkheim and the Law,* edited by Steven Lukes and Andrew T. Scull. Oxford: Martin Robertson.

Elam, Diane, and Robin Wiegman, eds. 1995. *Feminism Beside Itself.* New York: Routledge.

Elton, Charles Isaac. 1867. *The Tenures of Kent*. London: James Parker.

Emmett, Anthony. 1985. The rise of nationalism in SWA/Namibia, 1915–1966. Ph.D. Diss. Witwatersrand University.

Ennew, Judith. 1980. *The Western Isles Today*. Cambridge: Cambridge University Press.

Espeland, Wendy. 1994. Legally mediated identity: The National Environmental Policy Act and the bureaucratic construction of interests. *Law and Society Review* 28 (5):1149–79.

European Space Agency. 1989. Twenty-five years of European Cooperation in space—Celebratory ceremony on 19 April 1989. Special issue of the *ESA Bulletin*, no. 58:7–39.

Evans, Ivan. 1986. The political economy of a state apparatus: The Department of Native Affairs in the transition from segregation to Apartheid in South Africa. Ph.D. diss., University of Wisconsin.

Evans-Pritchard, E. E. 1940. *The Nuer: A Description of the Modes of Livelihood and Political Institutions of a Nilotic People*. Oxford: Clarendon Press.

Everitt, Alan Milner. 1986. *Continuity and Colonization: The Evolution of Kentish Settlement*. Leicester: Leicester University Press.

Ezorsky, Gertrude. 1984. Hannah Arendt's view of totalitarianism and the Holocaust. *Philosophical Forum* 15 (1):63–81.

Faier, Elizabeth. 1997. Looking in/Acting out: Gender, modernity, and the (re)production of the Palestinian family. *Political and Legal Anthropology Review* 20 (2):1–15.

———. 1999a. Global moderns: Democracy discourses and Palestinian social activism in Haifa, Israel. *City and Society, Annual Review* 1998:149–66.

———. 1999b. Improvising modernity: Organizations, gender, and the culture of Palestinian activism in Haifa, Israel. Ph.D. diss., Department of Anthropology, Indiana University.

Faitelson, Alex. 1996. *Heroism and Bravery in Lithuania, 1941–1945*. Jerusalem: Gefen.

Faith, Nicholas. 1990. *The World the Railways Made*. New York: Carroll and Graf.

Fallers, L. F. 1969. *Law without Precedent*. Chicago: University of Chicago Press.

Fallows, James. 1987. A damaged culture. *Atlantic Monthly*. November:49–58.

Fanon, Frantz. 1967. *The Wretched of the Earth*. Harmondsworth: Penguin.

Fardon, Richard. 1985. Introduction: A sense of relevance. In *Power and Knowledge: Anthropological and Sociological Approaches*, edited by Richard Fardon. Edinburgh: Scottish Academic Press.

Farson, Negley. 1940. *Behind God's Back*. New York: Harcourt, Brace.

Fattah, Ezzat. 1994. From victimization by the state to victimization by crime: A side-effect of transition to democracy? In *New Definitions of Crime in Societies in Transition to Democracy*, edited by Uwe Ewald. Bonn: Forum Verlag Godesberg.

Faubion, James D., ed. 1995. *Rethinking the Subject*. Boulder, Colo.: Westview Press.

Fein, Helen. 1979. *Accounting for Genocide*. New York: Free Press.

Feldman, Allan. 1991. *Formations of Violence*. Chicago: University of Chicago Press.

Ferguson, James. 1994. *The Anti-Politics Machine: "Development," Depoliticization, and Bureaucratic Power in Lesotho*. Minneapolis: University of Minnesota Press.

Fernea, Elizabeth Warnock, and Mary Evelyn Hocking, eds. 1992. *The Struggle for Peace: Israelis and Palestinians*. Austin: University of Texas Press.

Feyerabend, Paul. 1975. *Against Method*. London: Verso.

Fiawoo, D. K. 1971. From cult to "church": A study of some aspects of religious change in Ghana. *Ghana Review of Sociology*.

Field, Margaret Joyce. 1948. *Akim-Kotoku: An Oman of the Gold Coast*. London: Crown Agents for the Colonies.

Fitzgerald, Louise, Kimberly Lonsway, and Diane Payne. n.d. It never happened, but she must have asked for it: The cultural mythology of sexual victimization. Unpublished manuscript.

Fitzpatrick, Peter. 1992. *The Mythology of Modern Law*. London: Routledge.

Forsythe, Diana. 1982. *Urban-Rural Migration, Change, and Conflict in an Orkney Island Community*. London: Social Science Research Council.

Fortes, Meyer, and E. E. Evans-Pritchard, eds. 1940. *African Political Systems*. London: Oxford University Press for the International African Institute.

Foster, George. 1963. The dyadic contract in Tzintzuntzan, II: Patron-client relationship. *American Anthropologist* 65:1280–95.

Foucault, Michel. 1972. *The Archaeology of Knowledge*. Translated by A. M. Sheridan Smith. New York: Pantheon.

——. 1975. *The Birth of the Clinic: An Archaeology of Medical Perception*. Translated by A. M. Sheridan Smith. New York: Vintage.

——. 1980. *Power/Knowledge: Selected Interviews and Other Writings, 1972–1977*, edited by Colin Gordon. New York: Pantheon.

Fox, Richard. 1990. Hindu nationalism in the making, or the rise of the Hindian. In, Richard Fox, ed., *Nationalist Ideologies and the Production of National Cultures*. Washington, D.C.: American Anthropological Association, 63–80.

——, ed. 1991. Introduction. In *Recapturing Anthropology: Working in the Present*. Santa Fe, N.M.: School of American Research Press.

Freeman, James M. 1989. *Hearts of Sorrow: Vietnamese American Lives*. Stanford, Calif.: Stanford University Press.

——. 1995. *Changing Identities: Vietnamese Americans, 1975–1995*. Needham Heights, Mass.: Allyn and Bacon.

Freeman, James M., and Nguyen Dinh Huu. 1996. Repatriated to Vietnam: Children without parents. *Practicing Anthropology* 18 (1):28–32.

Freyd, Jennifer. 1996. *Betrayal Trauma*. Cambridge: Harvard University Press.

Friedlander, Saul. 1992. Introduction to *Probing the Limits of Representation: Nazism and the Final Solution*, edited by Saul Friedlander. Cambridge: Harvard University Press.

Friedman, Phillip. 1980. *Roads to Extinction: Essays on the Holocaust*. New York: Jewish Publication Society of America.

Frohmann, Lisa, and Elizabeth Mertz. 1994. Legal reform and social construction: Violence, gender, and the law. *Law and Social Inquiry* 19:829–51.

Fuchs, Stephan. 1992. *The Professional Quest for Truth: A Social Theory of Science and Knowledge*. Albany: State University of New York Press.

Fukuyama, Francis. 1993. *The End of History and the Last Man*. New York: Basic Books.

Furcinitti, Laura. 1993. Humanity in distress. *ARCWP Newsletter* 4 (4):7–13.

Furian, Gilbert. 1992. *Der Richter und Sein Lenker: Politische Justiz in der DDR*. Berlin: Das Neue Berlin Verlagsgesellschaft GmbH.

Galanter, Marc. 1974. Why the 'haves' come out ahead: Speculations on the limits of legal change. *Law and Society Review* 9 (1):95–160.

Galison, Peter, and B. Hevly, eds. 1992. *Big Science: The Growth of Large-Scale Research*. Stanford, Calif.: Stanford University Press.

Gallagher, Dennis. 1994. Durable solutions in a new political era. *Journal of International Affairs* 47 (2):429–50.

Galtung, Johan. 1989. *Europe in the Making*. New York: Crane Russak.

Geertz, Clifford. 1995. *After the Fact*. Cambridge: Harvard University Press.

George, Stephen. 1990a. *An Awkward Partner: Britain in the European Community*. New York: Oxford University Press.

———. 1990b. Social understanding and the inscription of self. In *Cultural Psychology: Essays on Comparative Human Development*, edited by James Stigler, Richard Shweder, and Gilbert Herdt. Cambridge: Cambridge University Press.

Gergen, Kenneth. 1991. *The Saturated Self: Dilemmas of Identity in Contemporary Life*. New York: Basic Books.

Gerlach, Luther P., and Betty Radcliffe. 1979. Can independence survive interdependence? *Futurics* 3 (3):181–206.

Gert, Bernard. 1976. *Moral Rules*. New York: Oxford University Press.

Giddens, Anthony. 1979. *Central Problems in Social Theory: Action, Structure and Contradiction in Social Analysis*. Berkeley: University of California Press.

———. 1981. *Central Problems in Sociological Theory*. Berkeley: University of California Press.

———. 1984. *The Constitution of Society*. Berkeley: University of California Press.

———. 1985. *The Nation-State and Violence*. Berkeley: University of California Press.

Gilbert, Martin. 1996. *The Boys: The Story of 732 Young Concentration Camp Survivors*. New York: Henry Holt.

Gilmore, David, ed. 1987. *Honor and Shame and the Unity of the Mediterranean*. Washington, D.C.: American Anthropological Association.

Ginat, Joseph. 1987. *Blood Disputes among Bedouin and Rural Arab Societies*. Pittsburgh: University of Pittsburgh Press.

Glazer, Ilsa, and Wahiba Abu Ras. 1994. On aggression, human rights, and hegemonic discourse: The case of a murder for family honor in Israel. *Sex Roles: A Journal of Research* 30 (3/4):269–89.

Gluckman, Max. 1963. *Order and Rebellion in Tribal Africa*. New York: Free Press.

Goffman, Erving. 1959. *The Presentation of Everyday Life*. London: Allen Lane.

———. 1971. *Relations in Public*. New York: Basic.

———. 1974. *Frame Analysis*. Cambridge: Harvard University Press.

Goldblatt, I. 1971. *History of South West Africa*. Cape Town: Juta.

Goldhagen, Daniel. 1996. *Hitler's Willing Executioners: Ordinary Germans and the Holocaust*. New York: Knopf.

Goodale, Mark. 1998. *Legal Turbulence: Toward an Alternative Jurisprudence*. LL.M. thesis, University of Wisconsin Law School.

Gooding, Susan S. 1994. Place, race, and names: Layered identities in *United States v. Oregon, Confederated Tribes of the Colville Reservation, Plaintiff-Intervenor*. *Law and Society Review* 28 (5):1181–229.

———. 1997a. Imagined spaces—Storied places: A case study of the Colville Tribes and the evolution of treaty fishing rights. *Droit et cultures* 33 (1):53–95.

———. 1997b. Civil right—Criminal knowledge: Ceremony and the sacred in the Indian fishing rights conflict in the Pacific Northwest. Paper presented at the 1997 Law and Society Association Annual Meeting, St. Louis, Mo.

Goodrich, Peter, and Yifat Hachamovitch. 1991. Time out of mind: An introduction to the semiotics of common law. In *Dangerous Supplements*, edited by Peter Fitzpatrick. London: Pluto Press.

Goodwin-Gill, Guy. 1983. *The Refugee in International Law*. Oxford: Clarendon Press.

Gordon, Robert J. 1988. Apartheid's anthropologists: On the genealogy of Afrikaner anthropology. *American Ethnologist* 15 (3):535–53.

———. 1992. *The Bushman Myth*. Boulder, Colo.: Westview Press.

———. 1993. The venal Hottentot Venus and the great claim to being. *African Studies* 51 (2):185–202.

Gorz, André. 1982. *Farewell to the Working Class*. Translated by Michael Sonenscher. Boston: South End Press.

Gottlieb, Roger. 1990. The concept of resistance: Resistance during the Holocaust. In *Thinking the Unthinkable: Meanings of the Holocaust*, edited by Roger Gottlieb. Mahwah, N.J.: Paulist Press.

Gow, Anne Wagley. 1991. Protection of asylum seekers in Hong Kong: Detention, screening and repatriation. Working paper submitted to the United Nations Economic and Social Council, Commission on Human Rights. Berkeley: Human Rights Advocates.

Graham, Dee, with Edna I. Rawlings and Roberta K. Rigsby. 1994. *Loving To Survive: Sexual Terror, Men's Violence, and Women's Lives*. New York: New York University Press.

Gray, John. 1993. *Beyond the New Right: Markets, Government and the Common Environment*. London: Routledge.

Grayson, Richard. 1997. Everything compares to New Jersey. *New York Times* 16 Aug. 1997:21.

Green, Laurie. 1997. Disturbing religious assemblies: The challenge to segregated churches in the Memphis Freedom Movement, 1960–1965. Paper presented at the 1997 Law and Society Association Annual Meeting, St. Louis, Mo.

Green, Linda. 1994. Fear as a way of life. *Cultural Anthropology* 9 (2):227–56.

Greene, Sandra E. 1996. *Gender, Ethnicity, and Social Change on the Upper Slave Coast: A History of the Anlo-Ewe.* Portsmouth, N.H.: Heinemann.

Greenhouse, Carol J. 1996. *A Moment's Notice: Time Politics Across Cultures.* Ithaca, N.Y.: Cornell University Press.

Griffiths, John. 1986. What is legal pluralism? *Journal of Legal Pluralism* 24:1–56.

Grimm, Hans. [1929] 1970. *Das Deutsche Suedwester Buch.* Lippoldsberg: Klosterhaus.

———. 1973. *Geschichten Aus Suedwestafrika: Luderitzland.* Lippoldsberg: Klosterhaus.

Grosz, Elizabeth. 1994. *Volatile Bodies.* Bloomington: Indiana University Press.

Guattari, Félix. 1995. Chaosophy. Edited by Sylvère Lotringer. New York: Semiotext(e).

Gugler, Josef. 1988. *The Urbanization of the Third World.* New York: Oxford University Press.

Gupta, Akhil. 1995. Blurred boundaries: The discourse of corruption, the culture of politics, and the imagined state. *American Ethnologist* 22 (2):375–402.

———. 1998. *Postcolonial Developments: Agriculture in the Making of Modern India.* Durham, N.C.: Duke University Press.

Gupta, Akhil, and James Ferguson. 1997. Discipline and practice: "The field" as site, method, and location in anthropology. In *Anthropological Locations: Boundaries and Grounds of a Field Science,* edited by Akhil Gupta and James Ferguson. Berkeley: University of California Press.

Gutman, Yisrael. 1989. *The Jews of Warsaw, 1930–1943.* Bloomington: Indiana University Press.

Haarhoff, Dorian. 1971. *Knowledge and Human Interests.* Translated by Jeremy J. Shapiro. Boston: Beacon Press.

———. 1991. *The Wild South West.* Johannesburg: Witwatersrand University Press.

Habermas, Jürgen. 1976. *Legitimation Crisis.* Translated by Thomas McCarthy. Cambridge: Polity Press.

———. 1990. *Moral Consciousness and Communicative Action.* Translated by Christian Lenhardt and Shierry Weber Nicholson. Cambridge: MIT Press.

Hagendijk, Rob. 1990. Structuration theory, constructivism, and scientific change. In *Theories of Science in Society,* edited by Susan E. Cozzens and Thomas F. Gieryn. Bloomington: Indiana University Press.

Hahn, C. L., H. Vedder, and L. Fourie. 1928. *The Native Tribes of South West Africa.* Cape Town: Cape Times.

Hailey, Lord, n.d. The administration of South West Africa. Typescript.

Hammoudi, Abdellah. 1993. *The Victim and Its Masks.* Chicago: University of Chicago Press.

Hanks, L. M. 1968. American aid is damaging Thai society. *Trans-Action* 5:29–34.

———. 1975. The Thai social order as entourage and circle. In *Change and Persistence in*

Thai Society: Essays in Honor of Lauriston Sharp, edited by G. W. Skinner and A. T. Kirsch. Ithaca, N.Y.: Cornell University Press.

Hann, C. M., ed. 1993. *Socialism: Ideals, Ideologies, and Local Practice*. London: Routledge.

Hannerz, Ulf. 1981. The management of danger. *Ethnos* 46 (1–2):19–46.

Hannerz, Ulf, and Orvar Löfgren. 1994. The nation in the global village. Special issue: Nordic Cultural Studies, edited by Erkki Vainikkala and Katarina Eskola. *Cultural Studies* 8 (2):198–207.

Hart, Donn V. 1977. *Compadrinazgo: Ritual Kinship in the Philippines*. DeKalb: Northern Illinois University Press.

Harvey, David. 1989. *The Condition of Postmodernity*. Cambridge, Mass.: Blackwell.

Hasso, Frances. 1998. The "women's front": Nationalism, feminism, and modernity in Palestine. *Gender and Society* 12 (4):441–65.

Hastrup, Kirsten. 1993. Hunger and the hardness of fact. *Man* 28 (4):727–39.

Headland, Ronald. 1992. *Messages of Murder: A Study of the Einsatzgruppen of the Security Police and the Security Service*. Rutherford, N.J.: Fairleigh Dickinson University Press.

Heelas, Paul, and Paul Morris, eds. 1992. *The Values of the Enterprise Culture: The Moral Debate*. London: Routledge.

Henderson, Heather. 1989. *The Victorian Self: Autobiography and Biblical Narrative*. Ithaca, N.Y.: Cornell University Press.

Herman, Judith Lewis. 1992. *Trauma and Recovery*. New York: Basic Books.

Herzfeld, Michael. 1980. Honour and shame: Problems in the comparative analysis of moral systems. *Man* 15:339–51.

———. 1987. *Anthropology through the Looking Glass: Critical Ethnography in the Margins of Europe*. Cambridge: Cambridge University Press.

———. 1990. *A Place in History*. Princeton, N.J.: Princeton University Press.

———. 1991. Silence, submission, and subversion: Toward a poetics of womanhood. In *Contested Identities. Gender and Kinship in Modern Greece*, edited by Peter Loizos and Evthymios Papataxiarchis. Princeton, N.J.: Princeton University Press.

———. 1992. *The Social Production of Indifference: Explaining the Symbolic Roots of Western Bureaucracy*. New York: Berg.

———. 1997. *Cultural Intimacy: Social Poetics in the Nation-State*. New York: Routledge.

Hess, David. 1992. Introduction to the new ethnography and the anthropology of science and technology. In *Knowledge and Society: The Anthropology of Science and Technology*, vol. 9, edited by David J. Hess and Linda L. Layne. Arie Rip, series editor. Greenwich, Conn.: JAI Press.

Heuer, Uwe-Jens, and Gerhard Riege. 1992. *Der Rechtsstaat—Eine Legende?* Baden-Baden: Nomos Verlagsgesellschaft.

Heyman, Josiah, ed. 1999. *States and Illegal Practices*. Oxford: Berg.

Hilberg, Raul. 1985. *The Destruction of the European Jews*. New York: Holmes and Meier.

———. 1992. *Perpetrators, Victims, Bystanders: The Jewish Catastrophe*. New York: Harper Collins.

Hobsbawm, Eric. 1990. *Nations and Nationalism since 1780*. Cambridge: Cambridge University Press.

Hodgson, Dorothy L. 1997. Embodying the contradictions of modernity: Gender and spirit possession among Maasai in Tanzania. In *Cultural Encounters: Gender at the Intersection of the Local and the Global in Africa*, edited by Maria Grosz-Ngate and Omari Kokole. New York: Routledge.

Holborn, Louise W. 1975. *Refugees: A Problem of our Time; The Work of the United Nations High Commissioner for Refugees, 1951–1972*. 2 vols. Metuchen, N.J.: Scarecrow Press.

Hollnsteiner, Mary R. 1963. *The Dynamics of Power in a Philippine Municipality*. Manila: University of the Philippines, Community Development Research Council Publication.

Holmes, Douglas. 1993. Illicit discourse. In *Perilous States: Conversations on Culture, Politics, and Nation*, edited by George E. Marcus. Chicago: University of Chicago Press.

——. 2000. *Integral Europe: Fast-Capitalism, Multiculturalism, Neofascism*. Princeton, N.J.: Princeton University Press.

Holmes, George. 1962. *The Later Middle Ages, 1272–1485*. New York: Norton.

Holston, James. 1993. *The Modernist City: An Anthropological Critique of Brasília*. Chicago: University of Chicago Press.

Horn, Pamela. 1984. *The Changing Countryside in Victorian and Edwardian England and Wales*. London: Athlone Press.

Horton, Robin. 1967. African traditional thought and western science. *Africa* 37:50–71, 155–85.

Huggins, Martha K. 1985. *From Slavery to Vagrancy in Brazil*. New Brunswick, N.J.: Rutgers University Press.

Humphrey, Caroline. 1993. Creating a culture of disillusionment: Consumption in Moscow, a chronicle of changing times. In *Worlds Apart*, edited by D. Miller. New York: Routledge.

——. 1998. Marx went away but Karl stayed behind. Updated edition of *Karl Marx Collective: Economy, Society, and Religion in a Siberian Collective Farm*. Ann Arbor: University of Michigan Press.

Humphreys, Sally. 1985. Law as discourse. *History and Anthropology*. 1:241–64.

Hutt, Thomas. 1993. Probleme beim Aufbau einer staatsanwaltschaftlichen Ermittlungsbehoerde in den neuen Bundeslaendern. In *Politisch-gesellschaftlicher Umbruch, Kriminalitaet, Straftrechtspflege*, edited by Guenther Kaiser and Joerg-Martin Jehle. Heidelberg: Kriminalistik Pub.

Hymes, Dell, ed. 1990. *Reinventing Anthropology*. New York: Pantheon Books.

Inglehart, Ronald. 1990. *Culture Shift in Advanced Industrial Society*. Princeton, N.J.: Princeton University Press.

Jackson, Stephen. 1999. Making Sense: Facts, tracts, and secret knowledge. Ph.D. diss. prospectus, Princeton University.

Jessup, Frank. 1974. *A History of Kent*. London: Phillimore.

Johnston, Richard J. 1991. *A Question of Place: Exploring the Practice of Human Geography*. Oxford: Blackwell.

Joppke, Christian. 1995. Intellectuals, nationalism, and the exit from communism: The case of East Germany. *Comparative Studies in Society and History* 37 (April).

Juristen fuer die deutsche Rechtsangleichung. 1990. Paper presented at the Vereinigung demokratischer Juristen, Strasberg-Nord.

Kandiyotti, Deniz, ed. 1991. *Women, Islam, and the State*. Philadelphia, Pa.: Temple University Press.

Kane, Stephanie C. 1994. *The Phantom Gringo Boat*. Washington, D.C.: Smithsonian.

Kapchan, Deborah. 1994. *Gender on the Market: Moroccan Women and Revoicing of Tradition*. Philadelphia: University of Pennsylvania Press.

Karp, Ivan, and Kent Maynard. 1983. Reading the Nuer. *Current Anthropology* 24:481–503.

Keane, Webb. 1997. *Signs of Recognition: Powers and Hazards of Representation in an Indonesian Society*. Berkeley: University of California Press.

Kearney, Michael. 1996. *Reconceptualizing the Peasantry: Anthropology in Global Perspective*. Boulder, Colo.: Westview Press.

Keely, Charles B., and Sharon Stanton Russell. 1994. Responses of industrial countries to asylum seekers. *Journal of International Affairs* 47 (2):399–417.

Keesing, Roger. 1994. Theories of culture revisited. In *Assessing Cultural Anthropology*, edited by Robert Borofsky. New York: McGraw-Hill.

Kellett, John R. 1969. *The Impact of Railways on Victorian Cities*. London: Routledge and Kegan Paul.

Kennedy, Duncan. 1993. *Sexy Dressing Etc.: Essays on the Power and Politics of Cultural Identity*. Cambridge: Harvard University Press.

Kenny, Michael, and David Kertzer, eds. 1983. *Urban Life in Mediterranean Europe: Anthropological Perspectives*. Urbana: University of Illinois Press.

Kent Action Group. 1993. Response of the Kent Action Group to the Union Railway Proposed Route for the Channel Tunnel Rail Link. Council for the Protection of Rural England, Ashford, Kent.

King, P. 1989. Gleaners, farmers, and the failure of legal sanctions in England, 1750–1850. *Past and Present* 125:116–50.

Klee, Ernst, Willi Dressen, and Volker Riess. 1991. *The Good Old Days: The Holocaust as Seen by Its Perpetrators and Bystanders*. New York: Simon and Schuster.

Kleinman, Arthur. 1986. *Social Origins of Distress and Disease: Depression, Neurasthenia, and Pain in Modern China*. New Haven, Conn.: Yale University Press.

Knorr-Cetina, Karin, and Michael Mulkay, eds. 1983. *Science Observed: Perspectives on the Social Study of Science*. London: Sage.

Koenigsberger, H. G. 1989. Composite states, representative institutions, and the American Revolution. *Historical Research* 62:135–53.

Kon, Igor. 1996. Moral Culture. In *Russian Culture at the Crossroads: Paradoxes of*

Postcommunist Consciousness, edited by Dmitri N. Shalin. Boulder, Colo.: Westview Press.

Kotze, Carol. 1984. The establishment of a government in Ovamboland, 1915–1925. M.A. thesis, University of South Africa, Pretoria.

Kramer, Fritz. 1993. *The Red Fez: Art and Spirit Possession in Africa*. London: Verso.

Kressel, Gideon. 1981. Sororicide/filiacide: Homicide for family honour. *Current Anthropology* 22 (2):141–52.

Krohn-Hansen, Christian. 1994. The anthropology of violent interaction. *Journal of Anthropological Research* 50 (4):367–81.

Kuhn, Thomas. 1970. *The Structure of Scientific Revolutions*. 2d ed. International Encyclopedia of Science. Chicago: The University of Chicago Press.

Lacan, Jacques. 1977. *Écrits: A Selection*. Translated by Alan Sheridan. London: Tavistock Publications.

Laclau, Ernesto. 1990. Post-Marxism without apologies. In *New Reflections on the Revolution of Our Time*. Edited by Ernesto Laclau. London: Verso.

Laclau, Ernesto, and Chantal Mouffe. 1985. *Hegemony and Socialist Strategy*. London: Verso.

Laczo, Mona. 2000. Holding on to hope. *Diakrona* 51 (Jan. 7).

Lan, David. 1985. *Guns and Rain: Guerrillas and Spirit Mediums in Zimbabwe*. Berkeley: University of California Press.

Landé, Carl H. 1965. *Leaders, Factions, and Parties. The Structure of Philippine Politics*. Southeast Asia studies monograph, no. 6. New Haven, Conn.: Yale University Press.

——. 1977. Networks and groups in Southeast Asia: Some observations on the group theory of politics. In *Friends, Followers, and Factions: A Reader in Political Clientism*, edited by Stefen W. Schmidt, Laura Guasti, Carl H. Landé, and James C. Scott. Berkeley: University of California Press.

Lang, Berel. 1990. *Act and Idea in the Nazi Genocide*. Chicago: Chicago University Press.

Langer, Lawrence. 1993. Tainted legacy: Remembering the Warsaw ghetto. *Tikkun* (May/June):37–40; 85–87.

Latour, Bruno. 1993. *We Have Never Been Modern*. Translated by Catherine Porter. Cambridge: Harvard University Press.

Latour, Bruno, and Steve Woolgar. 1979. *Laboratory Life: The Construction of Scientific Facts*. Princeton, N.J.: Princeton University Press.

Lavie, Smadar. 1990. *The Poetics of Military Occupation*. Berkeley: University of California Press.

Lazarus-Black, Mindie. 1994. *Legitimate Acts and Illegal Encounters: Law and Society in Antigua and Barbuda*. Washington, D.C.: Smithsonian.

Lazarus-Black, Mindie, and Susan Hirsch, eds. 1994. *Contested States*. New York: Routledge.

Ledeneva, Alena. 1998. *Russia's Economy of Favors: Blat, Networking, and Informal Exchange*. Cambridge: Cambridge University Press.

Leonhard, Wolfgang. 1979. *Die Revolution Entlaesst Ihre Kinder*. Munich: Heyne Verlag.

Levi, Werner. 1980. Law and politics in the international society. In *The Sociology of Law*, edited by William M. Evan. New York: Free Press.

Lewin, Carroll McC. 1993. Negotiated selves in the Holocaust. *Ethos* 21 (3):295–318.

Lionnet, Françoise. 1989. *Autobiographical Voices: Race, Gender, Self-Portraiture*. Ithaca, N.Y.: Cornell University Press.

Llewellyn, Karl N., and E. Adamson Hoebel. 1941. *The Cheyenne Way: Conflict and Case Law in Primitive Jurisprudence*. Norman: University of Oklahoma Press.

Loescher, Gil. 1993. The international refugee regime. *Journal of International Affairs* 47 (2):351–77.

Longdon, Norman, editor. 1989. *ESA Annual Report 1988*. Noordwijk, Netherlands: ESA Publications Division.

Longdon, Norman, and Duc Guyenne, editors. 1984. *Twenty Years of European Cooperation in Space: An ESA Report*. Noordwijk, Netherlands: ESA Publications Division.

Loughry, Maryanne, and Ruth Esquillo. 1994. *In Whose Best Interest?* Bangkok: Jesuit Refugee Service.

Lowenthal, David. 1994. European and English landscapes as national symbols. In *Geography and National Identity*, edited by D. Hooson. Oxford: Blackwell.

Lugones, Maria. 1990. Playfulness, "world"-travelling, and loving perception. In *Making Face, Making Soul: Haciendo Caras*, edited by Gloria Anzaldua. San Francisco: Aunt Lute Foundation.

Lüst, Reimar. 1987. *Europe and Space*. ESA Publication BR-35. Noordwijk, Netherlands: ESA Publications Division.

Lustick, Ian. [1980] 1982. *Arabs in the Jewish State: Israel's Control of a National Minority*. Austin: University of Texas Press.

Lynch, Michael. 1985. *Art and Artifact in Laboratory Science: A Study of Shop Work and Shop Talk in Research Laboratory*. London: Routledge and Kegan Paul.

MacCannell, Dean. 1992. *Empty Meeting Grounds*. New York: Routledge.

MacDonagh, O. 1980. "Pre-transformations": Victorian Britain. In *Law and Social Control*, edited by Eugene Kamenka and Alice Erh-Soon Tay. New York: St. Martin's Press.

MacDougall, Hugh A. 1982. *Racial Myth in English History: Trojans, Teutons, and Anglo-Saxons*. Hanover, N.H.: University Press of New England.

MacFarlane, Alan. 1978. *The Origins of English Individualism*. Oxford: Basil Blackwell.

Major, Alan P. 1981. *A New Dictionary of Kent Dialect*. Rainham, England: Meresborough Books.

Malinowski, Bronislaw, 1945. *The Dynamics of Culture Change*. New Haven, Conn.: Yale University Press.

Malkki, Liisa H. 1995. *Purity and Exile: Violence, Memory, and National Cosmology among Hutu Refugees in Tanzania*. Chicago: University of Chicago Press.

——. 1997. Newsstand culture: Transitory phenomena and the fieldwork tradition. In *Anthropological Locations: Boundaries and Grounds of a Field Science*, edited by Akhil Gupta and James Ferguson. Berkeley: University of California Press.

Mallory, C. S. 1971. Some aspects of the mission policy and practice of the Church of the Province of South Africa in Ovamboland. M.A. thesis, Rhodes University, Grahamstown.

Mander, John. 1963. *Great Britain or Little England?* Harmondsworth: Penguin.

Marcos, Ferdinand. 1960. Directive-Sp-0236. Aug. 11. Manila: Republic of the Philippines.

Marcus, George, ed. 1983. *Elites: Ethnographic Issues*. Albuquerque: University of New Mexico Press.

——. 1993. *Perilous States: Conversations on Culture, Politics, and Nation*. Chicago: University of Chicago Press.

Marcus, George, and Michael Fischer. 1986. *Anthropology as Cultural Critique*. Chicago: University of Chicago Press.

Marinina, Aleksandra. 1997. *Playing on Foreign Turf?* [Igra Na Chuzhom Pole]. Moscow: EKSMO.

Marrus, Michael. 1987. *The Holocaust in History*. Hanover, N.H.: University Press of New England.

Marshall, Ruth. 1995. Final act: Closing down the CPA. *Refugees* (1):9–14.

Martin, Emily. 1994. *Flexible Bodies: Tracking Immunity in American Culture from the Days of Polio to the Age of AIDS*. Boston: Beacon.

Marx, Karl. 1977. *Capital: A Critique of Political Economy*. Vol. 1. Translated by Ben Fowkes. New York: Vintage Books.

Masalha, Nur. 1993. Introduction to *The Palestinians in Israel: Is Israel the State of All Its Citizens and "Absentees"?*, edited by Nur Masalha. Haifa: Galilee Center for Social Research.

Masquelier, Adeline. 1993. Narratives of power, images of wealth: The ritual economy of Bori in the market. In *Modernity and Its Malcontents: Ritual and Power in Postcolonial Africa*, edited by Jean Comaroff and John L. Comaroff. Chicago: University of Chicago Press.

Matory, J. Lorand. 1993. Government by seduction: History and the trope of "mounting" in Oyo-Yoruba religion. In *Modernity and Its Malcontents: Ritual and Power in Postcolonial Africa*, edited by Jean Comaroff and John Comaroff. Chicago: University of Chicago Press.

——. 1994. *Sex and the Empire That Is No More: Gender and the Politics of Metaphor in Oyo Yoruba Religion*. Minneapolis: University of Minnesota Press.

Mattenklodt, Wilhelm. 1931. *Fugitive in the Jungle*. Boston: Little, Brown.

Maupoil, Bernard. [1943] 1961. *La géomancie à l'ancienne Côte des Esclaves*. Paris: Institut d'Ethnologie.

Mbuende, Kaire. 1986. *Namibia: The Broken Shield*. Lund: Liber.

McCallin, Margaret. 1992. *Living in Detention: A Review of the Psychosocial Well-Being of Vietnamese Children in the Hong Kong Detention Centres.* Geneva: International Catholic Child Bureau.

McCarthy, T. 1978. *The Critical Theory of Jürgen Habermas.* Cambridge: MIT Press.

McDonald, Maryon. 1993. The construction of difference: An anthropological approach to stereotypes. In *Inside European Identities: Ethnography in Western Europe,* edited by Sharon Macdonald. Oxford: Berg.

———. 1996. Unity in diversity: Moralities in the construction of Europe. *Social Anthropology* 4 (1):47–60.

McFaul, Michael, and Tova Perlmutter, eds. 1995. *Privatization, Conversion, and Enterprise Reform in Russia.* Boulder, Colo.: Westview Press.

McIntosh, K. 1975. *Fordwich the Lost Port.* Canterbury, England: McIntosh.

Meier, J. S. 1993. Notes from the underground: Integrating psychological and legal perspectives on domestic violence in theory and practice. *Hofstra Law Review* 21:1296–366.

Memmi, Albert. 1967. *The Colonizer and the Colonized.* Boston: Beacon.

Merry, Sally Engle. 1988. Legal pluralism. *Law and Society Review* 22 (5):869–96.

———. 1992. Anthropology, Law, and Transnational Processes. *Annual Review of Anthropology* 21:357–79.

Merton, Robert. 1973. In *Sociology of Science,* edited by Barry Barnes. Harmondsworth: Penguin.

Mertz, Elizabeth. 1987. Science and relativism: An historical view of anthropology's unresolved dilemma. *Anthropology and Humanism Quarterly* 12 (2):30–37.

———. 1988. The uses of history: Language, ideology and law in the United States and South Africa. *Law and Society Review* 22 (4):661–85.

———. 1992. Language, law, and social meanings: Linguistic/anthropological contributions to the study of law. *Law and Society Review* 26 (2):413–45.

———. 1994a. Legal loci and places in the heart: Community and identity in sociolegal studies. *Law and Society Review* 28:971–92.

———. 1994b. A new social constructionism for sociolegal studies. *Law and Society Review* 28:1243–265.

———. 1998. Linguistic ideology and praxis in U.S. law school classrooms. In *Language Ideologies,* edited by Bambi Schieffelin, Kathryn Woolard, and Paul Kroskrity. Oxford: Oxford University Press.

Mertz, Elizabeth, and Kimberly Lonsway. 1998. The power of denial: Individual and cultural constructions of child sexual abuse. *Northwestern University Law Review* 92 (4):1415–458.

Mertz, Elizabeth, with Wamucii Njogu and Susan Gooding. 1998. What difference does difference make? The challenge for legal education. *Journal of Legal Education* 48:1–87.

Mingay, Gordan E. 1989a. "Rural war": The life and times of Captain Swing. In *The Unquiet Countryside,* edited by G. E. Mingay. London: Routledge.

——, ed. 1989b. *The Rural Idyll*. London: Routledge.

——. 1990. *A Social History of the English Countryside*. London: Routledge.

Moghadam, Valentine M. 1993. *Modernizing Women: Gender and Social Change in the Middle East*. Boulder, Colo.: Lynne Rienner Press.

——. 1997. Women's NGOs in the Middle East and North Africa: Constraints, opportunities, and priorities. In *Organizing Women: Formal and Informal Women's Groups in the Middle East*, edited by Dawn Chatty and Annika Rabo. Oxford: Berg.

Moi, Toril. 1986. Introduction to *The Kristeva Reader*. Edited by Toril Moi and translated by Seán Hand. Oxford: Blackwell.

Moleah, Alfred. 1983. Namibia, the Struggle for Liberation. Wilmington, Del.: Disa Press.

Montejo, Victor. 1999. *Voices from Exile: Violence and Survival in Modern Maya History*. University of Oklahoma Press.

Moore, Sally Falk. 1973. Law and social change: The semi-autonomous social field as an appropriate subject of study. *Law and Society Review* 7 (4):719–46.

——. 1978. *Law as Process: An Anthropological Approach*. London: Routledge and Kegan Paul.

——. 1986. *Social Facts and Fabrications: "Customary" Law on Kilimanjaro, 1880–1980*. Cambridge: Cambridge University Press.

——, ed. 1993. Moralizing States. American Ethnological Society monograph no. 5. Arlington, VA: American Anthropological Association.

Mougne, Christine. 1989. Difficult decisions. *Refugees* (Nov.):37.

——. 1990. The tide is turning. *Refugees* (Dec.):25.

Mueller, Ingo. 1989. Furchtbare Juristen. Munich: Kindler Verlags.

Mulkay, Michael. 1975. Norms and ideology in science. *Social Science Information* 15:637–56.

Munn, Nancy. 1986. *The Fame of Gawa*. Durham, N.C.: Duke University Press.

Muntarbhorn, Vitit. 1992. *The Status of Refugees in Asia*. Oxford: Oxford University Press.

Mya Than and Joseph L. H. Tan, eds. 1993. *Vietnam's Dilemmas and Options*. Singapore: ASEAN Economic Research Unit, Institute of Southeast Asian Studies.

Nader, Laura. 1974. Up the anthropologist: Perspectives gained from studying up. In *Reinventing Anthropology*, edited by Dell Hymes. New York: Random House.

——. 1999. Thinking public interest anthropology, 1890s–1990s. *General Anthropology* 5 (1):7–9.

Nagengast, Carole. 1991. *Reluctant Socialists, Rural Entrepreneurs: Class, Culture, and the Polish State*. Boulder, Colo.: Westview Press.

Nash, June. 2001. *Mayan Vision: The Quest for Autonomy in an Age of Globalization*. New York: Routledge.

Nash, June, and María Patricia Fernández-Kelly, eds. 1983. *Women, Men, and the International Division of Labor*. Albany: State University of New York Press.

Neher, Clark D. 1985. Political clientism and instability in the Philippines. *Asian Affairs: An American Review* 12:1–23.

Nelson, Diane. 1999. *The Finger in the Wound: Ethnicity, Nation, and Gender in the Body Politic of Quincentennial Guatemala.* Berkeley: University of California Press.

Nelson, Lynn D., and Irina Y. Kuzes. 1995. *Radical Reform in Yeltsin's Russia: Political, Economic and Social Dimensions.* Armonk, N.Y.: M. E. Sharpe.

Neu, Patricia. 1993. *Needs Assessment of Arab Israeli Non-Governmental Organizations for an Inter-Agency Support Mechanism.* Shafa'amr, Israel: Galilee Society for Health Research and Services.

Nguyen Dinh Huu and James M. Freeman. 1992. Disrupted childhood: Unaccompanied minors in Southeast Asian refugee camps. Summary of fact-finding trip to Hong Kong, Philippines, Thailand, Malaysia, Singapore, Indonesia. San Jose, California: Aid to Refugee Children Without Parents.

——. 1993. Nowhere to return: The crisis of repatriated unaccompanied minors without parents. Summary report of the ARCWP fact-finding team on the situation of unaccompanied minors in Vietnam. San Jose, California: Aid To Refugee Children Without Parents.

——. 1994. Without a trace: The repatriation of Vietnamese unaccompanied minors, 1994. The 1994 summary Report of the ARCWP fact-finding team on the situation of repatriated unaccompanied minors in Vietnam. San Jose, California: Aid To Refugee Children Without Parents.

Nguyen Thanh Ha. 1994. Life of a repatriated unaccompanied minor. *ARCWP Newsletter* 7 (winter):7–9.

Nichols, Alan, and Paul White. 1993. *Refugee Dilemmas: Reviewing the Comprehensive Plan of Action for Vietnamese asylum seekers.* Manila: LAWASIA.

Nordstrom, Carolyn, and JoAnn Martin, eds. 1992. *The Paths to Domination, Resistance, and Terror.* Berkeley: University of California Press.

——. 2000a. Out of the shadows. In *Authority and Intervention in Africa*, edited by Thomas Callaghy, Ron Kassimir, and Robert Latham. New York: Cambridge University Press.

——. 2000b. Shadows and sovereigns. *Theory, Culture, and Society* 17 (4):35–54.

Nordstrom, Carolyn R. n.d. War, peace, and shadow powers: The licit, the illicit, and the unknown. Unpublished ms.

Nugent, Nicholas. 1996. *Vietnam: The Second Revolution.* Brighton, U.K.: In Print.

Nye, Robert. 1984. *Crime, Madness and Politics in Modern France.* Princeton, N.J.: Princeton University Press.

Ochs, Elinor. 1988. *Culture and Language Development: Language Acquisition and Language Socialization in a Samoan Village.* Cambridge: Cambridge University Press.

Ofer, Dalia. 1995. Everyday life of Jews under Nazi occupation: Methodological issues. *Holocaust and Genocide Studies* 9 (1):42–69.

Ogata, Sadako. 1994. Interview with Sadako Ogata, the United Nations High Commissioner for Refugees. 1994. *Journal of International Affairs* 47 (2):419–28.

Olivier, Martinus J. 1961. Inboorlingbeleid in die mandaatgebied van Suidwes-Afrika. Ph.D. diss. Stellenbosch University.

Olwig, Karen Fog, and Kirsten Hastrup, eds. 1997. *Siting Culture: The Shifting Anthropological Object.* London: Routledge.

Ong, Aihwa. 1999. *Flexible Citizenship.* Durham, N.C.: Duke University Press.

——. n.d. Graduated sovereignty in Southeastern Asia: Theory, culture, and sovereignty. Unpublished manuscript.

Ortner, Sherry B. 1984. Theory in anthropology since the sixties. *Comparative Studies in Society and History* 26:126–66.

——. 1995. Resistance and the problem of ethnographic refusal. *Comparative Studies in Science and History* 37:173–93.

Osborne, Peter, ed. 1991. *Socialism and the Limits of Liberalism.* London: Verso.

Owusu, Maxwell. 1995. Culture, colonialism, and African democracy: Problems and prospects. In *Africa in World History: Old, New, Then, and Now,* edited by Michael W. Coy Jr. and Leonard Plotnicov. Ethnology Monographs, no. 16. Pittsburgh: Department of Anthropology, University of Pittsburgh.

Parnell, Phillip C. 1988. *Escalating Disputes: Social Participation and Change in the Oaxacan Highlands.* Tucson: University of Arizona Press.

——. 1992. Time and irony in Manila squatter movements. In *The Paths to Domination, Resistance, and Terror,* edited by Carolyn Nordstrom and Joann Martin. Berkeley: University of California Press.

Parry, Jonathan, and Maurice Bloch, eds. 1989. *Money and the Minority of Exchange.* Cambridge: Cambridge University Press.

Peck, Abraham. 1987. The agony of the Lodz ghetto. In *Simon Wisenthal Annual 4,* edited by H. Friedlander and Sybil Milton. White Plains, N.Y.: Kraus.

Perechodnik, Calel. 1996. *Am I a Murderer?: Testament of a Jewish Ghetto Policeman.* Edited and translated by Frank Fox. Boulder, Colo.: Westview Press.

Peretz, Don, and Gideon Doron. 1997. *The Government and Politics of Israel.* 3d ed. Boulder, Colo.: Westview Press.

Peretz, Don, and Sammy Smooha. 1989. Israel's twelfth Knesset election: An all-loser game. *Middle East Journal* 43 (3):388–406.

Peristiany, J. G. [1966] 1974. Introduction to *Honour and Shame: The Values of Mediterranean Society,* edited by J. G. Peristiany. Chicago: University of Chicago Press.

Pesmen, Dale. 1996. "Do not have a hundred rubles, have instead a hundred friends": Money and sentiment in a Perestroika-Post-Soviet Siberian city." In *Irish Journal of Anthropology* 1:3–22.

——. 2000. *Russia and Soul: An Exploration.* Ithaca, N.Y.: Cornell University Press.

Peteet, Julie M. 1991. *Gender in Crisis: Women and the Palestinian Resistance Movement.* New York: Columbia University Press.

Peters, Emrys. 1990. *The Bedouin of Cyrenaica,* edited by Jack Goody and Emanuel Marx. Cambridge: Cambridge University Press.

Pienaar, Sara. 1987. *South Africa and International Relations between the Two World Wars*. Johannesburg: Witwatersrand University Press.

Postone, Moishe. 1993. *Time, Labor, and Social Domination*. Cambridge: Cambridge University Press.

Poyer, Lin. 1993. *The Ngatik Massacre: History and Identity on a Micronesian Atoll*. Washington, D.C.: Smithsonian.

Quigley, John. 1990. The transformation of Eastern Europe and the convergence of socialist and capitalist Law. *Willamette Law Review* 26 (4):937–56.

Rabinowitz, Dan. 1997. *Overlooking Nazareth: The Ethnography of Exclusion in Galilee*. Cambridge: Cambridge University Press.

Raedel, Fritz. 1947. Die Wirtschaft und die Arbeiterfrage Suedwestafrikas. Ph.D. diss. Stellenbosch University.

Rafael, Vicente L. 1993. *Contracting Colonialism: Translation and Christian Conversion in Tagalog Society under Early Spanish Rule*. Durham, N.C.: Duke University Press.

Rapport, Nigel J. 1993. *Diverse World-Views in an English Village*. Edinburgh: Edinburgh University Press.

Rattner, Arye. 1994. The margins of justice attitudes towards the law and the legal system among Jews and Arabs in Israel. *International Journal of Public Opinion Research* 6 (4):358–70.

Reed, Michael. 1984. Anglo-Saxon charter bounders. In *Discovering Past Landscapes*, edited by Michael Reed. London: Croom Helm.

Rekhess, Elie. 1990. Arabs in a Jewish state: Images versus reality. *Middle East Insight* 8 (1):3–9.

Ressler, Everett M., Neil Boothby, and Daniel J. Steinbock. 1988. *Unaccompanied Children: Care and Protection in Wars, Natural Disasters, and Refugee Movements*. New York: Oxford University Press.

Restivo, Sal. 1988. Modern science as a social problem. *Social Problems* 35 (3):206–25.

Richardson, Michael. 1979. How many died? *Far Eastern Economic Review* 106 (43):34.

Ries, Nancy. 1997. *Russian Talk: Culture and Conversation during Perestroika*. Ithaca, N.Y.: Cornell University Press.

Ringelbaum, Emmanuel. 1974. *Notes from the Warsaw Ghetto: The Journal of Emmanuel Ringelbaum*. Edited and translated by Jacob Sloan. New York: Schocken Books.

Rivera, Temario. 1991. Class, the state, and foreign capital: The politics of Philippine industrialization, 1950–1986. Ph.D. diss. University of Wisconsin, Madison.

Robinson, W. Courtland. 1998. *Terms of Refuge: The Indochinese Exodus and the International Response*. New York: Zed Books.

Roland, Charles. 1992. *Courage under Siege: Starvation, Disease, and Death in the Warsaw Ghetto*. Oxford: Oxford University Press.

Roniger, Luis, and Ayse Gunes-Ayata. 1994. *Democracy, Clientism, and Civil Society*. Boulder, Colo.: Lynne Rienner Publishers.

Rootes, Alan. 1980. *Front Line County: Kent at War, 1939–1945*. London: Robert Hale.

Rosaldo, Renalto. 1993. *Culture and Truth*. Boston: Beacon Press.

Rose, Gillian. 1993. *Feminism and Geography: The Limits of Geographical Knowledge*. Minneapolis: University of Minnesota Press.

Rosenthal, Judy. 1993. Gods, democracy, and ethnicity in Togo. Unpublished paper presented at the annual meeting of the American Anthropological Association, Washington, D.C.

———. 1995. The signifying crab. *Cultural Anthropology* 10 (4):581–86.

———. 1997. Foreign tongues and domestic bodies: Gendered cultural regions and regional sacred flows. In *Gendered Encounters: Challenging Cultural Boundaries and Social Hierarchies in Africa*, edited by Maria Grosz-Ngate and Omari Kokole. New York: Routledge.

———. 1998. *Possession, Ecstasy, and Law in Ewe Voodoo*. Charlottesville: University Press of Virginia.

Roskies, David. 1984. *Against the Apocalypse: Responses to Catastrophe in Modern Jewish Culture*. Cambridge: Harvard University Press.

Rouch, Jean. 1954–55. *Les Maitres Fous*. Film.

Ruggie, John Gerald. 1993. Territoriality and beyond: Problematizing modernity in international relations. *International Organization* 47 (1):139–74.

Rumbaut, Ruben. 1995. Vietnamese, Laotian, and Cambodian Americans. In *Asian Americans: Contemporary Issues and Trends*, edited by Pyong Gap Min. Thousand Oaks, California: Sage Publications.

Russo, Arturo. 1993. The definition of a scientific policy: ESRO's satellite programme in 1969–1973. ESA HSR-6. Noordwijk, Netherlands: ESA Publications Division.

Sa'ar, Amalia. 1998. Carefully on the margins: Christian Palestinians in Haifa between nation and state. *American Ethnologist* 25 (2):215–39.

Sa'di, Ahmad H. 1996. Minority resistance to state control: Towards a re-analysis of Palestinian political activity in Israel. *Social Identities* 2 (3):395–412.

Sacks, Oliver. 1995. *An Anthropologist on Mars*. New York: Alfred A. Knopf.

Sandys, Charles F. S. A. [1851] 1981. *A History of Gavelkind and Other Remarkable Customs of Kent*. London: John Russel Smith.

Sangren, P. Steven. 1988. Rhetoric and the authority of ethnography: "Postmodernism" and the social reproduction of texts. *Current Anthropology* 29 (3):405–36.

Sarat, Austin, and Thomas Kearns, eds. 1992. *Law's Violence*. Ann Arbor: University of Michigan Press.

Savage, Michael. 1989. Spatial differences in modern Britain. In *Restructuring Britain: The Changing Social Structure*, edited by C. Hamnett, L. McDowell, and P. Sarre. London: Sage.

Scarry, Elaine. 1985. *The Body in Pain: The Making and Unmaking of the World*. New York: Oxford University Press.

Scheffler, Wolfgang. 1985. The forgotten part of the "Final Solution": The liquidation of the ghettos. *Simon Wisenthal Annual* 4, edited by H. Friedlander and Sybil Milton. White Plains, N.Y.: Kraus.

Schieffelin, Bambi. 1990. *The Give and Take of Everyday Life: Language Socialization of Kaluli Children*. Cambridge: Cambridge University Press.

Schieffelin, Bambi, and Elinor Ochs. 1986. *Language Socialization across Cultures*. Cambridge: Cambridge University Press.

Schirmer, Jennifer. 1999. *Guatemalan Military Project: A Violence Called Democracy*. Philadelphia: University of Pennsylvania Press.

Schivelbusch, Wolfgang. 1986. *The Railway Journey: The Industrialization of Time and Space in the Nineteenth Century*. Berkeley: University of California Press.

Schmidt-Lauber, Brigitte. 1998. "Die verkehrte Hautfarbe" Ethnizitaet deutscher Namibier als Alltagpraxis. Berlin: Dietrich Reimer.

Schoeneburg, K-H. 1995. Gesellschaftliche Umbrueche und Verfassung (1919, 1933, 1949, 1968, and 1990). In Gesellschaftliche Umbrueche und politischer Umgang mit den Schatten der Vergangenheit in 20. Jahrhundert. Jena: Hausdruckerei der Friedrich-Schiller-Universitaet.

Scott, James. 1977. *The Moral Economy of the Peasant: Rebellion and Subsistence in Southeast Asia*. New Haven, Conn.: Yale University Press.

———. 1998. *Seeing Like a State: How Certain Schemes to Improve the Human Condition Have Failed*. New Haven, Conn.: Yale University Press.

Scott, James, and Benedict J. Kerkvliet. 1977. How traditional rural patrons lose legitimacy: A theory with special reference to Southeast Asia. In *Friends, Followers, and Factions: A Reader in Political Clientism*, edited by Stefen W. Schmidt, Laura Guasti, Carl H. Landé, and James C. Scott. Berkeley: University of California Press.

Sheate, W. R. 1992. Lobbying for effective environmental assessment. *Long Range Planning* 25 (4):90–98.

Shlapentokh, Vladimir. 1996. Early feudalism: The best parallel for contemporary Russia. *Europe-Asia Studies* 48 (3):393–411.

Shoard, Marion. 1987. *This Land Is Our Land: The Struggle for Britain's Countryside*. London: Paladin Grafton Books.

Shokeid, Moshe. 1980. Ethnic identity and the position of women among Arabs in an Israeli town. *Ethnic and Racial Studies* 3 (2):188–205.

Shore, Cris. 2000. *Building Europe: The Cultural Politics of European Integration*. London: Routledge.

Shweder, Richard. 1990. Cultural psychology—What is it? In *Cultural Psychology: Essays on Comparative Human Development*, edited by James Stigler, Richard Shweder, and Gilbert Herdt. Cambridge: Cambridge University Press.

Siegrist, Hannes. 1994. The professions, state, and government in theory and history. In *Governments and Professional Education*, edited by Tony Becher. Bristol, Pa.: Open University Press.

Silverstein, Michael. 1993. Metapragmatic discourse and metapragmatic function. In *Reflexive Language: Reported Speech and Metapragmatics*, edited by John Lucy. Cambridge: Cambridge University Press.

Simons, Jack. 1949. The law and its administration. In *Handbook on Race Relations in South Africa*, edited by E. Hellmann. New York: Oxford University Press.

Skinner, Elliot. 1995. The importance of legitimacy for African institutional stability: The Mossi Naam. In *Africa in World History: Old, New, Then, and Now*, edited by Michael W. Coy Jr. and Leonard Plotnicov. Ethnology Monographs, no. 16. Pittsburgh: Department of Anthropology, University of Pittsburgh.

Sklar, Richard. 1995. On democracy in Africa. In *Africa in World History: Old, New, Then, and Now*, edited by Michael W. Coy Jr. and Leonard Plotnicov. Ethnology Monographs, no. 16. Pittsburgh: Department of Anthropology, University of Pittsburgh.

Skočpol, Theda. 1985. Bringing the state back in: Strategies of analysis in current research. In *Bringing the State Back*, edited by Peter B. Evans, Dietrich Reuschemeyer, and Theda Skočpol. Cambridge: Cambridge University Press.

Sluka, Jeff, ed. 1999. *Death Squad: The Anthropology of State Terror*. Philadelphia: University of Pennsylvania Press.

Smooha, Sammy. 1990. Minority status in an ethnic democracy: The status of the Arab minority in Israel. *Ethnic and Racial Studies* 13 (3):389–413.

Spivak, Gayatri Chakravorty. 1993. Woman in difference. In *Outside in the Teaching Machine*. New York: Routledge.

Starr, June, and Jane Collier, eds. 1989. *History and Power in the Study of Law*. Ithaca, N.Y.: Cornell University Press.

Steedly, Mary Margaret. 1993. *Hanging without a Rope*. Princeton, N.J.: Princeton University Press.

Stephen, Lynn. 2001. *Zapata Lives! Histories and Cultural Politics in Southern Mexico*. Berkeley: University of California Press.

Stephens, Sharon. 1993. The making of an invisible event: Assessing risks and negotiating identities in post-Chernobyl Norway. Paper presented at the Annual Meeting of the American Anthropological Association, Washington, D.C.

———. 1995. Children and the politics of culture in late capitalism. In *Children and the Politics of Culture*, edited by Sharon Stephens. Princeton, N.J.: Princeton University Press.

Stoll, David. 1993. *Between Two Armies in the Ixil Towns of Guatemala*. New York: Columbia University Press.

Stoller, Paul. 1989. *Fusion of the Worlds: An Ethnography of Possession among the Songhay of Niger*. Chicago: University of Chicago Press.

———. 1992. *The Cinematic Griot: The Ethnography of Jean Rouch*. Chicago: University of Chicago Press.

Strathern, Marilyn. 1985. Knowing power and being equivocal: Three Melanesian constructs. In *Power and Knowledge: Anthropological and Sociological Approaches*, edited by R. Fardon. Edinburgh: Scottish Academic Press.

———. 1987a. Introduction to *Dealing with Inequality: Analysing Gender Relations in Melanesia and Beyond*. Edited by M. Strathern. Cambridge: Cambridge University Press.

——. 1987b. Out of context: The persuasive fictions of anthropology. *Current Anthropology* 28 (3):252–81.

——. 1988. *The Gender of the Gift.* Berkeley: University of California Press.

——. 1995a. Nostalgia and the new genetics. In *Rhetorics of Self-making,* edited by D. Battaglia. Berkeley: University of California Press.

——. 1995b. The nice thing about culture is that everyone has it. In *Shifting Contexts: Transformations in Anthropological Knowledge,* edited by Marilyn Strathern. New York: Routledge.

——, ed. 1995c. *Shifting Contexts: Transformations in Anthropological Knowledge.* New York: Routledge.

Strentz, Thomas. 1982. The Stockholm Syndrome: Law enforcement policy and hostage behavior. In *Victims of Terrorism,* edited by Frank M. Ochberg and David A. Soskis. Boulder, Colo.: Westview Press.

Swanepoel, P. 1972. *Polisie Avonture in Suidwes-Afrika.* Johannesburg: Perskor.

Swanson, Maynard. 1967. South West Africa in trust, 1915–1939. In *Britain and Germany in Africa,* edited by P. Gifford and W. R. Louis. New Haven, Conn.: Yale University Press.

Tambiah, Stanley. 1986. *Sri Lanka: Ethnic Fratricide and the Dismantling of Democracy.* Chicago: University of Chicago Press.

——. 1997. *Leveling Crowds: Ethnonationalist Conflicts and Collective Violence in South Asia.* Berkeley: University of California Press.

Taussig, Michael. 1980. *The Devil and Commodity Fetishism in South America.* Chapel Hill: University of North Carolina Press.

——. 1987. *Shamanism, Colonialism, and the Wild Man: A Study in Terror and Healing.* Chicago: University of Chicago Press.

——. 1992. *The Nervous System.* New York: Routledge.

——. 1993. *Mimesis and Alterity: A Particular History of the Senses.* New York: Routledge.

——. 1997. *The Magic of the State.* New York: Routledge.

Taylor, Charles. 1989. *Sources of the Self: The Making of the Modern Identity.* Cambridge: Harvard University Press.

Thébaud, Françoise. 1994. The Great War and the triumph of sexual division. In *Toward a Cultural Identity in the Twentieth Century. A History of Women in the West,* vol. 5, edited by Françoise Thébaud. General editors: Georges Duby and Michelle Perrot. Cambridge: Belknap Press of Harvard University Press.

Thomas, Nicholas. 1994. *Colonialism's Culture.* Princeton, N.J.: Princeton University Press.

Thompson, Edward P. 1975. *Whigs and Hunters.* London: Allen Lane.

——. 1991. *Customs in Common.* New York: New Press.

Thongchai Winichakul. 1994. *Siam Mapped: A History of the Geo-Body of a Nation.* Honolulu: University of Hawaii Press.

Thrift, Nigel. 1990. Transport and communication, 1730–1914. In *An Historical Geography of England and Wales,* 2d ed., edited by R. A. Dodgshon and R. A. Butlin. London: Academic Press.

Tory, Avraham. 1990. *Surviving the Holocaust: The Kovno Ghetto*. Cambridge: Harvard University Press.

Traweek, Sharon. 1988. *Beamtimes and Lifetimes: The World of High Energy Physicists*. Cambridge: Harvard University Press.

Trouillot, Michel-Rolph. 1991. Anthropology and the savage slot: The poetics and politics of otherness. In *Recapturing Anthropology*, edited by Richard Fox. Albuquerque, N.M.: School of American Research Press.

——. 2001. The anthropology of the state in the age of globalization: Close encounters of a deceptive kind. *Current Anthropology* (spring 2001):1–27.

Trunk, Isaiah. 1972. *Judenrat: The Jewish Councils in Eastern Europe under Nazi Occupation*. New York: Macmillan.

Tsing, Anna Lowenhaupt. 1993. *In the Realm of the Diamond Queen*. Princeton, N.J.: Princeton University Press.

Turner, Michael. 1984. The landscape of parliamentary enclosure. In *Discovering Past Landscapes*, edited by Michael Reed. London: Croom Helm.

Turner, Victor. 1969. *The Ritual Process*. Harmondsworth: Penguin.

Twitchett, Kenneth J. 1980. European regionalism in perspective. In *European Cooperation Today*, edited by Kenneth Twitchett. London: Europa Publications.

Unger, Roberto Mangabeira. 1976. *Law in Modern Society: Toward a Criticism of Social Theory*. New York: Free Press.

United Nations Institute for Namibia. 1980. *The Legal System of Namibia: Past, Current, and Future Perspectives*. Lusaka: UNIN.

Urry, John. 1990. Mass tourism and the rise and fall of the seaside resort. In *The Tourist Gaze: Leisure and Travel in Contemporary Society*. London: Sage.

Van der Veer, Guus. 1992. *Counseling and Therapy with Refugees*. New York: John Wiley.

Van Maanen, John, and Stephen R. Barley. 1984. Occupational communities: Culture and control in organizations. In *Research in Organizational Behavior*, vol. 6, edited by Barry Staw and Larry Cummings. Greenwich, Conn.: JAI Press.

Varenne, Hervé. 1993. The question of European nationalism. In *Cultural Change and the New Europe: Perspectives on the European Community*, edited by Thomas M. Wilson and M. Estellie Smith. Boulder, Colo.: Westview Press.

Vayda, Andrew P. 1994. Actions, variations, and change: The emerging anti-essentialist view in anthropology. In *Assessing Cultural Anthropology*, edited by Robert Borofsky. New York: McGraw-Hill.

Verdery, Katherine. 1992a. Hobsbawm in the East. *Anthropology Today* 8:8–10.

——. 1992b. The transition from socialism: Anthropology and Eastern Europe. Lewis Henry Morgan Lectures. University of Rochester.

——. 1993. Whither "nation" and "nationalism"? *Daedalus* 122:3, 37–46.

——. 1996. *What Was Socialism and What Comes Next?* Princeton, N.J.: Princeton University Press.

Verger, Pierre. 1957. *Notes sur le culte des Orisa et Vodun à Bahia: la Baie de tous les saints au Brésil et à l'ancienne Côte des esclaves en Afrique*. Dakar: IFAN.

———. 1968. *Flux et reflux de la traite des négres entre le Golfe de Bénin et Bahia de Todos os Santos, du XVIIe au XIXe siècle*. Paris: Mouton.

Vickerman, R. W. 1991. Transport infrastructure in the European Community: New developments, regional implications, and evaluation. In *Infrastructure and Regional Development*, edited by R. W. Vickerman. London: Pion.

Villacorte, Wilfrido V. 1994. The curse of the weak state: Leadership imperatives for the Ramos government. *Contemporary Southeast Asia* 16:67–92, 439–58.

Vincent, Joan. 1991. Engaging historicism. In *Recapturing Anthropology*, edited by Richard Fox. Albuquerque, N.M.: School of American Research Press.

Viswanathan, Gauri. 1993. Raymond Williams and British colonialism: The limits of metropolitan cultural theory. In *Views Beyond the Border Country: Raymond Williams and Cultural Politics*, edited by D. L. Dworkin and L. G. Roman. London: Routledge.

Wagoner, Paula L. 1997. Surveying justice: The problematics of overlapping jurisdictions in Indian Country. *Droit et cultures* 33 (1):21–52.

Wain, Barry. 1981. *The Refused: The Agony of the Indochinese Refugees*. New York: Simon and Schuster.

Walker, Oliver. 1949. *Kaffirs Are Lively*. London: Victor Gollancz.

Waller, P. J. 1983. *Town, City, and Nation England: 1850–1914*. Oxford: Oxford University Press.

Walsh, Kevin. 1992. *The Representation of the Past: Museums and Heritage in the Post-Modern World*. London: Routledge.

Warren, Kay B. 1989. *The Symbolism of Subordination: Indigenous Identity in a Guatemalan Town*. Austin: University of Texas Press.

———. 1993a. Introduction to *The Violence Within: Cultural and Political Opposition in Divided Nations*, edited by Kay B. Warren. Boulder, Colo.: Westview Press.

———. 1993b. Interpreting *La Violencia* in Guatemala. In *The Violence Within*, edited by Kay B. Warren. Boulder, Colo.: Westview Press.

———. 1998. *Indigenous Movements and Their Critics: Pan-Maya Activism in Guatemala*. Princeton, N.J.: Princeton University Press.

———. 1999. "Death squads and wider complicities: Dilemmas for the anthropology of violence. In *Death Squad: The Anthropology of State Terror*, edited by Jeffrey Sluka. Philadelphia: University of Pennsylvania Press.

———. 2001. Telling truths: Taking David Stoll and the Rigoberta Menchú exposé seriously. In *The Rigoberta Menchú Controversy*, edited by Arturo Arias. Minneapolis: University of Minnesota Press.

Waterbury, John. 1970. *The Commander of the Faithful: The Moroccan Political Elite—A Study in Segmented Politics*. New York: Columbia University Press.

Weber, Max. 1946. *From Max Weber: Essays in Sociology*. Translated, edited, and with an introduction by H. H. Gerth and C. Wright Mills. New York: Oxford University Press.

———. 1958. *The Protestant Ethic and the Spirit of Capitalism*. Translated by Talcott Parsons. New York: Charles Scribner's Sons.

Wedel, Janine R. 1999. *Collision and Collusion: The Strange Case of Western Aid to Eastern Europe.* New York: St. Martin's Press.

Weisberg, Jacob, 1999. Cold war without end. *New York Times Magazine Section,* 29 November:116–58.

Welaratna, Usha. 1993. *Beyond the Killing Fields: Voices of Nine Cambodian Survivors in America.* Stanford, Calif.: Stanford University Press.

Wellington, John. 1967. *South West Africa and Its Human Issues.* Cape Town: Oxford University Press.

Wells, Julia. 1986. The war of degradation: Black women's struggle against Orange Free State Pass Laws, 1913. In *Banditry, Rebellion and Social Protest in Africa,* edited by Donald Crummey. Portsmouth, N.H.: Heinemann.

Werbner, Richard. 1991. *Tears of the Dead: The Social Biography of an African Family.* Edinburgh: Edinburgh University for the International African Institute.

Wertsch, James V., ed. 1985. *Culture, Communication, and Cognition: Vygotskion Perspectives.* Cambridge: Cambridge University Press.

Weston, Kath. 1998. *Longslowburn: Sexuality and Social Science.* New York: Routledge.

Williams, Patricia. 1991. *The Alchemy of Race and Rights.* Cambridge: Harvard University Press.

Williams, Raymond. 1973. *The Country and the City.* New York: Oxford.

Williamson, Tom, and Liz Bellamy. 1987. *Property and Landscape: A Social History of Land Ownership and the English Countryside.* London: George Philip.

Wilson, Thomas M., and M. Estellie Smith, eds. 1993. *Cultural Change and the New Europe: Perspectives on the European Community.* Boulder, Colo.: Westview Press.

Witney, K. P. 1982. *The Kingdom of Kent.* London: Phillimore.

Wolff, Friedrich. 1990. Ueberlegungen eines Rechtanwaltes zur Verantwortung des Juristen fuer die deutsche Rechtsangleichung. Paper presented at the Vereinigung demokratischer Juristen, Strasberg-Nord.

Wood, Davida. 1993. Politics of identity in a Palestinian village in Israel. In *The Violence Within: Cultural and Political Opposition in Divided States,* edited by Kay B. Warren. Boulder, Colo.: Westview Press.

Worpole, K. 1994. The new "city states." In *Altered States: Postmodernism, Politics, Culture,* edited by M. Perryman. London: Lawrence and Wishart.

Wright, Patrick. 1985. *On Living in an Old Country.* London: Verso.

Yahil, Leni. 1991. *The Holocaust: The Fate of the European Jewry.* New York: Oxford University Press.

Yurchak, Alexei. 1997. The cynical reason of late socialism: Power, pretense, and the Anekdot. *Public Culture* 9 (22):161–88.

Zabusky, Stacia E. 1992. Multiple contexts, multiple meanings: Scientists in the European Space Agency. In *Knowledge and Society: The Anthropology of Science and Technology,* vol. 9, edited by David J. Hess and Linda L. Layne. Arie Rip, series editor. Greenwich, Conn.: JAI Press.

——. 1995. *Launching Europe: An Ethnography of European Cooperation in Space Science.* Princeton, N.J.: Princeton University Press.

——. 2000. Boundaries at work: Discourses of belonging in the European Space Agency. In *An Anthropology of the European Union: Building, Imagining, and Experiencing the New Europe,* edited by Irène Bellier and Thomas M. Wilson. Oxford: Berg.

——. n.d. Aspiration and ideology in the construction of community: American scientists defend utopia, 1978–85. Unpublished manuscript.

Žižek, Slavoj. 1993. *Tarrying with the Negative: Kant, Hegel, and the Critique of Ideology.* Durham, N.C.: Duke University Press.

Zolberg, Aristide R., Astri Suhrke, and Sergio Aguayo. 1989. *Escape from Violence: Conflict and the Refugee Crisis in the Developing World.* New York: Oxford University Press.

Zonabend, Françoise. 1993. *The Nuclear Peninsula.* Translated by J. A. Underwood. Cambridge: Cambridge University Press.

Zuckerman, Yitzhak. 1993. *A Surplus of Memory: Chronicle of the Warsaw Ghetto Uprising.* Berkeley: University of California Press.

Zureik, Elia. 1988. Crime, justice, and underdevelopment: The Palestinians under Israeli control. *International Journal of Middle East Studies* 20:411–42.

Index

323, 335–338; transformations of, 326–330. *See also* Atikevodu (spirit possession order); Ritual(s)

Vulnerability, 127–128

Warsaw (Poland), 41, 47–49

Warsaw Uprising (1943), 49, 57

Wehrmacht (German army), 41, 47

Windhoek Advertiser (Nambian newspaper), 74, 75, 77

Women, 14, 179–184, 187–188, 204–207; demonstrations of, 194–199; and domestic activism, 199–203; empowering of, 185, 202; and honor killings, 189–194; and power, 178; status of, 186, 195–196

Work, 139–140, 292, 294; rescue through, 44–47, 49, 50, 54, 58. *See also* Labor

Workers, 70

Library of Congress Cataloging-in-Publication Data

Ethnography in unstable places: everyday lives in contexts
of dramatic political change/edited by Carol J. Greenhouse,
Elizabeth Mertz, and Kay B. Warren.

p. cm.   Includes bibliographical references and index.

ISBN 0-8223-2833-x (cloth: alk. paper)

ISBN 0-8223-2848-8 (pbk.: alk. paper)

1. Political stability—Social aspects—Case studies.

2. Social structure—Political aspects—Case studies.

I. Greenhouse, Carol J., II. Mertz, Elizabeth. III. Warren, Kay B.

JC330.2.E74 2002   305.8—dc21   2001053188